)F HIG⁻   ⁻ICATION
)ARK

R

URBAN AND REGIONAL STUDIES NO. 8

Land Policy in Planning

URBAN AND REGIONAL STUDIES

Series Editors: Gordon Cherry and Anthony Travis

Land Policy in Planning

NATHANIEL LICHFIELD
and
HAIM DARIN-DRABKIN

London
GEORGE ALLEN & UNWIN
Boston   Sydney

First published in 1980

GEORGE ALLEN & UNWIN LTD
40 Museum Street, London WC1A 1LU

© George Allen & Unwin (Publishers) Ltd, 1980

British Library Cataloguing in Publication Data

Lichfield, Nathaniel
    Land policy in planning. – (Urban and regional
    studies; no. 8).
    1. Land use – Planning – Great Britain – History
    2. Environmental policy – Great Britain – History
    I. Title   II. Darin-Drabkin, Haim   III. Series
    333.7'0941   HD596   80-40698

ISBN 0-04-333017-7

Set in 10 on 11 point Times by Computacomp (UK) Ltd. Fort
William, Scotland and printed in Great Britain by Lowe & Brydone
Limited, Thetford, Norfolk

Contents

In Memoriam

It is a sad privilege for an author to have to dedicate a book to the memory of his co-author.

Haim Darin-Drabkin died unexpectedly in November 1979. Happily he was able to see our book in its final typescript and so to make his full contribution to it; without this the result would have been much the poorer.

Land Policy in Planning was the last of the major contributions which this distinguished scholar made to his subject. We who worked with him on the book will cherish that memory.

NL

Acknowledgements

Our appreciation must first go to the Leverhulme Trust Foundation, which made the study possible by providing a research grant for the year 1975–6. This enabled Dr Haim Darin-Drabkin to spend the best part of the year with his co-author, Professor Nathaniel Lichfield, in University College London (UCL), and enabled them to finance a research team to assist with the study. These were Bernard Bourdillon, who stayed with the project throughout, and Frank Schaffer, Stephen Shifferes and Honor Chapman, all of whom worked on the project on a part-time basis.

During the year the team collaborated in the following way. Lichfield gave the overall concept and treatment in a summary of the book and initiated Chapters 1, 2, 8 and 9. Darin-Drabkin prepared the appendix on foreign experience and its summary in Chapter 7, assisted by Stephen Shifferes. Bernard Bourdillon participated throughout, initiating Chapters 3, 4 and 6, and acting as the secretary of the group. Frank Schaffer initiated the review of British land policy in Chapter 5. All members worked very closely throughout and enriched the ongoing discussion on all the work as it evolved. Lichfield worked with all the researchers and revised the whole (except the appendix) on the basis of accumulated drafts.

The final note of appreciation must go to the secretaries who battled with successive versions: Mimi Hollander, Barbara Doherty and Annabelle Disson; to the School of Architecture and Planning in UCL which accommodated us in the Planning Methodology Research Unit; and to Nathaniel Lichfield & Partners, who were very tolerant towards their senior partner's preoccupations.

Part One

What is Land Policy?

Chapter 1

The Issue and the Treatment

1.1 LAND POLICY IN BRITAIN TODAY

Since 1970 there has been a revival in Britain of controversy over issues relating to land in planning to a dimension not known since the 1940s. In retrospect the events can now be seen as some kind of drama – or, as will emerge, of tragicomedy – in which there are acts yet to be written.[1]

The opening act was seen in the phenomenal rise in land values and prices in the late 1960s, leading to large profits for landowners and developers, with the community as a whole suffering. For one thing the price of housing land escalated, leading to high prices for dwellings, eroding the standard of living of all new purchasers of dwellings, particularly young people. For another, except through general taxation, the community at large had no means of benefiting directly from the increases in such land values; and many thought that general taxation was insufficient and that landowners should be more heavily penalised because of the special place of land in the economy as a production and consumption good.

The above led to widespread and deeply felt grievances. Amidst the mounting concern and discussion, the second act now seems to have had its opening in the panic measures of the Conservative government, which in 1973 introduced both the development gains tax and also control over the rents of offices and shops, thus undermining the profitability of the development companies which were then at the peak of their boom. In retrospect these measures appear to have been the straw which broke the camel's back of property development, some other straws being inflated building costs, rising interest rates, the slackening of consumer demand which came with economic recession, and so on.

In consequence the development industry, including the property development companies and the primary and secondary banks which had financed them so heavily, responded by cascading into bankruptcy after bankruptcy. This, together with the deepening of the economic recession, had by 1975 virtually brought the development industry, particularly in commercial development, to a standstill. Thus the market responded to the charge of inflated land prices by itself undermining their basis, and in many cases for the first time since the 1930s gave development land a negative development value.

Our description of these two acts in the drama relate to what has happened to land, properties and development. But while this is of great importance and relevance, it is not our primary focus, which is the implications for planning, or more precisely the implementation of plans. And in both acts of the drama there were such implications.

In the first, for example, since authorities had to buy land for public services at market values related to the inflated prices, the cost of such services also escalated, leading in many circumstances to either shortfall in their provision or facilities which were sub-standard or badly located. In the second act the collapse of the economy and the development industry has removed from the scene much of the development on which authorities rely for plan implementation, and indeed undermined the socio/economic/political viability of many plans.

This set the curtain for the third act, with the return to power of the Labour Party in 1974 possessing an election manifesto containing drastic proposals for dealing with the land problem:[2] their third attempt following the repeal by the Conservatives of the financial measures in the Town and County Planning Act, 1947, and then the Land Commission Act, 1967. Their election policies were brought to fruition in the White Paper on *Land* in 1974[3] which foreshadowed the Community Land Act (CLA), 1975, and the Development Land Tax Act (DLTA), 1976.

Together these cumbersome measures had simple twin aims: to increase the powers of local authorities to take over land for private development as a contribution towards more positive planning; and of local and central government to recoup a large measure of the increase in the value of such land arising from planning permissions. In their ultimate fruition, which could take some years, the Acts envisaged the passing through local authority hands of all land for development and renewal in the country, together with the passing into public hands of all rises in land values which resulted from such development. In essence it was Henry George's single tax as a curtain-raiser to municipalisation of all development land.

To the devotees of the Community Land scheme the final curtain would appear to have come down on the vexed problems of land policy in Britain. But there are many reasons for thinking that this will not turn out to be the case. The Acts will not be conclusive in this respect, this for various reasons: they cover only part of our land policy; they are only in the first stage and the really controversial issues are yet to come; there is the Conservative threat to repeal; the Community Land Act itself has structural weaknesses; and the bureaucratic complexity clearly apparent in the Development Land Tax Act is an ominous reminder of the reasons leading to the repeal of the similar provisions in the 1947 and 1967 Acts mentioned above.

But there is another reason for the Community Land scheme being unstable. Its social/economic/political context is based on a philosophy which was conceived in economic boom, *not* economic slump.[4] Yet the very collapse of the land and development industries as we have known them since the Second World War, deriving from both the economic recession and the collapse of institutions, make essential some attempt at revival on some new basis, for effective operation in the new social and economic climate of the 1970s and beyond. Thus for this reason alone the land policy measures conceived in 1973 (at a time when the collapse and its implications were not yet upon us) cannot be left entirely in their present form.

Thus it is timely to explore the land policy issue in the current social, political and economic context. We do so against two background matters. First, ever since the seminal products of the Second World War thinking on the subject in Britain, the Uthwatt Report leading to the Town and Country Planning Act, 1947, and the controversies surrounding them, there has not been the attention that the topic deserves in this country: the bewildering acts in our drama might not have unfolded in the same way had we been more prepared. And second, the treatment of the subject cannot be carried out on the lines of the debates of the 1940s since the context of the topic has changed so much since then: in economic growth and then decline, population spread, social ethics and the theory, practice and process of urban and regional planning.

Thus the scene is set for our treatment in this book of land policy in planning. But before proceeding, there are two important curtain-raisers to reveal in this chapter: what we here mean by 'planning' and 'land policy'. Before doing so it is useful to emphasise one point. While our focus is on Britain it is relevant to add that a concern similar to that which surrounds the topic in Britain is clearly proceeding throughout the world. This was brought out clearly by the United National International Conference on Human Settlements in 1976.[5] Here not only was *land* a central focus of debate but it clearly became a primary and dominant issue throughout the discussions. It certainly triggered off conflicting views between the countries, but more important it enabled forward-looking resolutions to be passed in which there was substantial agreement.[6] All this enables us to bring to bear on the issues in Britain some review of what is happening around the world in land policy.

1.2   WHAT IS PLANNING?[7]

The evolution of land policy just described is intimately bound up with the evolution of town and country planning in Britain; indeed, so closely related are they that until the passing of the Community Land Act most of the land policies relating to planning were embodied in town and country planning legislation. This being so, it is important to be clear just what is meant by 'planning' in this book. A brief account now follows.

All the world over central and local governments undertake planning (i.e. predicting the future in order to formulate normative policies to influence it). They do so in respect of their roles in society alongside the planning for its roles by the non-government sectors. In government the planning is undertaken for many sectors (e.g. education, health, welfare, highways, airports) with appropriate methodology and techniques. Some are short term, some long, some highly centralised, some highly diffused, some integrated with other sectors and some not. In parallel with this sectoral planning is carried out the planning of our towns and regions, with which we are here concerned. This is distinct in its techniques, approaches, kinds of plan, kinds of implementation tools, and so on from sectoral planning. It is also distinct in another important respect: by definition it seeks plans which integrate all the sectoral activities in terms of the implications for one all pervasive element, land use and development, and in so doing has regard not just to sectors but to the whole community.

Such planning is described by various adjectives to distinguish it from other kinds (e.g. national, economic or regional development planning). But even so it does not have one distinctive title and is commonly described by various adjectives, such as town and country, urban and regional, spatial, physical, land use, environmental, development or human settlement planning. On many occasions the terms are used interchangeably and could be defined to mean the same thing. But in theory and practice they have different connotations. For example, town and country or land-use planning tends to convey a preoccupation with the allocation of uses on the earth's surface; urban and regional planning more popularly denotes socioeconomic activities associated with land use; human settlement planning conveys an all-embracing concern with the human, social, economic, environmental and political aspects of the living together of people in rural or urban concentrations.

But while the terms can be used to mean the same thing, they do in fact reflect a continuing search for appropriate descriptions of an activity which does not remain constant but is evolving through time, both in any particular country and across the world. Such evolution has been very pronounced in Britain, which during this century has seen a change from the early tentative concern of the Town Planning Act, 1909, to one as practised during the 1970s, and which now possesses one of the most sophisticated systems of planning in the world. A brief review of its evolution in Britain will demonstrate the advance that has been made.

For reasons which have never been fully established, Britain is by common consent a leading country in the evolution of its urban planning system, both as innovator and as exporter – perhaps it was the early consciousness of the squalor of the urban system built by the first industrial revolution in the world; perhaps the long tradition of good management of the land in the British land-owning aristocracy; perhaps the system of property in land which recognised obligations as well as rights. But whatever the reason, the Second World War saw in Britain the innovation of a revolutionary system of town and country planning (whereas in some other countries the war saw very little change): it was called 'development planning', the term we will subsequently use. Following experience of twenty years of such development planning there has been introduced the well-known Mark II style of development plan, which has influenced practice throughout the world. Accordingly it is of relevance for this book to note some trends in this advanced system. This is considered under three heads: scope, method and practice.

The *scope* of planning is certainly widening as the demands on it grow in terms of the problems and the opportunities which need to be tackled. Some examples will illustrate. While the aim of fusing the physical, social and economic aspects of development planning has been pursued, so far it has not yet been fully successful, but the trend is certainly to try and make it so. There has been success in introducing into the plan the policies which are not site-specific (i.e. indicating the attitudes of the authorities on particular matters when making future decisions) alongside the more concrete proposals which *are* site-specific. There has certainly been a widening of the scope of the planning to make it an integral feature of the corporate planning of local authorities, whereby all their activities are seen comprehensively with development planning as one strand; indeed, urban planning and urban management or governance are seen as an interrelated process. In passing, since we are dealing with 'scope', it should be added that parallel moves have not been made in central government, where ministries are the big brothers of the local authority departments, and in this sense should, in theory, mirror local corporate thinking.

Coming to planning *method*, there seems to be consolidation in certain critical respects. There continues the use to suit circumstances of a variety of plan-making instruments within the overall development plan (such as key diagrams, local plans, action area plans) without reliance on one particular type of plan. Planning decisions are incorporated with the day-to-day decisions of the municipalities or central government and are not seen as being distinct. And the widest array of professional skills are being brought to bear, so that multi-disciplinary team work is the common and not rare feature in planning offices. But as against this there is continuing weakness in ensuring that there is implementation in accordance with planning policies, so that gaps continue to emerge between what is proposed and what in fact occurs on the ground.

But despite the pre-eminence of British planning there is none the less dissatisfaction with the practise of development planning as a whole, which is growing rather than decreasing. A few illustrations will be given.[8]

For one thing it is weakened by having been evolved as a local government operation, without a comparable system in support at the national and regional levels; there is still in Britain no co-ordinated national development planning of the economic or physical development kind, though particular sectors have their plans and programmes (e.g. motorways, electricity power stations, national parks, location of industry). There is still uncertainty as to the level at which regional planning should be carried out – as a bridge between the local and the national; should it be from central government down or local government up? And perhaps in consequence open regional planning has no teeth; in practice regional departments of central government act in co-ordination with power to implement their policies, using as a framework the regional strategies prepared by Regional Economic Planning Councils with their aid, the Council being nominated by government with no powers at its disposal. Then at the local planning authority level there is continuing tension and friction between the two tiers which were created in 1974: the strategic or county level, and the local or district levels. Politically and professionally the wars go on. This tension, and also the regional uncertainty, is part and parcel of a groundswell towards greater devolution from the centre to the locality, as a reaction against planning from above.

Finally, the public who are affected by the plans are becoming increasingly vocal and powerful, both as against their elected representatives and against the planning bureaucracy, using the powers for participation given them in the 1970s. But there are still unclarified difficulties in the manner in which this power is to be used in the ongoing planning situation, which adds to the confusion and ineffectiveness of the planning system itself. This is not simply a feature of the people flexing their muscles against elected representatives at whose representation of their interests they are cavilling, but also some doubt as to the value which the planning system provides for the considerable costs that it involves: in the unconscionable delays and frustrations in the working of the controls over development and in the denials to development in a country with a slack economy. And there is some scepticism as to whether this sophisticated planning system is in reality improving the 'quality of life'.

Thus even this most sophisticated of all local development planning systems has far from settled down in its new look, and accordingly it cannot be taken of necessity as *the* marker for the future. Indeed, there are rumblings which could indicate further changes in the near future. Politically, the lower-tier district councils as a whole are wishing to see the shift of power to themselves which the county councils as a whole are resisting, pressing for retention of the present system which gives them the strategic role. But their conflicts could be put into the melting-pot again, since the Labour government in 1978 indicated some dissatisfaction with the Tory-created system of local government reform which was effected in 1974 and set up a review some twenty-five years after the initial probes in this direction by the post-war Labour administration.[9]

The reasons behind this evolution in the scope of planning are too complex to trace here but one generalisation might be attempted; it reflects the continuing awareness that the subject-matter of the planning, the human settlement, is rich, complex and varied and requires ever more concern with the fundamentals of human society. Thus while there was an awareness in the early days of British planning of the social and economic issues in the civic design for the expansion of a town, the knowledge of the issues was amateur rather than professional. And it has needed the education of generations of students and practitioners in the field to bring into the arena the social, economic, cultural, political and other issues to an ever-increasing professional level.

But whatever the level, one thread runs through.[10] This is that the planning is essentially concerned with preparing for the carrying out of *development*, i.e. change of use on the physical surface of the earth as the platform for man's changing activities on it (see section 4.3.2). It is for this reason that the planning with which we are concerned in this book will be termed 'development planning'. But this term is also properly used for the planning of the economy at the national and regional scale, leading to national and regional development plans, and visualises a different connotation of the term 'development': i.e. those changes in social and economic structure which affect the capacity to produce, and which in turn affect the economic growth of that country. This provides a rich source for confusion, which we try and clarify below (section 3.1). Here a preliminary statement is needed for this and the following chapter.

If a simple distinction were to be made between these two meanings, it would be that the development plan for towns and regions has as its essential focus the *physical development* on the land, for it is here that the influence of such planning is brought to bear in *implementation*, thus earning and justifying the title *physical*. By contrast, in socioeconomic development planning, *implementation* is sought more through policies relating to financial controls, taxation, direct government activity and financing, and so on.

Thus in physical *development planning* we are concerned with a means to an end, which is the utilisation of the physical infrastructure for production in factories, consumption in dwellings, health in hospitals, education in schools, and so on. Thus we are concerned with the relationships between the socioeconomic activities and the physical infrastructure. For this purpose it is necessary to explore the plans which are being made for these activities, by the sectoral planners in housing, health, education, etc., which is *development planning* in the sense of *socioeconomic structure*. But the two roles in society are distinct, though in many circumstances, because of particular institutional arrangements, they are very closely related, as when a local authority is responsible for health, education, housing services as well as physical planning.

Clearly all such kinds of development planning are interlinked. Policies at the upper levels constrain what can be done at the lower; and conditions at the lower level constrain what can be done at the higher. This could relate to levels within the planning for towns and regions themselves (county versus district plans, for example) or between the physical development plans of towns and regions and the socioeconomic planning at the regional and national levels.

In effect, therefore, development planning for towns and regions is a summary in terms of the utilisation of the earth's surface of the various kinds of socioeconomic planning for sectors at the local, regional or national level. But while in this book we will need to have regard to the clear interlinking, we are primarily concerned with the local physical development plans.

And on this distinction a final point might be made. All those concerned with predicting and offering policies to guide the future (in any sphere or capacity) have common links in that they are all engaged in a generic process called 'planning'. As far as they are applying this planning to different fields, they must of necessity adapt their theory and practice; educational planning is by no means the same thing as urban and regional planning. None the less they must be mutually aware of the planning practice of the others, since it is critical that the various plans be brought into some relationship with one another, for otherwise they are mutually self-defeating.

1.3   ROLE OF LAND POLICY IN PLANNING

Having described what we mean by *planning* in this book, it is now necessary to explore the role of *land policy* within this planning.

As a term *land policy* is not new.[11] But in recent years its coinage has widened, with growing attention both in the literature as well as in practice. This increasing usage has demonstrated that the term has a very wide-ranging variety of meanings, something brought out in four studies with the term *land policy* in the title, each covering a wide, differing and valuable range of topics.[12] For some it is used indistinguishably from *land-use policy*; for some it is associated with land reform; for others it is the policy of government in relation to the land which it owns.

The diffuseness is emphasised by the fact that none of these four studies attempts a definition of the term. But even where there is a definition, the treatment of the contents is still very wide and varied.[13] It is perhaps at its widest where under *urban* land policy the *minimal* scope is where government intervenes in regulating urban land resources under the ten headings of land tenure, public land management, land title registration, land laws and courts, property taxation, property valuation, public goods, public utilities, public transport highways, and government property management. And the scope goes beyond the minimal when government is more actively involved in owning, using and developing urban land resources; there could then be seven additional components, such as urban government structure, urban government finance, urban government and central government relations, central government fiscal and monetary policies, housing policies, regional development policies and urban planning control.[14]

But even where a very narrow definition is adopted, the subject itself seems too lusty to contain. For example, an enquiry into *land tenure* was interpreted by the authors as a significant contribution to the meaning and application of land policy, covering such items as national and urban land policies, national land management, land-use planning, development procedures, compensation, valuation and rating, land-disposal arrangements, and land development accounting.[15]

These wide-ranging treatments clearly cover policies which go beyond the focus of *land*; indeed, it is difficult not to do so, as we see below (section 1.3). But perhaps another reason for lack of sharpness in treatment is the common identification of *land policy* with *all government* policies to do with *land*, simply because it is *government* which introduces and implements the policies. On this approach, land policy would cover the function of government in making laws affecting land (real property and taxation) and thereby also *private* land policy as between private property interests; in setting up and operating an urban and regional planning system for controlling land use and development; as user of land for public purposes (government offices, civic centres and social overheads); as developer of land for public purposes (infrastructure, roads, airports, etc.); as controller of activities on land for government programmes (housing, etc.).

On this it is relevant to note that the focus of the United Nations was narrower in its recommendations for national action following the Vancouver 1972 Conference on Human Settlements.[16] In order that land be used in the interests of society as a whole, it recommended action in relation to land-resource management, control of land-use changes, recapturing plus value, public ownership, patterns of ownership, increase in usable land and information needs.

Thus not only is the term not at all precisely used but, and perhaps for that reason, it can mean many different things: it is sufficiently wide to encompass *anything* to do with the *use* of land, be it in private or public occupation; or government regulations relating to the use of land, for example zoning or green belts; or *land reform*, particularly in countries which are breaking out of traditional social institutions and land tenure. All these concerns are of relevance to land, leading to many possible definitions of *land policy*. But for that very reason, given these conflicting concepts, it is clearly necessary for anyone concerned with land policy for particular objectives to give at the outset his statement on the meaning of land policy in pursuit of those objectives. Ours is the planning described above (see section 1.2). We therefore give our understanding on its role in planning, as employed in this book. This now follows.

In our description of development planning for towns and regions, as visualised here, we concluded in section 1.2 that it is a 'summarisation in terms of the utilisation of the earth's surface of the various kinds of planning, which are proceeding in respect of society's function'. In order for such planning to be able to influence the future, government must take steps to place in the hand of the authorities powers to initiate, stimulate, guide, regulate or prevent ongoing activities towards that future. This in brief we can call *plan implementation*. This process of preparing and implementing plans is, with other related activities in our *planning system* (see section 4.3), within the scope of what we call *planning*. To carry out this complex and lengthy process, in the open way demanded of it in contemporary practice, needs a *planning process*. There are many models for this purpose in the literature, to which we turn below (section 2.8). Here it is necessary only to consider how *policy* comes into the process.

There is general agreement that policies are designed 'to give direction, coherence and continuity to the courses of action, for which the decision-making body is responsible'.[17] There is also much discussion on the appropriate methodology for devising the policies. This is not necessary for us to pursue here.[18] We simply need note that the purpose of policy-making is to give effect to policy in practice by the use of measures (tools, instruments), and that policy should flow from explicit goals or objectives, for without them the policy becomes implicit and tends to degenerate to techniques without logic. What is not so generally agreed is *how* the goals and objectives are to be formulated. Should they come from ethical normative values or opinions? Or should they emerge from the findings of specific study of facts, predictions, problems, opportunity and constraints?[19] If the former is followed, the goals could be quite unrelated to reality and their non-feasibility would undermine credibility. This is less likely in the latter approach.

By the same token, the measures (tools, instruments) will vary according to how the goals and objectives are set. In the former case they are related to aims, in the latter to achievable objectives. Prepared this way they can be seen as leading to *programmes* for the *implementation* of policy relating to the utilisation of the earth's surface, which we can term *land-use policy*. And since *land use* in our kind of development planning is signified by *development*, we can describe the tools or instruments needed for the purpose of *implementation* as *development policy measures*. Familiar examples are the stimulus of an economy in an area of economic decline, provision of factory sites in a growing area, control of density and layout on an urban site, and the prohibition of urban development on farmland in order to keep a 'green belt'.

Within these overall *development policy measures* some relate specifically to the land itself and become *land-policy measures*. Clear examples are the acquisition of land by government to enable current unsuitable ownership patterns to be pooled, together with the compensation basis for such acquisition; or the control by government of the use of land without the need to take land. A general aim, i.e. policy, is to ensure that land needed for urban and regional development is supplied in needed quantities, appropriate locations, appropriate tenure, at the right time and at appropriate prices, having regard to efficiency and equity in the allocation of resources, in pursuit of the targets in urban and regional plans. And land-policy measures (tools, instruments) are needed to implement the policy. In popular usage it is these *measures* which become the *land policies*. They should not be confused, but to do so is easy; in this book we tend also to use the two interchangeably.

From this viewpoint and for our purpose in this book, *land policy* and *land-policy measures* can be defined as that part of *development policy* and *development policy measures* which are related to the *role* of land in the *implementation* of urban and regional plans.

But since land is the platform for all human activities, including physical development, there is in this concept clearly some difficulty of distinguishing where land policy finishes and the remainder of development policy begins. Some examples will illustrate. Clearly the buying of land for compulsory pooling of ownership as a basis for renewal is land policy. Equally the granting of subsidies or low-interest loans for the promotion of factories in areas of economic decline can also be considered as land policy, on the proposition that industrialists will bid for land which they would otherwise not afford. But some doubt arises in the case of, for example, a tax per employee in congested areas or a bonus per employee in depressed areas (to depress or stimulate employment); or taxes on vehicles in congested areas (as an aid to minimising traffic problems). But none the less the distinction is worth pursuing, because of the unique quality and special role of land in all our development and planning activities.[20] It is these qualities which give the special substance of land policy, to which we now turn.

1.4   THE SUBSTANCE OF LAND POLICY

1.4.1   UNIQUENESS OF LAND

It is a commonplace that land is unique, in the sense of being significantly different from all other aspects of economic, social and political life. And just because it is unique in this way it attracts to it policies the substance of which are themselves unique. For one thing land is the platform of all human activities, which, the telling exceptions apart (e.g. space travel) can barely exist otherwise. For another it is God-given or the gift of Nature, and its original qualities are found without the use of man-made resources. From this flows a third feature, the unique qualities as a factor of production compared with others: it is fixed in location, immovable, incapable of expansion of supply (with minor interesting exceptions such as reclamation). Then it has a special place in society in that, for example, no state can be said to be independent which does not have control over its own land, and no individual can be said to be independent who does not have freedom of access to a part of that land; it is over possession of land which people have fought for centuries. Because of this special place in society it is difficult to grant an individual absolute ownership of any portion of the land as against the rest of society, as he might have with a motor-car, television set, and so on.

And finally, just because the land is God- or Nature-given, the contrast, between the passive role of land ownership and the relentless activity required of those concerned with production, has always raised questions as to the entitlement of the increase in the *plus value* of land which flows from increasing population growth and economic activity.

1.4.2   MEANING OF LAND

The very meaning of land is seen differently by various sectors of society and their accompanying professional skills.

In physical geography, land is the *terra firma* on which settlements are created, and it is its physical qualities which are of interest in its use. Since each parcel of land is fixed in location and cannot be transported, the policies must be site-specific; and just because land is permanent, its qualities which are capable of erosion are not replaceable and therefore the policies must aim towards conservation.

In economics, land is a natural resource and, as such, is costless in terms of production. But *terra firma* is only one such natural resource, and policies are also needed for the minerals below, the waters surrounding, the fauna and flora attached and the life-giving light, air, sunshine, etc., on which they depend. The substance is therefore wider than in physical geography. Land and other natural resources enter economic life as a commodity on which an entrepreneur lays out production costs to release goods and services for consumption, and thus has cost, value and price.

To a lawyer, raw land as opposed to the man-made improvements on it (infrastructure and buildings) cannot be handled separately since they are, in fact, used jointly; to him *land* therefore includes all man-made improvements.

And compounded from the above, society has its own attitude. Freedom of access to land is a critical base for independence as a state. Enduring stewardship of the land is its way of protecting future generations. The palpable conflict between the freedom to use land by its owners and possessors, according to their own objectives, and the consequences for society raises the need for social control of the utilisation of the land.

1.4.3   PROPRIETARY RIGHTS AND OBLIGATIONS IN LAND[22]

But if to the lawyer the content of *land* is tangible, in that it includes the physical surface and all man-made improvements which are fixtures, none the less he has a more abstract view of the ownership and possession of the land and its improvements. To him land is not the object itself; it is the rights and obligations of parties in relation to the object which are the substance of his legal concern, which must include the legal and institutional framework of the ownership of land in its various tenures, the transfer of such ownership and tenure, and the social control over them by society.

Each such bundle of rights and obligations is seen as a *proprietary land unit* with its individual rights and obligations to others. These have matured over the centuries to give rise to the system of counterbalancing privileges which enable individual owners and possessors to pursue their individual objectives in some kind of harmony over which the Courts hold the ring according to the laws of the country. It is this accumulation of statute, case law, etc., which although administered by the legislature and judiciary can be regarded as *private land policy* designed over time to facilitate the continued use, enjoyment and development of proprietary rights, be they owned by private individuals or corporations or public bodies.[23]

1.5   SOME EXCLUSIONS FROM LAND POLICY IN THIS BOOK

Given this concept, it follows that there must be some exclusions from popular usage in our coverage of land policy in this book. These are enumerated at the outset so that the scope of treatment is seen:

1   *Land-use policy.* As seen above (see section 1.3), our concern is with the *implementation* of land-use plans and not with plan-making. Our concern is therefore not with the policies in such plans which can be called *land-use policies*, embracing in the adjective those others which are used as synonyms to describe urban and regional planning (see section 1.2).
2   *Rural land reform.* Land policies which relate to the utilisation of rural land as such (e.g. reforms in tenure, co-operative production and marketing, etc.) would be included as having relevance to the *implementation* of rural development plans. But that land reform would be excluded which had as its prime aim the redistribution of wealth without direct relevance to such implementation.
3   *Natural resource policies.* While natural resources other than land (e.g. water, air, fish) could well come within the definition of 'land', as seen by the economist (see section 1.3), they are not typically a primary focus in

implementation of development plans. Unless they were (and water could well be) they would be excluded.

4 *Economic development*. Also excluded would be those policies which have a bearing on the economy as a whole (e.g. import controls, welfare grants and taxation) which are not specifically aimed at the implementation of local development plans.

5 *General taxation*. Also excluded would be general taxation, whose aims are not specific for development. Thus a distinction would be made between the general real property rate or tax in that it merely collects revenue, as opposed to a specific tax applied to land, for example on vacant land to stimulate development.

To some, these exclusions from *land policy* will seem arbitrary. But they are not, in that they flow from the concept which is the criterion for the exclusion. Other concepts would produce a different treatment. But it is just the absence of any concept which allows for the inclusion of all policies relating to land in the loosely used definition of *land policy*.

But having excluded certain policies from our treatment of land policy, it is relevant to add that even so we will have to deal with their *side-effects* on the use of land, since these may feed back into land policy as defined here, and thus enter our concern. Some examples are: rural land reform could advance or retard migration to the towns, as could rationing of water as between farmers and urban dwellers in deserts; national economic development and taxation could result in changes in land use and thus in redistribution of wealth; and control over environmental pollution could influence land-use plans.

1.6 CATEGORIES OF LAND POLICY AND MEASURES

Having defined land policy restrictively for our purpose, we none the less need to recognise that even within this apparently limited scope there are a large number and a great variety of such policies. This arises in the nature of things. The policies have grown intermittently over decades in this century, at a time of rapid and vigorous physical, social and economic change; Parliament has introduced successive measures aimed at tackling particular problems as they have arisen, and has rarely taken the opportunity to tidy up as it has gone along, so that there is the interplay of established and new policies; and as we have seen (see section 1.1), the measures introduced by Parliament have reflected the political complexion of the day, not only in the nature of the majority political party but also in the counterpoint in the symphony of political influences (see section 2.9).

The result is that, currently, there is an accumulation of land-policy measures of bewildering richness. This would be so even if we confined our attention for the purpose of this book to land policies in Britain. But we have not. As will appear below (section 1.7), one of our ways of illuminating the requirements in Britain has been to review the foreign experience and to distil its implications for Britain. Thus the richness is even greater. In this situation the very categorisation adopted can itself be meaningful in terms of clarifying the subject-matter in hand; for example, one essay in the classification of that most rudimentary of facts in planning, land use, shows the great deal that can be done in clarification by distinguishing between the directly observable factors, their appraisal and an indication of what might be done about them.[24]

But we have not been so ambitious. Rather, from empirical study of ruling land policies in Britain and abroad (see Chapters 5–7 and the appendix), we have recognised three broad sub-divisions in descending order of specificity in control over development (direct control, indirect control and general influence) and then found sub-division, as follows:

Direct control over development
1 Control over specific development without taking land.
2 Control over specific development by taking land.
3 Control over specific development by direct public-authority participation.

Fiscal control over development
4 Influence over general development by fiscal measures.
5 Influence over specific development by fiscal measures.

General influence over development
6 General influence on the land market.

This is sufficient for the British experience, for here we go into detail in discussion (Chapters 5 and 6). But for the foreign experience, where there is a broad review without as much detail (in the appendix), there is a sub-categorisation aimed at showing for each measure something of the manner of application in the country in question. This is done by showing for each of the measures the specific power or detailed specification of a particular policy and then, for each where applicable, the conditions attached to each type of measure (namely, the scope of application, agency of application, timing of application, basis of land value which is relevant, the method of financing and the enforcement means). Then there is a further specific breakdown of the conditions in each of the different categories, where such illumination can be taken further.

1.7 OUTLINE OF TREATMENT

Our focus is land policy for the purpose of urban and regional planning in Britain. Our treatment is based upon three questions addressed to the British case, raised respectively in Parts I, II and II, namely: What is land policy? What kind of land policy? Which land policy? Part I addresses itself to the question of 'What is land policy?' laying the conceptual basis of the treatment on the following lines. As popularly used the term itself has many different meanings and it is particular aspects only which are of relevance for this book (see section 1.3). In brief these relate to land policy seen as a tool for the *implementation of urban and regional development plans*, and not, for example, in the sense of land reform, which has regard mainly to objectives of social justice and economic development.

As a context we therefore describe urban and regional development planning in Britain. It has many synonyms (town and country, environmental, city and regional, settlement land use, physical development). None of the synonyms is adequate and we adopt the term 'development planning' to describe the field, both because it is the official description in Britain and also it most clearly describes the concept of urban and regional planning. To emphasise the concept, in this book we sometimes use 'planned development'.[25]

Such planning the world over is both an art and a science of growing complexity, involving more and more professionals of diverse skill, and more and more sections of the population. But it is not so much as an art or a science that it is significant as when it becomes part of a government machine with a view to the *implementation* of plans.

Thus it is necessary to explain what is meant by the *implementation* of plans. This becomes a major undertaking since the literature, theory and practice of plan implementation is a neglected field, and the particular interpretation relevant for our treatment needs to be worked out (see Chapter 2). The particular emphasis is not on the *process* of plan implementation. While this is included in a brief overview (section 2.1), the emphasis for our purpose is on *how* the implementation process *should* affect plan-making, given the intention to prepare plans which are, as far as can be foreseen in the plan-making stage, capable of implementation. For this purpose a model for plan implementation is first set up (section 2.3), then an array of plan-implementation measures (section 2.5). The choice of suitable implementation measures is then described (section 2.6), leading to a review of the typical reasons for failure in plan implementation. This leads to the core of Chapter 2: how to plan with an eye to implementation (section 2.8). Since an important feature here is the feasibility testing of the plans as they are being made, this is amplified (section 2.9). In essence, therefore, we are continually aiming at closing the gap which emerges between planning and implementation, all the time striving to lift the constraints on implementation rather than biding too tamely by them. In this one of the ever-prevailing constraints is the role of politics throughout the whole of the process. Accordingly, the chapter closes with an attempt to clarify this complex area (section 2.9).

In our model for plan implementation we recognise two major influences: the activities of development agencies which are concerned with developing and renewing the urban fabric, and are the main agents of plan implementation; and the implementation authorities who attempt to steer and regulate their activities towards 'planned development'. This leads us to clarify the role of the development process in planning (Chapter 3). Having shown the meaning of the term in national, urban and local planning (section 3.1), its relation to socioeconomic life (section 3.2) and the nature of the process (sections 3.3–3.6) we go on to the core of the chapter: why is there a need for planning intervention in the land market, which, left to itself without government planning, has built, and does in fact build, towns and regions (section 3.7). This leads to a description of the means of planned intervention in the land market (section 3.8) which then becomes the basis for a description of the various kinds of land policy which are available for plan implementation, following the categories set out earlier (section 1.6). Interventions of these kinds in the land and development market bring their counter-pressures on planning, with which the chapter closes (section 3.11).

Having set the conceptual context in Part I, we then proceed to ask in Part II which policies should be introduced in Britain in amendment to those already existing?

As a preliminary, the contemporary context of planned development in Britain today is described in Chapter 4, first in relation to its social and economic context (section 4.1), then to features in the contemporary development process (section

4.2) and then to our contemporary planning system (section 4.3). This is followed by an empirical review of impediments to plan implementation in Britain. This has not been attempted by case study but rather on the broad brush: by introducing seven major planning objectives in post-war Britain and describing the programme for each as set out as well as impediments as they have occurred in practice (section 4.4).

Then going on to land policy, we start with its evolution in Britain until 1974 (sections 5.1–5.3) and then (section 5.4) summarise those current in 1974, i.e. prior to the introduction of the Labour Government's White Paper on *Land* setting out the principles of its community land legislation. We then turn to an examination of the shortcomings of British land policy, seen from the viewpoint of plan implementation, in Britain prior to the community land legislation of 1975–6. Conclusions are presented on impediments to implementation (section 5.5). We then (section 5.6) present the same story by concentrating on one particular and critical facet: the continuing search for solutions to the compensation-betterment issue in planning, i.e. the financial adjustments between authority on the one hand and landowners on the other, in trying to find an equitable manner of compensating landowners for the infringement of their rights in the interests of planning, and extracting from landowners some of the benefits they derive from growth and action by the community. We then close with some criteria for needed changes in land policy as it existed in 1975 (section 5.7).

This then is the situation left after the first two attempts by Labour to introduce drastic reforms in 1947 and 1967, and the reversal of those attempts by succeeding Conservative governments, which was the threshold for the new attempts of the community land scheme of 1975–6.

This community land scheme for England is then described in Chapter 6: the politico-economic context (section 6.1), its provisions (section 6.2), its implications for both planning and development (section 6.3) and its implications for the development process in the private sector, showing potential effects on the planning and development process (section 6.4). The question is then posed as to whether it will help or hinder implementation (section 6.5). Then the community land scheme for Wales is described, bringing out its significant differences from that in England (section 6.6). The chapter then concludes by making suggestions for not going on to implement the community land scheme as fully envisaged but having some partial scheme (section 6.7). The corollory is that the community land scheme is shown to be an incomplete answer to the land-policy question.

In Chapter 7 we move from Britain to a review of contemporary land policy abroad, based on the review in the appendix of the experience, practice and thinking on such measures around the world. The reasoning is as follows. While the concentration is on Britain we have sought to learn from abroad: what means are used there, what is their experience and what are their proposals?

But caution is needed in considering the applicability of such concepts and measures to Britain. Countries are highly individual in this respect, much more so than in respect of, say, land-use policies, because of variations in the willingness of different societies to intervene in the market process with a view to facilitating plan implementation; differences in the legal and institutional foundations on which such land-policy measures are grafted and in the levels of professional competence with which such policies are understood and employed. Thus Chapter 7 is selective of foreign experience in relation to Britain's needs.

Part II is thus an attempt to answer the question as to what kind of land policies should be proposed for Britain, by looking at the issue from the different vantage-points in Chapters 4–7. From this it is possible to reach conclusions on the new land policies required. This is given in Chapter 8. As a preliminary, the objectives of British land policy are restated: in essence the move from negative to positive planning (section 8.2); and the starting-point noted for the proposed changes in 1978, with the community land scheme in its initial stages. Then the actual proposals are enumerated, first as regards allocation (section 8.4) and then distribution (section 8.5), ending with a note on the appropriate manpower for the job (section 8.6).

These proposals are not meant to be specific recommendations for general adoption, but rather an extension to the current shopping-list. But if they are to be thought of in this way, then the particular manner of their grafting on to current land policies in Britain needs to be considered. This is the focus of Part III, 'Which land policy?'

It is first noted that there is a need for improved selection in land policy (section 9.1), followed by a review of possible approaches (section 9.2). Whatever the approach, there is needed a formal process for land-policy selection, which can be tried out, in detail or in principle, in particular instances and tested on plan review. A model for the purpose is presented (section 9.3). It is based on principles presented in the preceding chapters: the need to close the planning-implementation gap; the recognition that the implementation measures affect the plan proposals, if the plan is intended for implementation; there is accordingly a choice of ends–means packages; and in practice the evaluation of both ends and means in plan proposals should be carried out together.

The book ends with a case study of how particular land policies rather than others could be chosen in practice in a major project of urban renewal.

REFERENCES: CHAPTER 1

1 For an account see Royal Town Planning Institute (1975), DoE (1975a), and Lichfield (1976a).
2 Labour Party (1973). For preliminary thinking in the Labour Party see Lipsey (1973), and Brocklebank *et al.* (1973).
3 DoE (1974).
4 Lichfield (1976a).
5 Habitat/UN Conference (1976).
6 ibid., pp. 61–9.
7 This section relies on Lichfield (1978a).
8 For a broader review see Lichfield (1979b).
9 DoE (1978a).
10 This relies on Lichfield (1979a).
11 Ratcliff (1949), Renne (1958), Johnson and Barlowe (1954).
12 Land Economics Institute (1960), Clawson (1973), Ratcliffe (1976), and Dunkerley *et al.* (1977).
13 Archer (1971).
14 Commission of Inquiry into Land Tenures (1976).
15 Habitat/UN Conference (1976).
16 United Nations, Department of Economic and Social Affairs (1973).
17 Vickers (1965, p. 25), Solesbury (1974, p. 54).
18 Vickers (1965), Solesbury (1974), Bauer and Gergen (1968).
19 Lichfield *et al.* (1975, ch. 2).
20 See, for example, Renne (1958), Johnson and Barlowe (1954).
21 Barlowe (1958), and Denman and Prodano (1972).

22   McAuslan (1975).
23   See, for example, Barlowe (1958).
24   Guttenberg (1959).
25   For reasoning, see Lichfield (1956, part I).

Chapter 2

The Implementation of Development Plans

2.1 AN OVERVIEW OF PLAN IMPLEMENTATION

In this chapter we are concerned not so much with how to implement plans which have been prepared but rather with the preparation of plans with a view to their implementation: i.e. with those factors which arise in the plan-making process which, if tackled appropriately, enhance the prospects of the implementation of the plan which is being prepared.

But in order to give some perspective to plan-making studied in this way, it is useful at the outset to give an overview of plan implementation, as a context for subsequent discussion. This is done by reference to a typical but hypothetical example; and to make the example as straightforward as possible, it relates to the process of building a new town in accordance with a plan. This process can be divided into the following stages.[1]

2.1.1 PLAN-MAKING[2]

Here we include the well-tried practice of designing the plan for the new town. Typically, it is conducted first at the macro level (to decide by national or regional study and appraisal the case for the new town, its size, character, rate of growth, etc.), leading to the selection of a specific site, followed by the micro planning on the site (preparing the actual development plan for the town itself, to be built over phases).

2.1.2 DEVELOPMENT PLANNING[3]

By development is meant bringing together all the factors of production (the land, the various development agencies, the construction industry, finance) needed for the city building, matched to the needs and demands of the users. In essence the aim is to ensure that the factors will be available for the execution of the town plan in stages, it being recognised that should any of the factors not be present, or the demand (need backed by ability and willingness to pay, be it of the public or private sector), then the town cannot be built as planned.

2.1.3 CONSTRUCTION

The culmination of the development planning is the preparation of a series of development briefs (of varying orders of complexity) as guides to the professionals concerned with the design of the project plans: the architects, engineers, quantity surveyors, and so on. The latter will then proceed in accordance with these instructions to prepare the contract drawings for the construction force, the building and civil engineering contractors, who will work under the supervision of the project designers. This phase is completed when the finished works are handed over for occupation.

2.1.4 OCCUPATION/OPERATION/OWNERSHIP OF THE FINISHED WORKS[4]

When occupation begins in accordance with the planned intentions, the particular phase of the planned development can be said to have been completed. But then begins the long process of continued occupation (the operation of the development) which could be in accordance with the intentions (houses which continue to be used as such) or not (turned into offices). With such occupation, be it in the public or private sector, there is also the administration by the owners of the real property which is being created, with all its rights and obligations.

2.1.5 GOVERNMENT[5]

Public agencies, including the municipality, could well be the owners of many of the assets which have been created, for occupation by others (as in housing), or by themselves (municipal offices), or on behalf of the public at large (e.g. open spaces, car parks, etc.). But in addition to this kind of occupation/ownership function (more closely related to the preceding category), there is also the administration of government services for the community as a whole, on the basis of some form of constitution (e.g. elected or nominated government). For this purpose there is the need to raise income (e.g. from local taxes or from central government subvention) and the disbursement of such income in operating municipal-type services.

2.1.6 OVERVIEW

If this be the total process, then the actual implementation of the plans made in the first phase can be said to have been carried out throughout the remainder. As indicated, this is not our direct concern in this chapter. Rather, we are seeking to consider the implications for the first phase, plan-making, of the various facets of the implementation process. But for the purpose of exposition our example has related to a new town only; this is only a special example of our wider concern, implementation of plans for human settlements as a whole.

2.2 ARE PLANS MEANT TO BE IMPLEMENTED?

It is axiomatic that the purpose of plan-making is to show that a possible future exists which would be preferable to that which would otherwise occur, and at which therefore it would be desirable to aim. To some it is sufficient if the plan is some kind of a guideline or exhortation which people should be following. But to others the plan is meant for implementation, i.e. a target to which the future is to be steered by the decision-takers concerned. That is the stand taken in this book.

Clearly there is some value in the former kind of plan, one not necessarily intended for implementation. Like a beacon it will show the way and give hope. Furthermore, in the absence of any other plan, it fills a gap and so acquires its own authority. But by the same token it can be frustrating, as the following indicates: 'However admirable it may be, plans which cannot be realised are positively harmful. They stand in the way of more realistic plans, and cause needless worries to people who fear that their interest may be affected.'[6]

The mere fact that it has been necessary for government to make this statement in Britain as recently as 1967 emphasises the point. But the point relates to more than a division of view. It reveals also the sheer difficulties of producing urban and regional plans that are capable of implementation and, even given that, of the difficulties of following them through. And the result is only too apparent in countries around the world: that far too many urban and regional plans are never implemented, or at best are only implemented in part.

One cause, which is central to the focus of this book, is that the two have often been regarded as distinct as opposed to interrelated aspects of a total planning process.[7] Another is that much more attention has been given, in theory and in practice, to plan-making as opposed to plan implementation. One consequence of this separation, and disproportionate attention to plan-making, has been the neglect of plan implementation in literature and practice.

There is even much uncertainty as to just what is meant by *plan implementation*.[8] If this is the case, it is necessary to start by offering a concept at the outset. That is provided in the next section.

2.3   A MODEL FOR PLAN IMPLEMENTATION IN DEVELOPMENT PLANNING

2.3.1   THE MODEL

Some perspective on what is meant by *plan implementation* can be gathered by considering what happens in cities and regions if they are not planned at all. Borrowing an insight from the systems approach to planning, we start by recognising that cities and their regions can be regarded as a series of interrelated sub-systems of socioeconomic activities.[9] One possible categorisation of such activities is into those to do with the home (residential) and those carried on outside the home (production of goods and services; their consumption in shopping, education, leisure, entertainment, etc.). And for people to be able to enjoy both sets of activities, there is need for transportation of various kinds between all these locations by various modes (motor-cars, buses, cycling, walking) and also for communication between locations without transportation (e.g. telephone, radio, television, etc.).

These interrelated activities and physical systems have evolved, grown and declined over centuries without land-use planning under the pressure of the socioeconomic forces giving rise to activities such as the growth of population, changes in the means of livelihood, enlargement of human activity through increase of education, culture and leisure. Such evolution can take place without any change in the physical structure or absorption of more land by, for example, the increased density of occupation of socioeconomic activities in established structures, or of given numbers of vehicles on roads, or changes in the use of the structures to accommodate the more intense activity.

For this set of socioeconomic sub-systems to operate at all, there is needed a physical fabric to support it. While this can be presented in many ways, one typology is to note seven distinct elements:[10] there is the land on which all human settlement is founded; the minerals beneath the land which are the prime source of fossil energy; other natural resources which are necessary for life (sun, air, wind) and are also energy sources; the man-made buildings and their surrounding places for living, work and recreation; the infrastructure for servicing those buildings and places (the pipes carrying water, sewerage, gas, electricity, etc.); modes of transportation to convey people to and from various fixed points such as home to work, home to school; the communication along wires or through the air which enables people to have transaction with one another without the need to travel, and which is therefore a substitute for it.

But in urban history this is clearly minimal compared with the changes in the physical fabric accommodating the socioeconomic activity, giving rise to its expansion at the fringes, rehabilitation of older fabric, redevelopment for higher densities, etc., with their impact on land and other natural resources. All these changes have been the result of a series of (small or large, isolated or interrelated, public or private) development projects of various kinds via the development process (which brings together the factors of production for physical development and the consumers of that development).[11]

Thus over the centuries there has been this continuing interplay between the constraints and opportunities offered by the relatively rigid nature of the development fabric and the less rigid activities which have changed continuously and have sought to accommodate themselves within the fabric. And in the process of such change there is a consequential impact on the utilisation of the earth's surface (and its substrata and skies) and also on the other attributes of nature, man's natural environment, in his ever-growing 'pollution' of them.

This process of change and adaptation takes place in accordance with certain reasonably well-understood laws of behaviour which we have come to call the 'market system', within which units of demand interact with units of supply, to result in change in the production of wealth (development) and the distribution of its product. While the operations of this system differ as between economies and their stages of development, it can be regarded as a common thread running through all kinds of societies, be they more or less collectivised in their ownership of the means of production, distribution and consumption. In the 'mixed economies' there is that particular kind of interplay in which the private and public sectors have their own decided roles. Thus in a mixed economy the 'market' has been said to 'plan' the allocation and distribution of resources according to its own principles.[12] Then the question arises: what is understood by the implementation of the markets' 'plans'? Clearly this is not simply the workings of the market itself but the results of these workings. Such results are very widespread: in achieving physical development, in the activities in that development, in the management of the assets and activity created, in the municipal and government services needed for them, and in the interaction between all this and the corresponding elements in the remainder of the urban area (see section 2.1).

From this point we now consider the injection of development planning into the market system planning. From the outline of such planning above (see section 1.2) its role can be seen as intervening into the 'market process' so that the evolution of the cities and regions can be directed towards a future which would not otherwise emerge, and to be the best of alternative possible futures which have been considered. And it is in order to influence such future that we have the process of development planning, which aims at steering the future by means of 'planned development'.

The above analogy from 'market planning' enables us to see how 'planned development' would implement plans. For example, it would mean influencing the changes in the physical fabric which would otherwise evolve in a 'non-planned' way, and in the nature, intensity and location of the socioeconomic activities which would aim at adapting itself to that fabric. In the last resort, since the whole purpose of the physical fabric is to serve as a base for socioeconomic activities, plan implementation can only have meaning in its impact on such activities.

But if the plan is 'implemented' by exercising this influence, it is apparent that it is the producers and consumers of the physical fabric who are the implementation agencies for seeing that the plans themselves are in fact carried out. Plan implementation can take place only when these agents go along in their responses to the forces of change, be it in the carrying out of physical development or in the socioeconomic activities related to development.

From the logic of this model, it is thus not true to say 'Town and country planning policies and the laws that support them are a paradox' on the grounds that 'Planners do not plan the use of land and resources within the competence of their own executive powers. As planners their authority is over the use of powers lying in the hands of others. They plan the control of property power over land and resources, not the use and discharge of that power.'[13] On the contrary, it is seen that this is no paradox but the very intention: the marriage of the land and development 'market' which plans for and carries out the development itself for individual private and public units within the constraints of the plan-implementation authorities who are working to plans prepared for the whole community.[14]

2.3.2   THE IMPACTS FROM IMPLEMENTATION

From the preceding it is seen that the implementation of plans is achieved by the physical changes which result, providing the opportunity for a new balance in the socioeconomic, physical and natural resource sub-systems. But it is not the physical change which is of direct concern to the people affected so much as the implications for their way of life. These implications might be called the *impacts of plan implementation*.[15] These we now go on to consider, first in relation to their nature and then as to their location. As we shall see, they can be either *direct* or *indirect* (the latter are also called *'side-effects'*).

Prior to implementation of the physical output of a plan, there would be a way of life in the community in question made up of its ongoing socioeconomic activities whereby public and private services are produced for consumption, utilising in the process the physical fabric of the community and its natural resources. At the point of change of the physical fabric (more precisely when this is occupied for the purpose for which it was intended) the physical change (physical impact) on both natural and man-made resources would give rise to a change in the socioeconomic activity (activity impact). Ultimately there is the repercussion on the people concerned, or their well-being (welfare impact).[16]

Since the development process can take many years these impacts occur gradually. Some instances will be given. First, prior to the point of physical change leading to the different repercussions, there would be a period during which it would be known that physical change was to occur, with consequential reactions in anticipation by the people concerned. To exemplify, in the knowledge that a motorway is to be built in a few years' time, some will be attracted to nearby villages for higher potential accessibility but be repelled from dwellings immediately adjoining the motorway for fear of the noise. For an urban motorway the prospect of acquisition of dwellings would tend to impel owners and occupiers to move (preferring relocation when they chose rather than when directed). But for the identical reasons they would find it difficult to dispose of the property, or if disposing would need to accept lower prices then prevailed prior to the notification that the urban motorway would be built on that route. This is the well-known phenomenon of 'blight' whereby anticipation of measures for plan implementation erode established and prospective property values.

Second, during construction of the physical change (from the point in time when the builders get on to the site) there would be activity and natural resource impacts which would be temporary over the period of construction, following which their immediate cause would be removed.

Third, following the completion of the development, there would be activity and natural resource impacts in adjustment to the new physical situation. These changes would not come as a complete surprise, for their likelihood would have been predicted in the plan-making process, when the physical change would have been planned to facilitate desired changes in socioeconomic activities. But the result might not be what was predicted or planned: for example, high-income groups could occupy dwellings proposed for lower-income groups; and much more traffic than envisaged could be generated on a new road. This is inevitable since from their complex nature it is apparent that prediction of such impacts is not an easy task, particularly when it is local impacts which are under scrutiny over a long time horizon. This is so even for what might be called the 'first-round impacts', those which are traceable from the physical impact in question. But all first-round effects have ripples and chain reactions, and prediction is even more difficult for these further effects, where almost insurmountable technical difficulties arise.

We now turn to the location of the impacts. For physical change intended on particular land there will be on-site physical impacts. In anticipation of the change there will be the blight on the property in question, of the kind described. During construction there will clearly be displacement on on-site uses. And on occupation of the completed development, there will be a change in on-site socioeconomic activities.

But all the changes in socioeconomic activities, (prospective, displacement and post-construction) will have direct effects on adjoining land, so that impacts there will be linked to the on-site impacts. Anticipated blight on old houses earmarked for redevelopment will spread to adjoining property, with lowering of land values if the change is expected to depress the local market, and by raising of land values if slum clearance of the remaining pocket is proposed in a well-established middle-class residential area. Impacts on adjoining land during the construction stage speak for themselves, where noise, unsightly appearance, dust and dirt will all have their ramifications. And the completed development will result in adjustments between the prospective users and their neighbours.

But the ramifications could occur well away from the site in question. The anticipated change could well set up a chain reaction. Prospects of office employment on a site currently covered by houses could influence prospective shopping development; construction of a particular site could adversely affect distant properties on roads through which the lorries destined for the construction site would need to travel; the exploitation of a particular site for a use which previously did not exist could lead to the abandonment of development proposals for similar uses on sites in other parts of the town; refusal to permit shopping development on a particular site could enhance the prospects of another site.

Thus the impacts from plan implementation on particular sites, negative or positive, could be widespread in their ramifications, in their nature, over time and geographically. And taken together such impacts could clearly be either adverse or beneficial in nature and therefore have a differential effect on different sectors of the community. It is the prediction, measurement and categorisation of these impacts (economic, social, environmental, etc.) which is the focus of *plan evaluation*.[17]

2.3.3   ROLE OF THE VARIOUS ACTORS IN THE MODEL

If this be the model, it implies the following. *Planning* includes *plan-making*, *plan implementation*, and *plan review*. During the *planning process* these are interactive, and conclusions from *ex post* evaluation of implementation feed back into plan-making in the next round. This applies both in 'market planning' and in planned development. But there is a difference in the actors who contribute to either plan-making or plan implementation.

In the former, economic units in the market, the private or public firms, both plan and implement by their decisions; they are the *implementation agencies*. But in *planned development* the *plan-making authorities* are devising policies and programmes to stimulate, steer and regulate the *implementation agencies* who would be developing and operating in the 'market'; and it is as *implementation authorities* that they are giving effect to these policies and programmes in controlling and supplementing the *implementation agencies*.

In this regard it is apparent that our model portrays an over-simplified situation in practice. For any particular locality there could be a number of *plan-making* and also *plan-implementation* authorities working concurrently (for example, the regional and local authority plan-makers; the central and local government plan implementers). And all these are planning for and guiding a host of implementation and operation agencies. Thus the matrix of relationships is a very rich one, both on the plan-making and plan-implementation levels.

Taking the same approach as above, let us first consider the 'market-planned' town or region. The *implementation agencies*, whether they are in the private or public sector, act in the classic role of entrepreneurs in economics whereby they bring together the various factors of production (land, the building industry, financial investment in both the short and the long term), performing the role of the 'development industry'. But since they are producing the development for consumption, their own or someone else's, they need to consider and deal with another range of actors (be these the direct consumers of the finished development in terms of occupation − operators − or the less direct consumers as absentee owners). Each kind of consumer needs its own kind of financing, which is obtained from a variety of lending agencies. And the whole of the consumption market is influenced by the brokers, public-relations media, development promoters of particular towns, etc., who are attempting to bridge the gap between producers and consumers.

But these various actors who make up the *implementation agencies* are also *plan-makers* for their own activities, in the sense that they make some forward-looking provision for their intended activities. This could be simple, as in the case of the owner-occupier who builds his house, or the building society which makes its lending strategy for housing finance; or complicated, as in the case of a nationalised board for railways which makes its long-term plans for its sector.

Such plans are the warp and woof of the urban and regional plans which are prepared for a community. But here there are also many actors. Any local authority making its own plan will work within a hierarchy of plan-making bodies which, in addition to itself, may embrace policies, plans and programmes at the national and regional levels, planning authorities of adjoining towns with joint concerns, to perhaps the plan-makers of the neighbourhoods who are 'doing it themselves' through public participation. And all these plan-making bodies are at the centre of a web of other actors who are making their contribution in the ongoing process, such as interest or pressure groups, employers, trade unions, and so on.

Finally, come the *plan-implementation* authorities, who are responsible for seeing the urban and regional plan into effect. Here again a hierarchy can be seen at work. For example, in Britain the local authority function in this regard can be divided in a complex way in a two-tier local authority system which is then subject to ministerial control, which in turn can be shared functionally with other ministries (who exercise a sectoral plan-making role, as in the Ministry of Transport).

We have thus different groups of actors in the plan-implementation model, and each group can contain various institutions in any particular instance. But equally well one institution can combine the role of various actions. A clear example is the local authority which is a plan-making and plan-implementation authority as well as a development agency in carrying out 'positive planning' in, for example, town-centre redevelopment. Another is the new town development corporation, which both makes plans and implements by being the major development agency in its town. But this combination of role does not obscure the differentiation of role. A case in point is the potential conflict where a local authority in new town central-area development is maximising land value as landowners and controlling its own development as plan implementers.

This completes our over-brief review of the actors in this array of planning and implementation agencies. All those mentioned are the decision-making units, be they the individual home-builder or the Secretary of State. But throughout are found the various professionals (planners, architects, managers, etc.) who are not only concerned with advising particular institutions which they serve (as employee, consultant, etc.) but also make their own contribution through the independent professional and academic exchange which they are continually having in meetings, discussions, symposia, journals and so on.

Given this array, it is no wonder that the empirical aspects of implementation are difficult to disentangle from studies of practice.

2.3.4   VARIATIONS IN MODEL AS BETWEEN COUNTRIES AND WITHIN COUNTRIES

As indicated above, our conceptual model is intended to apply generally as an approach. But it is clear that many and perhaps all the variables will take on a particular emphasis in different countries, and indeed as between parts of countries. For example, the very socioeconomic forces which give rise to the pressures for development, and in turn to the physical change brought about by development, are the determinants of the rate of development which is in demand and which must be catered for. A rapid rate of development in a situation of inadequacy in the various actors in plan implementation (institutions, financing, professionals, etc.) will create quite different conditions from a situation of slack development pressures whereby all these actors are in adequate supply and operation. Another example is the variation in the political commitment as between countries to plan implementation.

In some there could exist all the needed laws and institutions, but plan implementation becomes a dead letter because of the unwillingness of government to pursue a plan when faced with decisions of expediency, or the unwillingness of the Courts to enforce a plan because of likely political tensions.

It is for the countries concerned to draw conclusions on their relative strengths and weaknesses as they affect the workings of the model. But here there is need to bring out one particular feature which is the common concern of the professionals involved in plan-making and plan implementation: namely, the nature of the planning system within which they are working in their own country.

By a *planning system* is meant something more than just the planning process, i.e. plan-making, plan implementation and review. In one formulation it comprises in addition the interrelated elements of co-ordination of public decisions, appropriate political, ministerial and professional machinery, participation by the public which is affected, and means of communication among all parties to the process.[18] To make some obvious points, there is all the difference in the world in plan implementation between localities which have or do not have co-ordination in decisions by central and/or local government departments; availability or non-availability of public officials who are professionally equipped in comprehending the development process; and whether or not the public is brought into the picture, be it in terms of information or decision involvement. But less obvious, though just as profound, is the varied machinery of plan-making, implementation and review which is embodied in the statute, constitution and administrative law of the country.

2.4   PLAN-MAKING WITH A VIEW TO IMPLEMENTATION

2.4.1   GENERAL

The difference in the statutory planning process in different countries can be seen clearly in one particular difference in plan-making, between what is generally called the 'master plan' and the 'development plan'. The former envisages some end-state for the town or region but does not face up to questions as to *how* the end-state will be reached, by *whom*, *when*, at *what costs*, etc. The latter does not start with the end-state but the present, and proceeds towards some provisionally formulative end-state by phases of development, the earlier being seen with greater clarity than the latter, and thereby addressing itself to the questions just posed in the plan-making stage.

Clearly the process of plan-making under each of these types of plan will have different implications for implementation. This is an instance of what was indicated above: that if we are to have successful plan implementation, we must begin with a policy, plan or programme which has been devised with an eye to enhancing its prospects for implementation. Otherwise the failures for plan implementation could lie in the plan-*making*. This viewpoint is so obvious that emphasis would appear hardly necessary. For example, the engineer or architect hardly needs to be told that in presenting his design for a structure it is assumed that in the design he has taken into account the conditions necessary for erecting the structure; it is the omissions from this practice (as in the Sydney Opera House) which go to make the point. It is equally obvious that even given the wish to include implementation feasibility in the plan-making, the very process is abundantly more difficult. But the point none the less needs emphasising, since there is in all urban and regional planning an element of utopianism which makes a virtue of providing a picture of what is not realistically obtainable, and in so doing tends to aim at lighting a beacon for men's hopes and aspirations rather than implementation.

In the nature of these difficulties it is not easy to prescribe just *how* plan-making can be improved with an eye to its implementation prospects. We are some way from either having firm conclusions from empirical case studies of the impediments to be overcome, or from agreeing a conceptual model for implementation of the kind indicated above. Accordingly, we here proceed on more cautious lines of showing how to increase the consciousness for the causes of failure or success in plan implementation by offering some simple guidelines in a check-list of procedures for improving 'implementability' in the plan-making stages. None of these are very startling or novel in themselves but it is the full consciousness of them in practice and their interrelation which can make the impact.

2.4.2   FAILURES AND SUCCESS IN PLAN IMPLEMENTATION[19]

The above discussion on the context for the choice of plan-implementation measures has at several points touched upon constraints on choice which are imposed upon the implementation authority by the 'outside world'. It is of interest to enlarge on this point here, since the inability to appreciate the nature of these constraints on implementation must often lie at the root of the failure to implement plans. We do so by pointing out some factors which can give rise to failure. By definition, if the causes of failure can be overcome, then implementation is on to the path of success. The potential cause of failure needs to be overcome, or the potential success exploited, for otherwise each attempt to implement a plan ends in failure; and each failure makes it more difficult to succeed the next time.

Technical inadequacy of plan
For plan implementation to be successful there must be a plan which is sensible.

This requires, for example, that (i) the studies which have been carried out reflect reality; (ii) the conclusions from the studies are sound as to the problems and opportunities which are present; (iii) the alternative possible futures which have been devised for evaluation are likely to be attractive to the people concerned; (iv) the mode of choice between alternative futures would appear reasonable; and (v) the actual choice can be justified. Unless there is some confidence in these and other aspects of the plan-making process, then confidence is undermined in the attempts to implement the plan. It is in this context that the positive role of public participation in plan-making can be so important.

Insufficient legal framework

Whatever the amount of influence which is used for plan implementation, there must be some foundation in law for the actual interventions which are proposed. If this does not exist, then the measures themselves can be successfully challenged in the Courts. In this respect much depends upon whether the constitution of the country is written or not. In the latter case each implementation measure must be backed up by specific statute or administrative law, so that the legality of the powers can be checked precisely. But where the constitution is written there is a continuing need for reinterpretation in the light of the legality of new measures. This results in the kind of running battles so familiar in the USA.[20] But issues of this kind are not unknown where there is no written constitution. The accumulation of planning powers in Britain, for example, and the nature of their use by authorities and bureaucracies, have risen to such dimensions that there is fear that they may be undermining the fundamental rights to the individual allowed by the British Constitution.[21]

Inadequate institutions

As indicated above, this can apply both to the development and operating institutions and also those concerned with plan-making and plan implementation. In developed countries, institution-building could involve simplifying and rationalising a top-heavy bureaucratic structure. In developing countries, where appropriate institutions do not exist, an initial step in the plan-making process could be the building of the institutions required, without which it is futile to start.

Not in accord with high- or lower-level authorities

Since any plan is part of a vertical chain of plans (from national to local) it clearly must have some vertical relationship with them. If they are in accord, then less resistance can be expected to their implementation than if the reverse applies, since the collaboration is needed, or certainly the absence of resistance, of the other authorities, be they at the higher or lower levels.

Inadequacy or maldistribution of economic resources

The implementation of a plan necessarily requires resources at the disposal of the development and operating agencies, for otherwise little could happen on the ground. But given adequate total resources, there may be failures owing to maldistribution between agencies. This could arise where the purpose of the planning is to transfer resources to ends which the market would not provide for, for example in the slowing down of expansion in order to provide more social overheads or amenities, or less environmental pollution, and so on.

Inadequate financial resources for compensation
While financial resources are clearly linked with the economic resources considered under the previous head, there is a special constraint in plan implementation relating to the capacity for financial adjustments between the planning/implementation agency and land- and property-owners. This arises where the introduction of a plan aims at intervening in the patterns of land and property ownership and thus changing the values which currently prevail, and which could be expected to prevail without the introduction of the plan. Where intervention would result in the diminution of some established or prospective values (be they privately or publicly owned), then there is raised the issue of compensation for the diminution of value, at levels dictated by law. Failure in implementation can then arise through the authorities having inadequate funds for the purpose.

But failure can also arise in another respect in this context. Where the compensation provisions are light in terms of the financial resources required from the authorities, they are necessarily heavy in terms of losses to be experienced by the landowners. This will lead to the land market refusing to operate under normal supply and demand conditions, and so opting out of the business of the development process which is at the root of city-building.

Lack of political backing
However well equipped the plan-making and plan implementation under the previous heads, it is all a preparation for the political backing of implementation, and it is here that failure so often occurs. For example, there could be agreement (by decision-makers) to the proposals in a plan, but reluctance at the point where resistance emerges to its implementation from those adversely affected; here often arises the well-known dichotomy between the short-term view of the politician interested in re-election and the longer-term view necessarily involved in planning for a community.

Lack of public backing
But even if there is political backing by the elected representatives, there still needs to be backing by those who have elected them, and on whose behalf the plan is ultimately prepared, the public at large. These are not only the residents of the planned area but also those non-residents who use it for other purposes, e.g. work, recreation or leisure, be it from nearby or far away.

The achievement of such public backing is now carried out through the process of 'public participation'. This requires not merely informing the public of what is proceeding but involving them, so that they may exercise their views and opinions on the various issues which arise in the plan-making and plan-implementation process. To some extent this is achieved indirectly by consultations with sectoral or representative groups (e.g. industry, commerce, nature-lovers, shoppers) who would speak for their sectors. But in addition, and beyond this, there is a need to involve the public direct by appropriate machinery devised for the purpose, e.g. exhibitions, meetings, questionnaires and discussion groups.

2.4.3   PROCEDURES FOR IMPROVING PROSPECTS OF PLAN-MAKING DURING IMPLEMENTATION

A model of the plan-making process

Following this review of the likely sources of failure in plan implementation, we now turn to the question: how should these considerations affect the process of plan-making? This question is of critical interest for the proposition in our approach: that plans are meant to be implemented. The comments to be made in this respect could be of general character. In order to make them more explicit we introduce a model of the plan-making process in Figure 2.1 as a framework to indicate how and where this process would be affected.

Figure 2.1

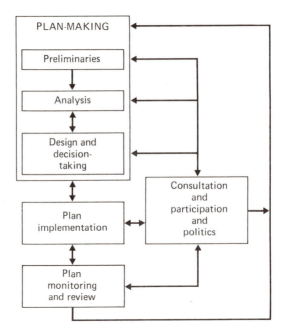

Very many models of the plan-making process are put forward in the practice and literature of planning.[22] While all their proponents would agree that such a process should not be an accidental or random set of activities but have some systemic sequence of steps (that is, be rational), there is disagreement as to, for example, the particular steps, their proper sequencing and relative weights. Thus there cannot be said to exist one generalised planning model which could be regarded as representative of all the variety. Accordingly we have adopted a synthetic model for the purpose of exposition based upon a review of what is practised and written. In this we see implementation as one aspect of a continuing *planning process* which starts with plan-making and then proceeds through implementation to monitoring, review and alteration as necessary of the original plans, policies or programmes. While it is convenient to describe it as a linear process, it is hardly necessary to add that in practice it could be recursive, cyclical, iterative and having feedback loops. This aspect is brought out in part in Figure 2.1, which also shows how consultation, participation and politics run throughout the total planning process.

Checklist of procedures for improving prospects of plan implementation
Within the synthetic model of the planning process just described we now particularise its steps and bring out as a check-list particular aspects where the process would be affected if, during it, a particular eye was given to the implementation of the plan being prepared. The comments made are clearly examples and not intended to be comprehensive of all that can be done in this respect.

1   *Preliminaries*
1.1 *Preliminary recognition and definition of issues.* In selecting the issues which are to be dealt with in the plan, have regard to those which are susceptible to influence through plan implementation, which in turn requires appreciation of the range of such measures which are available (see section 2.5 below).
1.2 *Decision to act and definition of planning task.* Here it is necessary to formulate with the plan-implementation authorities the approach to, and levels of, intervention which they contemplate as policy, and accordingly the way in which they intend and are able to use the range of implementation measures available. A necessary consideration here is the nature of the implementation agencies which are likely to be available. Variations in these matters will lead to variations in prospects for implementation of particular proposals.
1.3 *The planning context.* The review of plans, policies and programmes of higher-level authorities, including some appreciation of their robustness, will provide the context for ensuring that the local proposals are not likely to fail because of the failure of receiving higher-level approvals and support.
1.4 *Select plan and study areas.* While 'study areas' will be selected to provide the most effective way of understanding local problems, etc., it is only the 'planning area' over which the implementation authority will have its direct powers, supplemented by the higher-level plan-making authorities. Clearly this is critical in whether or not the plan-implementation authority will have powers of implementation; and clearly this will lead to consideration of the need for collaboration in this regard with adjoining authorities.

2   *Analysis*
2.1 *Review of data collection for analysis and forecasting.* In carrying out this critical step, regard should be had to data needed not only for plan-making but also for implementation (for example, land ownership, plans of local firms, etc.).
2.2 *Topic studies and forecasts.* It is here that the possibility arises of ensuring that the studies to be carried out are strictly relevant to the issues of the area, and its problems and opportunities, and thus to the realities of the remedial measures which are to be proposed.

2.3   *Identification of problems and opportunities.* This is the most critical step in the synthesis from the preceding action, since it identifies just where the programme is to operate if it is to tackle the underlying problems of the area and take advantage of its latent possibilities. A programme which fails to have adequate regard to these matters will not attract the support needed for implementation.

2.4   *Identification of objectives.* But the prospects of tackling the problems effectively and taking advantage of the opportunities will be undermined unless the planning objectives can be traced back to this base. This is in contrast to formulation of operation objectives from a prior definition of goals (weighted or not) since while these may be strong on aspiration they may not have a base in the realities of the area, and so fail to be acceptable for implementation.

2.5   *Identify implementation measures available.* A realistic enumeration and review of the implementation measures which are available (treating this in the broadest sense) is a critical step in ensuring that there is some means of bringing about the proposals which are to be generated (see Chapter 4).

2.6   *Identify constraints.* Since it is the constraints of various kinds on the possible action to be taken which will undermine any effective execution of that action, a clear definition of the constraints is essential. But in this it is also clearly necessary to have regard to the 'degree of constraint' since none are absolute (in the sense that all can be overcome at a cost), in order that the benefits of relaxing constraints against the cost of so doing can be considered during the plan-making.

2.7   *Formulation of operational criteria for planning.* Since the culmination of the design and decision-taking in plan-making leads to tests of various kinds, to lead to the adoption of a particular strategy from the alternatives available, it is clearly necessary for the operational criteria adopted in the planning to have fullest regard to the nature of these tests. To the extent that they do not, features are being built in which will fail to be accepted in the later tests, and by definition therefore fail to be strong on implementability.

3   *Planning and decision-taking*

3.1   *Generation of alternatives.* There are many ways of approaching the delimitation of ranges to be explored in the formulation of alternative proposals and strategies. In terms of implementability it is important in this selection not to stray too far beyond what is likely to be capable of implementation. This can be achieved if the alternatives are sketched out in relation to the findings of the studies carried out under the heading of 'analysis', since these are all geared towards implementability. For example, given particular planning objectives derived from problems and opportunities, what are the various ways of achieving some solution to these objectives?

3.2   *Consistency tests on alternatives.* This is clearly a critical step in ensuring a sensible relationship between certain of the necessary ingredients in the plan (such as consistency between the population to be provided for and the job opportunities which will be available for the economically active population).

3.3   *Testing for feasibility of alternatives.* As regards implementation, this is clearly the most critical test, since from its conclusions there will emerge the best possible indication available at the plan-making stage of whether the plan or strategy is likely to be implementable, and also the aspects on which there will be more doubt. Accordingly, the tests must cover all relevant aspects, such as effective legal framework, institutions, political backing, economic resources, demand, financing resources, and so on.

3.4   *Testing for open-endedness and flexibility.* However careful the prediction in the plan-making process, there must always be a large degree of uncertainty relating to the future, which thus makes it difficult to be confident about the plan proposals which are to be implemented beyond the immediate future. This uncertainty will also extend to the implementation measures and their feasibility. In terms of implementation, unless this flexibility is provided for, there could be obstruction to implementation of proposals to be generated later in modification of those in the original plans. The tests, however, are quite different from those for feasibility. Whereas for feasibility it is the practicability in respect of known measures and constraints which is being studied, in flexibility it is the potential barriers to implementation.

3.5   *Testing for acceptability.* Following the previous tests comes that for choosing the plan which is deemed by the decision-makers to be the most acceptable to them and their community. For this some criterion is necessary as to which plan would be the 'best'. Examples would be that which could be achieved with the lowest capital and operating cost and therefore would be the least burden on rates and taxes; or that which would give the least net overall cost; or that which would give the maximum benefit to the under-privileged sections of the community. From this it is clear that the plan to be chosen for implementation will depend on the choice criterion adopted.

It is also clear that a plan adopted on any particular criteria might not prove to be completely acceptable to the community as a whole, or to local sections of it, which would thus raise barriers to successful implementation. Some forewarning can be obtained on this in the evaluation analysis by pinpointing those groups of the community which would be adversely affected under each of the alternatives, and drawing conclusions in relation to these groups in respect of each.[23] Thus it could be predicted that if plan *A*, adopted on the least-cost basis, did little compared with plan *B* to ameliorate the conditions of the poor or a minority group, it would attract greater opposition from these groups than plan *B*, which would frustrate implementation. Thus from the evaluation there can be determined the general likelihood of 'acceptability of the alternatives', as a measure of friction that would arise from implementation.

3.6   *Decision-taking on the preferred plan.* The preceding tests will have offered the basis for a decision from the alternatives available. Clearly not all sections of the population will find the final choice acceptable. Accordingly, to enhance the prospects of implementability, it is necessary to be able to demonstrate that the preferred plan is superior to others; or if this cannot be done, it is necessary to have convincing reasons as to why it should be preferred to others which stand up better on the tests.

3.7   *Draft preferred plan, strategy, etc.* From the preceding it follows that the preferred plan or strategy can then be drafted in the necessary detail with some confidence that it will have the maximum chances of acceptability and implementability.

3.8   *Formulate the development programme.* On the basis of the chosen plan, policy or strategy the programme should be developed by specifying the *timing* of investment and action, the *agency* responsible for carrying it out, in central or local government or in the private sector, and the *expenditure* (capital and operating) required, with an indication of revenues to be earned. In addition there will be a series of policies which are to be used as a guide for day-to-day decisions by the plan-implementation authority. This will imply a commitment by the various agencies to the programme and policies and the necessary mobilisation of their resources, an implication which will have been explored in the various tests, consultations, and so on.

Testing for feasibility of implementation

Reasons for feasibility testing

In the earlier sections of this chapter we attempted to clarify the considerations which have a bearing on the implementation of plans; an understanding of the process and of the impacts of implementation; an array of the measures available; the context for choosing the measures; and a warning of the typical causes of failure in the issue of the measures. We then drew the considerations together in making them operational in relation to plan-making, using a synthetic model for the purpose.

Clearly, the more systematically the implementation considerations are borne in mind in the plan-making process, the more chance will there be that the various plan alternatives are feasible, i.e. practicable in terms of implementation. But however systematic, analytical and quantitative this process might be, the feasibility of any particular alternative cannot be ensured, simply because in urban and regional planning we are dealing with very complex situations which are only amenable to a degree of operational precision. Accordingly we urged above the necessity to 'test' the alternatives which have been generated for their feasibility, alongside all kinds of other tests which may be carried out in relation to other aspects of plan-making.[24]

An array of feasibility tests

We now enumerate a series of tests for feasibility which are designed to check the degree to which the plans which have emerged are likely to cause problems in implementation. They are not random. First, they flow from the implementation considerations outlined in earlier sections of this chapter; and furthermore they are listed in an order which reflects the plan-making process itself, so that if the tests were carried out in this order the earlier tests would be addressed to the earlier parts of the process, and so on.

1   *Higher-level direction.* Most plans are made in a situation where there is concurrent higher-level plan-making. Thus the initial question arises: does the plan in question accord with the views of the higher-level authorities, in terms, for example, of their goals, assumptions, forecasts, constraints and policies? If not, there will be friction in implementation. In making the test it is necessary, therefore, to elicit what these higher-level views are. The fact that they have not been expressly formulated, as is often the case, does not mean

that the test can be avoided; the views which have not been expressed will soon enough be formulated when faced with the plan in question.

2   *Lower-level aims.* In most plans there are also concurrent 'lower-level' plan-making, as in a district *vis-à-vis* a county, or a landowner *vis-à-vis* a district, or transport or housing department *vis-à-vis* a planning department. This brings in the reverse process to that just described. But whereas the higher-level direction must be sought, the lower-level aims need not be accommodated, since in principle the higher level would direct the lower. But in practice non-feasibility could arise through the lower-level authorities having responsibility for implementation which they will not exercise under direction, or having commitments which they cannot abandon even though not in line with the higher-level plan.

3   *Planning authority's directive.* In the initial stages of the plan-making process the plan-making authority may or may not have expressly formulated its goals, objectives, aims and constraints as a guideline to the professional team. If they have, then the test is to see the degree of accordance with these directions.[25] But where they have not, then they will do so in the ongoing dialogue between the authorities and the professionals in the plan-making. The tests would then be applied when the occasion arises.

4   *Constraints from context studies.* So far we have considered constraints which are external to the professionals in plan-making, but now come those which are generated by them in the studies for the plan. For example, is the land allocated for development suitable in topographical, geological and locational attributes? Will there be an economic demand for the accommodation to be generated? Will the economic resources be available for implementation? The answers to these questions will emerge from the plan-making process, if the studies to be carried out have been set up in a way to enable the answers to be produced.

5   *Solutions to planning problems and grasping of opportunities.* A major output from the planning studies is the definition of the current and emerging problems in the area which needs to be tackled (i.e. the gaps between what is or will be, and what ought to be and the opportunities which need to be grasped). It is the way the plan does this which is of importance to those using the area, for whatever their views of planning is, it is their experience of the problems and their eye on the opportunities which makes them vocal. It is for this reason that in some versions of the planning process it is not the operationalisation of decision-makers or community goals which lead to the definition of the planning objectives but the identification of the problems and opportunities which are moulded by the goals and aims of the decision-maker.[26] Thus an important test is to indicate the degree to which the plans will resolve current and potential problems and group opportunities. The more they do, the higher the acceptability and therefore the greater the ease in implementation in this respect.

6   *Availability of implementation measures.* Each plan can be seen as an indication of the change which is visualised by the planners over some period in the future from the conditions which exist, or which might otherwise exist if there were no plans. It is to effect this change that implementation measures of the kind discussed above are needed. Accordingly, a critical test is the availability of such measures, and their effectiveness for the purpose.

7 *Availability of institutions.* If the measures are to be used, then there must be available the agencies and institutions to use them at the appropriate level in budget, quality and skills of manpower, and so on. These should relate to the development and operating agencies needed to build and run the town in question, as well as the plan-implementation authority (as opposed to the plan-making authority) needed to guide the future in accordance with the plans. The test will investigate whether or not they are available or are likely to be available at the appropriate level.

8 *Acceptability by the public at large.* In this test we are concerned with the public at large, including representatives of groups (e.g. motorists' associations), in their capacity as consumers of the goods and services which would be generated as outputs of the plan as implemented. For example, those in need of housing must feel that adequate provision is planned in terms of number, location, quality, price, etc., and that there are appropriate building, financing, etc., agencies to produce the houses.

Just what the public or any groups will have to say in practice about a plan on the occasion of its publication or implementation it is impossible to predict; there will be so many considerations. What can be done is to predict the impact of the plan proposals upon the various groups in the community (as residents, motorists, shoppers, workers, etc.) in order to gauge how they are likely to be affected under the plans, since this will be a measure of their likely reaction. The test for this must bring out the changes which can be expected in the way of life of the people affected (adequate homes, inadequate roads for cars, etc.) and also their reaction to it, in terms of their perception of how their own objectives will be advanced or retarded. This would be the viewpoint from which they will judge whether the plans will bring them advantage or disadvantage. But since any individual could be represented in many groups, it follows that he may not have a single view on acceptability.

9 *Political acceptability.* All the preceding tests will have produced answers which will be of relevance to the political decision-takers in considering their attitude to the plans. For example, it would tell them whether these are (i) likely to be in accord with higher- or lower-level agencies; (ii) follow their own directives; (iii) be based upon the realities of the area in question, its problems and opportunities; (iv) be capable of implementation in terms of measures and institutions; (v) and do the minimum of harm and the maximum of good to the public at large in terms of ways of life and the values held. These are all essential ingredients to the considerations which political decision-takers have to face up to. Thus having exposed the ingredients it is possible to make some test as to whether the decision-takers are likely to find the plans acceptable on these considerations. This is the essence of politics in planning, to which we return below (section 2.9).

10 *Degrees of feasibility.* Although the term 'feasibility' suggests a *yes* or *no* situation, that the plan may be impracticable or not, in reality there are degrees of feasibility. This arises for at least two reasons.

First, the various plan elements to be tested are not all of equal weight as regards feasibility in implementation. For example, some lower-level aims can be overridden, as they are in everyday planning practice; political non-acceptability can be transformed overnight with the election to power of another party; slack economic demand for housing can be stiffened by direct government subsidy which makes the demand effective.

Second, from this it follows that the tests will reveal or confirm conclusions of various significance for the feasibility of implementation. Some would offer no threat at all (an implementation measure not being available but readily secured); some offer a modest threat (a need to build an institution); some offer a major threat (inadequacy of financial resources to the implementing authority).

The result of the tests on the critical bottlenecks will thus reveal the 'degree of non-feasibility' and thus the aspects in which there will be serious or less serious problems arising in implementation. A conclusion that the plan is non-feasible on an item should not necessarily lead to the abandonment of the item or plan but rather to the attempt at reformulation, using the tests as a feedback to show the kind of modification needed to achieve plan implementation. This would show the cost of relaxing the particular implementation constraint. The cost might prove manageable, or it could still be decided that it was too high, with the plan being declared 'non-feasible'.

In any work on this kind of reformulation certain principles must be recalled. Not all feasibility tests apply to all elements of a plan, and therefore inadequacy in certain respects will not necessarily imperil the whole plan. But in so far as the plan is meant to hang together as a whole, failure in realisation in one component could have repercussions throughout. Furthermore, where several of the potential failure items apply to a particular element of the plan, it is normally only sufficient for one item to break down for that particular element to be entirely prejudiced.

Consultation, participation throughout

Consultation with other groups, agencies, authorities throughout
So far we have mentioned discrete stages of the planning process. But throughout all stages there would be discussions with all the other agencies which are involved. These will be varied and numerous: those concerned with development (landowners, developers, financial institutions); with operation (industrialists, transport undertakings, municipal departments, nationalised boards); other planning authorities (of the same tier, or higher or lower in level). In this context the discussions will bring out any implications for implementation.

Involving the public throughout
Above, acceptability of the plan to the public has been discussed in terms of the impacts on particular groups. But in common experience resistance to plans is widespread through all groups (if only through dislike of change) and thus could be encountered even from groups who would be advantaged in the long term but can only see specific short-term disadvantage, or are resisting particular aspects of a plan which they would welcome on the whole. This again creates friction in implementation. Accordingly, an overriding aid to implementation is the bringing of the public into the planning process from its inception, so that they might understand what is going on and not simply react from lack of information and irritation with bureaucracy.

This involvement of the public is part of the 'learning process'. In this process it is important to ensure that the issues and questions raised with the public at any moment during plan-making are relevant at that stage and not to others. Thus different questions would be raised at successive stages. These should accordingly relate also to implementation, whose implications should be considered throughout the process, not simply at the end. In this way the resistance for implementation will be considered at the appropriate time and the lessons learned for incorporation in plan-making.

Working with the decision-makers throughout
Finally, there is the recognition that the planning process as practised by professionals is an input to decision-making by government at central and local levels and must therefore be carried out in close collaboration with government. The form of collaboration, and the interplay between professionals and politicians, will vary from country to country, and within countries, and so makes for difficult generalisation, except on one point: disregard will be fatal for plan implementation.

2.5   CHOOSING THE IMPLEMENTATION MEASURE

2.5.1   GENERAL

In the preceding section we have shown how plans can be prepared with an enhanced eye to their prospects of implementability. In this process, at various points there is the need to review the range of implementation measures which are available in the particular circumstances, in order to ensure that the plan is designed to be implemented in accordance with this range. Since this particular step is of critical importance in ensuring the maximum prospects for implementation, we dwell further on it in this section.

2.5.2   A CATEGORISATION OF PLAN-IMPLEMENTATION MEASURES

In the model of plan implementation described above (see section 2.3) two sets of actors are involved: the implementation agencies, and authorities. Here it is our purpose to review the implementation measures available to the latter rather than the former.

For the purpose of this review we are not concerned just with those measures which conventionally are recognised as available for plan implementation but also with those which are available for the general purposes of government and have been and can be adapted for the purposes of plan implementation. As the powers are of a miscellaneous kind it is useful to categorise them. This is now done under five headings, starting with those measures which require the least formality in legal power, rising up the scale to those requiring the most.

1   *General influence over the developers and operators*
Even a plan without implementation teeth can have an influence on implementation agencies, if in the absence of any other it offers a sensible context for their decisions. This is 'indicative planning', which has had its own successes.[27]
But quite a different example of what might be done under this heading is the

pressure that can be exerted by consumer groups on the producers of goods and services, in this case the implementation agencies, securing adjustments in their practice. This kind of influence grows the more 'educated' are those who can be potentially influenced. To encourage such an attitude in the adult population clearly requires considerable resources. The attitude could be made the more effective, the younger that the 'education' starts in the environmental and associated fields. Given adults who have spent their school years in absorbing knowledge about the environmental field, the higher would their standards be in what they are able to press for.

Pressures of this kind could arise in response to proposals by developers and operators, leading to conflict situations in development control. But the pressures can become the more pointed if those making them have alternative policies which they would like to see put forward. When such policies are represented in urban and regional plans for the area in question, we have what has become known as 'advocacy planning'.[28]

Also in this category of plan-implementation measures come the activities of individuals, whose personal role can be so critical. They have various names in the literature: the 'reticulist', 'animateur' or 'change agent',[29] whose job it is to not only see the possibilities of action but also by personal intervention to ensure that the action takes place; or the 'transactive planner'[30] who proceeds by a process of mutual learning between the client and expert groups, in which interpersonal relations acquire central importance.

2 *Organisational*

Individual agencies in development and operation make their own decisions on criteria suited to their own objectives but none the less can have advantage in collaboration and co-operation. Thus is opened a wide field for the use of *co-ordination* as an implementation measure.

This is potentially very powerful in the public sector when ministries within a government co-ordinate their decisions, with a view to achieving a more effective purpose, cutting out waste, and so on; or different levels of government ensure that they are not frustrating another in separately taken decisions.

But possibilities by co-ordination are not confined to the public sector. Private-sector developers and operators, as, for example, industrialists and house-builders, while remaining in open competition, could none the less have advantage in operating common policies or joining to avoid wasted resources. For example, in the common use of infrastructure they will be combining to overcome the opposition of a planning authority concerned with waste of resources.

3 *Fiscal influence*

In its everyday work government is concerned with raising revenue by taxation of various kinds, for example on income, wealth, property, land, etc. Even where such taxation is not specifically aimed at development policy, it can influence the carrying out of development: for example, by 'side-effects', as where relatively high levels of local property taxation in the centre of cities will tend to encourage dispersal.

But taxation could be also development-specific and so used more directly as a plan-implementation measure. Examples are the levy of local taxes to finance a sea wall which will protect a restricted number of properties, or taxation of vacant land to stimulate new development in accordance with a plan.

Taxation apart, there are a large array of financial incentives introduced by government which can have like effects. Without the aid of housing subsidies there would be much less development of housing for low-income groups than envisaged in a plan; and without the deterrent of high car park charges in the centres of cities, there would be more tendency for cars to enter than could be catered for by proposed roads.

4   *Direct intervention*

The specific taxation, subsidy, etc., measures just noted, which could be aimed specifically at the implementation of particular proposals, are a lead to our next group, which is entirely devoted to this purpose. They are the specific means whereby an implementation authority aims to influence the development or operations which will be carried out in practice on the ground.

First among these comes the *negative* control over the carrying out of development and operation, stemming from the legal requirement that development must receive a specific sanction by planning permit, thus giving the authorities direct control which can be aimed at plan implementation. Practice here varies between countries. In some the 'permit' is fairly automatic if the proposal is in conformity with the specifics of an approved legal scheme. In others, notably Britain, there is no such legal framework, and each application is judged on its merits against the background of a legal plan and other material considerations. Such powers, of refusal of permission, or permission with conditions, can be extended in particular cases by making 'planning agreements' whereby the developers seeking permission undertake to contribute to the general welfare of the community in various ways, as a *quid pro quo* for development permission. This can either be formal under specific agreements, or informal whereby there is a voluntary agreement in the negotiations to abide by certain conditions.

Clearly such *negative* influence can be very restrictive of the enterprise and activities of implementation agencies such as developers, entrepreneurs, business, and so on. Thus by the same token the sharing of such control, or relaxation of control, can provide a stimulus to the implementation agencies – to contribute to what is called 'releasing enterprise'. From this it is but a short step to trying to provide the environment and conditions which are favourable to enterprise, for example useful data and information, awareness of opportunities, introduction to relevant sources, helpful infrastructure, training and education.

In this sense *negative* rapidly turns to *positive*. But in addition there is the more conventional form of what is called *positive planning*. This can be of various kinds. At the simplest there is the means of assembling land by the plan-implementation authority, either by voluntary or compulsory purchase, in order to secure better development or redevelopment than could be obtained under market processes. In addition there is the direct carrying out by the authorities of physical development. In part this relates to those public goods which the authority needs to undertake since otherwise they are unlikely to be provided by the private sector (e.g. utilities, communications, transportation, social facilities in the form of schools, etc.). In part there is intervention in sectors where private agencies might be expected to operate, for example in erecting shops and offices in town centres, theatres and so on. Major instances of this kind are the new towns fostered by government which are largely products of public enterprise on the proposition that otherwise they would not be provided; *ad hoc* bodies, such as the Highlands and Islands Board, aim at the redevelopment and regeneration of regions by large-scale public development and associated activity.

5 *Personal direction*

Whereas the measures under the preceding section relate to intervention in the location, shape, intensity, etc., of physical development or related activities, our final section relates to that directed at the individual or group. 'Directed at physical' would be the proscription of certain kinds of educational establishments. 'Directed at activities' would be the banning of particular undesirable forms altogether, either absolutely or in particular locations, as, for example, with parking on the streets.

Less familiar in mixed economies but not unknown in others is the licence needed by the individual to leave his established home or established job for another. This direct control over the mobility and occupation of the individual can clearly be used in the implementation of certain policies. While the idea of this kind of control would be unacceptable in most societies, where it does exist it could conceivably be used as the ultimate measure for plan implementation.

2.5.3 CONTEXT FOR CHOICE OF IMPLEMENTATION MEASURES

The preceding review shows there is a wide range of potential implementation measures available for use in any planning situation. But clearly all such situations are not the same: there will be variations as between the countries, as between authorities in countries and over time in any particular locality. Accordingly, there will need to be a choice made between those measures for use in particular circumstances. Just how such choice would be taken on a particular measure is a topic we explore below (section 5.4). As a preliminary we sketch out here the context which would have a bearing on such choice.

In essence the aim is to comprehend the environment in which implementation will be taking place, in order to visualise what kind of policies, plans and programmes are likely to have a chance of success, and which of failure, and to prepare accordingly. Put more formally, the aim would be to find the context for a strategy for implementation.

Logic behind the planned intervention

Given that the implementation of plans is an intervention into the ongoing political economy which would otherwise build the cities, the starting-point is the approach to planned intervention of the authority concerned. Does it want, for example, to exercise a light hand on the tiller to avoid the worst excesses of 'market' operations, or a heavy hand in attempting to mould these forces towards predetermined social objectives, be they in a plan or not? Is there a specific rationale for intervention in each implementation decision, as, for example, to minimise the social cost and maximise the social benefits arising from the enterprise? Whatever the degree of intervention, can it be backed up by law, or does it rely on other forces in the society, for example on political weight (as where the poor or ethnic minorities cannot be compelled to abide by the prevailing law of the land for fear of violent revolution) or on undue influence, bribery or corruption (which circumvent legal processes)? Is the economy of the country or locality insufficiently thriving to permit planned intervention for a social goal which would undermine the profitability of the enterprise and so result in its removal elsewhere, to the detriment of the national or local economy?

The kind of plan to be implemented

In any particular country at any time there would be plans at different levels, and in some at all levels (national, regional and local). As indicated above, the very means of implementation for the different levels of plans must vary. For example, a plan at the national level would require implementation by direct government action or national-level investment or policy (e.g. on transportation networks, coastal protection, open farmland, etc.), whereas at the other end of the scale implementation in an 'action area' involves the carrying out of the physical development itself in a reasonably short space of time by public and private agencies.

The development/operating agencies which are available

Given that the ultimate implementation of a plan must rest with the development and operating agencies on the ground, for it is these at which the planning intervention is aimed, it follows that much must depend on the nature of the agencies available for the purpose. Given an active land market which would be responsive to the guidance in a plan, there would be less need for positive intervention in terms of making land available at the right price, time, etc., but more need for ensuring that the plan was not threatened through speculation. Given private-sector development companies which were capable and experienced in acting as development entrepreneurs, there would be less need for a public body to undertake this role. But where such entrepreneurs are either non-existent or inexperienced, as in a developing country, then there is a need to set up appropriate institutions for the purpose. Similar considerations apply to the operating agencies, as, for example, to the management and administration of open space or car parks, or the running of schools or hospitals; unless these are adequate, implementation in the physical sense could produce assets which would be wastefully or ineffectively administered.

Strength of plan-implementation agencies

Institution-building may also be necessary in the plan-implementation agencies which are available for intervention in the ongoing economy. It is one thing if they have the administrative and professional capacity to undertake the task and yet another if they do not. Partly this is a matter of professional manpower; in Western Europe a city can have staff of several hundred in its planning and building departments, whereas in a developing country there could merely be a handful. But it is partly also within the competence of the authority itself to administer the implementation measures in a manner which can be efficient, fair and not open to abuse. Strong measures in the hands of a weak authority with inadequate manpower can cause considerable costs in frustrating the development or operating agencies, and therefore must be counterproductive in plan implementation.

Implementation powers available

But whatever the institutional and manpower set up, a critical element is seen to be the powers which they have been given by law for the purpose of implementation. Given inadequate powers and finance, their intervention level could be ineffective in having to rely solely on measures which relate just to influence or organisation. How crippling such a limitation would be would vary with the particular society in which they are operating; in some, influence could go further than power, whereas in others it could not.

Degree of overlapping and co-ordination between public authorities

Planning as an arm of government is a relatively late arrival to the government machine and inevitably finds that it is encroaching on the sectoral planning measures of various ministries and public bodies. In the very nature of government such incremental additions to the machine and bureaucracy are rarely accepted as occasions for amending the legislative stockpile, for such understandable reasons as the pressures on the legislative machine, the vested interests of the established departments, and the weakness of planning as a government activity in terms of political backing, budgets, and so on. As a result there is often a lack of co-ordination between public-agency decisions. This alone can frustrate the use of plan-implementation measures and so condition their choice.

But by the same token here lies an opportunity for the increase of implementation powers simply through the rationalisation of the government machine: to cut out waste and friction and to increase concentration on the real objectives of the community. This lies at the base of recent developments towards government corporate planning; the more the achievement here, the more effective the use of the implementation measures, even though distributed among many agencies.

2.6   THE IMPLEMENTATION PROCESS

2.6.1   CARRYING OUT THE PROGRAMME

The starting-point

From the model of the plan-making process which was described above, it is seen that this ends with the formulation of the phased programme for the implementation of the plan – which has been designed with an eye to implementation. The nature of the programme will naturally vary as between towns. For example, in the new town it could consist of a series of discrete development projects, whereas in the established town the package of projects will be more varied, and there will also be more development control policies which are to be used as a guide for day-to-day decisions.

It is from this starting-point that the implementation process can be said to begin, though in practice there are many instances where such implementation is initiated in advance of the plan or programme being effected, simply because the decisions cannot wait. This is a specific instance of implementation without the benefit of a plan, to which we turn below.

Collaboration in carrying out the programme by agencies
The actual carrying out of the programme and policies by the various agencies on a day-by-day basis through the development and operation process is the critical step to be followed in implementation. This requires that each agency and the people within them are aware of how their actions should reflect the agreed plan in their daily decisions and routines.

React to initiatives as they arise
By definition the above programme will relate to action which could be foreseen within the plan-making process. But as new circumstances arise, implementation authorities should consider taking other action. For example, if a large local firm threatens to close, the local authority might consider taking action not previously contemplated in the plan or programme; or new proposals might be considered if central government empowers the local authority with new implementation measures.

The response of the authority should be guided by the framework of the plan or programme but the flexibility of reinterpreting earlier decisions should be preserved.

Take initiative to stimulate activity
In addition to reacting to initiatives, authorities should also consider where they can intervene to stimulate activity, where this is seen to be slack. This can take many forms. For example, an authority could seek to exploit its own role as an important institution in the economy of its own area, for example by increasing consumer demand for goods and services by direct purchase of their requirements within their area. They could provide the catalyst of an economic development officer, who would act in an entrepreneurial way. They could provide information to assist informed action. They could provide professional services, especially for small firms, in law, accountancy, and so on. They could scan their control practices (bye-laws, planning, environment, etc.) to see whether relaxation could stimulate economic activity without imperilling health, safety, the environment, and so on.

Co-ordinating the various activities
It is apparent that there is a great variety in the measures available for implementation and in the authorities who wield them. Just because of this, there is an enormous role for co-ordination by the local authority, not just for tidiness but for ensuring greater overall effectiveness. The cutting out of red tape, waste, overlapping, etc., can both release resources and make for greater efficiency in their use.

This particular role can best be exercised by the authority visualising itself as a *plan-implementation authority*, as opposed to its role as an economic agency concerned with the direct stimulus of the economy. As an implementation authority, it is overseeing all such agencies, including itself in its various departments.

2.6.2   DECISION-MAKING DURING THE IMPLEMENTATION PROCESS

Commitment to implementation
As described above, in the principles and practice of plan-making there is

tremendous scope for involvement of others by the plan-making authority and its professional advisers. There are the interest groups who must be consulted so that their viewpoints and needs can be reflected; the public who need to be informed, invited to comment and be involved in decision-making through 'public participation'. If this 'involvement' process is carried through, there is some assurance that the plan has been made in the knowledge of the views of all those concerned. And there is some assurance of involvement in plan adoption if the particular minister charged with approval of a local authority plan on behalf of the government consults with his fellow ministers and their departments, so that the collective view of government is taken into account prior to making the decision, including those who have control over economic and financial resources.

Given such involvement in plan-making and adoption, it is something of a surprise to find that in practice there seems little commitment to the implementation of the plan by those who have been so involved. This might be expected from those whose views have not been fully reflected in the plan (perhaps because they were in the minority, or had objections which had to be overridden in the general interest). But it is more surprising that even authorities who have in fact approved and adopted the plan at the end of this process are often not willing to make the commitment to carry it through and to follow its guidelines on issues as they arise. They will feel free to depart from the plan under the stress of particular decisions; and the sister departments of the minister approving the plan will not feel themselves committed to the policies which the plan enshrines, and nor will the financial and economic resources be pledged to its implementation in accordance with the programme set out.

Put more positively, if a plan is prepared as carefully as the above process indicates, and if the approval process is carried out seriously, then it might be expected that all the ministries and local government departments concerned would from that point on be working together administratively to implement the plan: by co-ordinating their policies, regulatory controls, development, budgets, land policies, taxation policies, financial incentives and disincentives, and all the other array of implementation measures which were described above. And it might be expected that there would be the political commitment to see the plan through, i.e. the decision to back the plan and programme at the political level even though there can be seen to be some political disadvantage in the short term in so doing.

There will be many reasons in practice why full commitment in this sense cannot be achieved. But so often there is no commitment at all, or just lip-service to it. This is perhaps the biggest reason for failure in plan implementation.

Role of ongoing implementation decisions

But even if there were a plan which had been carefully prepared with an eye to implementation as well as *full commitment* to its programme, it should not imply that the plan is to be carried through, come what may, as though it were a blueprint for construction which could not be departed from. Indeed, the plan and its programme will in a sense be dated at the time of approval, if not before, simply because they were devised as a plan for a future which is by definition uncertain, and therefore cannot be said to have envisaged all possible contingencies. We thus need to consider the role of ongoing decisions under the plan which may be taking place many years after the plan itself was formulated and adopted.

The decisions in question can be of many kinds. Traditionally in urban and regional planning they are of the kind described as 'negative', in that they relate to reactions to initiatives taken by implementation agencies in carrying out development, as described above. Then there come the 'positive planning measures', which is the term given to decisions by public agencies (the plan-making authority or others) to carry out development in accordance with the plan, either for its own sake or as a catalyst/framework for other development agencies. Or the decision could relate to financial incentives or disincentives devised by a national government for the advancement of regional policy. In all this, what regard should be had to the plan?

To some the answer is clear. The plan has certain policies, proposals and programmes and is therefore sacrosanct, and all decisions must be made accordingly, and the onus of proof must be on those who wish to do otherwise to show why this should not be so. Against this can be argued the following.

While such an approach is the essence of 'commitment' of the kind described above, it nevertheless does not recognise the genuine possibility that any proposal which does not accord with the plan may be superior to it, and accordingly should be accepted even if at variance with the plan. This could arise for reasons such as the following:

(a)   The level of generality at which the studies for the plan will have been carried out may be insufficient to cope with specific development issues as they arise. A typical instance here is in the fact that any development agency will prepare its own plan for its land with much greater care than could conceivably be visualised by a plan-making authority, and therefore may have come up with conclusions when making their application for permit which need to be given adequate attention.

(b)   Assumptions which have been made in plan-making could be shown to be incorrect by later events, such as in the rate of growth of population, housing demand, etc., or in the policies of higher-level authorities which have in themselves been changed for good reason (for example, in regional planning or sectoral planning of highways, airports, etc.).

Given these possibilites, the role of the ongoing implementation decisions then become not so much one of following the prescribed policies because they have been approved (and to which there is, it is hoped, commitment) but rather as a testing of the approved policies in the light of contemporary events and pressures. In essence, therefore, each such decision is a 'review' of the plan with a view to answering the same fundamental question that is raised on formal review of the plan: namely, should it be altered in the light of hindsight? Clearly the approach and techniques in such a decision review must be different from that of the formal comprehensive review (see section 2.7) but none the less the attitude should persist: would a departure from the originally formulated policies, proposals and programmes give greater net benefit to the community compared with implementing what was originally visualised? If the answer is in the affirmative, then there is a case for modifying the plan.

This again introduces a planning balance-sheet approach. In this case regard must be had to two kinds of cost. First are those already incurred in implementing the plan as originally proposed which would be scrapped by a decision leading to reversal. Up to a certain point the advantages would justify the scrapping of such costs. But there is none the less a 'point of no return' in plan implementation which needs to be observed. Second, there are the potential costs which come from the pressure to observe equity as between owners following an initial decision to depart from the plan. Here a particular development could well show a net benefit over the plan. But if it can be predicted that the decision would be regarded as a precedent in equity, and therefore there would follow an accumulation of such decisions which in total might not convey net benefits, then there is justification for resisting the initial proposal which would create the precedent.

Enforcement of decisions

Any decision of the kind just described is simply a piece of paper which is yet to be acted upon. If the ensuing action is in accord with the decision, then the plan is implemented in the manner described. But if on the other hand the decision is ignored, and the development agency, ministry department, etc., proceeds to act in accordance with its original intentions, then clearly the plan is not implemented *in practice*. It is here that the need for enforcement procedures arises, those which enable the implementing authority to ensure that its decisions are not flouted.

Of itself this provides a huge potential for failure in plan implementation. It could arise simply through inadequate manpower in the employ of the implementing authority to carry out the necessary inspection and supervision. There could be wholesale flouting of decisions (or even the refusal to ask for permission) simply because it is recognised that the implementing authority does not have the political will or intention to carry out the enforcement procedures. Or the society may be one in which flouting of the law occurs through bribery in the right places. Seen this way, the enforcement procedures which are in fact pursued are clearly a vital link in implementation.

2.7   MONITORING AND REVIEW OF IMPLEMENTATION

The review of plans as an ongoing process is by now well established in the planning process and is well documented.[31] It stems from the recognition that plan-making must have regard to a future which is inevitably uncertain in so many different dimensions, so that assumptions, predictions, etc., stand a good chance of being found lacking in the light of experience. Accordingly, it is necessary to have ongoing monitoring of selected aspects of the development and planning process, with a view to establishing differences in assumptions, facts, experience, values, etc., from those encountered in the original plan-making stage as a basis for considering whether or not the original policies, plan, programme, etc., ought to be adjusted in the light of experience.

From what has been said above, it is clear that all this applies with equal if not greater strength to the processes of *plan implementation*. There is little theory to go on: principles and practice are immature; and experience in plan implementation has been so disappointing as to carry with it the assurance that there is a tremendous amount to be learnt from ongoing practice. In putting forward the remedies both sides of the gap will need to be kept in mind: adjustment of the proposals and adjustment of the implementation measures. We thus have a review of implementation and a continuing attempt to close the planning–implementation gap.

In this review there is a need to consider the effectiveness of the plan-implementation measures which have been adopted. While this aspect will have been considered in their selection at that stage, there can only be prediction, *not* certainties. Accordingly, the review stages give the opportunity for testing predictions on the effectiveness of measures and for making necessary adjustments to them in the ongoing process of implementation.

But there is more to be gained from implementation review than just modification of a particular plan, programme, and so on. Taking all such reviews together we can look critically at the successes and failures of plan implementation, with diagnosis, as the empirical base for extending our understanding of theory and practice in plan implementation.

2.8   CLOSING THE PLANNING–IMPLEMENTATION GAP

The main point of this chapter is that if plans are to be prepared with a view to implementation, the implications of implementation should be considered throughout the planning process, in order to ensure as far as practicable that the plan which is recommended will be feasible for implementation. The plan will then have a maximum chance of influencing the future, in the directions chosen by the plan-makers and decision-takers.

From this it follows that a plan produced on these prescriptions could be very timid and grey, simply because it was completely conditioned by its being run through the feasibility tests described above. As such, it might seem unexciting compared with a bold and imaginative plan, but which is quite unlikely to be implemented because it disregards the critical constraints, and while conveying possibilities would not be likely to have much influence on the future.

This duality has always been a feature of urban and regional planning. Those professionally or politically concerned with making a new future wish to be bold and imaginative in departing from the limitations to contemporary life which they see around them. But at the same time they know that there is no future, professionally or politically, in the continuing production of plans which are not implemented – all too many of them. This duality came into unhappy prominence in the first round of development plans under the Town and Country Planning Act, 1947. The Act itself was born in the post-war socialist administration dedicated to changing the face of Britain which attracted general enthusiasm as compensation for the sacrifices of the Second World War. But by the very fact of the war our resources for introducing significant change were limited. Since it was one of the very notable and praiseworthy features of the initial development plan process that there needed to be strict regard to resource constraints,[32] and since the plans had to be approved by a central government which was very conscious of resource constraints, the results were too grey for a Britain wishing to see itself transformed.

Clearly either of the two extremes described are undesirable. We do not wish to have impracticable or grey plans. We thus cannot avoid the dual objective: to plan as imaginatively and boldly as possible, in order to create a future which is better than the present or past, but at the same time to recognise the limitations of feasibility. Thus in practice there is always a 'planning–implementation gap' for certain elements of the plan proposals.

To close the gap completely at the time of plan preparation, i.e. to accept all limitations in implementation, would probably result in a grey plan. Thus the aim should be to do something bolder. This involves some kind of strategy in itself. For example, there should be a close study of the possibilities brought out through existing degrees of feasibility. And it should be recognised that the gap as visualised at any time need not be that which will appear when a particular plan proposal is to be implemented, since over time the tendency would be to increase or decrease the measures available for plan implementation. Thus the ongoing struggle of plan implementation must mean a learning process for those concerned, so that the better use of plan-implementation skills to achieve better plans can be expected in the future. In this, given that the real restrictions on implementation measures are in the powers and resources available for direct intervention (see section 2.5.2, no. 4), plan-makers and implementers should work more with the other kinds of implementation measures described above which do not rely on powers or resources (see sections 2.5.1 and 2.5.2).

In all this, one difficulty for the plan implementers is that all concerned tend to resist rather than welcome change: for one thing there is caution over physical developments which involve vast investments and last a long time, and for another there is the protection of interests which might be threatened. Thus there is a premium on changes which are familiar, and tried and tested. In such circumstances the new is not easy to introduce, even though it is fairly clear that it will be an improvement on the traditional or more familiar. But the innovation itself can often break the ice. A notable example in Britain was the building of the shopping centre in Stevenage new town. As the first of the mall-pedestrian precincts in Britain, it aroused great opposition from the prospective shopkeepers, who thought shops on pedestrian ways (as opposed to traffic streets) would undermine trade. But the persistent battle fought by the development corporation and its advisers won; and pedestrian shopping centres in Britain have flourished ever since.

Thus the measurement of a gap which is acceptable at any moment in time is not easy, and neither are the ways of closing the gap between the acceptable and the unacceptable. But this gap, and what to do about it in practice, is the crux of plan implementation. Unless it is handled effectively, then planning must continue to suffer, from either being too timid for the opportunities or too ambitious for the world to swallow. We return to this important matter below, when we explore it in depth in relation to land policy (see Chapter 9).

2.9 POLITICS AND PLANNING

So far in this broad review there has been only the briefest mention of politics. The reason for its omission is not its irrelevance; indeed, it is so vital and all-pervasive throughout the whole process of plan-making and implementation that it could hardly be slotted into any of the particular aspects of plan implementation which have been dealt with in previous sections. It is accordingly treated in the broadest way in this section.[33]

2.9.1   THE SCOPE OF POLITICS IN PLANNING

The nature of this political element in planning (as in other spheres) is not a simple one. It is made up of many strains. Two are described in exemplification.

Perhaps the most popular is that identified with 'party politics' wherein it is the battles between the majority and opposition parties in the British system of government which are all-important; the opposition party tends to oppose all that the majority party proposes, following lines taken on each major issue before open debate by a party caucus, from which professional advisers are normally excluded. Thus the outcome of 'party politics' is that decisions are taken by the party in power. But in the present British electoral system this is not necessarily the party of the majority in terms of votes but that of the majority of elected delegates. Thus the decisions may go with a minority of voters.

But the party in power is not homogeneous, so that the way in which its power is exercised is not always predictable. Within the same ruling party in central government a land-use planning issue could be decided by the relative powers of departmental ministers in the Cabinet (Industry versus Education, Environment versus Health, etc.), with ministerial power being a product perhaps of departmental size, personality of the minister in question, his popularity in the party hierarchy, and seniority in departmental weight. Similar manifestations can be seen as between the various departments in a municipality, and indeed between the chief officers of those departments in their relationships with the elected members. And moving outside government, power and its influence on planning decisions can also be a function of that pressure group, lobby, appointed representative, etc., which has influence, money and ability to be forceful.

Compared with this strain of politics by power or influence,[34] there is the more traditional concept of politics as the art of wise and rational government, allocating scarce resources to achieve ends which are in the interests of the total community.[35] While similar to the approach of economics, it differs in that within its calculus there are considerations which are outside the realms of economics.[36] In this sense there is some similarity between politics and planning, with planning being a means of pointing to wise decisions affecting the future and indicating 'who gets what, when and how'.[37]

This latter concept of politics includes in its analysis factors which are outside the contributions of particular disciplines (like economics, planning, sociology, architecture). It should be possible to distinguish the factors which are 'political' and those which are not. In common usage the term 'political' is meant to include anything which enters into a planning decision in practice but which cannot be neatly categorised into the compartments of other spheres. It is the vast untidy residual of factors which can be used to justify weights given by the political decision-makers to elements in planning decisions, so leading in a certain direction without the need to define and clarify what the weights are and why they have been adopted.

Given this possible wide scope of politics in planning, but no authoritative lead from political science,[38] there is some difficulty in indicating just what the role of politics in implementation might be. Just because of this lack of clarity, it is useful to proceed, as when introducing implementation above (section 2.3), by devising some model aimed at explaining the political process.

2.9.2   A MODEL OF THE POLITICAL PROCESS IN PLANNING

In discussing politics and planning we are really discussing politics and government, since we are concerned here with intervention by government in the making, implementation and operation of development plans. To go further, in dealing with government intervention we are concerned with the relationship between government and the people it represents.

This relationship could be simply described by the word 'democracy'. But as a review of the 'democratic' systems of various Western countries will show, this form of government in itself has many variations: compare the local power of cantons in Switzerland with the highly centralised power of the British government, its Cabinet and Prime Minister.[39]

From the various models available, we are assuming here the current British form of democratic government, of which the key features are as follows: the elections to the lower House of an individual by a local electorate, with the individual chosen by a local party group and not imposed from a central party list; with government by majority party, perhaps supported by small groups from other opposition parties; with the majority political party having the power of administering services centrally throughout the country by virtue of appointing ministers, leading to a division of responsibility between members of the legislature and of the executive; where the local authorities are elected on the same democratic principles; where they could have the same or a different political complexion from central government; and where the local and central civil service is appointed and remains in office without automatic change of the higher-level personnel on a political change of government.

Based on these assumptions there follows a diagrammatic representation of the influences brought to bear on the government of the day, be it central or local, at any moment in time, and thereby influencing the decisions taken.

As represented in Figure 2.2, those *taking* the decisions are the politicians in power, who interact with the politicians not in power. Affecting their internal interaction are a large number of influences, which can be traced in the diagram by reference to the numbers shown, those on the left-hand side being mainly 'the economy' and those on the right being mainly 'government':

Economy
1   The people as a whole in the country, born and unborn.
2   The electorate as a whole, representing the people.
3   Representatives of large elements of those people as producers, e.g. trade unions, employers' associations.
4   Representatives of interest and pressure groups, e.g. amenity societies, road building lobby, cyclists, and so on.
5   Representatives of the people as a whole in their capacity as consumers.
6   Big business straddling international boundaries, in conglomerates.

Government
7   Ministers and managers of the central government departments.
8   Local authorities around the country.
9   The managers of the statutory undertakings and nationalised boards throughout the country.
10 International governments.

Figure 2.2   *Influences in political decision-making*

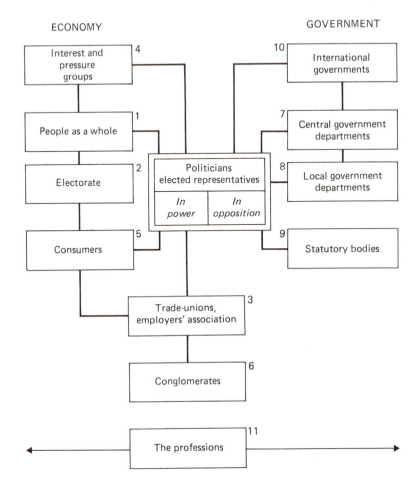

Note: The lines are meant to indicate the range of groups having influence on elected representatives and the interaction between those groups. All have their professional advisers who interact both when acting for their clients and also between themselves and their own groups.

Professions

11 The professional personnel of different kinds who advise or manage for any of the groups described, be it for central government, trade unions, interest groups, nationalised boards, etc., and who interact independently of their employers, between individuals and between groups.

From this array, which does not pretend to be comprehensive, it can be seen that the ultimate decision-*takers* are receiving impulses from and presumably giving impulses to a vast array of organisations continuously throughout their political life. The communication of the impulses is undertaken in a variety of ways, be it *via* the open media (newspapers, television, radio, etc.), or the less open method of series of meetings and discussions or the still less open use of correspondence and the personal meetings and lobbyings which are constantly in progress. And these impulses are by no means unidirectional (between the groups and the politicians) but are interacting in diverse, complex ways. For example, the interest and pressure groups will have their own professional advisers who will be in lateral communication with the advisers of central and local government; while the government is elected periodically by the electorate, the public as a whole could be influencing government throughout its life directly or indirectly (through interest groups, consumer associations, public participation, etc.); and indeed minorities who have no electoral role at all (e.g. new immigrants) could none the less have considerable influence on particular issues.

Figure 2.2 gives point to the contrast made between 'decision-*taking*' and 'decision-*making*'. Whereas there can be no question that the 'taking' of a decision rests formally with the politicians in power, the 'making' of the decision is a complicated compound of the innumerable influences described. Although in some fields of activity in the country there can be seen the relationship between the decision which is *taken* and the variety of influences which contribute towards its *making, decision-taking* models in planning are not at all clearly formulated in this respect. Just how this bewildering array of influences works in practice, to result in particular decisions on particular issues, is something which might be unravelled only by painstaking case study with access to a great deal of information which is not normally available. This is shown in the fact that there are comparatively few notable case studies which have been made of the planning process as in fact it is carried out (compared with the rationalisation of what in fact occurs).[40] It is also shown from a perusal of the decision letters on local inquiries of the Secretary of State for the Environment and of the reasoning behind those decisions offered by the reports of the Inspectorate.[41] Given the highly central role and long experience of the DoE in planning, it might be expected that there would emerge from these letters and reports some clear framework of influences behind the decisions which have been taken. That this is not so is perhaps due to this bewildering array of influences at work in the decision-making and the absence of a clear decision-making process.

By the same token it is also very difficult to crystallise from this picture the answer to the question posed in this section: what is the role of politics in planning? In a sense it is all politics: the exercise of power and influence on the making of decisions, all revolving around the issue of 'who gets what, when and how'. But even if we attempt to narrow the question to the role of the *politician* in planning, in order to clarify the respective roles of the politician-manager-professional, the structure is still not clear. However, what we can do is to attempt to throw some light on some of the questions in this field which are highly relevant and controversial in theory and practice in planning, and to see where this model leads us to.

2.9.3   SOME QUESTIONS ON POLITICS IN PLANNING

What is the role of the politician in planning?
Since land-use planning is part of government, as is education, health, etc., the

role of the politician in planning is no different in principle from his role in these other spheres. He is the decision-taker, chosen by the electorate to act on behalf of the people of the country, in accordance with the laws and the constitution. As such he is continually aware that politics is the 'art of the possible', that the contributory factors to any decision are made up of a vast complex of interacting influences which he must somehow resolve in his mind to lead him to a decision which he can defend. As such he is a broker 'mediating, adjusting and putting views in sufficient harmony for action'.[42]

The *taking* of the decision for action (or inaction) is clearly the culmination of a process of *making* the decision in which all the influences described in the above model can be brought to bear. Sometimes the decision is *made* in an encapsulated form in a half-hour's telephone call – sometimes after a long formal process when all aspects have been considered with the aid of experts, with interest groups, hearing evidence, etc., leading to conclusions and consultation.[43]

In any such case the intellectual demands on the political decision-taker are very heavy, given that he is earnestly trying to discharge his responsibilities by taking account of all the factors that are relevant to the decision and giving them proper consideration and weight in relation to one another. It is this which poses a question about the role of the politician in planning – not that he is performing the wrong role as a decision-taker, but that he may be performing it without having the analytical decision-taking equipment for this very responsible task, and therefore in a manner which is out of step with the 'rational models' pursued by planners. Just how wide the gap can be is seen by comparing the analysis that went into the Report of the Roskill Commission and the reasoning which the government of the day adopted in giving its decision against the Roskill recommendation,[44] or by considering the implications of the Crossman *Diaries*[45] for the way in which ministerial and Cabinet decision-taking is pursued. This is not to say that the politicians should necessarily find a rational decision-making model for their work. Perhaps this is impossible or undesirable. But we must recognise for its practical implications the disparity between the approach of the professional and the politician in their parallel work in this field.

What are the criteria for political decision-taking?
Given that the role of the politicians is to take decisions which can be defended in the 'general interest of the community', and given that in any decision there must be a large number of conflicting interests and views to be taken into account, what are the criteria to be adopted by the politician in his role of 'broker-mediator'?

To find an answer we must start from the recognition that any attempt to define what can be called 'the general interest of the community' produces a very confusing picture, leading many to the despairing answer that there is no possibility of defining what is in the 'public interest'.[46] However, other answers might be introduced.

One conclusion, from case studies, is that the public interest is simply the resultant of the conflicting pressure exerted by sectors of the public.[47] This could very well be a description of reality. But this model of decision-taking does attract the doubt that large groups of the population cannot be represented in this 'market-place of pressure' simply because they may not be at all vocal (like children or the unborn generation), and may not have the resources to express their views via the media, public-relations experts, professional advisers, influential connections in the corridors of power, and so on. Thus political decisions of this kind can be expedient on a day-to-day basis in recognising reality, but are open to criticism as not representing those who do not exert pressure as 'decision-makers'.

Another approach flows from the assumption that the elected representatives have been elected to govern, i.e. to take decisions, and that the criterion lies simply in their personal view, according to their conscience, of what ought to be done. In this they would be clearly sensitive to public opinion, pressures and advice, etc., but would not seek to explain their decisions in these terms. But this model of the individual politician acting according to his conscience must be quite rare in contemporary government, where 'party politics' is so powerful. In the House of Commons, for example, the free vote is the rarity, and it is the vote according to the party whip, determined by the party managers, which is decisive. Here the relationship between the conclusions of the party management and the wider array of the pressures and interests of the public is not so apparent, since the party might be following a mandate from those who elected it, which could be a minority in the British kind of democracy; or it might be following a line which is not even clearly linked to the views of its electorate, as, for example, where it is simply expressing a view of opposition to the other party, or perhaps a view which, however genuine, is going beyond or falls short of its election mandate.

These comments, relating to central government political decision-taking, applies to an increasing extent to local government, where the trend is certainly towards more caucus decisions as opposed to the free vote according to conscience. And further confusion arises when a district council wishes, in a planning decision, to follow its majority party line only to find that the strategic authority, on the same decision-taking criterion, wishes to follow another line, and the relevant central government department yet another. In such cases, which are not uncommon in planning, it would be very difficult to show which of the three possible decisions would accord with the 'general interest'.

This brief review of possible political decision-taking criteria adds weight to the conclusion from the preceding section: on the gap between the planner's rational modes which give rise to his recommendations and those of the politician in taking decisions.

What is the role of the professional in planning vis-à-vis *the politician?*
By the 'professional in planning' we do not mean simply the generalist land-use planner but all those skills which contribute, be it the social scientist (economist, sociologist, etc.), those who carry out construction (architect, engineer, surveyor, etc.), the accountants, the administrators or lawyers. To be sure there are differences between these professions as to their roles *vis-à-vis* the politician, the clearest distinction being seen between the administrators and the remainder, the administrators being the most closely identified with the politicians in assisting in the formulation of policies and their execution.[48] But for our purposes here a common treatment on roles is possible.

The classical distinction is one between ends and means. The politician has the privilege of deciding on the kind of future to be aimed for in the community, in terms of such matters as the goals to be aimed at, the constraints limiting the range and nature of alternatives, the criteria for choice between them and the selection of means of implementation consistent with community *ethics*. And it is the function and duty of the professional to use his experience and skill to assist the politicians towards their value-laden ends.

But owing to the complexities and duration of the planning process, including the ends–means–ends chain in the planning process, the distinction does not hold in practice. Professionals often find themselves in the situation of using their planning experience and skill without specific direction from the politicians, though they would need in the end to obtain the politicians' approval to their proposals. Indeed, the very ease with which the professionals can carry out such tasks without direction or even with no direction at all[49] can lead them to take upon themselves many of the privileges which a non-technocratic democracy would reserve to the politicians. And many professionals take advantage of the opportunity, perhaps because of their technocratic leanings, or because of their drive for action despite absence of political guidance, or because of their party political attitudes which leads them to wish to impose where they can their own values and ideologies on the community.

Here then is a source of actual and potential conflict in terms of 'values' which can arise through sins of omission from the politician and of commission from the professionals. And from this conflict there are generated interesting areas of discussion: Who in the end are the real policy-makers? Should the planner aim to be value-free? Can he in fact be value-free? Should there be 'advocacy planners', lending their skills to devise plans based not only on values of a client or employer but also on those which the planner himself chooses to adopt? Is the client of the planner in government service the government agency itself, or the community at large which the government is elected to represent? Should the planner play different roles at different times, choosing from three which have been suggested: apolitical and value-neutral; activist while avoiding the appearance; openly involved politically and activist?[50] Should planners remain politically neutral as individuals but politically involved as groups? These very questions show that the roles of the professions *vis-à-vis* the politicians have indeed become muddied compared with the classical models; and perhaps the muddying is due to the fact that the classical models themselves were too pure.

One contribution towards the clarification, and perhaps an alternative model, is as follows. Without question any government agency or private-sector client is free to give instructions in terms of goals, constraints, choice criteria, choice between alternatives and means of implementation. This is certainly their privilege and indeed, as a government planning agency, their responsibility. And equally clearly it is the duty of every professional to use his skill and experience to the best possible extent to give answers to the employer or client which reflect the instructions. But the professional also has a parallel duty to his professional ethic. To discharge this he should indicate alternative possibilities to the client/employer and the public which do not conform with the precise instructions. This would not necessarily aim to persuade that the alternative is the better course, but essentially is a means of showing the opportunity cost to the client of his own choice.

The following will illustrate. If a local authority sets a target of doubling the population in ten years, the professional could point out the disbenefits of such a course compared with a more modest rate of growth; if the constraint were to rule out certain kinds of alternative plans (increased public transport by bus as against full motorisation), then the opportunities lost in abandoning this possibility could be shown; if the criterion of choice between alternative plans was the least burden to the rates, then the opportunities lost by not having some stated increase in such burden could be indicated; and if the means of implementation for renewal were to be confined to a land-use plan within which existing landowners could develop, then the lost opportunities through public land assembly could be pointed out. In brief it is the duty of the professional to indicate other possibilities, and not simply those which follow the directions laid down by the politicians. In this way he is exposing to the clients/employers, and to the community at large, what possibilities exist outside those which the elected representatives are pursuing, and what is the opportunity cost in pursuing them.

Such a display of alternative possibilities could be presented in a manner which is provocative and excites disloyalty and counter-pressure (for example, by inciting the local press to publicise the professionals' alternatives where they differ from those of the authority). By such overt behaviour the professional would be openly fighting the political machinery. This is not intended. Rather, it is that the array of alternatives should be part of the ongoing advice which is given on a daily basis to the employer, or disseminated on an ongoing basis in a public consultation exercise. The professional obligation requires that the alternatives show the opportunities which are forgone in the political choice. Let the opposition parties or public battle for them should they so wish.

But if the opportunities forgone which are chosen for demonstration are not to be politically biased (e.g. towards the poor, or minorities, or local shopkeepers), how are they to be chosen? In practice this is not so difficult. In its nature the profession of urban and regional planning attempts to devise a future taking into account all groups in the community and all their objectives, and on their collective behalf struggles with sectional interests. Thus in its nature it seeks that future which would best achieve the 'general or public interest', to the best degree possible, and is not put off by the literature which explains that in theory the purest definition of the public interest is very elusive.[51] Planners recognise that the elixir is as difficult to find as the optimal in planning. They are content to 'satisfice': to achieve the best they can by reducing overall costs and maximising overall benefits, and by attempting to ensure a distribution of benefits and costs which has some basis in terms of 'social justice' and the criteria of the decision-makers.[52]

This built-in drive of the planners has been dismissed as a naive belief in a 'consensus society' in place of the reality, which is that society makes its decisions through conflict between groups, where the decision goes to the most powerful.[53] But this dismissal would appear to rest on some misunderstanding of the future which professional planners aim at. That society is built on conflict, between ages, between classes, present and past, present and future, is all too clear. It is brought home in the consideration of any typical application for permission to develop, which brings up the large number of conflicting interests which are involved and the arguments put forward by each to pursue its own advantage. But in the end a decision is in fact made on the application. This means that the 'who gets what, when and how' has also been decided, implicitly or explicitly.

In this context the planners' contribution is to propose intervention for the reasons described above (section 2.3), to try and *improve* upon the allocation and distribution of costs and benefits which would arise without the planned intervention. He does this simply because as a planner he has the professional need to look at all sectors of the community rather than just sectional interests; take account of present, past and future; and ensure that the unrepresented party in the political process is not neglected. In all this he does not assume that society is in consensus rather than in conflict. But just because it is in conflict he attempts to find the 'best' solution for society in the taking of that particular decision, to make the devision of spoils explicit rather than implicit in the general interest.

However inefficient the attempt is in practice (being bedevilled by sheer technical difficulties in predicting the outcomes of plans in conditions of uncertainty, crudity of measurement, of introducing the values of the future into a present which takes the decisions), the attempt is in the nature of a touchstone whereby the possible futures sought by others are placed in context. All this in the purest sense is the responsibility of the politician; he represents the public and as such should be just as all-embracing. But in reality he may not be so, for the reasons mentioned above (section 2.9.1) and in any case he has sought professional advice. In respect of the future of the towns and regions the planner is society's professional conscience, and he is the mirror which attempts to correct the distortions of political decision-taking, where the decisions should reflect what may not be the 'general interest'. That controversy surrounds the attempts, and that he is often wrong or misguided, is a function of the difficulties of the task. They do not disprove the point.

2.9.4 SOME CONCLUSIONS

Taking the above considerations into account, what conclusions can be drawn on the respective role of the politician and professional planners in decision-taking in planning?

The politicians in their decision-taking responsibility are at the receiving end of the vast array of information, influence and feedback pressures. Any individual confronted with this bewildering array is facing an enormous task in moving towards a sensible decision on any issue, which can then be defended in this conflict society in terms of its superiority over other possible decisions, and then defended again, following the passage of time, when the circumstances of change throw light with hindsight on the wisdom of the decision. Such difficulties are compounded in that elected representatives so often have to take decisions as members of a group rather than as individuals; they are inevitably working under pressures of time; in local government at least are only part time; and they do not have at hand the political-science techniques and tools for the job.

Yet they have the power to take the decisions, subject only to the Courts if they offend the law. And since it is the decision which matters in influencing the future in planning, not all the preliminary build up, there is this fundamental discrepancy: the politicians have the power but operate in an atmosphere which is less conducive to rational decision-taking than do the professionals who do not have the power. In this situation it is the task of the professional to facilitate the decision-taking operations. How can this be done?

Clearly the greatest contribution comes from the conventional role of the professional to assimilate the relevant factors as a basis for giving advice to the elected representatives, bearing in mind their goals, values, constraints, and so on. Sometimes the advice will be relatively passive, and sometimes by recommendations and active persuasion. But, it was argued above, there are also other contributions that can be made.

First, the professional influence could penetrate outside the line of communication between any particular employer/client and their professional advisers and be working also in and on any of the other groups in the constellation who are contributing to the decision-making. This can be done directly, as where a planning officer will meet with local community groups or pressure groups to communicate and inform; it can be done less directly in the ongoing communications between professionals, where the points of view of those advising all groups can be interchanged, verbally at conferences, meetings, etc., and in written communication by journals, etc. The better the mutual understanding, the better the professional contribution that can be made to the decision-making.

In addition there is the 'conscience role' described above of exposing the possible alternatives for action and the opportunity costs of not taking those alternatives. In this the professionals are putting forward possibilities which accord with their values as professionals; that are not neutral and value-free and do not represent their own ideologies, but instead attempt in some way to represent the values of the community as a whole, having regard to the concept of the 'public interest', however fuzzy that might be. In all this the professional will act in at least two ways. As the producer of information he is bound to present his studies, findings, recommendations, etc., in a written form which goes on the record as the contribution from his skill and experience. But in supplement he will act 'transactively' or as a 'reticulist', so that his influence and contribution can be put over in a more effective way (see section 2.5.2 no. 1 above).

Thus the politician and the professional, while working together on common problems, have distinctive roles, tools, techniques and, often, horizons. They just cannot do each other's job, and neither can do his own job without the other. It is the recognition of their distinctive roles, and their mutual interaction, which offers a basis for progression towards better decision-making. And on this both politicians and planners have considerable ground to make up. The planner is operating in a most difficult area of government and practice, which is comparatively new the world over and is changing rapidly and in which his profession is still immature compared with others. The politician, on the other hand, is working in a game which is as old as the hills and at which he needs the gifts of birth and experience rather than of long training. But in exercising his gifts he is faced with increasing complexities in an increasingly complex world, and one which is more and more exposed to a wider array of influences on any particular decision.

The path is strewn with many battles. Perhaps the biggest breakthrough for the planners would be to discover how their work can contribute effectively to the community's welfare, and be accepted as so doing.[54] And perhaps the biggest breakthrough for politicians would be when they replace the 'art of the possible' by the 'art of the impossible'.

In this complex world of planning it is the impossible which is needed to make the breakthrough.

REFERENCES: CHAPTER 2

1 For the general process see Lichfield (1956), and for new towns Schaffer (1970).
2 See, for example, Golany (1976).
3 See, for example, Lichfield (1956), and Apgar (1976).
4 See, for example, Thorncroft (1965).
5 See, for example, Levin (1976).
6 Town and Country Planning (1967).
7 Yone (1974).
8 For a review of possible meanings see Alterman (1975), Yone (1974), and Pressman and Wildavsky (1973).
9 Chadwick (1971), and McLoughlin (1969).
10 Lichfield and Marinov (1977).
11 Lichfield (1956, ch. 1).
12 Myrdal (1960, p. 1).
13 Denman (1978, p. 83).
14 Lichfield (1956, part 1).
15 This topic is covered by a wide range of literature on what is called 'impact analysis'. See, for example, McEvoy and Dietz (1977).
16 See Lichfield *et al.* (1975, ch. 1).
17 Lichfield and Marinov (1977).
18 Lichfield (1976b).
19 Here we conceptualise from the model. The same issue has been tackled differently by testing actual plans and programmes on a simpler conceptual model. See Alexander (1979).
20 See Haar (1959).
21 Jowell (1977b).
22 Lichfield *et al.* (1975, pp. 30–1).
23 Nathaniel Lichfield & Partners (1977).
24 Lichfield (1970).
25 For a review of methods see Lichfield *et al.* (1975, pp. 52–5).
26 Ibid, pp. 25–30.
27 As used in the literature on French central and regional planning.
28 Davidoff (1965).
29 As used in popular discussion.
30 Friedmann (1973).
31 Department of the Environment (1977b).
32 See Lichfield (1956, part 5).
33 The literature is diverse but not specifically articulated for urban and regional planning. Some exceptions are Allison (1975), Catanese (1974), Gregory (1971), Altschuler (1956), Meyerson and Banfield (1955), Rabinowitz (1969), and Walker (1941).
34 See Self (1975, p. 104), who distinguishes between the two terms, and prefers 'influence' to the more usual 'power': 'Politics works through the structure of influence.'
35 For example, Simon (1947).
36 Margolis (1978), and Self (1975).
37 Beckman (1964).
38 Allison (1975, chs 7–8) reviews both the orthodox and the heterodox in political theory and planning. But he cannot as a result be specific on the role of politics in planning.
39 Self (1975, p. 104): 'There is no one consistent and adequate theory of democracy which can explain or justify political behaviour in modern westernised states.' He suggests (p. 105) four categories in describing the elements in a composite theory of democracy: majoritarian representative leadership, pluralism (balance of interests), classical political populism, and modern consumer populism.
40 For example, Gregory (1971), and Altschuler (1956).
41 See issues of *Journal of Planning and Environmental Law*, *The Estates Gazette*.
42 See Beckman (1964, p. 253).
43 For examples of long-drawn-out consideration see Commission on the Third London Airport (1971), DoE (1973c), and DoE (1978b).
44 House of Commons, *Hansard*, vol. 830, 1971–2, cols 446–55 'Third London Airport'.
45 Crossman (1975–7).

46 Schubert (1960).
47 Altschuler (1956).
48 Self (1977, ch. 5).
49 As, for example, in many of the consultant studies for planning new towns in Britain, prior to the setting up of the New Town Development Corporation.
50 Catanese (1974, pp. 141–54).
51 Arrow (1951).
52 See Lichfield (1971).
53 See Simmie (1974).
54 Lichfield (1979b).

Chapter 3

The Development Process in Planning

In the preceding chapter we described a model for development plan implementation (section 2.3) which showed that the plan is implemented if physical development is carried out in accordance with its proposals or policies, and if the physical development is then operated accordingly. In this conceptualisation a clear division can be seen between the implementation in terms of the physical development and the subsequent use of that development: control over the former and therefore implementation possibilities are so much stronger than over the latter. In practice this is borne out by planning permits being couched in quite precise terms in relation to the physical development but with only loose prescriptions, if any, on the activities to take place within the physical development on completion. Indeed, the Courts have tended to rule against such activities being included.[1]

It is for such reasons that the concentration in land-use planning is on the physical development rather than on the activities, which is a justification for the description 'physical planning'; implementation of activities in accordance with plans must be achieved in the main by other means, for example educational policy in respect of running schools, licensing for the carrying on of businesses in cinemas, shops, offices, and so on. For this reason we will in this chapter concentrate on such physical development in considering how the development process is affected by land-use planning. In so doing we will in essence be discussing 'planned development'. We do so by first comprehending the nature of physical development (sections 3.1–3.3), then the nature of the physical development process and special role of land within it (section 3.4). This leads on to an economic analysis of the land and development market (sections 3.5–3.6) as a preliminary to showing the need for planning intervention in the land market (section 3.7) and the land-policy means for doing so (sections 3.8–3.10). Then comes a concluding section on how market pressures affect planning (section 3.11).

3.1 THE MEANING OF DEVELOPMENT[2]

In land-use planning in Britain the term 'development' has an accepted and clear meaning: it is a term used to describe any land to which has become attached man-made fixtures through construction, the bricks and mortar (see section 4.3.2). The sub-division of such development which comprises the street and utility system is called 'improvement',[3] this being the infrastructure for the construction of buildings, etc., which completes the development. With these terms are linked the verbs 'to develop' or 'to improve', which convey the process of 'development' or 'improvement' which brings about the end-state of the process, the 'development' or 'improvement'.

However, in national or regional planning the term 'development' has quite a different connotation and one which is not so readily agreed.[4] In the context of a developing country 'development' carries with it the idea that the particular country needs and/or wishes to 'catch up' with developed countries in terms of growth in the output of its economy and thereby consumption and welfare. Sometimes this is simply referred to as 'economic growth'. But this means different things to different people.[5] Most narrowly it relates to output as defined in national-income statistics, i.e. product which is exchanged in the market. More broadly it means all goods and services, including those not exchanged, whether included in gross domestic product or not. Whatever the varying meanings, the common-sense aim in a developing country is to have more of all the goods and services needed for human enjoyment and satisfaction, as a basis for raising standards of living by distribution of the increased output around the population, in accordance with the prevailing principles of equity and social justice.

But to achieve such growth, whether it be defined strictly or more broadly, it is recognised that the developing country needs an input called 'development'.[6] But again the precise meaning is subject to discussion. It has been interpreted narrowly, in parallel with the interpretation of 'economic growth', to mean the input of capital investment required to increase the efficiency of the productive processes, and therefore the volume of output; or more widely in the social and economic structure of the developing countries which provides the 'capacity to produce', amounting to a 'mechanism which will produce self-sustaining and cumulative indigenous improvement'.[7] This capacity is not only related simply to changes in productive factors but also to structural changes across the whole of the society, in social and political arrangements, institutions, and finally, and perhaps most important of all, in human development, in the education, health and attitudes of the people.

From this it follows that while 'growth' and 'development' tend to be used somewhat interchangeably, they are not the same and may not even always proceed together. There could be growth without development (e.g. in oil output whose revenues are pumped into overseas investment and not to create social-overhead capital or infrastructure at home). And there might conceivably be development without growth, if the latter be strictly defined as output in terms of national product, as in the production of healthier and better-educated people, who then use their new attributes for leisure and pleasure and not for the production of goods and services which are exchanged in the economy. But even here the very development could involve growth in infrastructure since all but the simplest of pleasures consume some goods and services which require production.

However, when we turn to land-use planning, the terms 'growth' and 'development' have quite different meanings from those just described, though their relationship can be seen. The focus of land-use planning is the shaping of the future of human settlements. It is essentially concerned with the use of the earth's surface, i.e. with the physical structures, spaces and infrastructure to be provided or not provided on that surface. These are the physical frameworks for the human activities which make up our settlements.

In this context 'development' relates to these physical manifestations on the earth's surface or beneath the surface (e.g. mineral extraction). Thus in land-use planning, to 'develop' is to produce the built environment within the total environment, and the term 'development' describes the finished product in terms of the actual artefacts themselves. And in this context 'growth' is simply the expansion of the artefacts, be it on virgin fields where no such development has taken place before, or in replacement of former development by the process of urban renewal.

But the contrast which would appear to emerge between the terms *growth* and *development* at these different levels is not as sharp as it appears. At the local and sub-regional level the concern of land-use planning is fundamentally not with the artefacts but with the human activities in the environment; in preparing the plans for the physical development it is the activities to be accommodated (the utilisation of the land) which are the main subject of study, and in considering the output of the planning it is the activities which would result which are the primary concern. Thus 'physical development' has its socioeconomic implications. And from the regional and national level the growth with which that development is concerned cannot take place without the contributions of the buildings and infrastructure provided by the physical development. Increases in productivity and output cannot be provided without the built fabric which is to house the machinery and the labour; and nor can improvements in the internal distribution system of a country (and thereby trade) take place without the improvement in the transportation network, ports, airports, and so on.

Looked at this way growth in the local and sub-regional sense relates not simply to the enlargement of the physical fabric as such, but rather to the expansion in the population and the social and economic activities (both for production and consumption) which will take place in the expanded fabric, both as to quantity and nature. Thus the physical development in local and sub-regional planning is a means for this growth.

To conclude this exploration, while the terms 'development' and 'growth' are used to convey different things, they convey one common function at all planning levels: how can *development* be carried out to achieve *growth* which is satisfactory in volume, kind of impact and distribution?

3.2   PHYSICAL DEVELOPMENT IN SOCIOECONOMIC LIFE

As just indicated, for *growth* to take place in a community, there is the need for *development*, both in the broad structural sense and also in the more narrow sense of *physical* development in infrastructure and buildings. The constituents of growth give rise to demand for new development in, for example, factories and offices for production or dwellings and shops for consumption; and the public sector provides out of its resources the social-overhead capital and infrastructure required to balance the private-sector development, for otherwise there could be 'private affluence and public squalor'.[8]

The rate of production and consumption of this *physical development* is clearly a function of the growth rate of the economy, as can be seen at times of depression and stagnation where the rate of such development is drastically reduced. But in fact the fluctuations of the development industry at times of boom or slump tend to be greater than those of the economy as a whole, since unlike goods of short life duration the development industries are concerned with providing marginal changes to the overall stock of development which endures despite the fluctuation in the economy; overall demand has only to change slightly to alter profoundly the demand for the marginal changes in physical development.

This introduces another role for the public sector in the production of physical development: not only as a development agency but also as government, through its fiscal policy, which may or may not be part of an overall economic national and regional policy. For example, to raise revenue it has a taxation system directed both at land and property in particular (death duties, local rates, development gains/capital gains taxes, etc.) and less directly through other kinds of taxation (corporation, income, vehicle-licensing) or subsidies (such as inducements for less-developed regions).

These, then, are the socioeconomic forces in any society which give rise to the pressures for change in its physical development, both in the creation of new stock and the renewal of old. Given this relationship, it is clear that it is these forces which in effect build the cities and regions. And it is in the attempt to explain the manner in which these forces work and the results they produce that there has grown up a vast body of literature on urban and regional geography, economics and sociology which present theories underlying urban and regional change.[9] They show that the need and demand for physical development to which they give rise is governed and influenced by a wide range of factors. The stock of development and the development process may be said to be the physical manifestation of the geography and topography of an area, its institutions, practices, traditions, laws and economic state. As one statement has it, 'Land utilisation takes place within three frameworks: the physical, the institutional and the economic,'[10] to which could be added the social and political.

The framework is ever-changing. The development of technology has had a fundamental effect on man's relationship with land and has 'increased the economic supply of land far beyond earlier potentialities' since modern society 'is characterised by the expanded accelerated use of natural resources to satisfy human wants'.[11] These descriptions depict the link between the broader and narrower meaning of development – between the broad historical trends in society and their physical manifestations in specific physical development. And they pinpoint the critical problems or urban development. With necessary affluence and population, pressures on land supply grow, with its 'scarcity' being dictated by the balance between increased demand, technical advance, and the resources to resolve the conflicts.[12]

3.3   THE PHYSICAL DEVELOPMENT PROCESS

The preceding section has described what might be called the 'macro determinants' of land-use change. But for these influences to work it is necessary for the micro process to operate, whereby the factors of production concerned with physical development (land, construction industry, finance) are wielded by the entrepreneur (developer) to satisfy economic demand by public and/or private consumers.[13]

While this process represents that of the typical firm in the textbooks in economics, or of the typical public agency in the textbooks on public-sector management, as a process it has distinct characteristics. The greatest is its complex and long-drawn-out nature compared with, for example, production in agriculture. Typically the process consists of a series of stages within the overall model of implementation given above (section 2.3): maturing, project planning, construction and occupation. And while any particular development would proceed along its own individual lines, a typical project might go as follows.[14]

The preliminary stage lies in the general maturing of circumstances which will make realisable a change in the use of the land in the not too distant future: an increase in the number of people requiring accommodation; an improvement, through the building of a road, in the accessibility of the land; the extension of public utility services to it; the establishment of a factory nearby which makes the location convenient for the dwellings of the factory workers. The maturing of the circumstances may be stimulated or retarded by any owner of the land, but it may well be independent of action by him.

The process begins effectively when, against the background of these maturing circumstances, the idea takes shape that a change in use might one day be possible on a site which at the time is perhaps a field, or is covered with property that is approaching the end of its economic life. For the change to come about, the freehold of the site, or a sufficient leasehold interest, must be owned, or become capable of being owned, by persons who are prepared to develop; and before work is begun it may pass through the hands of several people, including land speculators – purchasers who do not intend to use or develop it but only to make a profit on resale.

Before work can take place it will be necessary to remove any obstruction to their smooth execution. There may be subsidiary legal interests to be terminated or made terminable at short notice, rights of way to be diverted, rights of adjoining owners to be negotiated away, boundaries to be adjusted, and additional land to be acquired to improve the shape of the holding.

One or more of the actors who are interested in the development would prepare the development scheme: the surveys of the site, the designs and drawings, the estimates of costs and returns. In its preparation there will be discussion of the possibilities of development with the bye-law, drainage, planning and licensing authorities, and perhaps with government departments. At some stage there will be the formal applications for the permissions and consents of all public authorities.

Before a contract for construction is let, contract drawings, specifications and quantities must be ready, tenders invited and agreements made between parties who are to participate in the carrying out of the development. Possibilities will have been explored of borrowing money, both to finance the works (bridging) and on long-term loan for the eventual owner.

When the time is judged right the works will be executed. Where the accommodation is not to be used by the developer there may be 'pre-lets', or negotiations for disposal will be initiated during the construction.

The process terminates when the works are completed and the new accommodation is fully or substantially in occupation and use. It will start again as renewal: when maturing circumstances make realisable a further change in the use of the land and buildings, or of the land only upon demolition of the buildings.

From this description of the physical development process it is apparent that there are many parties involved: there might be the original landowner or any subsequent purchaser of the land; the private or public developer of various kinds who undertakes the process; the building industry, including firms, labour, those supplying the material, those producing them; the institutions lending finance; the ultimate occupiers, whatever the tenure; and the ultimate consumers of the services provided, e.g. shoppers as opposed to retailers. And all these parties are supported by an array of professionals: the town planners, economists, surveyors, valuers, financial analysts, architects, engineers, quantity surveyors; lawyers, estate agents, and so on.

All these production factors taken together constitute what has come to be called the 'development industry'. Taken collectively they are the ultimate 'builders' of our towns.

3.4 THE SPECIAL ROLE OF LAND IN DEVELOPMENT

Against this background it is of relevance to note that there is little evidence to support the suggestion that 'property rights in land settle the land use'.[15] But none the less in the development process and in land-use planning *land* does play a special role compared with the other factors of production. In order to understand the recurring debate over land, and the reasons for land policy, it is necessary to grasp the nature of this role. We have initiated this when illustrating the diverse attributes of land which need to be considered in the *substance* of land policy (section 1.4). We now go on to consider again these special qualities of land, but this time for their particular significance in *development*.[16]

In terms of geography since the total supply of land is by and large fixed (i.e. subject to erosion and accretion) there is special concern that land be conserved and used as efficiently as possible, which gives a special meaning to its 'scarcity' as a resource. It is particularly scarce in urban as opposed to rural settlement, and urban development increases the intensity of land use in building high and so provides a substitute for additional quantities of land. But against this, raw land is physically non-depreciable over time (except for minerals and the top soil used by agriculture), unlike virtually all other commodities, including the structures built on land.

To the economist the fact that land is stationary and not transportable makes it hardly possible to talk of a national or regional market for land in the same way as is the case in the market for motor-cars; so that the price of land is fixed by the demand for land in certain locations, *not* by general supply and demand.

As a factor of production land 'is distinguished from capital and labour because ... it exists in the natural order of things and no labour has been expended on its production'.[17] It is 'the complex of natural opportunities offered to labour and capital'.[18] This is essentially an abstract, analytical definition; it divides the virgin, given thing, the natural resource, from all that has been done upon it to exploit its inherent wealth and make it more productive. However, 'land under the foot of human settlements, primitive and sophisticated, is so inextricably mixed with the works of men upon it that to identify the virgin substance is impossible'.[19] And land, in its virgin state, is not often used directly, even in agriculture: 'except in cases of such extensive uses as grazing or wild hay production, land improvements must ordinarily be made before the land is ready for man's use. Labour and capital must be expended for cleaning, removing stumps, and levelling, draining, or irrigating the land, depending upon its location and character'.[20] While it is not easy to separate 'land' from all the man-made improvements to it, such as buildings, fertilisation and infrastructure, this distinction is fundamental in land economics. Following this distinction, raw land is, in essence, 'costless' in terms of resources. However, it is a necessary ingredient of any human activity and commands a price in the market as do other commodities.

To the lawyer the definition of land is empirical. He 'looks at the whole thing, improved, developed, worked upon. ... Thus to the lawyer land means not only the natural soil and waters, the solum, but all buildings, roads, fences, shafts, ditches and all erections and excavations which are physically attached to or identified with the soil',[21] being 'the sum total of the natural and man-made resources over which possession of the earth's surface gives control'.[22] When compared with other forms of property, land ('real' as opposed to 'personal' property) is characterised by special concepts (proprietary rights and obligations) and tenure (whereby there can be possession as well as ownership). Thus for any particular parcel of land there is the lawyers' bundle of rights and obligations which make up the 'proprietary land unit' that is 'an area of land used as a single entity and co-extensive in its physical dimensions with vested rights of property, to use, to dispose, to alienate'.[23] This bundle will include the implications of the law of nuisance, positive or restrictive covenants, etc., which are included in *private land policy*, i.e. as between owners, protected by the Courts. Not only are these complex in themselves but where evolved over centuries in certain countries have resulted in very complex tenure patterns, particularly where such laws relate not to one code but to several.[24]

Furthermore, land is subject to special kinds of social controls over its use and development, having regard to the social and political implications, which has generated a special field of concern, the social control of land use, within which is land-use planning.[25]

Land thus presents complexities in development, simply because of its special characteristics. Therefore, the handling of land as a factor of production in itself becomes complex, as will be shown in the economic discussion which follows.

3.5   THE ECONOMICS OF THE LAND AND DEVELOPMENT MARKET

Having just described the nature of land and physical development in the physical development process, we now go on to present an economic analysis of this process, concentrating on the special role of two key factors in the process, the developer and the landowner. This leads to a discussion on the relationship between 'land use' and 'land value' in the land market. By 'land market' we have in mind the classic definition which connotes all real-estate transactions for sites and new and established stock, carried out not in 'any particular marketplace in which things are bought and sold, but the whole of any region in which buyers and sellers are in such free intercourse with one another that the price of the same goods tends to equalise easily and quickly'.[26]

Land finds its way into the maturing stage of development from those using it for its current use to those who have in mind its use for development, through the exchange process in the land market; groups of buyers and groups of sellers compete against each other and the land changes hands at a price decided by the interaction of market forces. Here the special nature of land comes to the forefront. For most goods, in a perfectly functioning free market, prices are the result of the interaction of demand and supply, where the demand function depicts the willingness to pay for various quantities of a commodity at stated prices and the supply function depicts the willingness to produce these quantities at those prices. However, since land is a gift of nature and has no labour expended in its production (except for the improvements), it is costless in terms of resources. How then is the price of land set? In essence the answer is to be found in rent theory: in the famous discussion on agricultural rent, as to whether the high price of corn was caused by high land rents or vice versa.[27] We now answer this question in relation to urban development, seen from the viewpoints of the developer and the landowner.

In the development process it is the developer as entrepreneur who is the key in initiating and carrying through the development process. He may be of many different kinds: as, for example, the individual building his own house; the 'speculative' builder of houses for mass sale; the industrialist owner-occupier; the industrial-estate company who provides sites on improved land for factories; the public sector in the form of the local authority providing houses, national boards providing infrastructure, the government department building a trunk road, barracks, military training ground, and so on.

For exposition we pick out the typical private-sector developer. He will operate on a profit-maximising basis within the constraints of having to compete for the inputs which he cannot do without.[28] A simple example will illustrate how the market works. An essential input to the development is the land, or rather the proprietary rights in the land. Assuming he needs to buy or rent land, how does he go about the selection? From his knowledge of trends the developer will consider alternative projects on alternative sites and select between them on the basis of maximum profitability per unit of investment. For this he will estimate the net return to him on each site, excluding land cost, which would be the difference between the value of the completed development less the cost of inputs (including normal profit) all discounted to a common date.[29] There will be left a residue which is the maximum he would be able to pay for the land, on a rental or capital basis, and not forgo the chance to partake in the development and reap normal profits.

This is the answer given in land economics and valuation theory, in what is known as the *residual approach*.[30] The question then arises as to how much of this he will in fact pay. In principle he will be prepared to have to pay it all: competition within the development industry will drive developers' profits down to the normal rates for entrepreneurial endeavour. This theory is supported empirically.[31] In a study of residential development the developers estimate the total selling price of the envisaged development and deduct from this the total building costs (site preparation costs, erection costs, taxes, financial costs and normal profits) to ascertain the amount they would be prepared to spend to buy the land. But owing to imperfections in the market the bid which actually secures the land would be somewhere between the ceiling price of the developer and the floor price of the landowner.[32]

We now turn to the landowner. What factors dictate whether he will sell, and at what price?

The first question is answered by the opportunity cost of doing so: he will dispose of his land to the developer if this would reap higher rewards than retaining it for its present use. His estimate of higher rewards would need to embrace the costs of removal: financial, family, psychological.

As to the second question, the price, competition within the groups of developers will allow the landowner to require the highest price for the land which any of the group would offer in competition. This would be the developer who can see the greatest margin between the estimated final demand price for the developed land less the costs of developing it ready for final use; this is the development value, the 'residual value' of the land.[33] This arises because the developer uses land as a stock in trade and he must buy land or go out of business; rather than go without the land (and a normal level of profits from using it), he will be willing to pay up to the level at which he is only left with the normal profits. For his part, the landowner, if he has no need to sell the land, can hold on, especially if prices are rising. He has the 'monopoly' position for *his* land. But he cannot ask more than the best bid from the developers if there is other land which the developers can obtain.

Thus the final price of improved land will be dictated (under given overall demand circumstances) by the use made of the land and the suitability of the land for that use. The suitability of land for a particular use will be influenced by such things as technical suitability (drainage, flatness, subsoil), accessibility to functionally related activities (in the case of housing, the closeness of shops, work, etc.), the availability of infrastructure, and so on.

Since different pieces of land may be more or less suitable for a certain land use, the price may be expected to vary as between different plots of land even though they are in the same use. For example, there will be more business at a filling station on a main road than on a country lane, so that the proprietor of the busier station will be willing to pay a greater price for land. In a competitive market the relative land price should settle down in such a way that both proprietors are left with the same profits – normal profits. Thus there will be large variations in land prices within the same use, since this price will vary spatially, as a location rent.[34]

So far the discussion has placed greater stress on demand than supply in the formation of land values. This would accord with the idea that the supply of land is passive – that the total supply of land is given by nature and that little can be done to alter it. However, this aggregate supply of land is not as critical as the supply of land through the development process, in which land is made ready for and supplied to final users, sometimes termed 'economic supply'. It follows that this economic supply is governed by the behaviour of those involved in the development process: those who decide what should go where, by bringing together the various factors of development such as land, labour and capital and supplying the land for development.

In this, landowners may take an active role in dictating the use of land and the supply of land to the market in order to increase their wealth. They may do so as entrepreneurs and initiate the development of their land, or as speculators when they keep their land off the market for the purpose of gain.

In some circumstances a landowner can do worse than keep his land vacant and off the market. As stated above, land does not appreciate with time; if it is not used, it is not 'worn out' simply by the passage of time. Put another way, there are no true maintenance costs of land which burden the holder of vacant land, though there are institutional costs, such as the real or opportunity cost of the capital tied up and any taxes which may be payable. To put against these costs are the hopes of an increase in value over time.

> Vacant land is usually more valuable than the land with a building on it because it allows the most profitable kind of building to be built on it. The most profitable kind of building changes from time to time in an unpredictable way. Developed land also has the disadvantage that it is often let for significant periods at fixed rents.[35]

The person who is deciding whether to sell a piece of land to a developer or to hold it vacant has, in essence, a simple choice. If on retention he expects the value to rise by more than the interest on the capital (taking account of inflation), then it is worth his while to keep it vacant.

This reasoning would also apply to the land dealer, who buys with the intention of selling and not developing, popularly called the 'land speculator'. Although he has attracted much public anger in recent years, there are those who defend his role as useful.[36] Thus, for example, 'high prices are caused by high demand and limited supply, not by speculators' profits', and:

> a speculator who makes a profit must buy when the price is low and sell when the price is high. In buying when cheap he prevents the bottom dropping out of a falling market. By selling when the price is high he prevents the price from going through the roof. Speculators bring the price down when it is too high and earn profits in return for the judgements and risk-taking. The profits are evidence that they are doing their 'socially useful' job of reducing the swings of the price level and strengthening the elements of stability.

There are arguments which may be raised against this. But whether or not the land hoarders' or land speculators' role is useful in the market, they clearly have an anti-social role in terms of land prices. Speculators can exacerbate fluctuations by buying on a rising tide, and by their purchases maintain that tide whenever there is an underlying upwards trend in land prices, due, for example, to the growing pressures on land, fall in money value due to inflation, and absence of other good investments. In such conditions there is the incentive to bank land which is not ripe for development at an early stage and hold it until demand rises sufficiently to compensate. And there is also the tendency, with the planning machinery limiting the land available to any particular use, of speculation taking advantage of and exacerbating the demand/supply situation in one particular use. If the absolute land requirement of such use is not particularly large, small changes in supply may have large effects on the price: 'In large and older cities ... there is often a shortage of property in locations suitable for redevelopment ... And speculative holding of the properties by owners who want to get as much as possible of the profits of development, is important in limiting supply.'[37]

3.6   RELATION BETWEEN LAND USE AND LAND VALUE THROUGH TIME

In the preceding section we have shown how land use and land value run together at that point in time when a successful bid by competing developers will secure the transfer of the land from the owner for development. This bid is then an indicator of the value of the land in the market at that point in time, on the basis of discounted costs and revenues for the development which are envisaged in the successful bid.

But clearly this is just one point in time over the long evolution of that particular parcel of land from its original farming condition through to urban development. This time period is lengthy not only because of the slow maturing to change in land utilisation, in response to the changing economic, social and demographic circumstances of the country (both the overall growth and in shifts between interregional and intra-city locations), but also because of the considerable length of time which is involved in the development process (see section 3.3) which is needed to effect these changes in land utilisation through development. Thus the question arises: what is the relation between land use and land value at other times than at the point of the successful bid? We provide an answer by considering the typical evolution of a parcel of farmland through to its development and beyond.[38]

While urban development is many years away, the value of the land will be based upon its current use as farmland, reflecting its fertility, condition, etc., on the principles of economic rent (see section 3.5). We call this 'current use value'.

But as urban development approaches (for example, through the expansion of a nearby town, building of a new motorway which increases accessibility to the city) developers and speculators become interested in the land and are prepared to make bids for it which reflect the potential use for development. At that point in time there cannot be know with certainty the 'demand' for the development (i.e. the kind of development and price), nor the cost of providing it, nor the timing; and if planning permissions need to be obtained, it cannot be known whether the applications would be successful. Accordingly, at that point in time the potential use must be uncertain, and therefore the estimates of value based on that use, on the principles described above (section 3.5). All this justifies the term 'hope value' for the uncertain potential value which is additional to the current use value.

During this maturing period any purchaser of the land for potential use at 'hope value' might be disposed to terminate the current use (farming) if there were advantage in doing so (higher rental values than for farming for a transitional use) or stimulus to do so (if there were taxation on potential use value). But this would be transitional only, in preparation for the time when the successful development bid would fix the use for development and initiate the development process to carry it out. During this period there could well be changes in the development proposal, since the price actually paid for the land would then become a determinant of the development rather than a residual on valuation which occurs during the bidding process. Thus it is when the development is initiated beyond the point of no return (for example, when construction starts) that the actual development value of the land can be firmly estimated. It will in fact only be decided when the development is completed and occupied; mishaps during the construction process, for example through strikes, bankruptcies, etc., can divert potential use and value even beyond this 'point of no return'.

Following the occupation of the new development, a new current use is established (normally, though not necessarily of the use for which the development was designed) and accordingly a new current use value arises. For all the reasons just indicated this will not necessarily be the value of the finished development which was estimated in the bidding process.

Once the new current use is established many buildings go through their whole lives without alteration or adaptation for other uses. Then their current use value will change under the pressures of demand and supply for that particular stock in that particular location and with changes in the value of money. They may increase or decline, and may go through cycles of increases and declines. But for many buildings there will be the possibility of a more profitable current use emerging before the end of their lives, so attracting higher current use values, as when houses become used for offices. In advance of this change there will be a potential use and potential use value in the manner described above for farmland; in valuation of this potential, allowance would need to be made for the costs of adaptation to the new use.

But there could be cases where the buildings do not continue in the use for which they were designed, and cannot find some other use, be it because they have become 'white elephants' in terms of contemporary demand (the huge cinemas of the 1930s) or because the demand for that particular building ceases even though the general needs continue (for example, high-rise flats which have become unpopular for families; local authority housing estates which have attracted vandalism, crime, etc., and are therefore shunned by potential residents). The current use value then veers to zero, with the land value becoming associated with any potential use for the land (which would necessarily involve the demolition of the structures which, in the instances given, would have long physical lives).

Despite long physical life these properties can be said to be 'economically obsolete' simply because the ongoing revenues from their occupation will be insufficient to pay the operating costs (rates, maintenance, etc.). This situation can arise for other kinds of obsolescence, be it locational (as where closing of a railway station will make a shop obsolete), environmental (as where otherwise sound dwellings become uninhabitable through pollution from adjoining factories or cement works), or functional (as where slum houses are regarded as no longer fit for human habitation).[39]

Whatever the reasons for the obsolescence, the cycle of redevelopment approaches. When it starts it parallels in most respects that of the cycle of development described above. Landowners and developers will be competing, with the redevelopment going to the successful bidder. But there is one significant difference in terms of land values. Whereas in farmland the residual valuation approach will typically reveal a surplus of finished value over costs of achieving that value, in urban redevelopment this need not necessarily be so. This arises because the difference between value and cost may not be sufficiently above the current use value of the standing property to make its demolition worth while. To be worth while the use value of the new development must exceed, by at least an allowance for the developer's profit, the combined cost of the new buildings and works and the current use value of the existing land and buildings. Until this point is reached the property as it exists has an economic life, and the opportunity cost to the owner in retaining that use is higher than the site bid he would obtain from developers. In such situations, if a public authority wishes to secure redevelopment for social objectives, some subsidy would be needed.

But given the situation where a successful bid is made and acted upon, then the whole cycle of redevelopment takes place, following the cycle described above on development on farmland.

And then the process will start up once again in the future. So the continuing relationship between land use and land value will go on.

3.7   THE NEED FOR PLANNING INTERVENTION IN THE LAND MARKET

The working through the price mechanism of the market in land and development, as just described (sections 3.5–3.6) is an instance of a more general situation in which the market, by its 'higgling', can be said to plan the allocation and distribution of resources by the 'automatic direction of economic life towards an inherent goal'.[40] In this, consumers decide by voting with their purchases just what economic activity they request from the producers; and the market allocates resources to the carrying out of that activity and also distributes the resultant income or wealth.[41] More particularly in relation to land, in response to the demand of consumers for the services offered, as expressed in price, the use and development of land is decided and the product is apportioned amongst those concerned with its ownership, development and occupation.[42]

Given that the market can operate freely (i.e. without its internal imperfections or the external direction of planning), the results of 'higgling' are not all that random. In general the price system leads to innovation and an efficient use of resources.[43] In the land market it gives rise to what might be called a 'natural use zoning': 'in response to the demands of consumers for the products and services of land, as expressed in price, land use has become arranged in certain patterns. Rent acts as sorter and arranger of this pattern.'[44] And furthermore, it has been claimed that 'natural use zoning' is not simply just one possibility as such but rather that:

> the utilisation of land is ultimately determined by the relative efficiencies of various uses in various locations. Efficiency and use is measured by rent-paying ability, the ability of a use to extract economic utility from a site. The process of adjustment in city structure to a most efficient land use pattern is through the competition of uses for the various locations. The use that can extract the greatest return from a given site will be the successful bidder. The out growth of this market process of competitive bidding for sites among potential users of land in an orderly pattern of land use spatially organised to perform most efficiently the economic functions that characterise urban life.[45]

However, it is recognised that the capacity of the market to perform socially valuable functions of this kind is limited by its well-known imperfections, so that 'It is needless to dwell on how imperfectly the market operates and how wide are the actual deviations from the perfect pattern of land uses.'[46] These imperfections have been described as follows:[47]

1 The commodity is not standardised, and the lack of transactions relating to even generally similar properties hampers the establishment of a firm market price.
2 There is no central source of timely and complete information which can act as a guide to traders.
3 Supply takes a long time to adjust to demand both because buildings take a long time to erect and when erected last a long time.
4 Action in response to market signals is delayed because the majority of buyers and sellers lack market experience and understanding.

This awareness of the potential for social usefulness of the land market, but at the same time of its limitations, has led to the argument that:

> the basic objective of city planning is to attain the same land use pattern that would emerge naturally from the processes of the urban real estate market under conditions of perfect competition. This statement assumes that the commodity, through local government agencies, competes in the market to provide for those public uses, such as schools and parks, for which the community is willing to pay.[48]

This leads to the suggestion that the role and objectives of city planning should be to remove the imperfections of the market.

This early conclusion from one admirer of the land market seems difficult to reconcile with a more recent one.[49] Starting from the proposition that it is for the planners to plan and the landowners to implement, and drawing the conclusion that this is at the root of the planners' weakness in implementation (all of which we have doubted above in section 2.3), the key to successful planning would be for planning authorities 'to provide landowners with all relevant information on the demands for land within the planned area and the nature of the uses which a given plan would generate and require; listen to and consider the landowner's proposal; get acquainted with the nature, extent and economies of the proprietary land units created in the land; and plan accordingly.'[50] While this clearly has advantages in securing valuable information and data for the planners (one of the main reasons for the proposal), there is little recognition that the proposals of landowners based on their 'proprietary land units' would be hardly adequate as the mosaic for a plan. For one thing such land holdings could be quite inefficient for contemporary development, both as to size and shape and also tenure. For another (as noted above in section 3.5) the landowner is only one party to the development process and therefore his 'proposals' can hardly be relied upon for implementation. For yet another there would be the imperfections in the land market, to which we have referred. And the doubt is increased by the suggestion that this is the key not simply to planning but to 'positive planning'.[51]

Coming back to the earlier suggestion, that it is the role and objectives of city planning to remove the imperfections of the market, it is relevant to note that urban and regional planning does to some degree in practice reduce such imperfections, in each of the four items mentioned. On (1) through planning conditions there is an increase in standardisation; on (2) the planning office provides a clearance house for all kinds of information, on (3) stimulated renewal advances the supply of land for redevelopment; and on (4) planning departments offer a great deal of valuable and free advice.[52]

However, to argue that in a mixed economy and welfare state the remedy of market imperfections is the 'basic objective of city planning' is to overlook at least two major points.[53] First, the imperfections in the land and development market go well beyond the four points just noted. Second, even on the four points, a simulation of the market in city planning offices would be well beyond what could be attempted there in both theory and practice. This can be illustrated simply by enumerating the additional market imperfections, which fall under six headings:

1   *Consumer sovereignty*

In the market the principle of 'consumer sovereignty' is held to be supreme. But it is generally agreed that unfettered vent to such consumer bidding is not always socially desirable (e.g. drugs, low-standard buildings) and there are 'merit wants' which government considers that people *should* have (e.g. compulsory schooling, minimum sanitation, etc.).[54] In addition there is the assertion that producers to a degree mould consumer demand.[55]

2   *Public-sector involvement*

First, in the 'market' described above it is recognised that the community (national and special agencies as well as local government) will enter into the market process by bidding for land for those facilities which the private sector will not be able to provide through lack of profits. However, in doing so, their bids cannot be made in terms of economic rent, i.e. for that use which will give the maximum surplus of value over cost. This arises because there is no way of placing market values of many of the public facilities provided, such as schools, open spaces, roads, and so on. For these, therefore, rent cannot act 'as sorter and arranger' of a pattern which under market influences would give the 'best use'. Where a poor authority must locate a school on land of inferior location and quality, simply because of its low tax base, it is difficult to see how this could be in the 'best interest of the community'.

Second, where a public agency provides a utility service as infrastructure for urban development, and charges for the product, it is rare that it does so in terms of market principles. Generally speaking it will aim to cover average and not marginal costs, and perhaps with cross-subsidisation. This particular element in the land improvement costs, therefore, is not based on market price, and could therefore, distort the land-use patterns.

Third, another source of distortion is in the price controls of government in the rental value of finished accommodation (housing, offices) which prevents the market from responding to price signals.

3   *Supply of development*

First, the land which enters into the market supply could be held in complex tenure patterns (ownership, possession, rights and obligations), embodied in what has come to be known as a 'proprietary land use'.[56] This means that the asking price and the bids relate to land whose use could very well be constrained in many institutional ways, thus militating against efficiency in development.

Second, coming to the bricks and mortar, urban development is long-lived, almost permanent, so that development-related decisions will influence the life and the shape of a city for a long time to come. Often these decisions are made by individuals, private companies, etc., and will reflect their feelings, or perhaps lack of feelings, about the past and the future. This clearly may not accord with the view of the future expressed by the community's decision-makers, who have responsibility for safeguarding the conditions of those yet to be born, and the heritage of the past.

4   Externalities

Even if the market were perfect, it would, by definition, fail to take into account externalities in the use of the land, i.e. those costs which the decision-makers in the development process create but have no need to incur, or those benefits for which they cannot charge.[57] But if the social costs and benefits do not enter into the private calculus of the market, they have no role in the rental bid which acts as the sorter and arranger of patterns. In other words, the higgling of the market will not reflect the costs and benefits to those outside the particular land transaction at issue, which is the rest of the community:

> Marginal private net product falls short of marginal social net product, because incidental services are performed to third parties from whom it is technically difficult to exact payment ... There are a number of others in which, owing to the technical difficulty of enforcing compensation for incidental disservices, marginal net product is greater than marginal social net product.[58]

5   Speculation

There are also the factors noted above (section 3.4) inherent in the special nature of land which facilitate speculation in the land market. While there could be some support for the view that land speculation is not entirely anti-social, none the less it is most important on occasions for the community to control excesses which flow from it.

6   Unequal incomes and wealth

Finally, there is the need to consider the implications of a market process which is based upon the distribution of income and wealth in the society, with its inequalities leading to inequalities of opportunity, and so on. Clearly the market signals will reflect the income distribution on the demand side (because certain sectors will not be able to afford to buy the output in terms of dwellings, anemities, etc.). To be sure, one way of countering this situation is to rely upon the ongoing and continuing efforts for redistribution of income and wealth, which is fought out in the political arena, and to look for the amelioration in this direction. But this is to ignore the possible influence of intervention by planning authorities, which, being part of government, cannot absolve themselves from the political issues involved.

In all that is presented above in this section, although there are many different formulations of the same material,[59] there is little that is controversial in principle. But there is considerable heat and controversy in the conclusions that are drawn as to how planning should respond in a mixed economy. Just how this is to be done is an extremely difficult question, not only for land but also for all aspects of the economy, in respect of which many similar arguments are used, varying from country to country.[60] Just how the *balance* is to be drawn is the lodestone of planning in a mixed economy. But before pursuing the balance in relation to land policy, we should just see how the issue is part of a very wide one.

3.8   THE LOGIC OF GOVERNMENT INTERVENTION

As a great generalisation, there would appear to be two driving-forces in government intervention: the search for greater efficiency in the production of goods and services, both public (e.g. defence) and private (e.g. against cartels); and the search for greater equity, social justice, etc., in the distribution of the product.

Another great generalisation would be that some economies give more emphasis to the drive for efficiency (those more closely geared to the capitalist ethic), whereas others have a greater drive, and perhaps starting-point, in social justice (to the point of socialisation of the means of production, distribution and exchange). But in no instances do these two twin aims exist independently. In any contemporary society the drive for efficiency is tempered with social justice (if only to avoid violent social revolution); and any starting-point on equity and distribution must also be concerned with efficiency, for otherwise there would be insufficient goods and services to distribute. Thus the necessity for considering both efficiency and equity is more than ideological.

The socioeconomic logic for state intervention can be argued from each of these twin viewpoints. In the capitalist economy a starting-point is the market, in which each individual and body preserves his own self-interest, making the best use of his resources according to his own criteria. But as we saw above (section 3.7), markets do not produce the best answer for society and accordingly government intervention is needed. It was recognised even by Adam Smith that government of necessity had a role to play and this is not denied today by the archpriests of freedom from government intervention,[61] whereas a much bigger role is recognised by others.[62]

A quite different logic for such intervention stems from those countries which have for various reasons become impatient with the capitalist mode of production and distribution and have therefore aimed for some socialist/communist/syndicalist/co-operative alternatives.[63] The array of possibilities here are very wide, both in the theory over the last two to three centuries, and the practice, as social revolutions arose in East Europe, China and Africa. But a general starting-point of the logic is the inefficiency of the capitalist system of markets (waste of resources, distortion through influence of producers on consumers, ignoring the social costs of economic growth, etc.), as well as the unacceptable face of capitalism in the maldistribution of the product (people divorced from the land, low incomes, public squalor amidst private affluence, etc.). But here again there is general acceptance that the societies which are motivated this way have so far not convincingly discovered the best way of combining social justice and efficiency in production; and the academic and political disputation, and the many different forms of socialist endeavour around the world, some in bitter conflict, are evidence that an agreed road has not yet been found.

The logic discussed so far has related to *market failure* in the workings of the economy in production and distribution. But there is another source of 'failure' which is common to both government intervention in the mixed economy and also in the more socialised economy. This relates to the recognition that the government is after all just a collection of people who are vested with enormous power as politicians or civil servants and advisers (the so-called bureaucrats) and furthermore are expected to exercise that power in a manner which is very demanding of them as individuals.

For example, politicians are expected to be able to make judgements on a vast array of pressing problems, and in accordance with criteria which are not readily indicated by prices, etc., but relate to the much more ambiguous political considerations of 'public interest'. And they are expected to do so in situations which inherently call for a long-term view but which in practice demand of them a short-term view in relation to their own elected period in office. Also bureaucrats find themselves in a difficult situation of needing to administer policies and programmes to serve public political ends, but without the criteria which are so readily offered in the market process (of return on investment, etc.). It is true that the complexity of task, scale of operation, etc., in the public sector may be no greater than that facing the manager of a big enterprise in the private sector, in a business he also does not own. But in contrast to the former, the latter has objectives and criteria of performance which can be more readily defined.

There thus arise instances of 'government failure' which can be set alongside those other better-known instances of 'market failure'. But the reasons for the failure are different from those of the market. This area is being explored by political scientists, economists and others, with a view to building up principles, theory and practice, in the government sector.[64]

But there is a third kind of potential failure. In principle government intervention in the market system is aimed at increasing economic freedom for the masses even while denying freedom to landowners and entrepreneurs. But unless its *balance* is just, there can be an unjustifiable denial of freedom, a tendency which can be exaggerated by government failure. This can be called *freedom failure*, which has reached horrifying dimensions in many contemporary societies. Any intervention which denies freedom without creating at least compensating freedoms for others can be suspect. And it is this sentiment which is one of the major arguments of those who see the growing power of the state, be it exercised in Parliament or by administrative law, as the great threat to individual freedom. It is this which is creating the new breed of 'liberals'.[65]

From this review the following emerges. There clearly is, and has been, *market failure*, which all agree needs to be tempered by government intervention. The dispute is over the extent and manner of the intervention. But in current knowledge such intervention cannot be relied upon readily and convincingly to find the appropriate balance in state interventions, appropriate in the sense of finding the right balance in efficiency and equity and also in protecting the freedom of individuals in the redistribution of rights.

This difficulty is compounded by the recognition that there can be no particular set of rules which will apply to all the varying conditions of situations in a particular country at any moment of time. Different sectors, geographical situations, programmes will require different criteria.

This difficulty in applying a general approach to the particular situation is severe in relation to land, just because of its unique qualities (section 1.4 above). To this we now turn in exemplification. But we do so by descending from the general overview of the world in this section to a very specific issue in relation to land policy.

3.9   THE DIVIDING-LINE BETWEEN PRIVATE AND PUBLIC LAND POLICY

3.9.1   THE LINE IN PRINCIPLE

If we superimpose, as it were, public land policy over the rights and obligations of the proprietary units (see section 1.3), we have in effect for any individual unit a particular kind of *tenure*, being the sum of those rights and obligatious which go with private ownership and possession of property together with those which go with the accumulation of state intervention powers.

The exact nature of the boundary line between the two is difficult to define, for it depends upon the degree of intervention which is being exercised and the nature of the intervention measures which are being used. This varies around the world as we see below (Chapter 7 and the Appendix). But it also varies from time to time in a particular country. The point can be demonstrated by reference to *externalities*, which are commonly regarded as the cornerstone for intervention, by government in the planning of human settlements *vis-à-vis* the market process,[66] and accordingly in the implementation of such planning through land policy.

We start with the proprietary land unit as defined above (section 1.3): that part of the physical surface of the earth which the land-tenure system has subdivided into an operating unit recognised in the law, having its unique bundle of rights and obligations. It is in the use of this unit in production or consumption that there arise the externalities which are mutually imposed on each other by the individual units. While there are various definitions of these mutual interactions, a general one is those costs which individual decision-makers have no need to incur, or benefits for which they cannot charge.

Some of the rights can be protected at law, as though they were part of the proprietary rights even though not specifically provided for in the deeds, for example the right to a quiet enjoyment in the use of property under the law of private nuisance. But there are other rights and obligations related to the use of real property which are provided for in general statute, where the government of the day has thought a matter of sufficient importance to warrant the granting of general rights and obligations, for example in the need to construct buildings to a certain standard or to avoid pollution of water courses, etc. To some extent the detailing of these rights and obligations is left to administrative law (e.g. bye-laws and regulations) and in other respects particular agreements are reached between authority and the landowners in relation to particular developments which then become proprietary rights and obligations (e.g. agreements under the Town and Country Planning Act, section 52).

Accordingly, it would be difficult in practice to define the rights and obligations of proprietary land units beyond those specifically spelled out in the deeds and recognised in land law, to which parties can none the less have recourse in the Courts. But to the extent that parties can, the bundle can be said to be within the realms of *private land policy* as interpreted by the Courts. It is in the area outside this fuzzy line that we are concerned with *public land policy*.

As part of the attack some are opening up the whole question of externalities in the following way:[67]

1   While it is not difficult to grasp the concept of external costs and benefits from Pigou's formulation, there are surprising differences in the literature in terms of precise definition.
2   But accepting any particular definition of externality, there are a range of conflicting prescriptions as to what might be done to correct divergence between private and net social costs and benefits.
3   Given agreement on the prescription to be adopted, there is considerable technical difficulty in quantifying the tax, subsidy, etc., which is involved.
4   Given this, it is necessary before adopting any particular intervention by government to be sure that the net benefits and costs to society justify the intervention, bearing in mind the total nature of the costs and benefits and their incidence.
5   This can be a taxing task in economic analysis, as many studies (section 3.10 below) show. But even so, it is more straightforward than attempting to predict the results in the market-place of introducing various kinds of remedies to close the divergence between the private and social costs.

It is because of such considerations that arguments are being developed for an alternative to government intervention in attempting to close the divergence between private and social costs and benefits. Instead, there should be an attempt made to make such externalities part of 'property' so that the costs and benefits can be resolved just as though the item under consideration were part of normal property rights, i.e. by negotiation between individuals and, if necessary, recourse to the Courts. The dividing-line between the proprietary rights and obligations which can be settled in this way, and those which fall traditionally to externalities, is a fuzzy one. Thus it is not difficult to visualise that many of the rights and obligations now dealt with as externalities by government intervention could come into the 'private' area. To do this the 'rights' and 'obligations' would need to be attached to property,[68] and furthermore the 'transaction costs' (costs of acquiring information, negotiation, charging, etc.) would need to be sufficiently reduced to make them amenable to bargaining. In this way government intervention, which however right in principle is so difficult in practice, is replaced by the time-honoured method of resolving rights and obligations as between parties, be these parties private individuals, public bodies, or a mixture of both.

But is this the solution? Even the advocates of this approach would not suggest that all externalities can be handled in this way, and there is thus left an area for the conventional application of government intervention to externalities. We therefore *still* have the question: even given a new definition of proprietary rights, to what extent should the government intervene beyond this?

There is certainly scope for trying to take out from public decisions certain items which could be dealt with more simply by market transactions. But even the severest critics of planning agree that some need for government intervention remains. For this there is certainly much to be learned in the public sector from the attacks on 'government' and 'freedom' failure.

Wherever the argument goes, all this has strong relevance in both urban and regional planning and land policy. In essence those concerned (government bodies and their professional advisers) have the difficult task of attempting to regulate market failure, and in so doing are subject to what is here called 'government' and 'freedom' failure. But for this they are not too well equipped. In the state of their art they do not have the necessary knowledge. Their methodology is beset by several weaknesses: their analysis is poor; the measurement of costs and benefits and their incidence is inadequate; criteria for decision are not well formulated and amount to an unhappy amalgam of professional planning criteria, political rules, administrative convenience, etc., not to say the outcome of political bargaining between local authorities, and so on and so forth. In brief, in planning and land policy there would seem to be no scope for significant extension of the market-place for the resolution or implementation of planning decisions. But there would certainly seem to be considerable leverage to be obtained in improving the basis for decisions.

3.9.2　FINANCIAL ADJUSTMENTS BETWEEN THE STATE AND INDIVIDUALS RESULTING FROM PUBLIC LAND POLICY

So far we have been discussing land policy in terms of its rights and obligations with the distinction between the *private* and the *public* sector. We now wish to take a glance at the financial implications resulting from the resolution of the rights and obligations in relation to proprietary land units.

Within the realm of *private land policy*, where the rights and obligations can be treated as matters of property, then the financial outcome is, as in other matters of property, the result of bargaining between buyers and sellers in the land market, with recourse to the Courts in matters of dispute, or to the arbitration of valuers and appraisers where the law is not at issue so much as, say, the quantum of the damage. In this respect both the Courts and the arbitration services have built up their own methods of assessment.

However, in the realm of *public land policy* the financial adjustments are not left to the Courts but are provided for in statute or in a constitution in general terms. This is the area of compensation and betterment, or 'windfalls', or 'wipe-outs' (see below). Here there is a complex array of provisions based not so much on the valuation of property rights as on the division of that value based on principles of equity as between the state and the citizen, and the extent to which the former should compensate for or claim betterment in respect of the degree to which the proposed change diminishes or enhances the value of property rights in the individual proprietary land unit. We return to this issue below and here merely note certain points of relevance to the line between private and public land policy.

First, while there may be a certain symmetry in the area of *private land policy* between the rights and obligations which are affected and the financial outcome (since on the whole we are dealing with market values for property rights and obligations), there is no such symmetry in the area of *public land policy*. Thus it could be that the state will in the public interest deprive a land unit of valuable rights of development but none the less consider that it has no financial obligation for compensation. And furthermore, the state may argue that having deprived landowner X of such rights, so that landowner Y will necessarily benefit to some degree by the potential shift in the value of such rights to his site, that it can accordingly claim the freedom to charge betterment on this site. From this it follows that any shift from the area of *public* to the area of *private* land policy carries with it a shift in the financial basis by which rights and obligations are bought and sold. Indeed, it is this very change in the basis of the financial adjustment which makes the shift from the public to the private sector in land policy so attractive to those who see strength in the workings of the land market economy as opposed to public-sector administration – and so unattractive to those who see the reverse.

A second point relates to the interaction between the rights and obligations as they exist and the financial adjustments of the kind just described. While in the public sector these need not be symmetrical, they are none the less interacting. Accordingly, when the individual owner of proprietary rights comes to exercise them in the market-place, he will be affected in his economic calculus and decisions by the value of such rights which can be obtained in the market-place when subjected to the financial adjustments imposed upon him by the state. To give the simple and familiar example, if a landowner cannot claim to himself the plus value from development but must pass this on to the state, then his propensity to develop will be so undermined that he will not be disposed to carry out his economic function of development. This then faces the state with the need to introduce land policy to ensure that such decisions do not undermine the development of the community by, for example, leaving undeveloped land which is of potential development value.

We now turn to examine in some detail the effect on the land market of such interventions.

3.10   EFFECT OF PLANNED INTERVENTION IN THE LAND MARKET THROUGH LAND POLICY

From the preceding section it is seen that a land market which is left to its own devices can hardly be expected (because of potential market failures) to produce an arrangement of land-use patterns and development which would be socially acceptable. It was further seen that, to remedy the imperfections, there is a need for urban and regional planning, aimed at producing a city which would be better than could be produced by market forces.

In brief, the 'best use' of land would not be left to the 'highest and/or best use' of the market,[69] but the market outcome would be controlled in terms of other objectives. It is not necessary here to suggest what these objectives should be, beyond what has already been said above (section 1.2). What is relevant instead is to amplify our introduction (section 1.3) on the role of land policy as a means of implementation to give effect to planned development.

3.10.1   CATEGORISATION OF DEVELOPMENT AND LAND POLICIES

As a preliminary we return to the comprehensive plan-implementation (development policy) measures which were categorised above. To recall, these were:

1   Influence over the developers and operators.

2   Organisation.
3   Financial influence.
4   Direct influence.
5   Personal direction.

But since we are here concerned with those measures relating more directly to land, i.e. land policy, we need to select from the total array of development policy measures. In this we have regard to our description of the role of land policy within development policy (section 1.3) and our categorisation of land policy measures (section 1.6) given above.

Direct control over development
1   Control over specific development without taking land.
2   Control over specific development by taking land.
3   Control over specific development by direct public-authority participation.

Fiscal control over development
4   Influence over general development by fiscal measures.
5   Influence over specific development by fiscal measures.

General influence over development
6   General influence on the land market.

Comparing these land policy categories with the development policy categories we find the following cross-classification:

1   General influence (land policy 6).
2   Organisational (nil).
3   Financial (land policy 4 and 5).
4   Direct development (land policy 1, 2 and 3).
5   Personal (nil).

However, for the purpose of exposition in tracing the repercussions of such land policy measures on the land market it is helpful to depart from the above categorisations to yet another cross-classification, i.e.

1   General influence (land policy 6).
2   Negative planning (land policy 1).
3   Positive planning (land policy 2 and 3).
4   Fiscal measures (land policy 4 and 5).

For each we give a general introduction and then show how the measure will affect land values, this being the expression of the market in the context of this chapter.[70]

3.10.2   GENERAL INFLUENCE (LAND POLICY 6)

Under this head come all the factors described in the preceding chapter relating to influence over developers and operators (section 2.5.1). But a particular kind of influence is amplified here: the improvement that planning can make to the particular imperfection in the land market relating to information (section 3.6). It does so because a planning office provides a clearance house for all kinds of relevant information which is of value to those operating in the market: in the unique area and sectoral studies carried out for plan preparation; and in the circulation of information about availability of land for development on the one hand and the plans and intentions of landowners and prospective developers on the other (through the network of contacts in the planning office to those in the market exchanging views with the planning authority).

In so doing the planning office reduces one kind of uncertainty which would otherwise prevail in the minds of those concerned in the market: in respect of facts about the current and future situation in the region and the intentions of others as regards development and operation. But it adds to another kind of uncertainty: that relating to the proposals of the planning authorities, their precise nature, when they will have effect, whether they are firm or are likely to be reversed. But these countervailing trends do not apply to each and every property. Accordingly, there will be more certainty about certain properties and less certainty about others. It is difficult to say in summary what the overall effect would be in terms of the stabilisation of the information underlying the market process.

3.10.3   NEGATIVE PLANNING (LAND POLICY 1)

Under this head comes the control over development which is a feature of the need for all development (except minutiae) to receive specific sanction from the planning authorities upon the lodging of an application (see section 4.3.2). Presumably such application would not have been made in the first instance had not the applicant visualised some opportunity to realise positive development value on the land, either on a virgin site or through rehabilitation or redevelopment. But he will not be able to realise the value until the permit is given. And since in making up its mind the authority has considerable discretion (in needing to have regard not only to the development plan, if in existence, but to other material considerations), there can be no certainty as to what the outcome would be. And while many cases are straightforward, there are many others in which the issue itself is fought over considerable periods, perhaps requiring an appeal to the Secretary of State, and involving many modifications of the original concepts.

But while the precise effect on the value of a particular property is not known until the permit is given, some prediction is possible. This will affect the levels of value in the market pending resolution of the uncertainty. These will fluctuate between a floor level which can be banked on (for example, current use value without permission to realise any additional development value) to a ceiling of 'hope value' (discounting the kind of development hoped for). Some instances of the kind of prediction are now suggested.

The simplest case is the allocation to fully developed land of a use similar to the current use, and where the property is not economically obsolete so that no redevelopment is proposed. The effect will be to make more certain the use and occupation of the property, since continued use without interference by a public authority is assured, as is the exclusion of surrounding uses which produce disharmony. Use values and investment values will be stabilised and will be enhanced through the greater certainty.

There will often be properties whose current use does not accord with the primary use of the area within which they fall; they will be non-conforming. Here uncertainty is introduced. The uncertainty is less in certain cases than in others. For example, where an old and dilapidated factory is being used for a noxious trade in a residential area, action by the authority to close the non-conforming use is much more likely than where there is a modern and substantial factory in the rear of a shopping centre; where the allocated use would *prima facie* permit of a more profitable use in the non-conforming properties than their current one (as, for example, where houses come within an industrial area), the market values of the non-conforming properties would be increased. But the use value for dwellings in such an area will diminish, since there is no future for that use and there is the likelihood of disharmonious uses being introduced.

Where the non-conforming uses are 'zoned down' in value the position is different. Where, for example, factories are included in a proposed residential area, the owners will not redevelop for the lower-value use, and action by the authority will be required if the factories are to go. But the authority may not in fact propose action (since the factories do not conflict with surrounding uses), but in such a case the use and investment value of the premises will diminish if only because of the uncertainty about possibilities of expansion.

As to the development values in general, where land, whether virgin or built-up, has development value but is not allocated for development, then its potential use value will be lowered. But if it is allocated to development, this value will be capable of realisation. But if allocated for a use which is less profitable than some other for which there is a demand, its value will be less than the full unfettered potential.

Of interest to those concerned with potential use and development values will be not only the uses which may be permitted but also the density of use, particularly in business areas. If there is the demand, higher density (to the appropriate level) will mean a higher development value. If a lower density only is permitted, the development value of the site is diminished.

3.10.4 POSITIVE PLANNING (LAND POLICY 2 AND 3)

Under this head comes the action by an implementation authority which attracted the title 'positive planning' on the introduction of the Town and Country Planning Act, 1947, to distinguish it from the 'negative planning' which had prevailed under the control by zoning and withholding of permission under the previous legislation, the Town and Country Planning Act, 1932. Generally speaking, the term is meant to cover the entry by authorities into the market either (i) to ensure that land is made available for development in the right place, at the right time and at the right price and tenure – incidentally thus helping to remedy another of the imperfections of the land market noted above (section 3.6), by the augmentation of supply; or (ii) to take over the development function itself, either on their own or as landowners in association with private developers and financiers, in order to have not only landlord control of building development but also that of a partner (see section 4.2.5). In such cases the influence on values in the market is much more decided than through negative planning, simply because there are more concrete proposals to be reckoned with. Some instances will again be given.

The simplest cases are those proposed development sites which are privately owned but are clearly intended for a specific public use or purpose involving public acquisition: the reservations, for example, for schools, open space, principal car parks and railway extensions. Simplicity of effect arises in these cases because of relative certainty: first, because the site will usually have been selected with some care; and second, because the implications of eventual public purchase are clearly appreciated in terms of expropriation and compensation. The effect will be most certain if it is known that the purchase will be fairly imminent, and less if it is not. If the scheme were to take up to twenty years to come about, and might then not even materialise (a public body is not bound to pursue its proposals) values may not be adversely affected. The market, and occupiers of property, do not always have complete confidence in the stated aims of public authorities, and may discount for a proposal which they think is so unrealistic that it is never likely to come about.

The use values to the occupiers of the affected properties will be diminished by the prospective disturbance, where this is expected to be fairly soon or where the time of intended acquisition is uncertain. The depreciation in value might be quite small, as where the properties have users who habitually take premises on short tenancies (as, for example, certain types of flats). But the use value to occupying industrialists or shopkeepers is more seriously diminished if their use seems likely to be disturbed.

Exchange values, whether for the purpose of occupation or investment, will probably be more seriously affected, even in those cases where the owner can look forward to compensation at full market value at the time of acquisition. For one thing purchasers are reluctant to buy (either for occupation or investment) property which is likely to be compulsorily acquired at some later date; and they find it more difficult to buy because banks, building societies, etc., are reluctant to lend. For another the owner himself similarly finds it difficult to borrow money on the property to finance a move to another site, and so is disposed to accept a lower price. For yet another when public acquisition of property is threatened, there is a natural tendency for occupiers and owners to have less interest in it than before, and for it to deteriorate in consequence and to become less valuable. Any reduction in value resulting from these factors may lead to compensation on eventual acquisition being lower than market value at the time the proposal was made known, for if the acquisition takes place after many years the negotiations for compensation must reflect the lowered value. So decided is this that some redress has been found necessary. The Town and Country Planning Act, 1947, section 51(3) states with regard to land designated in a plan that where interests in such land are valued for compulsory purchase no account shall be taken in calculating its value 'of any depreciation in the value of such interests which is attributable to the designation'.

Development value, which is to be prevented by a reservation from settling on particular land, may shift to other land where the demand for the use is capable of being satisfied, and where the planning authority would permit the value to be realised. The shift cannot be traced precisely. It will become palpable in the enhanced prospects of development on this other land compared with what would have been the prospects before the plan was made known. The threat of public acquisition of particular property today may therefore depreciate its value because of the expected compensation provisions. This is in contrast to the position in the last century and in the early part of this one, when owners often welcomed the prospects of being bought out by a public authority because, for various reasons, they received generous compensation and speculators bought up property on the line of road improvements in the expectation of profit. On the then existing arrangements for compensation, 'it has become notorious ... that the sums paid for the acquisition of property for public purposes, not only in contested but also in uncontested cases, have for many years past been in many cases excessive'.[71]

Reservations for public use may influence values of adjoining land. A simple example is the proposal for the public open space which would increase the use value and investment value of dwellings adjoining, as well as the development value of adjoining sites for dwellings. Another example is the reservation for a car park or bus station which would probably have the opposite effect on residential values because of possible injury to amenity. In such a case, or where a site is allocated to a wholesale market, a new railway station or municipal offices in an established residential area, the diminution of residential use value may be accompanied by an increase in development value. A retail or wholesale market, for example, will attract shopkeepers, restaurants and service industry to serve the people who would congregate there. A site for a new group of public buildings might attract a demand for office use.

New commercial development values which settle in this way will sometimes be entirely new to the area, as where a new retail market attracts new shoppers to the town. Sometimes they will be floating development values which are already present, as where the trends in development of a central shopping area are diverted to the fringes of a new bus station. Or it may be that the new values will replace current use values which are made to decline by the new reservation, or made to decline more rapidly than they otherwise would have done.

However, the impact on land values is frequently not as clear as indicated here, simply because the authorities have not yet worked out clearly their proposals and are indicating them only diagrammatically, as in structure plans. An illustration can again be given. Where the property that will be required for a road scheme is clearly indicated, as it might be where a new road is to run between two existing parallel streets, the property so shown can be said to be specifically reserved, and the values will be affected in the manner described. This is the exceptional case, however; most road proposals are shown diagrammatically and do not attempt to indicate the property that will be affected by them. When, therefore, the road is designed in detail, a deviation of line (for junctions, redevelopment adjoining the road, etc.) may affect properties away from the diagrammatic road line, and leave some undisturbed which appeared to be affected.

Comparable in its effect on values with diagrammatic road lines is the symbol indicating approximately where in a built-up area there will be a school reservation when more details have been worked out. Since the symbol conveys the intention to reserve a school site in its vicinity on the plan, occupiers and would-be purchasers of property in the vicinity, of the kind that might attract an acquiring authority, naturally have their minds exercised in the matter, so affecting values.

3.10.5   FISCAL MEASURES (LAND POLICY 4 AND 5)

So far in this section we have been primarily concerned with land policy measures aimed at facilitating the implementation of plans, and have noted their side-effects on land value, and accordingly on equity, economic efficiency, and so on. We now turn to fiscal measures, which have more direct economic repercussions on the workings of the land and development markets without specific reference to implementation of plans, but which will, by their effect on the development process, either help or hinder it. It is upon the effects on the development process generally that this section concentrates. The analysis is carried out primarily by a consideration of the effects of each measure on the two basic economic variables of *price* and *quantity*.

Price controls

The control of the final development price has been attempted from time to time. But its effects in terms of resource allocation have tended to undermine its distributive intention: Rent control is the one property price control which has remained for much longer in many places because of the unfavourable income redistributive effects of increases in rents. ... However, the general opinion of those who have looked closely at it ... is that in the long run it tends to have effects contrary to its objectives. The supply of privately rented housing tends to dry up as owners either let it deteriorate or convert it to owner occupation. There is little if any building of new housing for renting, unless new dwellings are specifically exempted from control. And the sitting tenants, who acquire an interest in the controlled property they occupy, become a privileged group whose composition is determined by historical procedure rather than by need.

Price control has also been exercised specifically in the case of public acquisition. This has been done primarily on the equity basis of allowing the community to avoid paying a price which includes the 'hope value' from the development it is about to undertake. One procedure in this case is to exclude from the market price only this hope value (as in new towns and comprehensive development area acquisition). As indicated above (section 3.7.3), in areas where compulsory purchase on this basis is certain, the price will be reduced below the free-market level. Thus for the authorities in question this certainly achieves the objective. But as a measure for reducing land price in general the scale of operation is barely significant enough. From the foreign experience reviewed below (Chapter 7) the general conclusion would seem to be that only if there is very widespread and certain public acquisition does the price paid for this acquisition influence the price of land in the same market.

From this and the preceding discussion some conclusions emerge:

1 Equity considerations can have undesirable results in allocation.
2 The control of the final price of development with no policy of stimulating supply will lead to shortages.
3 A land policy which controls the price of final development of land at some stage before the disposal of the final development will not necessarily lower the price of the final development. It will create profits for someone in the process. If the price control is not universal, it will lead to a shift of supply land from a controlled to an uncontrolled use.

Taxes on land

Taxes are enforced contributions collected from individuals by governments for a
public purpose and the common good with no return to the individual in the form
of special benefits. Taxes levied on property are charges that must be met if
owners are to maintain title to their property. The taxes may be levied in various
ways: on gross or net income; current use value or market value; on all land or
vacant land; land with or without improvements. The level of taxation may also
vary: at normal wealth- or income-tax rates; at a special rate; or one varying with
the length of ownership.

Before looking further it is worth distinguishing between allocative and
distributive effects. On the first, a tax is neutral if it does not affect decisions on the
allocation of resources. If it is not neutral and changes allocation, it is important to
understand what reallocative effects it does have, since these may be either
deleterious or beneficial. On the second, if a tax is levied on one person, he might,
through his economic decisions and actions, be able to shift the burden of the tax
to someone else: If taxes can be shifted so that their incidence, or 'final resting
place', is on someone other than the individual on whom the tax was originally
assessed, the actual tax burden is different from the apparent one. While the
difference is not necessarily harmful, since it was not intended, it could have
undesirable side-effects. If the effect were intended, it would be simpler to tax
directly the person on whom the burden finally rests.

Following these general comments we now concentrate on taxes on the value
of land independently of improvements. Such taxes may be levied on current use
value or potential use value. These two values differ to the extent of the (hoped-
for) development value – a difference which would be at a maximum just prior to
development. In what follows a tax on the potential use value of land is called a
site value tax (SVT), following normal parlance, as opposed to a *current use value
tax* (CUVT).

The SVT is one of the oldest of the proposed remedies of the ills inherent in the
urban land market. In its classic form it would involve a tax on the value of each
site no matter what its use, based on the value the site would have if it was
unimproved but all of the surrounding land was used as at the time of the
valuation. Such a value is quite independent of anything that the owner does to
affect the value of the property. It applies to all privately-owned land no matter
what its use.

In relation to SVT, it has been said that since all the earnings of land are in the
form of economic rent, certain types of costs falling on the landowner cannot be
passed on to consumers. It is generally argued that the tax cannot be shifted,
because shifting is possible, under reasonably competitive conditions, only if the
supply of sites is reduced. But the supply of land is, for all, perfectly inelastic.
Individual landowners will not respond to an increase in land taxes by
withdrawing their sites from the market, since doing so will not affect their tax
liability. Indeed, their only chance of reducing the burdensomeness of the tax
relative to their income streams is to seek to raise the latter by encouraging more
intensive use of the sites they own. Collectively, landowners cannot reduce the
stock of land: if individual landowners wish to liquidate in the face of higher
taxes, they must sell the sites to other owners.

Accordingly, SVT will increase supply, since land taxes stimulate building by
decreasing the price of land so that it becomes easier to acquire. The implication is

that SVT cannot be shifted and that it is neutral. This is arguable, but before giving reasons it is useful to look briefly at the current use value tax (CUVT), with which the site value tax is compared.

It has been suggested that what was said above concerning SVT would be true for CUVT, which is, in effect, levied on the actual rents accruing to land: Since the tax is levied on all rents, the relative profitability of different uses would be unaffected and thus there will be no allocative effects. Land will not be forced out of use because land which is very unprofitable will command little rent and so pay little tax. Thus there will be no change in the supply of goods which are produced with the aid of land and since there is no change in supply, there can be no change in prices. Against this it is argued that a tax levied on a gross rents basis, related to actual use, encourages withholding of sites from use entirely (rental value and tax equal zero) and more generally favours low return uses over high return uses. In other words, the CUVT is not neutral and the burden of tax can be shifted.

In a static situation with no general inflation in the price of land, the former could be correct. The post-tax profit-maximisation behaviour will be the same as the pre-tax behaviour, and so the tax cannot be passed on. The latter argument would seem to be more acceptable when there is an upward trend in land prices, when the landowner could hold land off the market as long as the absolute rise in market price per annum is sufficient to cover the costs of holding the land (the interest charges on the potential land price and the tax burden, which is zero in the case of a CUVT). Thus much depends on the valuation arithmetic of the particular case. But a site value land tax does secure less speculation than in the no-tax situation and it follows that it is not neutral. Economic behaviour is different before and after the tax. This applies only to redevelopment: the most important feature of the site value tax system would seem to be that it confronts the owners of property ripe for redevelopment with the redevelopment potential of their property by way of annual cash charges directly related to this redevelopment potential, and they cannot ignore these changes. But this would not necessarily be beneficial, since it could impose liquidity problems on those who are holding their land in an economically sub-optimal use, but to good 'social ends'. In this way, the site value tax system with its high tax charges on properties in redevelopment areas can virtually force the redevelopment of privately owned buildings of historic or architectural importance which the owners might otherwise have been willing to retain. Or, by stimulating and reinforcing market forces, the site value tax system has encouraged the concentration of the office redevelopment [in Sydney] into a relatively small area and it can be argued that this concentration has considerably reduced the amenity of this area for workers and visitors.

These arguments foster the view that an SVT system would have to take very full account of the planning proposals for an area in order not to encourage development counter to them, and indeed if adopted should have assessments based on 'planned values'. Such arguments are not nearly as forceful in the case of a CUVT. Such a tax will not of itself induce landowners to realise the development potential of their land.

While it has so far been assumed that, having decided on a tax base, the tax would be levied at the same proportionate rate throughout the land market, there are various possibilities for special taxes related, say, to specific uses or designed specifically for plan implementation. However, the conventional wisdom in the study of public finance is that it is usually more sensible to try to effect desirable non-fiscal ends by direct measures – for example, to reserve open space by actual public acquisition – rather than by manipulating major general taxes for this purpose, with attendant administrative difficulties and, frequently, unanticipated side effects.

Notwithstanding this, proposals have often been put forward for what are generally called *land-hoarding charges*: the special taxing of land which, although suitable for development, is being withheld from the market. The effects will depend on the way in which the charge is levied. For example, in 1973 a tax was proposed which would be levied at 30 per cent of the land value in each year that it was held vacant after the first three years following the granting of planning permission. Such a charge will have the long-run effect of deterring landowners from making premature planning applications; they will not do so until they are certain of being able to begin development within three years. Thus while such a tax would have the short-term effect of increasing land supply, it may be expected to reduce it marginally in the long term since there will always be some caution as to development prospects.

Taxes on improvements

Taxes on improvements, as opposed to those on the land, can in theory only be on the capital investment of the improvements or on the rents which go towards covering the costs of this investment. All rents over and above this theoretically accrue to the land as 'economic rent'.

Turning to the question of neutrality, in urban land, improvements are so important that the problems associated with utilising these improvements become the major issues of urban land utilisation. Building and other improvements, considered from the long-term point of view, are destructible, since they wear out in due time. Consequently, if taxes are levied on the value of improvements, the owner can do little to shift such taxes during the ordinary life of the improvement; but when the building or improvements need to be replaced, the owner will not replace it unless the reward for renewal is sufficient to justify such replacement with those in other alternative endeavours. ... A tax on the value of or income from improvements will lower the reward to renewal and will thus tend to delay it. As noted above, such a delay is tantamount to a reduction in the supply of improvements to land.

All this means is that a tax on improvements will not be neutral and the tax will be shifted. Many consequences follow from this: in the private production of goods and services it encourages the substitution of other inputs for real property and to a more limited degree for producer durables. To the extent that firms and industries are limited in their opportunities to effect such substitutions without raising costs of production above those of their direct and indirect competitors, the tax will tend to direct resources away from particular firms and industries.

However, the unneutrality of the property tax is, of course, far less objectionable to the degree that it offsets other unneutralities in the tax system. ... In regard to business inputs, for instance, it can be considered as a counterpart to the existing taxes on payrolls levied for social insurance purposes.

Following what was said above, there should be no difference between taxing the capital value of the improvements and taxing the net rents accruing to them.

However, in countries which do tax real property on rent income, the tax tends to be on gross rather than net rents, the difference between them being due to maintenance costs, and so on. While these costs (which reduce the capital value of improvements) are in essence allowed against taxes on the capital value of land improvements, they are not taken into account by a tax on gross rents. A rational property-owner would, under a gross rents tax, tend to reduce his operating and maintenance costs. This means that over and above the effects of the unneutrality of the property tax levied on net rents a gross rents tax will be an inducement to lower standard of operation and maintenance.

Levies
Levies differ from taxes in that they are not imposed annually but only under special circumstances relating to the land or improvements in question. The circumstances may be profits resulting from public decisions on land-use changes and development on the land (planning permission), from public investment in infrastructure either on or off the land, or from transactions reflecting the market pressures on land. For each of these there are variations in the specific levels chosen to delimit the capital gains (the levels might be the normal for all transactions, or might be special to land); there may be variation in the timing of the levy (at the time of sale, or lease, at development or at the time of granting planning permission).

The primary justification for this set of measures is to be found in considerations of equity: in essence that land values are created by the community (its decisions, actions and demands) rather than by the landowner; and furthermore that particular fortunate landowners should not benefit through planning decisions if others are denied the opportunity. Given this, the community has every right to recapture as much of the unearned increment as it chooses. It may do this to a variety of levels. It may see the whole value of land as 'fair game' and tax this through site value taxation; or it may consider bygones as bygones and impose a levy only on value *increases*, on development or disposal; and in either case it may wish to leave the landowner some proportion.

One way of collecting such a levy is through capital gains taxation. Most countries tax capital gains less heavily than annual income, and consequently encourage investment in assets that will increase the productive capacity of the nation. While there may be sound economic reasons for this in many cases, it is difficult to make such a case for land: more investment in *land* does not increase the productive capacity as such, unless associated with development. Discussions about the effects of land value increment levies on timing of land supply raise complex issues. But certain conclusions can be drawn. A levy which is assessed and also collected at the time of a planning permission can raise liquidity problems for the landowner or developer, through difficulty in borrowing, and so deter development. But if the levy were assessed but not collected till the gains were realised through development, and if the absolute amount of the levy due were not altered by delay, its discounted present equivalent may be reduced by delaying payment and therefore development. And the levy may deter people from making determined planning applications where the potential rewards for success are significantly reduced; the rational entrepreneur will equate the marginal costs of 'planning application effort' with the marginal gain of success, and a land value increment levy will reduce this marginal revenue and so reduce the effort made to gain planning permission. But on the other hand, the effect could be increased in the knowledge that the community share in the value increment may make it more willing to approve applications.

And where there is politically generated expectation of a reduction in the amount of the levy, then clearly landowners will defer selling and developers will defer development. This was seen in the financial provisions of the 1947 Act which aimed at imposing a levy of 100 per cent on gains from development. This complete expropriation of development gains removed the incentive to sell land. The landowners could expect nothing from development,

> so that they might as well sit tight and enjoy living on, and possibly farming, large areas of land which were needed for development. It is not surprising that they demanded some additional payment from developers to persuade them to sell. Developers had to pay this as well as pay the whole of the development value to the Crown, thus paying for it twice over.

Bearing this in mind it must be recognised that land policies are necessarily long-term policies: 'If they are not supported to some extent by the political parties which could form a government, landowners will take account of the possibility of a change in government in making their decisions.' In fact, in 1951 the Conservatives did gain power and repealed the financial provisions of the 1947 Act, so justifying the decision of any landowner who refused to part with his land. And history may be repeating itself with the Development Land Tax Act of 1976.

Charges for developers' requirements

A system by which developers contribute to the public costs of serving the land they are developing does not conform to the definition of a tax since it may be seen as payment in return for services to the individual developer. However, its effects will be similar to those of a tax or levy; in fact, the argument is the same as that followed when considering the effects of a levy on the timing of development.

It is assumed that the charge is related in some way to the actual cost of public provision. If so, it will not only have the effects on planning applications mentioned so far but is also likely to affect the kind of development for which application is made. This is because the charge would probably be related to the kind of development to take place and so need not have the same proportion of total development value as a capital gains tax.

The incidence of the charges depends on whether or not the residual approach to land price-setting would be realistic in that particular land market. If so, the price of land would be reduced by the capital cost of the improvements, as with any other increase in building costs. But it can be argued that these charges will be wholly passed on to the occupier, since by 'delaying development, the price at which development property can be sold increases enough to cover the cost. Developers will only operate when the margin between their buying and their selling price is sufficient to cover the costs. They can increase their selling price by delaying sale but can do little to influence the buying price.'

3.10.6   SIDE-EFFECTS

In the above discussion (sections 3.8.1–3.8.5) we have traced through the

Figure 3.1

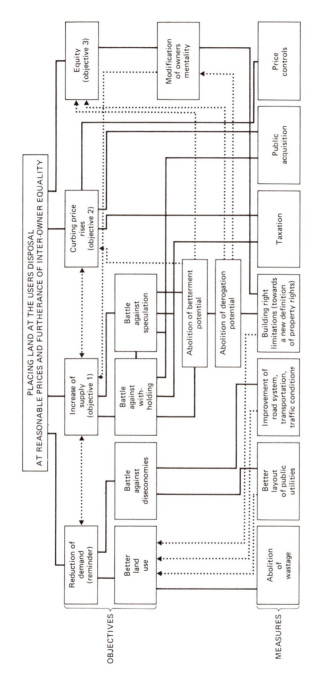

PLACING LAND AT THE USERS DISPOSAL
AT REASONABLE PRICES AND FURTHERANCE OF INTER-OWNER EQUALITY

OBJECTIVES

Reduction of demand (reminder)

Increase of supply (objective 1)

Curbing price rises (objective 2)

Equity (objective 3)

Modification of owners mentality

Battle against diseconomies

Battle against with-holding

Battle against speculation

Better land use

Abolition of betterment potential

Abolition of derogation potential

MEASURES

Abolition of wastage

Improvement of road system, transportation, traffic conditions

Better layout of public utilities

Building right limitations (towards a new definition of property rights)

Taxation

Public acquisition

Price controls

Source: Gilli, (1976, p.30).

repercussions of particular land policy measures on land values. In so doing we have, for reasons of space, been rather brief in analysis, relying on the references as a source of amplification. From these it will be seen how complex the repercussions can be. To give some guide here we close with a diagrammatic representation (Figure 3.1) of the side-effects of one such land policy, in the circumstances of France.[73]

The land policy in question has the following objective: to place at the users' disposal (public authorities and private developers) land at reasonable prices, furthering inter-owner quality. This involves three land policies and their measures, all to be carried out within the constraint of furtherance of equality between owners.

1   Reduce land demand, by greater efficiency in infrastructure development;
2   Increase land supply by resisting the withholding of land from the market, by taxation, public acquisition of land, curbing speculation; and
3   Act directly on prices to prevent excessive increase, by taxation, limit to compensation, price controls.

All these would have direct repercussions and side-effects ('fallouts') which would be interacting and interpenetrating. Figure 3.1 illustrates these.

3.11   MARKET PRESSURES IN PLANNING[74]

It was shown earlier in this chapter how development in a mixed economy may be said to operate through the medium of the market (section 3.5) leading to the need for planning intervention (section 3.6) in part through land policy (section 3.7). This being so, planning has to reckon with the market reacting adversely against its plans:

> If planners make a plan which happens to be disliked, say by a firm or a landlord, these do not simply submit but take evasive action. ... The point is that the market is not to be ordered around. Whatever planners may do, economic agents pursue their own goals, doing the best that they can in their own interests given the constraints that planners and others impose on them.

The principal reaction from the market comes from its underlying profit maximisation. If this can be advanced by putting pressures on the planning system, it is not surprising if it occurs; as long as the planning system influences land prices, it will be worth the while of the private sector to create these pressures. Their principal direction is to get the planning authority to allow high value uses, perhaps by rearranging the uses in their plans or by increasing permitted densities. The extent to which they are pursued will depend on the amount of possible gain (which, as recent British experience has shown, may be enormous) and on the flexibility of the planning authority, the appeals procedure, and so on.

But if these pressures are successful, they will divert the implementation of a plan and reduce its effectiveness, which could have serious effect for the community, as the following examples show.

The approval of higher densities than envisaged in a plan for particular land (which leads to higher land values for that land) may have a negative environmental impact, for example by creating more traffic congestion, and impose higher costs on the community in its relief. Alternatively, planning decisions to allow the change of residential land to commercial use in the inner city can also lead to a restricted supply there of residential land, as owners all expect that they, too, will benefit from such a change and thus refuse to develop their property residentially; the high prices prevent any further residential development, and the concomitant neglect of deteriorating property leads to blighted areas with harmful consequences for low-income groups. Or again, the conversion of agricultural land into urban use, which requires planning permission, if not carefully controlled, may lead to high land prices for adjoining agricultural land due to the expectation that such land might also be used for urban development. Such a situation in turn forces those seeking cheap land for housing to go even further from the city frontier, leading to buildings erected without services in isolated locations. This leads to higher infrastructure costs for an inefficient transportation network, and price increases in all the undeveloped land between the new projects and the urbanised area.

Thus planning in a mixed economy has to aim at *planned development*, which recognises the role of the market but seeks to control it towards social ends. We now turn to how this is attempted in Britain today.

REFERENCES: CHAPTER 3

1 Jowell (1977b).
2 This relies on Lichfield (1978b).
3 This is the English usage. In the USA the term would also include the buildings.
4 See, for example, Commission on International Development (1969).
5 See, for example, Olson and Landsberg (1975).
6 See, for example, Seers and Joy (1968).
7 Schiavo-Compo and Singer (1970, part I).
8 Galbraith (1958).
9 See, for example, Hauser and Schnore (1965).
10 Ely and Wehrwein (1940).
11 Renne (1958, p. 6).
12 Darin-Drabkin and Lichfield (1977).
13 For descriptions of the land development process, see Lichfield (1956), Hall *et al.* (1973), DoE (1975a), Davidson and Leonard (1976).
14 From Lichfield (1956).
15 Denman (1969).
16 For a treatment of this kind see Barlowe (1958).
17 Denman and Prodano (1972, p. 19).
18 Geiger (1936, p. 17).
19 Denman and Prodano (1972, p. 19).
20 Renne (1958, p. 225).
21 Denman and Prodano (1972, p. 19).
22 Barlowe (1958, p. 7).
23 Denman and Prodano (1972, p. 24).
24 As, for example, in Israel, where there is an amalgam of Turkish, British and Roman law.
25 Garner (1956).
26 Marshall (1927), quoting Cournot.
27 Ricardo (1911).
28 Turvey (1957), Newell (1977).

29 Lichfield (1958a).
30 Turvey (1957, chs 2 and 4), Newell (1977, ch. 5).
31 For empirical evidence see Hall *et al.* (1973, vol. II, ch. 7).
32 Turvey (1957).
33 Lichfield (1956, ch. 10), Newell (1977, ch. 5).
34 Alonso (1964).
35 Neutze (1973, p. 15).
36 Walters (1974).
37 Neutze (1973, p. 17).
38 Lichfield (1956, pp. 311–18).
39 Lichfield (1968).
40 Myrdal (1960, p. 1).
41 See, for example, Samuelson (1958).
42 Ely and Wehrwein (1940, p. 138).
43 See, for example Samuelson (1958).
44 Ely and Wehrwein (1940, p. 138).
45 Ratcliff (1949, p. 369).
46 Ibid, p. 384.
47 Ibid, p. 385. For a somewhat different formulation and discussion, see Turner (1977, pp. 35–41), and Harrison (1977, pp. 62–84).
48 Ratcliff (1949, p. 385). This view is not stated so strongly in Ratcliff (1961, p. 327).
49 Denman (1969, pp. 20–1), and Denman (1974, pp. 1–7).
50 Denman (1969, p. 21).
51 Denman (1978, p. 21).
52 Lichfield (1964b).
53 This section relies on Lichfield (1964b), and Foster (1973).
54 Musgrave (1959, ch. 1).
55 Galbraith (1958).
56 Denman and Prodano (1972, p. 24).
57 For a discussion, see Turvey (1957), Lichfield (1964b), Foster (1973), and Coase (1960).
58 Pigou (1948, p. 184).
59 See, for example, Bator (1956), Harrison (1977), and Turner (1977).
60 Shonfield (1965).
61 For example, Hayek (1979), Friedmann (1973), and Walters (1974).
62 For example, Baumol (1965), and Meade (1975).
63 See Vaizey (1977).
64 Shonfield (1965).
65 Hayek (1979).
66 See Baumol (1965). For a classic description, see Kapp (1950).
67 See Cheung (1978), Littlechild (1978).
68 Burton, in Cheung (1978, pp. 69–90).
69 Ashton (1939, pp. 54–60).
70 In the main sections 3.10.2–3.10.4 rely upon Lichfield (1956, ch. 24).
71 Ministry of Works and Planning (1942, para. 7).
72 There is a considerable literature which is drawn upon here.
73 Gilli (1976, p. 30).
74 This relies on Lichfield (1956, ch. 26), Neutze (1973, pp. 19–21), and Foster (1973, p. 133).

Part Two

Source of Land Policy

Chapter 4

The Process of Development Planning

4.1 THE SOCIAL AND ECONOMIC CONTEXT

In the preceding chapters we have been at pains to show how the process of development and of its planning are closely related. Physical development is the fabric underlying the social, economic and cultural development of a country; and development planning is the attempt to mould ongoing physical development in order to solve the problems of the country and to take advantage of opportunities in accordance with the country's objectives. Taking these two processes together, we have the concept of 'planned development'. Because of its constituent elements this process is undergoing continuing change under social, economic and political pressures. But since it is our purpose to look forward to land policies which might be introduced for the future, it is useful to have some description of contemporary planned development in Britain as our point of departure. This is attempted in this chapter.

But what is going on today in this connection is a 'still picture' in a moving film which covers a long time span. This is necessarily so, since the physical development which is the focus of our development planning is the most enduring artefact with which man has to deal. Thus in planning our cities and regions we are inevitably concerned with (i) a heritage which may have taken centuries to evolve; (ii) with the present, since it is the people now living in our settlements who are the ultimate clients in our planning; and (iii) with their children, since the physical development which we are shaping will endure for a long time.

Thus planned development at any particular time must look forward on the shoulders of the past, and on time scales which are unusually long for many other forms of human activity. Thus to provide some picture of the social and economic context of contemporary planned development, it is necessary to look at Britain in the past, even if ever so briefly.

One historical factor which still dictates much of the physical environment is the first industrial revolution. Its timing still sets Britain apart from the other countries of the world. This is so because it occurred here earlier than elsewhere, and British land policy must be capable of dealing with the problems of a huge outdated stock of development, as the following will indicate.

In the nineteenth century the population of England and Wales increased threefold,[1] and the major cities were established. In 1800 there were only eight towns with populations of more than 50,000, while in 1900 60 per cent of the population of 38 million was living in towns.[2] Added to this, it was the zenith of private enterprise. Little of this urban development was planned for current lifestyles. The dwellings followed the factories to areas which were often environmentally unsuitable for housing, and this housing was usually of a minimum standard. Densities were high and open space limited.[3] As a result 25 per cent of the dwellings in the United Kingdom are over sixty years old,[4] and some 15 per cent fall below the required minimum standard of fitness.[5] Of all countries in 1900 Britain had the highest percentage of urban population. Comparing this with the current urban population provides a rough index of obsolescence in urbanism. In 1950 Britain had the worst in the world, half as much again as France, the next highest.[6]

Other major historical influences on the stock of buildings in the United Kingdom were the two world wars. During 1939–45 the building of new homes came to a complete standstill, and there was little or no maintenance, while the population increased by 1½ million. When people returned afterwards, they faced a major problem of overcrowding.[7] In addition, the central areas of many British towns were blitzed. This massive destruction gave a new impetus to planning policies and problems. Long before the bombs had stopped falling there was serious consideration of the problems of renewal: 'The destruction wrought by bombing transformed the "rebuilding of Britain" from a socially desirable but somewhat visionary and vague ideal into a matter of practice and defined necessity.'[8]

The Second World War also affected regional development in Britain. For example, the depressed areas had been a serious problem prior to 1939, but with the outbreak of fighting the existence of industrial areas away from the metropolis became an advantage; the munitions factories gravitated towards these areas, and so provided massive amounts of factory space adaptable for civilian use after the war.

Since the war there has been a sustained pressure for change in the physical environment. The UK population increased from 45 million in 1945 to some 54 million in 1971.[9] But this gave rise to more development than the mere numbers suggest, through changes in the locational, demographic and economic characteristics of the population. Under planning, people have dispersed over the country. Reduction in family size has meant the demand for homes growing consistently faster than the overall population. Growth in the real standard of living has meant that people require better standards of housing and other urban attributes, as well as more cars. Car ownership per 1,000 of population has risen from about 46 in 1950 to 235 in 1972,[10] requiring growth and updating in transport network and infrastructure. There has been a marked shift in the balance between the tertiary sector (commercial and service) and manufacturing which has required an alteration in the character of many urban centres, and there has also been growth and change in the stock of shopping development through the 'retailing revolution'.[11]

An important element in this physical growth was the economic boom of the 1960s. The building of houses and offices reached record levels, being more profitable than investment in industry (thus distorting the economy and cramping economic growth); investment grew in land and land development with market prices for development land rising rapidly. Office rents in London also reached record levels (rising even higher when further office building there was virtually prohibited).[12] The prices of houses trebled, partly due to increased building costs, but largely due to the unsatisfied demand for houses and the readiness of the building societies, by then flush with funds, to grant mortgages.

Unhappily, the sustained growth since the First World War, with full employment over most of the period, came to an end in the early 1970s under the pressure of a variety of influences. There was the world-wide economic depression, exacerbated by the sudden rise in the price of oil. But more particularly for our purposes the development industry was hit very badly, on both the public and private fronts. On the former, the very downturn in the economy in Britain, with rising interest rates and inflation at levels not experienced in this century, all combined to impose limits in the amount of public-sector spending, and thereby on public development. Concurrently, the downturn in demand as a whole found the development industry with its development programme completely unprepared, and unable to cope with the losses caused by inflated costs of land and construction and high interest rates. This led to large-scale failures in the development industry and in the financial institutions supporting it, and a rapid erosion in the entrepreneurial contribution of the developers and the development companies.[13]

These features have continued throughout the late 1970s, though concurrently there is the expectation of some improvement, linked with the opportunities that will be offered by the sudden wealth from the discoveries of oil and gas under the seas surrounding Britain. But just how the British economy will fare into the 1980s is uncertain, since there are clearly structural weaknesses to be faced and it is most difficult to predict international prospects in trade and availability of financial capital. As always after the cataclysm comes the question: will there be a return to the 'normalcy' we have known?

4.2 CONTEMPORARY FEATURES IN THE DEVELOPMENT PROCESS

In Chapter 3 we described the role of the development process in planned development, and here we present some features of this process in contemporary Britain. We give the account by reference to the main factors of production in that process.

4.2.1 LAND[14]

Unlike some countries, there is in Britain no '*Domesday Book*' of land ownership, and there are surprising difficulties in establishing the facts, and indeed (in England and Wales as compared with Scotland) the facts also concerning the actual prices paid on land transfer. But for our purposes it is sufficient to note that there is a mixed economy in land ownership and, furthermore, that within the public and private sectors there is a range of estate sizes, from the small to the very large.

The public sector already owns a substantial area of land, and in some urban areas the proportion is high, possibly of the order of one-half if all public bodies are taken together. To take one example, perhaps extreme, of the 2,250 hectares in the London dockland study area, some 80 per cent is in public ownership of one kind or another.

In the private sector, alongside the diffusion of a 'propery-owning democracy', there still exists a stratum of very large landowners with very extensive rural holdings, while even in London much of the prime central area is still very much privately owned.

If there is a trend in the private/public composition of land ownership, it must surely be towards the public sector, with the increasing role of this sector in the economy of the country. More particularly, within the general growth, public agencies, and in particular local authorities, are assuming a relatively greater role in land ownership for development, and for this purpose have a steadily growing array of powers for compulsory purchase (forced sale) from the private sector.

As regards tenure in the development process, there has been the particular flavour in Britain of leasehold, originating in the main in the private sector and now heavily used in the public sector for new towns, urban redevelopment, and so on.

4.2.2   THE CONSTRUCTION INDUSTRY[15]

In this industry we include all those factors needed for the carrying out of building and civil engineering works on land: namely, the firms with their management structures, the building labour and the manufacturing and delivery systems for the building material needed. To be sure this industry has itself been undergoing very significant changes, under the pressures of, for example, rising prices of labour, capital and materials, and the need to adapt to modern as opposed to traditional methods of construction and production.

4.2.3   FINANCE[16]

A continuing feature of development is the need of all the actors concerned (both in production and consumption of the finished development, be they owners or owner-occupiers) for sources of finance outside their own resources. Thus there has grown up the complex system of money flows. In part this is for short-term bridging finance (to make the land available for development throughout the development process until completion, to finance the professionals preparing the preparatory planning, the works of the building and construction industry) and the long-term finance for those who will own the finished development as an investment.

Within all this a notable feature of contemporary development is the huge concentration of funds in the building societies (for house purchase) and in the financial institutions (the insurance companies, pension funds, property unit trusts, charities, etc.); and not only are these huge but by the logic of their sources they must tend to grow and grow.

But the same cannot be said of the resources available to local government for development. They are caught up in the paradox of ever-growing responsibilities, either imposed upon them by central government or of their own choosing, without corresponding growth in financial resources, be it in the real estate tax base for local rating assessment or in grants from central government. Thus while the public sector is taking on a growing role relative to the private in development, it cannot match the growth with the provision of funds from its own sources, and must rely more and more on the private sector.

4.2.4   THE DEVELOPER[17]

Until the early 1970s the striking feature of post-1945 development in Britain was the dramatic growth of the property development company: in function (compared with the property investment company of pre-1939 days); in size (becoming owners of vast assets because of the tendency to hold land for investment); and in operation (pioneering a sophistication in development practice in the international scene). But the collapse indicated in the preceding section has virtually transformed the scene, both by the elimination of many of the companies through failure (with many of the secondary financial institutions geared to property development) and by the abandonment of major development enterprises (except those in the pipeline) of the development companies still in operation. Many property companies have, in fact, turned from the post-war development to the pre-war investment function.

In parallel with this decline in importance of the developer as such there has been a relative increase in the development functions of the contractor and the financial institutions. As regards the former, certain of the major contractors have taken on in addition the development function (the contractor-developer) and also, in some cases, the financing. In addition some financing institutions have also been expanding their development function, choosing to use their own money for this purpose rather than lending it to developers. As such the process was the culmination of a transition whereby the financial institutions moved from lending to developers at fixed rates to participation in the profits from such development.

4.2.5 PARTNERSHIPS[18]

These changing roles in development have given rise to new combinations amongst the various actors, of which the contractor-financier and institution-developer have just been noted. A particular instance is the 'partnership agreement' of the landowner and developer, sometimes with the financier, which has grown up amongst public-sector developers, particularly in comprehensive development of new towns.

These current forms of partnership have changed considerably from their origins in the association between local authorities and developers which was born in the new legislation needed to cope with redevelopment of the blitzed areas after the Second World War. Since only a few authorities had previously coped with redevelopment of this magnitude, and then under local Acts (e.g. Birmingham, London), collaboration with the private sector was needed and desirable. But even here the know-how did not exist; the pre-war property company was an investor in already-standing bricks and mortar. But the development industry responded to the challenge and the new property development companies began to operate.

The basis for the collaboration was clearly one of freeholder/leaseholder. This resulted from the merging of the Labour government's principles (the land in public ownership and the rise in land values to the community) with the principles generated by the aristocratic landed estates over centuries, of fostering good estate management and development through freehold/leasehold. Thus the landed-estate principles became absorbed, almost without modification, by the socialist administration – who began to embark on 'positive planning', in the redevelopment of the bombed areas, and then in the blighted areas and the varied kinds of development in new towns, housing, and so on.[19]

Perhaps it was this injection from both the novel and traditional which led to the endurance in the succeeding years of the freehold/leasehold basis of local authority/new town development, even during the Conservative administration of 1951–64. Thus almost all of the major post-war development and redevelopment projects which were initiated by public enterprise took place with very little direct development by the local authorities.

In this there was joint collaboration between the authority and developer, each playing their distinctive roles, as follows:

1   The authority as landowner had the task of making the necessary land available, with powers to augment the supply by compulsory purchase, at prices controlled by law.
2   The authority as planner, developer and government had parallel contributions of various kinds: it determined the appropriate land uses on the basis of its planning of a wider area; it could project the investment by controlling competitive uses; it provided the necessary infrastructure such as roads and utilities to support the development and so affected its timing; it could provide all kinds of capital and revenue services within the development (car-parking, municipal buildings); it could take over certain elements of the completed development under municipal management; and it could offer a co-ordinating role for the various expenditures and activities of the other public agencies.
3   The developer was the classic entrepreneur. He brought in the know-how of the development process; he understood the market for which he was catering, and how to provide the right building at the right time in the right place; he understood the financial relationship of costs, rents, financing and taxes, he secured finance through the institutions who were prepared to back him as an entrepreneur of achievement or promise; and he provided property management of the completed development on behalf of himself and the landowner.

In this complicated process each actor pursued his own objectives in playing his distinctive role, while sharing with all the others the common objective of achieving a completed development which met the constraints and objectives of all parties concerned. Unless there could be mutual adjustment and agreement here, the partnership could not be reached and the development would not be started.

To meet this situation there were clearly all kinds of contracts needed between the various parties, in all sorts of permutations and combinations. Although starting with the simple freeholder/leaseholder arrangement of the traditional type, the form of association between the authorities and developers evolved significantly over the following twenty-five years. As indicated above, freehold/ leasehold relationships persisted throughout the Conservative administrations and were never seriously challenged (and it was the Labour administration that nibbled at the principle in leasehold reform).[20] But the contractual details did change. In the main these related to the financial shares between the freeholder, lessee and financier (rising rents to reflect growth and later inflation, fixed rates of interest in addition to equity shares, financing of the local authorities' land acquisition).[21]

Taken to the full, this shows the authority in a 'trading capacity' as opposed to a 'landlord capacity'. Such trading activities are a feature of a growing tendency of authorities to undertake partnerships with the private sector, not only in respect of development of land but also for conventional business activities, as in providing the finance for local enterprises.[22]

But the *partnership* concept can be taken further, i.e. in bringing together all the respective actors in development to produce the 'package deal' or the 'turnkey project'. Here one actor, or a consortium, undertakes to provide the total package from land assembly through to completed and occupied development, be it for a factory or shop at the one extreme or perhaps for a whole new town at the other. For this is needed a consortium or association of professional skills, equipped to provide all that is needed. Given the array of skills, and the need to conceive of and execute the turnkey operation as a whole, this is tantamount to taking on the role of 'project management': the undertaking by professionals of the managerial function for the whole operation, on behalf of the client, whoever that happens to be in the particular project.

4.3   THE CONTEMPORARY PLANNING SYSTEM

So far in discussing planning we have concentrated on two particular aspects, plan-making and plan implementation. But these two are in fact part of a much wider array of elements which, working together, make up a total planning system. Some contemporary features are now described briefly under a series of heads which, on one classification, constitute the major elements of the system.[23]

4.3.1   PLAN-MAKING

For this purpose plans are prepared at the national, local and regional levels by different institutions, and in our description it is convenient to link them.

Following the review of the nature of British planning above (section 1.2) we now summarise its plan-making in practice. At the national level, the government department concerned with planning – now the Department of the Environment – was created from various established ministries in 1970. This department is concerned with all aspects of urban and regional planning and the Secretary of State for the Environment (subject to the Cabinet) is the ultimate authority in the statutory planning framework.[24]

In 1974 the structure of local government was altered drastically; the previous arrangement had been in operation for ninety years and was out of date both organisationally and spatially. In England, for example, the number of local authorities was cut from 1,390 to 422 (excluding London). These new local authorities comprise two tiers; the county councils (six metropolitan and forty-seven non-metropolitan) and the district councils (thirty-six metropolitan and 333 non-metropolitan). Thus the reorganisation brought together for the first time many conurbations in one administration.[25]

Prior to this the planning system had been reshaped under the 1968 Town and Country Planning Act following the report of the Planning Advisory Group.[26] This adapted the former development plan system into a new one of structure and local plans.

The structure plans are intended as broad statements of policy concerning issues of key structural importance. They are concerned with looking forward over a period of fifteen years, explaining the aims underlying the plans and the strategy for achieving them.[27] Each county council is required to prepare a structure plan for its area. In doing this it has to consult with government departments, adjoining councils, district councils and interested bodies. The Secretary of State has to approve a plan following its examination and this gives central government the power to influence it in the light of national and regional considerations.

Prior to his doing so it is published and submitted to public scrutiny, leading to the Secretary of State conducting an 'examination in public' into a number of specific issues. Finally, the Secretary of State decides whether to approve the plan, with or without amendments.

In the structure plans the county councils identify certain priority areas ('action areas') in which they anticipate early development or redevelopment. For these areas district councils prepare action plans. Apart from this, the district also prepares local plans for large areas ('district plans') and for particular planning aspects ('subject plans'). These have to conform in general with the approved structure plan, but unlike the structure plan they deal with the details of development and provide the basis for development control. While the Secretary of State may 'call in' local plans for his own approval, it is hoped that approval by the authority (after public debate) will generally be sufficient.

At the national level plans are prepared under the auspices of the Department of the Environment. There was, in 1965, the second attempt to produce a national economic plan,[28] but this was thwarted by economic recession. There are, however, national plans for various sectors (such as hospitals, transport and national parks) produced by the relevant ministries.

At the next tier down come the regional plans or strategies. Before 1969 these were the responsibility of the Department of Economic Affairs, but they were later transferred to what became the Department of the Environment. They head regional economic planning boards that work with regional economic councils, nominated multidisciplinary teams that consider a wide range of issues in the regional context. Their purpose is to provide both a structure within which the local authorities can operate their planning machinery as well as a basis from which central government can operate its regional policy. But the system of regional planning is not embodied in legislation and the councils have no resources, staff or powers of implementation.

4.3.2 PLAN IMPLEMENTATION

Following the review of implementation measures above (section 2.5) we now highlight certain specific aspects of current British practice.

As development agencies the public sector plays a great part in implementation at all of the various levels of government hierarchy. There are the local authorities, principally the districts but also the counties; certain regional bodies, such as the Water Authorities, which are responsible for utilities on a regional basis; the various nationalised boards such as British Rail, British Steel, the National Coal Board, and so on; the New Town Development Corporations for the thirty-odd new towns in Britain, acting as a special kind of developer with loans from central government; and finally central government itself, for example in building the trunk roads.[29]

But more relevant for our purpose here are the implementation authorities. Here again the principal burden falls on the local authorities, divided between the county and district authorities in a complex way.[30] The level which has the least powers of implementation is the regional; the economic planning councils have no teeth, staff or investment resources and the regional departments of the ministries are really arms of central government. This operates controls directly, for example in office and industrial location policy.[31]

Within all this the aspect of implementation which characterises planning in the eyes of the public is development control by the county and district authorities in tandem. As this has not altered substantially since the 1947 Act, this may be seen as the direct descendant of the public-health bye-law controls of the last century, i.e. as a *social control* of land use.[32] It is this which is the cornerstone of plan implementation and which spearheads the limitation of rights attached to the ownership of land, where this is not 'taken' but left with the owner.

The power of this control stems from the requirement that, subject to certain exceptions which are not significant for our purpose, planning permission is required for the carrying out of any development of land.[33] For this purpose development is defined as 'the carrying out of building, engineering, mining or other operations in, on, over or under land, or the making of any material change in the use of any buildings or other land' subject to certain exceptions which are not of themselves significant for our purpose. Given that 'development' as here defined is proposed, an application for planning permission is required. When considering whether or not to grant permission, the authority 'shall have regard to the provisions of the development plan, so far as material to the application, and to any other material considerations'.[34] For this purpose the authority must enter into a complex set of consultations and discussions to ensure that all relevant considerations are taken into account.[35] Having considered the application in this way, the authorities may 'grant planning permission either unconditionally or subject to such conditions as they think fit; or ... may refuse planning permission'.[36] Or they 'may enter into an agreement with any person interested in land in their area for the purpose of restricting or regulating the development or use of the land'.[37] There is a right of appeal to the Secretary of State against an outright refusal or against conditions;[38] his decision is final except in matters of legal interpretation. If development occurs without planning permission or contrary to conditions, the authority may serve an enforcement notice 'requiring the breach to be remedied'.[39]

It is under this development control machinery, which absorbs the major part of the time and energy diverted to planning by authorities and ministries, that the physical development of the country is controlled.

4.3.3   CO-ORDINATION OF PUBLIC DECISIONS

Given the vast array of public agencies, their plan-making across major sectors in the country, and plan implementation of various kinds, it is evident that considerable contribution can be made to effectiveness through co-ordination, both horizontal and vertical. This is recognised in government activities in many ways. There is the elaborate system of consultative machinery which has been set up for central and local government for both plan-making and plan implementation, including the closely integrated central government regional machine in the various provincial capitals.

This ongoing co-ordination of government activities has been given a new dimension on the introduction of corporate planning in local government, with its attempts to integrate the planning and operational activities of the various departments, as regards objectives, priorities, spending, and so on.

4.3.4 APPROPRIATE POLITICAL AND ADMINISTRATIVE MACHINERY

In Chapter 2 the close interrelationship between the politicians and the professionals in plan-making and plan implementation was described. There was also mentioned the relationship between these two arms and the administrators and managers in central and local government who in a sense are a bridge between the politicians as policy-makers and implementers and the professional planners. It is in the relative contributions of these three arms that the success of the planning system depends.

But this complex machinery cannot be expected to work smoothly without some provision in education, training and selection of the appropriate manpower for the various tasks, for in the end it is on the quantity and quality of such manpower that all depends. This already exists in the education and training of the wide array of professional planning and developmental skills concerned in the process of planned development. But the needs do not stop there: the politicians and administrator-managers, both as legislators and executors, need to be well prepared, as do representatives of sections of the population, and also the general public, starting in the schools, so that they all may participate suitably in the ongoing discussions and consultations. Needless to say, the preparation for each group would not be uniform.

4.3.5 PARTICIPATION BY THE PUBLIC

Whereas much of the machinery needed for the collaboration just described is well established (e.g. between Parliament and the executive, between local authorities and departments, etc.), the participation by the public in planning operations is of much more recent origin.

Very full public discussion was seen, from the start in 1947, as an important feature of the new planning process. But the 1947 Act adopted the traditional method of publication of the plan to give objectors an opportunity of making written comments or, if they wished, of appearing before a ministry inspector at a local public inquiry. In addition, it was always open to a local authority to consult the public while the plan was being prepared if it could find an effective way of doing so. But few did, and the inquiries on planning appeals to the minister tended to become more and more formal (and more expensive) through the briefing counsel and the calling of an array of expert witnesses. With the dramatic rise in the number of planning applications,[40] the administration at both local and central levels was becoming hopelessly clogged by the mid-1960s.

As a result the degree of participation in the process by the citizen became almost negligible, and in 1968 new methods were introduced which required the local authority to publicise its proposals in the course of preparing a structure plan and take into account any representations it received *before* submitting the plan for the minister's approval. The procedure at any subsequent inquiry ordered by the minister was also simplified. The whole question was ventilated further in 1969.[41]

It is perhaps too early yet to judge how effective this new machinery will be. Much will depend on the way local authorities operate it in order to obtain the views of a representative cross-section of the public, as distinct from the numerous pressure groups that tend to dominate public meetings. Nevertheless, the signs are that people are beginning to show more interest in the planning process, and the growth of an informed public opinion should help significantly in the sometimes delicate task of resolving the conflicting views that surround major planning problems.

4.3.6 MEANS OF COMMUNICATION BETWEEN PARTIES

The preceding five elements of our planning system show how complex an array there is of agencies, activities, people, professionals, of various kinds and of different backgrounds, and laymen. Each must communicate with the others. For example, Parliament speaks to central and local government through statutes and administrative laws; the relevant departments talk to authorities through circulars and advisory memoranda; the plans themselves communicate to all affected in terms of proposals, priorities, and so on; professionals discuss with the decision-makers and the public in terms of their plans and reports; the representatives of the public communicate with the Secretary of State at public inquiries in terms of formalised procedures. These examples show how varied are the possible means of communication. Furthermore, since the various means have grown up in the form devised by their originators (statutes through the eyes and skill of the parliamentary draughtsmen and planning reports through those of the professional planners), there is something of a Tower of Babel.

Since all are involved in what can be seen as one vast plan-making and plan-implementation process, and since within the total activities there are an innumerable number of segmented decisions, each being a link in a continually evolving chain, there is clearly a need for some clear and intelligent communication of questions and answers. It is not to be wondered, therefore, that there is miscommunication between all those concerned. In terms of contemporary planning this must be one of the major areas requiring drastic reform.

4.3.7 SYSTEMIC THINKING

Having outlined the elements of the system it is necessary to add that a feature of contemporary planning is the surprising failure to see the interrelationship of various elements in full, and to act with this in mind. Indeed, the very complexity of the dialogue between plan-making and plan implementation, discussed above (Chapter 2), is some evidence of this.

But if the system is to work fully, then it can only be regarded in the *systemic* sense: in seeing the interrelationship between the parts.[42] Repercussions on plan content as a result of plan implementation, described above, is a case in point. Also of great relevance is the form and content of education for planners, bearing in mind the tasks that they will need to carry out in their professions, for which the education is equipping them. Also relevant is the link between the needs of society as seen by politicians and the people, and the means of meeting those needs as visualised and prepared by the professional planners.

4.4   CENTRAL GOVERNMENT/LOCAL GOVERNMENT FINANCE

As stated above (section 4.3.2), the local authorities are the principal plan-implementation agencies; it is on their financial structure that we concentrate in this section. The topic is vast,[43] and we consider here only those aspects related to the development process.

Local authorities obtain their finance for current and capital spending from three main sources – rates, government grants, and borrowing. In the financial year 1973–4 the authorities in England and Wales spent a total of some £13,500 million. Three-quarters of this was current spending on loan repayments, salaries, running expenses, etc., with capital-account spending on land and works making up the remaining quarter.

While in considering development we are generally concerned with the capital account, there is some relevant spending from the current account, for example housing, traffic management, education, highways, lighting, parking.

The distinction between capital and current (or revenue) expenditure is important because they are financed in very different ways. The revenue for the current account comes from the rates (25 per cent), government grants (40 per cent) and from fees, charges and miscellaneous sources (35 per cent), while the revenue for the capital account comes largely from loans (78 per cent) and from transfers. Only some 4 per cent of the capital income is in the form of government grants.

But while not large, these are very important in specific types of plan implementation. There are, for example, 75–100 per cent capital grants for major classified roads; and revenue subsidies for clearance and development in comprehensive development areas of some 50 per cent of the loss incurred. Again, there are specific housing subsidies for difficult sites and high buildings, which have heavily influenced the rise and fall of high-rise policy. In general, 'the nature of central government grants must have influenced the choice and extent of development; this has been especially significant for major roads'.[44]

But both in capital and revenue, local authority spending on plan implementation is tightly controlled by the central government.

On the first, in order to raise a loan, the local authority had originally to obtain authorisation (loan sanction) from the government, who can control both the purpose for which and the means by which money is borrowed. In 1971 the system of control was eased slightly and it became possible for authorities to borrow for a range of needs under a block loan sanction. However, 'key-sector borrowing', for which individual sanctions are still mandatory, includes most of education, housing, main roads and social services (including borrowing under the community land scheme).

On top of this, Treasury approval is required for every issue of local authority stock on the stock exchange; but this means of borrowing tends to be confined to the larger local authorities. Other sources of loans are temporary borrowing and the Public Works Loan Commission. This last tends to be a cheap way of borrowing, since it is financed by government loans, but it is open to local authorities for only a certain proportion of their funds.

Turning to revenue, rates are an important consideration in local government finance since they form the only revenue collected directly by and for the local authority. They are levied on the annual rental value of real property, i.e. the rent which might reasonably be received from year to year if the property were let on stated assumptions in the free market without legal restrictions. Agricultural land and buildings, churches, charitable institutions and public parks are exempt, as was empty property until 1966 when local authorities were given the discretionary power to include them.

But the rates are an inadequate revenue base, as may be seen simply by the fact that the 'rate support grant' from central government was, in 1974–5, greater than actual rate revenue.

Furthermore, while the local authorities decide what rate they will levy each year, there is substantial central government pressure to keep the rates down. And they have a peculiar way of engendering the wrath of rate-payers – probably because they are not taxed at source like income tax. All in all, they form a revenue base which is full of difficulties. They Layfield Committee[45] has recently reported with a series of proposals for improvements.

Thus a large part of local spending, perhaps four-fifths on average, is determined by central government, who uses this extensive control of spending (among other things) (a) to guide planning and implementation as it sees fit, and (b) to manipulate macroeconomic variables in the interests of the economy as a whole, and subject to the priorities ruling in national decisions. While such control may well be necessary, it has, from the more limited viewpoint of local policy and plan implementation, a high nuisance value. It would certainly seem that a land policy which comes near to 'balancing the books' is less likely to be subject to limitations and fluctuations due to attempts by central government to regulate the economy.

4.5 IMPEDIMENTS TO IMPLEMENTATION IN SOME MAJOR BRITISH PLANNING OBJECTIVES

4.5.1 THE APPROACH

Our review of planned development in Britain today has been made to set the scene for establishing in this section the impediments to the implementation of plans in Britain, as a lead into considering what land-policy changes should be made in the future. As indicated earlier (section 2.8), we see this issue as 'closing the planning–implementation gap'. To illuminate this point there are several possible approaches which could be followed in attempting to answer this question. For example, following the conceptual approach of Chapter 2, what are the possible causes of failure in plan implementation and how can they be avoided? Or, in order to establish the reasons for implementation failure, what has been the experience of particular plans over time? But the first is too theoretical for our purpose and on the second there is little empirical material in Britain on which to base conclusions.

But there is an alternative, a midway course between the conceptual analysis and empirical case study. In Britain there are certain major strands in our development planning since the Second World War which can be regarded as major objectives of our planning policies. They have all been fairly consistent throughout the period, though changes in the social, economic and political context have required alterations in the emphasis. Because of the central place of these objectives, their consistency, and their unified application throughout the country through the administration of the central government department concerned, we are able to use the objectives for our purpose of asking to what degree there have been implementation issues. We proceed to answer this in relation to particular programmes (city-centre redevelopment, housing renewal, green belts and new towns) which have been amongst the strongest. In each we first present a review of the programmes themselves and then show the nature of the impediments, bringing out, we hope, their very varied nature.

4.5.2   URBAN REDEVELOPMENT

The programme
As mentioned above (section 4.1) the bomb damage sustained during the Second World War gave city-centre planning a great impetus: there was both the need and the opportunity for comprehensive planning on a large scale. The machinery was created not only for bomb damage but also for obsolescence, and even before the specific problems of blitzed areas had been largely overcome, the renewal of obsolescence became an important objective, with an emphasis on comprehensive redevelopment as opposed to rehabilitation. In this it was assumed by the architects of the early legislation that the majority of the development would be undertaken by the public sector.[46] This was indeed so until the 1950s, when licensing control over building was abolished, unleashing pent-up demand in the private sector. Concurrently the change in the compensation provisions in the Planning Acts deterred the public sector, since it increased the cost of land to the local authorities. In the 1960s there was a general boom in the economy and development industry which, coupled with a large growth in the tertiary sector, enabled private enterprise to invest heavily in new commercial development in city centres, leading to increasing pressures for private central-area development. Large schemes were undertaken in many towns and cities and a great deal of demolition took place.[47] While it was possible to provide modern, convenient shopping areas, there was a heavy toll in terms of the cities which people knew, with many former occupiers (business and residents) being forced out of the area by increasing rents.

In terms of land policy the various Planning Acts passed since the late 1960s would seem to have provided all that was needed to support such a programme, i.e. through the power to buy up any areas in need of comprehensive development or, where such an operation was not necessary, through the power to grant planning permission for new buildings in place of old ones. Yet urban redevelopment is still the most neglected field of planned development, at any rate outside the central areas where redevelopment for commercial uses was financially profitable.

In part the neglect of urban redevelopment is due to the very complexity of the operation and the human disturbance to which it inevitably gives rise. But in part it is due to the financial issues involved, on which we concentrate. As indicated above (section 3.6), in redevelopment there is often a shortfall between the potential use value and the current use value, and a subsidy is needed if redevelopment is to take place. This was recognised in the 1944 and 1947 Acts in relation to the war-damaged ('blitz') and obsolete ('blight') areas by providing an Exchequer grant to meet any loss incurred by local authorities.[48] Although these specific grants were abolished in 1958 with the introduction of the new system for a 'general grant' to local authorities, they were reinstated in 1966. The 'blitz' grant was very generous for the initial period, covering up to 90 per cent of the annual loss on redevelopment, with the 'blight' grant being somewhat less. There is now a single grant of 50 per cent.

The basis of these grants is an Exchequer contribution for a limited number of years towards the annual deficit. The initial capital necessary for buying the land, clearing it and preparing it for development is borrowed (usually from government sources at the current rate of interest plus repayment of capital over a period of up to sixty years). Against the loan charges and other annual costs are credited rents and ground rents, and capital adjustments are made when land is sold, leased for a capital premium or 'appropriated' for local government services. The resulting annual deficit, if any, then qualifies for a grant for a period of years, by which time the operation may be showing a surplus. If not, it becomes thereafter a charge on the rates.

The impediments

It is thus the initial 'land-management' cost that is the important factor. The land (and any buildings on it) has to be bought, and the cost in urban areas can be quite high, even if bought at existing use value. Replanning congested housing areas usually means lower densities, more open space and other such facilities that yield little or no income, with the result that some of the land value is either destroyed or, by creating an overspill damand, is 'shifted' outside the area.

The land then has to be cleared – a slow process if people are living in the area and have to be found alternative accommodation – and new roads built or new services provided where necessary. Interest charges on capital have to be met during this long period of preparation, and only when it is complete can the authority organise the programme of building by the several agencies who will participate in the redevelopment. This includes negotiating leases with private developers and financial sources and arranging with perhaps several local authorities and statutory undertakings to play their part in a programme that has to be precisely timed – not an easy task in a period when capital expenditure is severely restricted. It needs careful forward planning and a measure of co-operation by other authorities that is not always forthcoming; and the cost of servicing the initial capital at high interest rates is the major factor that causes a deficit in the early years. Even with a 50 per cent Exchequer grant, the prospect of an initial deficit deters many authorities, particularly the smaller ones, from undertaking urban renewal on the scale needed.

Even in some of the larger cities, schemes started thirty years ago are still not complete because of the cost of some vital pieces of land, and redevelopment is frequently undertaken spasmodically, without, it would seem, proper relation to any wider plan or long-term programme. How far this is true, to what extent it is justified by local conditions and whether an improved financial policy would improve both planning and implementation, is difficult to establish.

The fact that in many towns extensive redevelopment of central shopping areas has taken place successfully with the co-operation of private developers only emphasises the point. These are mainly areas of high shopping values, where the profitability prospect has affected private finance. This adds force to the view that outside such areas land policy itself can be ineffective if the financial implications are not adequately dealt with. Thus finance, whether in terms of land values, development cost, disposal arrangements or the cost of capital itself, is an integral feature of a comprehensive land policy for urban redevelopment.

4.5.3   URBAN REHABILITATION

The programme
In retrospect the urban development of the mid-1950s to the mid-1970s constituted an enormous programme until its bottom fell out with the economic decline of the mid-1970s (section 4.1). But there were other factors working against major redevelopment schemes which were having their deterrent effect before the balloon burst. There was the great reaction felt the world over against disturbance to homes and businesses occasioned by the land acquisition and clearance preliminary to the redevelopment, without reasonable provision for relocation at reasonable cost, either on site or off site. There was the conservation movement which saw existing structures as assets to be protected if at all possible; whereas previously the retention of established property needed to be justified against the intention to redevelop, now the intention to redevelop needed to be justified in terms of the damage that would be caused.[49] A third factor was the move against the 'bigness' which was identified with redevelopment, in the main towards the smaller-scale unit, under the general ideology of 'small is beautiful'.[50] And finally there was the growing recognition of the need to protect our historic and architectural heritage to a greater degree than had been experienced, with the consequential strengthening of government machinery for the purpose.[51]

But despite all these pressures there can hardly be said to have been a significant urban rehabilitation programme, except for housing rehabilitation, to which we turn below (section 4.5.4). Yet despite the absence of a programme the search for rehabilitation as opposed to redevelopment is certainly one of the contemporary principles and accordingly we consider it here.

The impediments
There are two significant barriers to urban rehabilitation on any scale: (i) pooling of ownerships, and (ii) the propensity for financial loss.

On the former, whereas for redevelopment the sweeping away of former property-ownership boundaries and tenure seems to be necessary, since otherwise the benefits of comprehensive redevelopment are lost, the pooling of ownerships becomes necessary by one means or another. This is not so obvious in rehabilitation. By definition most of the property will remain in its existing boundaries, if not tenures, and the presumption is against comprehensive purchase of the whole but rather in favour of retention of individual occupation and ownerships. This situation would fit in quite well with a rehabilitation scheme, provided that all the individual owners are prepared to participate in the necessary works to their property and its environment, and the necessary extra costs which would fall on them, sometimes for benefits which do not appear to be worth while. And unless all the individual owners and occupiers collaborate, so that the rehabilitation is complete over the whole area in question, then the return to the individual owner who does rehabilitate will be the less, since he cannot capture the whole of the increased value which would otherwise be possible.

In this situation only compulsory measures against any recalcitrant owners will meet the needs of the situation. But there is a strong resistance to measures of this kind, on both policy and equity grounds.

As to the second difficulty, finance, the problem emerges from the logic of the economics of development described above (section 3.5).[52] In any renewal the high market value of the standing property offers a high threshold over which the potential site value must leap to a significant degree to make the redevelopment financially viable. In practice this occurs through the redevelopment attracting higher densities, more efficient layout, new uses which are more profitable, and so on. But little of this is possible in rehabilitation; and while such increased value could accrue on particular plots which are redeveloped, the increase would be offset by the loss in demolition for environmental improvements, for example open space, car parks, and so on. To this is added another factor: per unit of building area the costs of rehabilitation are high compared with the costs of redevelopment (because of the less efficient potential in the construction work) but at the same time the value per unit of rehabilitated accommodation is not as proportionately high as the new. Thus all in all the economics of rehabilitation are not favourable compared with the economics of redevelopment.

In brief, the impediments to urban rehabilitation are greater than those to urban redevelopment. For one thing they require more vigorous land-pooling measures. For another they require more subsidy to meet the shortfalls. But here it is ironic that while government subsidies for comprehensive redevelopment of the kind mentioned in the preceding section have been forthcoming, there has not been the corresponding generosity for rehabilitation.

4.5.4   HOUSING RENEWAL

The programme
In the field of housing, there was, prior to the Second World War, a substantial amount of slum clearance and redevelopment. But this was seriously checked by the war. Following the enforced neglect and deterioration of existing housing stock, the period immediately after was taken up with reducing the absolute shortage of dwellings and urban facilities.

It was not until the mid-1950s that clearance could generally be resumed. Since then (1955–71) 1¼ million houses have been demolished, and this programme has been continued. In 1956 it was estimated that, by the end of 1973, the number of slum houses would have declined from 1·8 million in 1967 to less than a million.[53]

Running alongside this programme of clearance and redevelopment has been the increasingly important programme of improvement. While in the Housing Acts of 1947 and 1959 the provisions for stimulating improvements formed only a very minor part of housing strategy, the Housing Acts of 1969 and 1974, introducing General Improvement Areas (GIAs) and Housing Action Areas (HAAs) respectively, altered the emphasis towards improvement.

A local authority can designate a GIA (without the consent of the Secretary of State), to which it may give grants to the costs of housing improvements, with the central government contributing 75 per cent of the local authority grant. The local authority may also spend up to £200 per dwelling on environmental works outside the dwelling, the central government paying some 50 per cent. The concept of the Housing Action Area is similar to the GIA, but the intention is that the action should be faster and more concentrated, the grant being higher. But there is still much to be done; there are still many unfit dwellings (12 per cent in 1971) and some 30 per cent of the housing stock needs £125 or more spent on repairs, or on supplying one or more of the basic amenities, or both.[54]

The impediments

The major problem with any clearance scheme for public housing is the cost of land. Bearing in mind the current use value of the property and the cost of demoliton, there is a large gap between the price of the site and, afterwards, its value for residential use by low-value dwellings.

This gap has to be met by subsidies from one source or another. Central government bears the majority of the cost of acquisition and clearance, but the part paid by local authorities (out of their rate fund or via the rent pool) is still high, for both 'renewal by demolition and reconstruction [are] too costly to be practicable'.[55]

Another impediment is the time taken for the whole process: 'The lengthy nature of the whole process results from the inherent complexities, the multiplicity of departments involved, the time taken for objections to be made by owners and for those to be considered by the local authority and the time taken in arranging, holding and deciding upon a local inquiry'.[56]

Furthermore, it is becoming increasingly recognised that residents have a strong attachment to their area of residence, however poor the conditions. Since there is usually a lowering in density on redevelopment, in gross neighbourhood if not in net site terms, it is generally physically impossible to rehouse all the residents in the same area. However, even if it is not impossible, there is a period of some years (while the decision procedure is concluded and then between the actual site purchase and the disposing of the final development) during which the inhabitants have to be housed elsewhere – and the 'community' breaks up. All this time-consuming procedure, and the uncertainty which it entails, encourages a general resistance of development and blights the area for some time before redevelopment occurs. All these problems have led to the recent emphasis on rehabilitation rather than redevelopment, principally through General Improvement Area and Housing Action Area measures.

On the former, it is too soon to make any real appraisal of the extent to which this policy has impediments, but some problems are already apparent. With regard to the external environmental improvements, it has been suggested that a grant of £200 per dwelling is inadequate to act as a catalyst to improvement of the dwellings by owners. But enforcement by the local authority is unpalatable, leading some local authorities to delay environmental improvements.

Another major problem has been that, even with the grant at 75 per cent, it was often not profitable for the landlord of rented property to improve his property. However, this situation has now been relieved, since under the fair rents system of the 1972 Housing Finance Act the landlord can charge increased rent if improvements are made; and there are rent rebates available to offset the effect of this increase on low-income tenants: 'How far this will encourage landlords (particularly the large numbers of elderly owners of one or two dwellings) to undertake improvement, however, remains to be seen.'[57]

As with GIAs, it is too soon to assess the extent of implementation problems for HAAs. However, the problems will probably be broadly similar to those of the GIA programme, with the grants being even less likely to be taken up in the stress areas. With both programmes enforcement is very difficult, involving long delay and the use of compulsory purchase orders, which are politically difficult in areas of owner-occupation and are expensive to the local authority.

4.5.5   GREEN BELT

The programme
The idea of a green belt for cities is of some vintage, but there has been a continuing search for its real purpose, as the following shows.

The pre-1939 objectives of a green-belt policy were varied. Instances were: (i) to promote regional balance through containment of the areas of major growth; (ii) 'to provide a reserve supply of public open spaces and of recreational areas and to establish a green belt or girdle of open space lands'[58] for urban dwellers; and (iii) to control urban growth to preserve and protect agricultural land.

However, in the early 1950s the concept of the *green belt* became more specific. Abercrombie saw it as a continuous 'green background' of some depth embedded at suitable places with building development (and not vice versa);[59] and the Scott Report envisaged the green belt as a tract of ordinary countryside where normal rural occupations continued (and where the farmer was the normal custodian) as well as providing facilities for the nearby town dwellers.[60] In the event, the 1944 *Greater London Plan* proposed a green belt up to ten miles wide, aimed at restricting urban growth while actively encouraging agricultural and recreational possibilities and enhancing the beauty of the area. And following the 1947 Act, conurbations other than London used the new powers of control to restrict urban development, but there was little conformity of objective. In 1955, in answer to this, the minister put forward the most clearly defined official statement on the purposes and nature of green belts.[61] They could be used to:

1   check the growth of a large built-up area;
2   prevent the merging of two neighbouring towns; and
3   assist in the preserving of the special character of a town.

In the early 1960s the policy of strict prohibition on development in the green belt was relaxed and the emphasis shifted towards amenity conservation. An analysis of the development plans had revealed that the rate of local dispersal had been underestimated and that there was insufficient room for expansion. Therefore, local authorities were asked to consider what areas might be suitable for housing, and certain sites were identified almost immediately. In practice, the shift was made earlier, with certain planning appeals being allowed. With this movement there was also one towards an emphasis on fine countryside in the belt and permission for some building on land of little amenity value.

There was thus a return to the ideas of the Scott Committee, given in the *South East Study* as follows:

> All land in the green belt should have a positive purpose; whether it be its quality as farm land, its mineral resources, its special scenic values, its suitability for public open space ... or for those land uses generated by the main built-up area which cannot suitably be located within it − such as reservoirs and institutions needing larger areas of open land around them.

The impediments

The South East Joint Planning Team were able to say that the London green belt had achieved all its objectives for Greater London. However, 'the full measure of success is difficult to judge since the assumptions on which the Greater London Plan [of 1944] were based were invalidated in the early years'.[63]

Inasmuch as the green belt has constituted an area of sterilised land acting as a buffer to urban expansion, its implementation by planning controls has been broadly successful. Even so, the South East Joint Planning Team felt that its very inflexibility is a drawback. Unless the outer boundaries of a town, where there is pressure for expansion, can be enforced for the period of the plan, either the green belt will have to be pushed back, leading to increased pressure on the 'white' land (i.e. land not allocated for development) or in the long run there will be development in the green belt, thus devaluing the concept.

Coming to the more positive side, the aim of conserving and promoting amenity and ensuring that all parts of the green belt have beneficial uses is also faced with certain problems. The

> other land use controls (such as designation of Areas of Outstanding Natural Beauty) and land ownership usually act more positively than green belt procedures in preserving attractive countryside. To some degree this is because the areas of land involved are smaller in extent, and are sometimes overseen by statutory bodies ... but it is also because the purpose of the additional land use controls are often more clearly defined.[64]

The present policy is to allow development on a limited number of sites which do not fulfil other positive purposes. With such development there is a substantial financial gain to the landowner, and this gives him an incentive to allow his land to deteriorate. A local authority is obviously more likely to allow development on derelict than on 'positive' green belt.

Furthermore, the effectiveness of the green belt depends on the willingness of the various public bodies and statutory undertakings to co-operate with each other and with the minister concerned. This is especially so since much green-belt land is owned by government and service departments which are often outside the control and influence of local authority planning departments. For these reasons land belonging to government and service departments has detracted from, rather than supported, the effectiveness of green belts.

4.5.6 NEW TOWNS[65]

The programme

The interrelatedness of the various principal strands of planning policy is very well illustrated by the new towns programme. Following several pre-1939 proposals, they were 'conceived as part of a national policy of land development [the Barlow report of 1940] and a regional town planning policy deriving from this [the Abercrombie Plan of 1944]'.[66] Together with green belts and regional economic policy, they were proposed as one means of overcoming the disadvantages of urban and economic over-concentration as exemplified by London and the South-east.

The detailed arrangements were considered by a Committee under the chairmanship of Lord Reith,[67] and the New Towns Act of 1946 followed very soon afterwards. It provided that:

1 The minister would decide when and where a new town was needed and would designate land for the purpose.
2 The minister would appoint a development corporation to plan and build each town which would be responsible to him and act under his direction and guidance.
3 The development corporation would have power, with the minister's consent, to buy compulsorily any of the land needed and would either build themselves or arrange for building by other appropriate authorities (including local authorities and statutory undertakings) or would dispose of suitable sites – normally leasehold – for approved private-enterprise building.
4 All finance needed by the development corporation would be provided by the government.

Later acts provided for transfer of the assets, when a town is substantially complete, to the Commission for the New Towns or to the local authority, and also required surpluses in the hands of the Commission and the development corporation to be paid to the government.

The basic function of the new towns was 'to relieve the housing pressures of London and other big cities'.[68] The congested nature of inner-city areas and their high densities pointed to the need for population dispersal. Bomb damage to urban fabric and unanticipated growth of populations and households were responsible for an acute shortage of housing. At the time it was felt that improved housing conditions in existing cities could only be obtained fast enough at unwarranted social and economic costs.

As indicated above (section 4.4.5), the green belts were needed because it was felt that the large cities had grown too much and that rapid peripheral expansion was undesirable. As to regional economic policy, new towns could be planned as growth poles in areas of economic depression. However, the effect of new towns as part of national policy and as a part of regional/local policy could often be in conflict; for example, 'the promotion of new centres of growth on growth poles within the South East will absorb some of the mobile industrial population which might have gone to the problem regions'.[69] Taking an example, a new factory requires an industrial development certificate before it is able to settle into a new town. The Department of Industry, however, has a prior and more compelling commitment in favour of development areas, so that unless a new town is situated there it may have difficulty in securing industry.

At the beginning of 1971 there were twenty-eight new towns in Britain. All were designated under the 1946 New Towns Act and therefore have been or are being planned and built by government-appointed development corporations: 'Their common administrative and financial basis is, however, about the only thing all the new towns have in common. Their origins, their locations and their objectives are exceedingly diverse.'[70] For convenience, they can be differentiated by their dates of designation.

The first group, commonly known as the mark-I new towns, consists of towns designated between 1946 and 1950. They fall into two sub-groups according to the purpose of designation: first, to achieve planned dispersal of population from overcrowded urban areas, or second, to aid regional development policies in development areas. Eight of the new towns fall into the first category, their function being to cope with the overspill population from London, three come into the second category, while two fall into both categories. Corby comes into neither category, having been initiated with the purpose of providing housing and commercial services for the nearby steelworks.

There was a significant break in time before the second group, the mark-II new towns, was started. In the 1950s only Cumbernauld, located near Glasgow, was designated. By 1961 it had become obvious that the programme of expanding towns was failing to deal adequately with the overspill problem of the major conurbations. Thirteen new towns have since been designated. In England and Wales, with one exception, all these were intended to solve the specific overspill problems of major conurbations. Some, while designated as overspill towns, also incidentally served the objective of promoting development areas and hence enjoyed all the incentives applicable to such areas. The two Scottish new towns of this era were both conceived as growth points in a comprehensive regional programme for Central Scotland.

Mark-I and mark-II new towns differ also in terms of size. The mark-I new towns, with the exception of two, had target populations of between 35,000 and 60,000. Very few were genuine green-field sites, most originating as villages or small market towns with existing populations between 5,000 and 10,000. Four designated new towns had substantial populations of between 15,000 and 25,000 at the date of designation. The mark-II new towns are more diversified, so that generalisation is more difficult. On the whole they differ from the mark-I new towns in that there is a sharp increase in the size of the town and in the size of the population. Several of the new towns started with a basic population of 100,000, and built up to 200,000 or 300,000. This reflects a general belief that a new town should start with a base population large enough to ensure adequate levels of shopping and other services.

The capital financing of development corporations is entirely the responsibility of the central government, the corporations not being able to borrow money independently. They are financed by a system of long-term Treasury loans repayable over a period of sixty years at current rates of interest. Neither the Treasury nor the minister can approve the advance of funds for any specific development proposal unless it is likely to secure a 'reasonable' rate of return on Exchequer investment. Strict financial control is exercised over the corporations by the ministry through detailed examinations of any proposed major spending and through supervision of the budgets submitted by the corporations.

The impediments[71]

In the new towns, the new town development corporations are the main, but not the sole, agencies. Their functions overlap considerably with, and are often dependent upon, the collaboration of local authorities. The development corporations must consult with and secure approvals from local district councils on building bye-laws, on plans for sewerage, open space and, sometimes, water. Similarly, negotiations are usually necessary with the county council for roads, surface-water drainage, education and health services; with statutory bodies concerned with utilities such as electricity and gas; with the Regional Boards for water and sewage disposal; with the Board of Trade on industrial developments, with the Ministries of Labour and Works on labour and materials; with the Agricultural Land Commissioner and the County Agricultural Executive Committees; and so on.

Matters are further complicated by the designation of development areas across local authority boundaries, sites for new towns being chosen for socioeconomic and technical reasons rather than subsequent ease of administration. All these complications call for great effort in co-ordination, which can be achieved but offers an impediment to effective development.

Development corporations receive loans and grants from the Department of the Environment for the carrying out of their development in new towns. But this covers only their own activities, and the question arises: who should bear the cost of the remaining development? Costs are imposed on the local authorities, for they are required to undertake the expansion of existing facilities and to provide new services. As local authorities are reluctant that the rate-payers within their areas should be made to meet such financial costs, the provision of these services by the local authority is often dependent on development corporations agreeing to pay 'a fair share' of the costs involved. Just what is a fair share is a matter of controversy, and the sharing of costs between local authorities and development corporations is often negotiated with the 'help' of the ministry. One complication is that corporations only have access to Exchequer loans charged at current rates of interest over sixty years, while local authorities are not similarly restricted and are able to obtain cheaper loans for shorter periods elsewhere.

Impediment also arises from this disparity in source of finance from various agencies for what should be a common development programme.

4.5.7   REGIONAL POLICY

The programme[72]

It is generally recognised that 'prosperous' Britain broadly consists of central England lying to the north and west of London and south and east of Liverpool and Manchester. However, the exact areas which are to be favoured in regional policy is a contentious issue. Up to 1960 the 'development areas' of the 1945 Act were maintained, these being broad areas characterised by old, heavy industry based on the coalfields. In the 1960 Local Employment Act the development areas were thrown overboard in favour of the idea of 'development districts' which habitually suffered unemployment of more than $4\frac{1}{2}$ per cent. This, however, was found to be unsatisfactory on a number of counts,[73] especially in that it was supposed to inhibit the generation of growth poles in the underdeveloped regions. There ensued a short period in which aid was concentrated on those areas which were considered to be potential growth zones, and in 1966 the Industrial Development Act did away with development districts and brought in development areas again. These were defined in a much wider sense than were the original areas.

Given this regional disparity, there is general agreement that the aim of regional policy is to promote the less prosperous regions by, for example, either reducing unemployment rates, or the exodus of population, or both.

The aid which has gone to these areas has taken a number of forms: there have been grants to industrialists of 40 per cent of the value of capital investments (20 per cent elsewhere); tax concessions in respect of Selective Employment Tax when this was in operation; retraining schemes; favourable treatment under the office development permit and industrial development certificate schemes; and finally influence via the nationalised industries.

The impediments[74]

One difficulty in implementing regional policy is in its conflict of objectives, at any one time and over time.

Before the implementation measures for regional policy may be used, it has to be decided just where they are to be aimed: for example, in the more distressed areas as a whole, or in growth points within these areas identified as being especially suitable for the reception of aid. The choice has varied from government to government, and is still contentious. The variation in policy is itself detrimental to success; in order to be successful regional policy measures must be long term and consistent.

Having chosen the location, the aid may take various forms. Since each could have different and often ill-understood effects, there is yet another impediment from uncertainty.

A reduction in taxation will tend to stimulate production but it will also increase the demand for imports, especially in the early years. This in turn will lead to greater activity in the congested areas. This effect may be offset to the extent that tax reductions decrease prices rather than increase profits or real wages; if so, exports to congested areas will be enhanced.

Capital grants have somewhat similar effects. They are most useful if the injection of public capital can stimulate a large amount of private investment. However, again this may lead to increased regional imports. It also tends to favour capital-intensive industries. While these make for a sound, commercially viable industrial area, they will do least to alleviate unemployment.

Negative controls are also used: the guidance of employment to locations according with regional policy was to be by (a) the granting of industrial development certificates (IDCs) and office development permits (ODPs), and (b) the granting of planning permission by local authorities. The power to grant IDCs and ODPs is regarded by the Department of Industry as the strongest implement in regional policy. It does not involve large sums of money and this is an obvious advantage; furthermore, it is highly flexible. There are, however, limits to which they may be pushed. Those firms who are refused may not expand, may go abroad or even stop operating, with a consequent loss to the economy as a whole.

There is a need for great skill in assessing each case to predict the effect. But since this lies in the controversial field of regional economics, the effectiveness of the implementation is not at all ensured.

REFERENCES: CHAPTER 4

1 Trantor (1973).
2 DoE (1976e, pp. 11, 23).
3 See, for example, Engels (1971).
4 DoE (1975e).
5 Ibid.
6 Lichfield (1962, pp. 22–34).
7 DoE (1976e, p. 29).
8 Cullingworth (1974, p. 29).
9 Office of Population Censuses and Surveys (1973).
10 DoE (1976e, p. 47).
11 Nathaniel Lichfield & Partners (1978).
12 DoE (1975a).
13 Marriott (1967), Lichfield (1976a), and Ambrose and Colenutt (1975).
14 See Massey and Catalanl (1978).
15 See Hillebrandt (1974), Turin (1975), and Bowley (1966).
16 See DoE (1975a).
17 This relies on Whitehouse (1964), Marriott (1967), and DoE (1975a).
18 This relies on DoE (1972b), and Lichfield (1976a).
19 Ministry of Town and Country Planning (1947), and Wells (1944).
20 Leasehold Reform Act of 1967.
21 Lichfield (1976a).
22 Minns and Thornley (1978).
23 Following the schema in Lichfield (1976b).
24 Central Office of Information (1978).
25 Local Government Act (1972), and DoE (1972a).
26 Planning Advisory Group (1965).
27 There is no comprehensive account. See, for example, Local Government Act (1972), DoE (1977a), Heap (1967), and Purdue (1977, ch. 2).
28 Department of Economic Affairs (1965).
29 Central Office of Information (1978).
30 Local Government Act (1972, sections 15 ff); and DoE (1973d).
31 Central Office of Information (1978).
32 Garner (1956).
33 Town and Country Planning Act (1971, Section 23).
34 Ibid, section 29.
35 McLoughlin (1973, pp. 88–9), and McAuslan (1975, pp. 369–80).
36 Town and Country Planning Act (1971, section 29).
37 Ibid, section 52.
38 Ibid, section 36.
39 Ibid, section 87.
40 DoE (1975g).
41 Ministry of Housing and Local Government (1969).
42 Lichfield (1979b).
43 See, for example, Chester (1951).
44 Holliday (1973).
45 DoE (1973c).
46 Cullingworth (1975, ch. 11).
47 Holliday (1973).
48 Lichfield (1956, ch. 15).
49 Johnson (1973).

50 Schumacher (1973).
51 *Town Planning Review*, vol. 46, no. 4, October 1975.
52 Needleman (1967).
53 Garner (1956).
54 Garner (1956).
55 National Economic Development Office (1971).
56 Cullingworth (1972, p. 73).
57 Ibid, p. 86.
58 Dalton (1939), quoted in Thomas (1970).
59 Abercrombie (1945).
60 Ministry of Works and Planning (1942a).
61 Ministry of Housing and Local Government (1955).
62 Ministry of Housing and Local Government (1964).
63 DoE (1971, vol. II).
64 Thomas (1970, pp. 87–8).
65 For a general history and *modus operandi*, see Schaffer (1970).
66 Merlin (1971).
67 Ministry of Town and Country Planning (1946).
68 Cullingworth (1974, p. 232).
69 McCrone (1969).
70 Hall (1973, p. 332).
71 See Schaffer (1970).
72 See McCrone (1969).
73 Ibid.
74 See Hall *et al.* (1975, ch. 6).

Chapter 5

Historical Review of Land Policies in Britain

5.1 THE EVOLUTION OF BRITISH LAND POLICY

As we saw above (section 3.8), land policy in Britain has in this century become intertwined with town and country planning in its control over land use. But in fact there were antecedents well before that. In this there were two important strands: the division of proprietary rights as between private landowners; and as between them as a class and the state.

In the first comes the common law controlling the rights and obligations as between owners, for example in the law on tenure, of trespass and nuisance, together with certain statutes, for example those relating to the right of light or relaxation of leasehold covenants.[1] Second comes the accumulation of many centuries of statute and administrative law, covering the manner in which property could be used and development carried out, together with the compulsory purchase of land by a public authority for a specific purpose defined by statute, as in the building of railways, roads, canals, parks, and so on.[2] And each of these provisions had its own code of financial adjustment between those who took away rights and those who suffered their denial, of the kind discussed below under *compensation and betterment* (section 5.6).

This amounted to a most impressive degree of intervention as between neighbouring land- and property-owners on the one hand, and they and authority on the other.[3] However, taken together they were found at the beginning of this century to be inadequate to meet social objectives in the control over urban expansion and more than inadequate as the century evolved for new objectives in urban renewal, environmental pollution, and so on. As regards the common law:

> The judicial development of the law, vigorous and imaginative though it has been, has been found wanting ... tied to concepts of property, possession and fault, the judges have been unable by their own strength to break out of the confines of the common law and tackle the broad problems of land use in an industrial and urbanised society ... The guarding of our environment has been found to require an activist, intrusive role to be played by the executive arm of government.[4]

And as regards state intervention, the miscellany of negative and positive powers proved to be too narrow and piecemeal for the job, so that a new code had to be evolved in town and country legislation which, taken as a whole, went much further than that practised before. Successive Town and Country Planning Acts have extended it, in the process creating what amounts to new tenures (with property remaining in private ownership with development rights virtually vested in the state), with authority aiming to control the workings of the land market through administrative law and practice which would appear to be outside the law.[5]

So vigorous is this state control that there has arisen the suggestion that the time has come for the rights of the individual to be protected by statute (privacy, quiet, and clean air, etc.) whose taking away by the state or developers would have to be specifically justified.[6]

Thus land policy in Britain can be said to have existed prior to town and country planning legislation. Its first main strand was 'private land policy', in which private landowners sought the conservation, use and development of their land and natural resources within the common law. The second strand was the increasing state intervention culminating in town and country planning legislation. But the two are uneasily running side by side and, while not in watertight compartments, are not integrated, to the disadvantage of each.

Under town planning land policy has certainly taken on new dimensions. Starting at the beginning of the century the first town planning bill introduced in 1908, enabling local authorities to prepare planning schemes for land in the vicinity of towns, included a betterment levy of 100 per cent – a figure that was reduced to 50 per cent by the House of Lords. The 1932 Planning Act provided for a 75 per cent betterment levy and enabled a wide range of restrictions on land use to be imposed without compensation. The Housing Act of 1935 introduced a new 'redevelopment area' procedure based on compulsory purchase of unsatisfactory urban areas.

Admittedly the procedures under these planning statutes were long and frustrating and the powers hedged about with so many qualifications that little appears to have got done, and certainly no betterment was collected. But the powers were there, the principles had already been accepted by Parliament, and when the time came to consider the post-war problems it was possible to build on this past experience and at the same time try to eliminate the factors that might, as ministers put it at the time, 'hamper, prejudice or delay'[7] the work of reconstruction.

5.2   LAND POLICY SINCE THE SECOND WORLD WAR

5.2.1   GENERAL REVIEW

The year 1943 marked an important step forward in Britain's planning history. It saw the appointment for the first time of a minister charged with the duty of 'securing consistency and continuity in the framing and execution of a national policy with respect to the use and development of land throughout England and Wales',[8] with a similar duty for Scotland being placed on the Secretary of State for Scotland. The words 'and execution' are particularly signficant. They emphasised the duty of ministers to see that planning policy was not merely adopted but also actually carried out. This placed on them the responsibility for bringing into operation measures adequate for the task of implementation, including land policy.

This implementation task thus included *land policy*. As indicated above (section 4.1), British land policy has had to be fashioned and operated within the framework of a mixed economy. In this much development is carried out by private enterprise, within a land system that is marked by a complicated pattern of ownership units, many of them small, and within a legal system under which therè may be several owners of different interests in the same parcel of land who each carry different rights and obligations.

As also indicated above, while since 1943 our planning process has long since been accepted by the major political parties in Britain, there are some planning objectives for which the implementation arrangements have not proved fully adequate (see section 4.4). And while many aspects of the land policy needed to support such implementation are also now generally accepted, there are some that continue to arouse political controversy.

This political element is the crucial one. The history of land policy in Britain can be summed up as the struggle to accommodate the rights of landowners to the needs of planning in a way that is politically acceptable, that provides a reasonable measure of equity (a matter on which there are widely differing opinions), and does not frustrate the normal development processes but on the contrary facilitates and encourages them within the framework of accepted planning objectives.

This chapter therefore examines the various land policies adopted in Britain during the years 1943–74, i.e. prior to the passing of the community land legislation in 1975–6, which is the subject of the next chapter. It concludes with criteria for improvement, as a curtain-raiser to considering in Chapter 6 whether the community land legislation does in fact meet our plan-implementation needs.

5.2.2 THE BARLOW REPORT

Not only were the strands of post-war land policy already partly woven by a long line of precedents, but the process of examining its effectiveness actually started before the war, i.e. with the Barlow Commission.[9] Having been set up to look into the problems arising from the drift of population southwards, primarily in search of work, the Commission inevitably found it necessary to take a close look at the system of local planning control then in operation. Amongst a host of related matters it concluded that a national planning authority was needed, with power to control the location of new industry, to move industry away from congested areas, possibly coupled with the building of new towns. The Barlow Report profoundly influenced the course of later policy.

In reviewing the operation of the Planning Acts then in force the Commission commented that 'the difficulties that are encountered by planning authorities under the existing system of compensation and betterment are so great as seriously to hamper the progress of planning throughout the country'.[10] Certain ideas had been put to the Commission, including one for the purchase by the government of all development rights in undeveloped land, very much on the lines adopted a few years later for the purchase by the state of coal royalties.[11] The Commission had not felt it within their province to make any recommendations on this and had accordingly recommended that the government should appoint a body of experts to examine the important issues of policy and finance involved in the question of compensation and betterment.

By the time the Commission's Report was published war had broken out and the wartime coalition government under Winston Churchill had set up a Cabinet Committee on Reconstruction Problems with a wide remit to examine the problems that would arise after the war.[12] Rumours of land speculation were already causing public uneasiness, and Lord Reith, then Minister of Works, was given the responsibility of studying the problems of physical reconstruction. He immediately appointed the Scott Committee to consider the problems of the rural areas and the Uthwatt Committee to examine the subject of compensation and betterment and, more generally, to advise on the steps to be taken to prevent the work of reconstruction after the war being prejudiced. Shortly afterwards the government announced its acceptance of the principle of *national* planning.[13]

5.2.3   THE UTHWATT REPORT

The Uthwatt Committee Report concerns itself solely with land policy. It contains a closely reasoned analysis that is the foundation of all land policy discussion and controversy since 1942, formed the basis of the legislation on land policy from 1944 to 1948 and has influenced all land policy since then. Before examining the later statutes, however, it is essential to recall the main features of the Report.

1   *National planning*[14]

The Committee set the scene by referring to the government's acceptance of the principle of national planning, and went on:

> We assume that it will be directed to ensuring that the best use is made of land with a view to securing economic efficiency for the community and well-being for the individual, and that it will be recognised that this involves the subordination to the public good of the personal interests and wishes of landowners. Unreserved acceptance of this conception of planning is vital to a successful reconstruction policy. ...
>
> In our analysis of the difficulties of compensation and betterment we begin with an appreciation of the fact that fundamentally the problem arises from the existing legal position with regard to the use of land, which attempts largely to preserve, in a highly developed economy, the purely individualistic approach to land ownership. That ... is no longer completely tenable in our present stage of development and it operates to prevent the proper and effective utilisation of our limited land resources.

2   *Shifting value*[15]

The Committee went on to explain that under a system of well-conceived planning the acquisition of land for the various requirements must proceed on the basis of selecting the most suitable land, irrespective of land value. A coastal area, a beauty spot, the fringe land surrounding existing towns, may all have a high building value for residential or industrial development, yet it may be in the national interest to forbid building. This was impracticable under the 1932 Act because of the liability placed on the local authority to compensate the landowners concerned for loss of development value.

Yet there was no overall loss. Wisely imposed planning control does not diminish the total sum of land values but merely redistributes them. Development to meet demand would take place somewhere else and the development value would 'shift' to that land. Thus, although there was obvious loss to the owner of the land which was prohibited from development, the compensation paid to him would be for value that had not really been destroyed at all but had 'shifted' to other land, as would also take place if land were taken out of the market for building purposes because it was needed for an open space or some other public purpose. Yet the land to which the value shifted could never be specifically identified, the increase in value could not be quantified nor proved, and the betterment accruing to its owners could never be collected.

This was the main reason for the unsatisfactory results under the 1932 system of local planning; and with the adoption of national planning, shifts of value would take place on a larger scale than in the past. The Committee concluded that 'if all the land of the country were in the ownership of a single person or body, the mere shifting of values would not call for any financial adjustments and the need for paying compensation or securing betterment would disappear'.

3   *Floating value*[16]

But in addition to 'shifting values' there was also the phenomenon of 'floating value', which led to over-valuation and consequent payment of excessive compensation, whether for restrictions on use or for purchase of land for public purposes. In support of this the Committee quoted from the professional evidence submitted and also from a Report in 1936 from the minister's advisory committee. They also gave their own explanation:

> Potential development value is by nature speculative. The hoped-for building may take place on the particular piece of land in question or it may take place elsewhere; it may come within five years or it may be twenty-five years. ... The present value at any time of the potential value of a piece of land is obtained by estimating whether and when development is likely to take place, including an estimate of the risk that other competing land may secure prior turn. ...
>   Potential value is necessarily a 'floating value' and it is impossible to predict with certainty where the 'float' will settle as sites are actually required for the purposes of development. When a piece of undeveloped land is compulsorily acquired, or development on it is prohibited, the owner received compensation for the loss of the values of a probability of the floating demand settling upon his piece of land. The probability is not capable of arithmetical quantification. In practice where this process is repeated indefinitely over a large area the sum of the probabilities as estimated greatly exceed the actual possibilities, because the 'float', limited as it is to actually occurring demand, can only settle on a proportion of the whole area. There is therefore over-valuation.

The Committee talks here not of real values but of the valuations for compensation purposes which even the professional valuers agreed could result in a 'bill for compensation ... likely greatly to exceed in the aggregate the amount of the real loss'.

4   *Exclusion of compensation*[17]

But apart from the payment of excessive compensation, there was the further and perhaps more fundamental question of whether any compensation should be paid at all for planning restrictions on the use of land. The Committee pointed out that for a hundred years owners of property had been compelled under bye-laws, etc., and to an increasing extent, to comply with compensation with certain requirements in the public interest. In support they quoted a judicial dictum, though recognising the different context: 'A mere negative prohibition, though it involves interference with an owner's enjoyment of property, does not, merely because it is obeyed, carry with it at common law any right to compensation.'[18] To some extent the principle was already in the 1932 Act, which, while providing generally for compensation for restrictions imposed by a planning scheme, enabled the minister to exclude any such payment for limitations on certain matters such as the density of development, restrictions which the Uthwatt Committee described as 'obligations which according to the social standard of the day are regarded as due to neighbours and fellow citizens.'

The definition of matters for which compensation was excluded showed that there is a very hazy line here between what counts as a limitation of rights to the owner of the land and what counts as the surrender of those rights to the state. This is an important distinction since in the second case the state is liable to pay compensation while in the first it is not. As the Uthwatt Committee stated:

> At what point does the public interest become such that a private individual ought to be called on to comply, at his own cost, with a restriction or requirement designed to secure the public interest? The history of the imposition of obligations without compensation has been to push that point progressively further on and to add to the list of requirements considered to be essential to the well-being of the community ... the view of the Legislature on these essential requirements for the well-being of the community has passed beyond the field of health and safety to that of convenience and amenity, as witness bye-laws in regard to advertisements and petrol filling stations.

The Committee concluded that going beyond certain restrictions (for example, to prohibit development altogether on certain land to meet the requirements of regional or national policy) amounted to taking away a proprietary interest in the land itself, and for this, as in the case of compulsory purchase, compensation was not unreasonable. The right to develop, and the increased land value that accrued as a result, was thus the key factor to be dealt with if a satisfactory basis was to be found for a national planning process.

5   *The development rights scheme*[19]

In the light of this analysis the Committee concluded that for unbuilt-on land outside the urban areas unification of these development rights or values under a single ownership was 'an essential minimum necessary to remove the conflict between public and private interest'. The Committee accordingly recommended the vesting in the state of all development rights in land outside built-up areas subject to compensation on the basis of a global sum representing the true value of all such rights, to be divided *pro rata* among all owners of development value. This would involve no interference with title or possession so long as the existing use continued. But when land was required either for public purposes or for private development, it recommended that the land itself should be bought by the state in order to amalgamate the 'owner's interest' and the development rights. The owner would receive current existing use value, plus compensation for severance or other injurious affection. In the case of private development the state would then grant an appropriate building lease to the developer; freehold disposal would be inconsistent with the permanence of the scheme. Only in the case of an owner building a house for his own occupation did the Committee recommend the grant of a licence to build instead of purchase and re-lease

6 *Reconstruction areas*[20]

In framing its recommendations on developed land – mainly urban areas – the Committee took as its starting-point government statements that had 'emphasised that post-war reconstruction should have as one of its aims the transformation of our towns and cities into more worthy centres of living, sufficient to meet the needs of modern civilisation and provide citizens with a healthy environment both for work and leisure'. The Committee assumed, therefore, that it should 'envisage plans on bold lines framed according to the dictates of good planning and involving, where necessary, a complete disregard for existing layouts'.

After explaining, with some detailed examples the magnitude and complication of the problems of urban-area redevelopment, the Committee rejected as quite ineffective the existing powers in the pre-war Planning and Housing Acts. For the purpose of reconstructing war-damaged areas, and the almost equally urgent task of securing the redevelopment of obsolete and unsatisfactory areas, the Committee considered it essential to 'invest the planning authority with the power to cut through the tangle of separate ownerships and boundary lines and make the whole of the land in the area immediately available for comprehensive replanning as a single unit'. The Committee accordingly recommended that the planning authority should be given the power to purchase the whole of such areas, by a simple and expeditious procedure. Also stressed was the need for adequate supporting finance, and while expressing no view on the extent to which the cost of such operations should fall on local resources or be borne by national funds, the Committee urged immediate consideration of the question.

7 *Urban betterment levy*[21]

As regards 'betterment' in urban areas, the Committee concluded that no *ad hoc* search for betterment due to planning or public improvements on particular land could succeed because it was impossible to segregate that particular element in a total increase of value. Therefore recommended was a levy on *all* increases in annual site value as revealed by quinquennial rating valuations, the levy to be at the rate of 75 per cent to take account of the fact that some element of the increase might be due to the skill and enterprise of the owner or occupier.

8 *Nationalisation of the reversion*

The Uthwatt Report contained a large number of other detailed recommendations, mainly concerned with the powers and procedure for land acquisition and the compensation to be paid. Some were adopted, but they are now mainly of historic interest and only marginally concern a current study of land policy. But there is one proposal in the Report that is worth a mention since it was long afterwards revived in no less than a *Times* leader, commenting that it 'deserves serious consideration and detailed development'.[22] This was a proposal

that all land in Britain be forthwith converted into leasehold interests held by the present proprietors as lessees of the State at a peppercorn rent for a uniform term of years as may reasonably, without payment of compensation, be regarded as equitable.

Since under leasehold tenure in Britain the ground lease (with certain exceptions) reverts without compensation to the freeholder, this 'unification of the reversion' would result in an eventual vesting of all property in the state.

The Committee commented that, intelligently administered, this unification would not hamper the operation of private enterprise in development or otherwise fetter the enjoyment of land; new leases would be granted as necessary and the machinery for the purpose would already be in operation under the proposed development rights scheme and reconstruction-area proposals. It is of interest that two of the five members had objections to it (one on technical grounds, one because he was opposed to nationalisation of land), the others commenting that 'they hold it to be the task of this generation to take stock of the possible needs and views of succeeding generations with respect to national planning. They wish to start time running in favour of succeeding generations'.[23]

5.3 POST-WAR LEGISLATION, 1943–75

5.3.1 GENERAL

The 'inside story' of the long discussions over the next four or five years, both among departments and in Cabinet, has now been published in the official history.[24] It is a fascinating study of the evolution of policy and gives a graphic account of the many difficulties which ministers and officials had to overcome before bills could be introduced in Parliament. One interesting feature is the wide measure of agreement which then prevailed among the main political parties on some of the important questions of principle, as is evidenced by the coalition government's 1944 White Paper *The Control of Land Use*. For our purpose it is sufficient to say that the Uthwatt Committee's development rights scheme and their proposals for dealing with war-damaged and other urban reconstruction areas were both adopted, with some modifications, but the proposal for an urban betterment levy was not.

It was this wartime coalition government which set the ball rolling with three significant Acts: (i) that of 1943 which established a new Minister in charge of the national land-use planning process; (ii) that of 1943 which made mandatory and not permissive the 1932 Act development control over the whole country; and (iii) the 1944 Act which introduced comprehensive redevelopment and grants for both blitzed and blighted areas.

But in 1945 it was a Labour government which was elected, and bent on a new post-war world. Their legislative product was of great significance. This section contains a largely factual summary of the main land policies which emerged in the series of interrelated Acts which together made up the new code for governing planning and reconstruction in the post-war period.

The second and third of the Coalition Acts were both replaced by the Town and Country Planning Act of 1947. Other Acts (such as the National Parks and Countryside Acts of 1949 and 1968, the Mineral Workings Act of 1952, the Caravans Acts of 1960 and 1968, and the Clean Air Act of 1956) all contained elements of land policy but dealt with specialised subjects which, although of great interest, did not add much of general application to the main stream of land policy. The Distribution of Industry Act of 1945 (which gave the Board of Trade direct control over the location of virtually all new industry) is important as an instrument of planning policy, and is of interest for the compensation–betterment issue to note that it provided no compensation on refusal of an industrial development certificate. And there were a number of other new statutory provisions which had important effects but are of minor concern to planning strategy as a whole.

It is therefore proposed to concentrate first on the New Towns Act and the related Town Development Act of 1952; then to deal with the land policy aspects of the Town and Country Planning Act of 1947, and the amendments made in 1953, 1954 and 1959; and finally, to examine the Land Commission Act of 1967 and its repeal in 1970. Throughout this period of change in land policy there have been the strong political overtones mentioned above (section 1.1) that sometimes obscure the reasons for the many changes and make analysis difficult and uncertain.

5.3.2   TOWN AND COUNTRY PLANNING ACTS, 1947, 1953, 1954 AND 1959[25]

The 1947 Act, which set out the new post-war planning system described above (section 4.3.1), in addition to having features which were significantly different from the pre-war planning system in the Town and Country Planning Act of 1932, extended land policy measures to ensure that the new planning objectives could be achieved.

One measure was the extension to the whole country of the pre-war powers of development control, which under the former system applied only in those areas where a resolution to plan had been introduced; it became mandatory and not permissive. But in addition the nature of the control was quite different. Whereas previously the rules for not granting permission were circumscribed in a 'planning scheme' which was in effect a local law for the area, under the 1947 Act development could only take place on the grant of a specific permit, each case being treated on its merits (see section 4.3.2). Again, the compensation for *injurious affection* on refusal or conditions was greatly used in favour of the authority. It is this particular feature which has transformed the whole of the planning system of Britain; whereas previously the landowner had the rights granted him in the local scheme, after 1947 the landowner had no rights until they were granted to him by the planning permit, except in the case of reinstatement.

This particular system of development control has persisted with very little change in law (except for the minutiae of rules and regulations and certain minor changes in successive Acts) from 1948 until the present day. And under it there have been administered endless thousands of development permits and refusals, and appeals to the minister. But there is reason to think that the development control system has been too enduring and has not reflected the significant changes in the social, economical and political climate since 1947. For example, the demolition of buildings was not included as development in the 1947 Act and is still not regarded as development (except where the buildings are listed as of historic or architectural interest) despite the significant changes in attitude towards the conservation of buildings of recent years.

This apparently negative control, which involved no taking of land except in rare circumstances at the option of the owner, had its positive aspect; since it enabled planning permission to be given where it was in accordance with the intentions of the development plan, which each local planning authority was required to prepare and submit to the minister for approval, it gave the authorities a powerful lever for influencing development. It thus relied basically for implementation on the private- or public-enterprise developer selecting suitable land and making his own arrangements to buy it in the land market, by agreement for the private sector and by agreement or compulsorily by the public sector. The developer could test the suitability of his choice of land by applying for planning permission, and if successful he could proceed with the development. Since the Second World War most of the development in Britain has been carried out in this way; accordingly, it has involved much time and effort by both local planning authorities and also the minister, to whom there is a right of appeal, against refusal of permission or the inclusion of a condition.

It was recognised, however, that while the land market had its own logic, it tended to produce 'piecemeal development', dictated by the particular land which developers were able and willing to buy, and perhaps consisting of one type of development, such as houses, without the supporting shops, services and employment opportunities needed to create a fully adequate environment. This might not result in the right volume, speed or balance of development from the community viewpoint. The 1947 Act accordingly gave local planning authorities wide powers to buy land, compulsorily where necessary with the minister's approval, for the purpose of 'securing its use in the manner proposed by the Plan'. In the parliamentary debates it was made clear that ministers fully intended the powers to be used to achieve properly balanced development.[26] This was the new 'positive planning'.

The development plans were required to contain a programme of development and to designate land for compulsory purchase. But in order to place some limit on the amount of land subject to a threat of compulsory purchase, the powers of designation extended only to land likely to be required within a period of ten years, or seven years in the case of agricultural land. The development plans had to be reviewed and revised every five years, and this enabled the programme to be 'rolled on' at each review, additional land being designated as necessary.

In addition the Act incorporated and extended the important provisions of the Town and Country Planning Act of 1944 enabling the local planning authorities to buy areas for comprehensive development or redevelopment. The 1944 Act had provided an Exchequer grant to meet losses incurred in redeveloping areas of war damage and the 1947 Act extended grants to other areas, although at a lower rate.

Thus, in terms of land policy, the Act was based primarily on a combination of categories (1), (2) and (3), with an element of both (4) and (5) (see section 1.6). This provided all the necessary powers for the implementation of plans but could work only with financial provisions aimed at a solution of the compensation–betterment problem. Otherwise, for example, landowners in, say, a green belt, where no development would be allowed, would suffer a loss because that is where most of the development value in an unplanned system would lie; whereas owners whose land was selected for development, and to which the development value 'shifted', would make a substantial gain. And the community would be liable for compensation without being able to collect betterment. For the solution the government decided to adopt the principle of the 'development rights scheme' recommended by the Uthwatt Committee, but with two modifications.

First, they applied it to all land, not only to 'unbuilt land'. The Uthwatt Committee had not explained why it had limited its proposals to land outside urban areas; built-on land frequently had a development value for more intensive development, and in any case the task of precisely delineating 'built-up areas' was virtually impossible, since they contained a certain amount of unbuilt-on land to which the same principles applied. After long discussions a sum of £300 million was provided for compensating landowners whose land held a development value in 1948. It would be distributed within three years, when all claims had been assessed and an equitable basis of distribution had been worked out. All owners would thus receive fair, but not excessive, compensation for any development value in their land at 1948. As a corollary any development value realised thereafter, through the grant of a planning permission, could reasonably be expected to accrue to the state. A Central Land Board was therefore set up to collect this 'development charge'.

These arrangements made it unnecessary, it was thought, to adopt the Uthwatt Committee's recommendation for a quinquennial levy on increases in the site value of all land already built on. The difficulties of valuing the site alone, excluding the building, were very considerable, and the proposal would have taxed all increases of value, whether for existing use or for a more intensive use. While recognising that such increases might in some cases be the result of public works (new roads, railways, bridges, etc.), most of them would be covered by the proposed development charge on new development and for the rest there were strong reasons for leaving property values for existing use to find their own levels. In any case the rights or wrongs of taxing existing use values were not part of the planning function and were best left for separate consideration by the taxing and rating authorities. The restriction of compensation on compulsory purchase to a 1939 level of value, introduced by the 1944 Act to counter possible wartime speculation in land and intended to last for five years, was itself repealed by the 1947 Act, very largely because 1938 values had by then become quite unrealistic.

The second modification to Uthwatt's recommendations concerned the Committee's suggestion that when a permission to develop was granted, the state should buy the land from the owner in order to merge his interests with the state-owned development rights, and then grant a lease for development at a price that included the new development value. This seemed to the government an unnecessary complication. For one thing the term 'development' necessarily included a wide range of operations, large and small, including changes of use without any actual building work, and purchase in all such cases was clearly undesirable.

This then was the basis of the development rights scheme of the 1947 Act. Although the scheme was frequently described as the 'purchase by the state of all development rights', as a matter of law the state acquired no interest in land as such. All it acquired was a right to refuse permission to develop without a liability to pay compensation, and a right to claim a development charge whenever permission to develop was granted. In legal terms there were no interests in land to 'merge'.

But none the less there was compensation for loss of rights, by providing a global sum for distribution, following the lines successfully adopted some years earlier for the purchase by the state of all coal royalties. For the compensation, £300 million was thought, on such evidence as was available, to be a fair value for the rights being taken over as at 1 April 1948. With interest rates then about 3 per cent, the annual income from the development charge – estimated at £9 million a year once the scheme was in full operation – would be sufficient to service the capital so that no cost would fall on the taxpayer. All subsequent development values would accrue to the state in perpetuity, thus providing a steady and increasing source of income; planning would no longer be inhibited or distorted by compensation problems; and the long-standing difficulties of collecting betterment resulting from planning operations – accepted by all parties as just and proper – would be solved once and for all.

Moreover, the scheme secured justice as between one owner and another – the one who received planning permission would not make a fortune from land value which was denied to the owner who was refused; all development values that had accrued to the date of the Act would be paid for, so there was no element of 'confiscation'; all owners would retain the full existing use value of their land or property, whether the value rose or fell with later market fluctuations, and on enforced sale would always receive enough to buy an equivalent property elsewhere (but perhaps not enough for full as opposed to statutory disturbance).

These criteria – thought essential both to equity and workability – were achieved, or intended to be achieved, by requiring the development charge to be the full difference between the existing use value of land and the value of the land with the permission to develop. As a result, a purchaser of land for development would not be able to sell at more than the existing use value and all land would therefore change hands in the market at or about that level. Wide publicity was given to the Act in the hope of ensuring that both owners and purchasers understood the position and negotiated with a full knowledge of the new law, though there was no formal control of sale prices and the parties were left to make whatever bargain suited them.

On a compulsory purchase by a public authority, however, the price was firmly fixed at existing use value plus a payment for disturbance and negotiations, and – if necessary – arbitration took place on that basis. By the Act the Central Land Board was given certain powers of purchase designed to enable it to step in and buy if a vendor was demanding an unreasonable price well above existing use value, thereby attempting to obtain some or all of the development value for himself and thus prejudicing the collection of the proper level of development charge.

Finally, to ensure that land needed for development was not kept from the market, extended powers of compulsory purchase were given to the local authorities to buy land to secure the 'proper planning' of the area to supplement the many other such powers available to them and other public authorities to buy for all statutory purposes, e.g. comprehensive development, new town building, and so on.

All in all this was a completely logical structure – too logical, some may argue with hindsight – within which properly planned development could take place and the new conception of 'positive planning' secured. But the logic was hampered by one important element: uncertainty. The distribution of the £300 million could not be made until all the claims had been examined and values settled. This, it was thought, would take about three years and under the Act the minister was then required to submit to Parliament a scheme for distribution. Some organisations were forecasting that owners would get only a minute proportion of their claims. Accordingly there was some reluctance to sell land for private development at existing use value until the amount payable on the claim was known. In the event the £300 million proved to be a remarkably close estimate.[27] Moreover, with the new planning machine beginning to work, permission being refused for development in proposed green-belt and other such areas, the 'shift of value' process was already beginning to operate and developers were turning their attention to land which had until then no prospect of development and therefore no valid claim on the £300 million. Here, too, it was said, owners were refusing to sell at around existing use value. This uncertainty was fostered by the fact that the detailed working of the scheme was based on the practice of valuation (of development charges and acquisition prices) with the knowledge that such valuation is not an exact science, with prices in the market varying, for example, according to the bargaining position of the parties concerned.

It was recognised that development charges, although theoretically 100 per cent, would in practice have to be fixed on the low rather than the high side, and there would thus always be margins within which private purchases could be negotiated. The Uthwatt Committee recognised this, and commented:

We are prepared to face the possibility or the probability that in order to clear the ground the intending developer may see that in some form or other the landowner gets more than he would on a compulsory acquisition. That possibility or probability cannot we think be effectively provided against and it is not worth while making the attempt.[28]

The Central Land Board also took a realistic view. As they told the Public Accounts Committee,[29] land for development was at that time temporarily commanding a greatly enhanced value because labour and materials were scarce and a building licence had to be obtained. The enhanced value was in reality the value to the developer of the building licence, which the Board decided as a matter of policy should be excluded from the assessment of development charge.

None the less the Board made a few compulsory purchase orders in an attempt to publicise the position and influence the land market into a more realistic understanding of the new arrangements. Not all were confirmed by the ministry, which found it 'a most disagreeable jurisdiction'.[30] The Central Land Board's powers of purchase were also challenged in the Courts, and although their actions were vindicated in the House of Lords,[31] it was a couple of years before the case reached that stage.

Meanwhile, local authorities were buying land extensively at existing use value for housing and other public purposes and new town development corporations were similarly negotiating purchases without difficulty. Very few compulsory orders had to be made. There is no record of any attempt by the local planning authorities to use their power to buy land compulsorily on the grounds that it was needed for development but was being kept from the market. Although numerous examples could be quoted – and indeed were – of owners who for one reason or other declined to sell, the ministry at that time denied there was any shortage of land for development: the resources of the building industry, it was said, were fully stretched, and under the transitional provisions of the Act there was enough land available for development to build 100,000 houses and 3,800 acres of factory and commercial building. The development charge, it was concluded, was not a deterrent to development.[32]

But in the absence of any contemporary monitoring, it is difficult to throw much light on the controversies surrounding the development rights scheme in the 1947 Act. And even this would not have been conclusive in that the scheme, to be repealed in 1953, was so short-lived, and the times so difficult in recovering from the then recent war. Perhaps the official history of the period, now in preparation,[33] may shed further light on the problems that arose in the administration of the Act in the first five years of its operation.

Its short life was to be killed in 1953 with the first of the three Acts unscrambling the compensation–betterment provisions of the 1947 Act, following the Conservative return to power in 1951. First, the Town and Country Planning Act of 1953 abolished development charges and repealed the power of the Central Land Board to buy land, thus restoring full development values to the owners of land for which planning permission was granted. Second, the Town and Country Planning Act of 1954 then suspended distribution of the £300 million and provided instead that it was the full agreed amount of any claim made under the 1947 Act which should be paid by central government on refusal of a planning permission to develop; land bought by a public authority would continue to be bought at existing use value, to which would be added the amount of the agreed claim, thus denying any development value accrued for any reason since 1948. All claims would be increased by one-seventh, representing tax-free interest for the seven years from 1948 to 1955.

The 'unscrambling' process was complicated because many changes of ownership had taken place since 1947, on sale, death, gift, expiration of leases, and so on. This involved intricate apportionments of the claims on the £300 million; and because under the 1947 Act they were personal property, detached as it were from the land, the Act had to reattach them to the land as part of the real estate. These, however, were mainly technical complications. The important results of the 1953 and 1954 Acts from the point of view of land policy and its effective administration were as follows:

1   The Acts preserved the power of a local planning authority to refuse planning permission without incurring any liability to pay compensation from its own resources. Any outstanding claim on the £300 million was met by the Exchequer. This led to the distinct danger that planning would be distorted not so much, as in the 1932 Act days, from fear of compensation as from authorities becoming indifferent to their impact on development value, simply because it was central government which would foot the bill for its sterilisation. In order to protect the Exchequer from unjustified claims the Act did in fact enable the minister to review any local authority decision that gave rise to a claim, but in doing so he was required by the Act to have regard to

the development plans; in the event planning decisions do not appear to have suffered any serious distortion.

2   The Acts abandoned the policy, inherent in the 1947 Act, of equity as between landowners. It became the luck of the draw. The owner on whose land private development was allowed could retain the full price he could obtain in the market; but on a refusal, or when land was needed for public purposes such as schools, playing fields, roads, buildings, etc., an owner received only existing use value plus the agreed amount of his 1947 Act claim (if any).

3   This 'two-price' system did not last long. By the third unscrambling Act, the Town and Country Planning Act of 1959, market value for compulsory purchase was restored, but the Act included some important reservations which precluded payment in some cases (not all) for any element of value which could be attributed to major public development, such as a new town, an expansion of a town under the Town Development Act, or comprehensive redevelopment. This also involved some highly artificial concepts involving the issue of 'certificates of alternative use' for assessing the value of land with planning permission for uses not experienced in the market, e.g. schools.

4   The Central Land Board, originally expected to be not only self-supporting but eventually to collect an increasing amount of revenue from development charges, became a body with the sole function of calculating and paying out the compensation claims. Later these functions were transferred to the ministry, and the Board was abolished. No further claims for payment were etertained after 1968.

To conclude on the land policy aspects of these three Conservative measures, the unscrambling of the financial provisions of the 1947 Act did not mean a return to the compensation and betterment situation of the 1932 Act. On betterment, the government gave up a substantial source of revenue, without any further possibilities until the Land Commission Act of 1967, itself to be short-lived. But on compensation there was an ingenious compromise. The government maintained the view that on paying out the compensation claims from the £300 million fund, albeit at 1948 levels, it in fact 'bought the development rights' of *all* undeveloped land, in built or unbuilt areas, whether or not it qualified for the 1947 Act claim. It could therefore justify continued refusal of permissions without compensation. From time to time there has been pressure to restore compensation on refusal to full market value[34] in order to 'restore equity', but this has always been refused. To accede to it would have destroyed the last important feature of the 1947 Act, completed the circle back to 1932 and recreated the very difficulties that had made planning virtually ineffective in pre-war days.

We must leave it to the historian to analyse the political reasoning that led the Conservative goernment in 1953 to repeal so much of the 1947 compensation–betterment solution; to extend the pre-war right of the state to control development value without payment of compensation; to deny full development value on land purchased compulsorily; and to abandon completely any idea of equity as between one landowner and another. It was the more surprising since the 1947 Act had followed closely the main basis of the coalition government's proposals in 1944 when in both the House of Commons and the House of Lords nobody had seriously disputed the equity of a development charge; any differences of opinion were on the percentage of the charge and other relatively small matters. But the most astonishing feature is that the government should have been willing to pay out up to £300 million – quite a sizeable sum in those days – without any compensating income by way of development charges from those clearly able to pay from increased land value on planning permission. And with hindsight, what a bad business deal it was, considering what happened to land values thereafter.

But whatever the reasoning, the Conservatives 'solved', quite ingeniously, the compensation–betterment dilemma. Since local authorities did not have to pay compensation on refusal of permission and were also able to buy land they needed at existing use value, then financially they had no cause to worry if betterment went to the landowner, particularly as, if levied, it would have gone to the Exchequer, not to the local authority itself. And from the central government viewpoint the issue was quite simple. The development charge was unpopular and not readily understood. It was said that it was holding up development. The economy was beginning to pick up and shortage of housing was a major issue. The minister (then Harold Macmillan) was anxious to achieve a target of 400,000 new houses (private and public) a year. Anything likely to impede this target had to be swept ruthlessly aside. Therefore, the development charge must go.

But the financial indifference to betterment was soon to be replaced by deep public concern for it. In the early 1950s few people would have predicted the rapid rise in land and property values of later years. Hitherto, with the building licence system in operation, land transactions had not taken place on a large scale, and on the whole prices were still reasonably modest. In the event, however, the building boom of the 1960s created large fortunes for some landowners and property companies and gave rise to public concern on the equity issues (landowners to society, landowner to landowner) and also about the effects on the economy as a whole.

5.3.3   THE LAND COMMISSION ACT OF 1967

It was this boom and public concern which the Labour government inherited on its return in the 1964 election. A first step was to follow the generally popular and overdue measure of taxing the previously untaxed profits from land. They included in the Finance Act of 1967 a capital gains tax on increases in certain existing use values and, by the Land Commission Act of 1967, made another attempt 'to secure that a substantial part of the development value created by the community returns to the community and that the burden of the cost of land for essential purpose is reduced'. This was to be secured by a betterment levy of 40 per cent (to be increased to 45 per cent and then 50 per cent at short intervals, with the possibility of further increases later).

But the Act also introduced a new land policy measure: to aid in securing that the right land was available at the right time for the implementation of national, regional and local plans. The objective was to supplement the local authority powers to facilitate an orderly programme of approved development. For this purpose a Land Commission, set up primarily to collect the betterment levy, was given power to buy land compulsorily, at a price net of betterment levy. A new expedited procedure for vesting title was provided in place of that of the 1947 Act and the Commission itself had some powers to develop such land, but in general it was expected that it would sell or lease to a suitable developer. In the case of houses a new form of freehold tenure was introduced called 'Crownhold' under which future increases in development values remained with the Crown.

But the Labour government in turn did not attempt to go back full circle to the 1947 Act provisions and there were important differences between the 1967 Land Commission Act and the 1947 Act. First, instead of attempting to exclude development value from market prices, by repealing the 1959 Act market value formula, the 1967 Act allowed prices to reach their own level and then claimed as betterment the prescribed percentage of the proceeds. Second, whereas the 1947 Act had relied largely on the local authorities to implement the plans, the 1967 Act supplemented them with the new powers of purchase given to the Land Commission. The reasoning here was that even with the 1947 powers the local authorities were still not willing and/or able to secure the orderly development visualised when introducing that Act. The Commission did not replace the powers of the local authorities, however, and had to secure planning permission for all development they undertook. It was stressed that, to be successful, the Land Commission would need the close co-operation of the local authorities. But this was not always forthcoming; where the friction lay is not easy to ascertain, but in some cases the Land Commission found itself having to conduct a formal appeal to its own minister against a refusal of planning permission. To do this effectively would have demanded a separate staff of planning experts in the Land Commission itself, in addition to those of the local authorities and the ministry: an obvious nonsense.

Establishing a new national organisation such as the Land Commission was an expensive business, but eventually, like the earlier Central Land Board, it would clearly have shown a high yield from betterment levy and the surplus on its land sales. Indeed, the Commission expressed the hope that it would be possible to use some of the future surplus to buy land for urban renewal and make it available at a price related to the new plan, thus helping to finance this expensive sphere of planning work. The opportunity never came, because the incoming Conservative government abolished the Land Commission in 1971 and betterment levy was repealed.

That the problem of betterment remained is illuminated by the following. The government estimate for the 1967 Act was that a betterment levy of only 40–50 per cent would, when in full operation, yield £80 million a year. The magnitude of the rise in development values over the twenty-year period since 1947 can be seen by comparison with the estimate of £9 million a year in 1948 from a levy of 100 per cent.

5.4   SUMMARY OF LAND POLICIES CURRENT IN 1974

Having reviewed the historical evolution of British land policy legislation and practice, we now go on to summarise the actual land policies as they existed prior to the passing of the community land legislation, under the categories introduced above (section 1.6). In this we are to some extent repeating material given in Chapter 4 and at the beginning of this chapter. Our purpose in doing so is to highlight the gaps in such land policies which amount to impediments in implementation (section 4.5.5) as a basis for the criteria for needed changes in current (pre-Community Land Act) land policy (section 5.6). It is this which is used to consider whether or not the community land legislation (discussed in Chapter 6) meets all the criteria.

5.4.1   CONTROL OVER SPECIFIC DEVELOPMENT WITHOUT TAKING LAND[35]

As noted above (section 4.3.2) development control is the backbone of plan implementation in the British planning system. This control, coupled with building regulations and the like, operates in respect of and affects all types of development, since it is used to ensure either that development does not occur if 'unsatisfactory'; or if it does, then it proceeds in accordance with conditions which will make it satisfactory.

As indicated above (section 5.3), although termed *negative* it has its *positive* side. Used constructively, under the names of 'planning', 'development' or 'design briefs',[36] it can secure 'good' development, for example if used with guidelines prepared by authorities as to what they would wish to see on the land in question.

But while planning control is the backbone, and has been practised under much the same legislative measures since the 1947 Act (see section 4.3.2), it cannot be suggested that the practice is stable or clear. Some examples will illustrate. While an authority, 'in dealing with the application, shall have regard to the provisions of the development plan, so far as material to the application, and to any other material considerations,'[37] it is not at all clear from the courts just what is 'material':[38] to what degree can non-conformity with the stated policy be regarded as justifying refusal, bearing in mind that policies are of necessity formulated only as guidelines to action and not as prescriptions for it;[39] what are the reasonable limits for planning conditions;[40] to what degree is judicial control over the administration of planning appropriate to contemporary planning.[41]

This unclarity in the legal context of development control is mirrored by similar uncertainty in professional practice. For one thing, the administrative machine had become overcumbersome and creaking, and thus required overhaul.[42] For another, recent commentaries by professionals concerned in the practice show a branch of study (planning) which is groping towards some purpose, as opposed to having reached it, and this after some thirty years of practice.[43]

The uncertainty can be further illustrated by the practice of recent years which has come to be known as *planning gain*. To grasp its nature requires a return to what was said above about the nature of planning permission in development control (section 4.3.2): 'where an application is made to a local planning authority for planning permission, that authority in dealing with its application, shall have regard to the provisions of the development plan so far as material to the application, and to any other material considerations'.[44] In making its decision the authority can refuse, grant, or grant subject to condition. In imposing conditions the authority would have been advised by the minister to have regard to the following tests.[45] Is the permission (a) necessary, (b) relevant to planning, (c) relevant to the development to be permitted, (d) enforceable, (e) precise, and (f) reasonable? Thus the discretion of the authority in imposing conditions is circumscribed. These constraints can, however, be avoided by an authority by entering into an agreement with owners which regulates or restricts the development or use of the land.[46] This principle was later generalised outside planning to enable local authorities and developers to make agreements about contributions to the cost of infrastructure services[47] and further strengthen practice in respect of housing development where the agreements could cover the provision of roads, public open spaces, land for schools, and so on.[48] In this way the circumscribed discretion of the planning condition by administrative direction was widened specifically by statute.

But none the less the nature of the agreements themselves were relatively circumscribed; perhaps a contributory cause was the need until 1968 for them to be ratified by the minister. But during the 1970s the subject-matter became wider and wider. Details became available following an investigation into practice of a sample of 28 per cent of English local authorities.[49] The result showed that planning permissions were being given with such agreed conditions as the specification of the use, public rights of way on the developer's land, dedication of land to public use, extinguishing an existing user, provision of community buildings, rehabilitation of property, provision of infrastructure, gift of site or buildings for residential use, commuted payments for car parking.

From these results it was apparent that the property boom, with its growing land profits to the landowners and developers, enabled greater concessions to be obtained for the authority, especially as they had sentiment on their side in having no chance other than planning gain or general taxation to recoup some betterment. But it was noted that 'the agreements reflected a more contemporary view of planning purposes – a view that recognises that planning must, to be effective, take into account criteria wider than land uses alone'.[50] However, these were wider than the Courts were prone to accept as within planning powers on those cases which had come before them. In brief they found that what might be called *amenity gain* involving traditional land-use considerations was within the law but that *social and economic* gains derived from planning were not (for example, where the use is required to create employment (industry and residential development), to obtain a 'social mix' (council housing in an office development) and other forms of 'social and economic engineering' through development control). Thus 'planning by agreement may be seen as a device to permit the evasion of the criteria that the Courts impose, and to release in development control the naked power that procedural justice attempts to restrain'.

For our purpose what may be concluded is that the achievement of planning gain through planning permission by agreement can, in fact, be very 'positive'. Whether or not the alleged excesses are outside the law is not for discussion here. But what is apparent is that the law would appear to be lagging behind what many could consider as reasonable in terms of contemporary objectives in urban and regional planning. But it could be that it is the law, or rather the interpretation of the law, which needs to change. It could be that this also would be included in the warning that here as in other aspects of our society the common-law system is in retreat, is being challenged and is being abandoned; and yet the rule of law must be preserved if we are to have a just society; and it is for the lawyers to find answers to the questions in a way which society finds helpful.[51]

5.4.2   CONTROL OVER SPECIFIC DEVELOPMENT BY TAKING LAND

In the preceding section we have seen that while the distinction between 'negative' planning and 'positive' planning has considerable ancestry and is a useful simplification, the dividing-line between them is somewhat tenuous. Here we are moving over the dividing-line by contrasting the taking of land with not doing so. In this the tenuousness is emphasised by what has come to be called 'inverse compulsory purchase' whereby even without taking land the authority has so circumscribed the property rights of an owner that he has power to require the authority to buy from him, examples being *purchase notices* where he has no remaining beneficial use for his property, or *enforced purchase* where the property is so blighted by restrictions that there is no reasonable market for the property.[52]

The distinction has of necessity been pursued in the USA, where the borderline of 'taking' has been tested in the Courts over the years because of the need to interpret the written constitution. In summary,

> the exercise of eminent domain has traditionally involved the taking of property for a public use.... The police power, as ordinarily understood in relation to private property, has involved the supression or limitation applied to the property in the owner's hands in order to protect the public health, safety, morals, or general welfare against dangers arising, or likely to arise, from the misemployment of the property. ... [And] one rule of thumb has been that property is taken by eminent domain because of the usefulness of the property in the hands of the public, but property is regulated by the police power because of its harmfulness in the hands of the owner.[53]

But while the issue of 'taking or not' is clearly of huge significance to an owner who does not wish to be disturbed, in practice the most important consideration is the difference in the compensation rights of the owner in each case. In the USA it is clear: for eminent domain compensation is paid to the owner whereas for exercise of the police power it is not.[54] On the same issue in Britain there is no such clear-cut line, the situation being determined in each parliamentary statute. For a general proposition we can go back to Uthwatt:[55]

1 Ownership of land does not carry with it an unqualified right of user.
2 Therefore restrictions based on the duties of neighbourliness may be imposed without involving the conception that the landowner is being deprived of any property or interest.
3 Therefore such restrictions can be imposed without liability to pay compensation.
4 But the point may be reached when the restrictions imposed extend beyond the obligations of neighbourliness.
5 At this stage the restrictions become equivalent to an expropriation of a proprietary right or interest and therefore (it will be claimed) should carry a right to compensation as such.

But while the principle is clear, the dividing-line of not taking or taking, as adopted in successive statutes, is not.[56] Apart from the interest in the line from the viewpoint of its effect on development and state infringement of proprietary rights, the practical outcome of the dividing-line is financial: what compensation flows? We return to this below (section 5.6). Here we turn to the control of development where taking becomes necessary. The public sector is empowered to purchase land, compulsorily or by agreement, under varied legislation. There are about one hundred separate such statutes, conferring powers for every function of the local authority and statutory undertakings.[57] But in parallel with these powers, and not replacing them, have grown up others which facilitate public purchase for planning, as distinct from the particular public purpose visualised by legislation geared to *ad hoc* powers. This is the focus of this section.[58]

In general legislation these planning types of powers began with the Housing Act, 1936, but gathered strength after the Second World War with the move towards 'positive' planning in the 1944 and 1947 Town and Country Planning Acts and in the New Towns and Town Development Acts. All these, taken together, empowered the local authorities or new town development corporations to *promote* general development in specific areas rather than simply *control* it on application for permission.

Because of the wide-reaching nature of this new, general power of compulsory purchase, the initial post-war measure, the Town and Country Planning Act, 1944, adopted a new principle. The choice of specific land could not be left directly to a compulsory purchase order, as in the case where the public purpose to which the land was to be put was clear. Instead, there was an intermediate stage in the procedure. The area in which 'positive planning' was to be examined had first to be settled by a 'declaratory order' approved by the minister: 'Where the Minister ... is satisfied that it is requisite, for the purpose of dealing satisfactorily with extensive war damage, in the area of a local planning authority, that a part or parts of their area ... should be laid out afresh and redeveloped as a whole, an order may be made by the Minister' declaring that the land designated by the order should be subject to compulsory purchase. Areas so designated became known as 'declaratory areas'.

The 1947 Town and Country Planning Act absorbed the 'declaratory order' into the procedure of the development plan system which it set up, and the 'declaratory area' became an 'area of comprehensive development'. These new areas could be defined for dealing not only with war damage but also with obsolete development, with new neighbourhoods or industrial areas on the periphery, or with any other purpose specified. Following approval by the minister, compulsory purchase orders could be made on any land so designated, the principle of purchase having been settled. Thus compulsory purchase of land for 'planning' was not possible (exceptions apart) without prior designation.

The need for prior designation was brought to an end by the Town and Country Planning Act of 1968, and the new procedure is now governed by the 1971 Town and Country Planning Act, a consolidating measure. The entity most akin to the comprehensive development area is the 'action area', which is to be indicated in the structure plan and fully worked out as a local plan, and the authorising enactment for compulsory purchase for planning purposes – now section 112 of the 1971 Act – reproduces the wide powers of the 1947 and earlier amending Acts. It empowers the Secretary of State to authorise a local planning authority to purchase land compulsorily within their area if he is satisfied on one of the following counts:

1   that the land is required in order to secure the treatment as a whole, by development, redevelopment or improvement; or partly by one and partly by another method, of the land or of any area within which the land is situated; or

2   that it is expedient in the public interest that the land should be held together with land so required; or
3   that the land is required for development or redevelopment, or both, as a whole for the purpose of providing for the relocation of population or industry or the replacement of open space in the course of the redevelopment or improvement, or both, of another area as a whole; or
4   that it is expedient to acquire the land immediately for a purpose which it is necessary to achieve in the interests of the proper planning of an area in which the land is situated.

There are other provisions which can be regarded as authorising enactments for compulsory purchase within the field of planning. For example, section 114 of the 1971 Act empowers the Secretary of State to authorise compulsory purchase of listed buildings if he considers they are not being properly looked after; section 113 authorises the Secretary of State to acquire compulsorily any land necessary for the public service.

As with the powers themselves, the compensation code has changed over the years, as described above (section 5.3.3).

Another important body of legislation closely related to planning comprises the Housing Acts under which the majority of slum clearance is done, and large new municipal housing estates have been built on land bought for the purpose. The 1957 Housing Act has two main parts dealing with the public acquisition of existing housing: part III allows local authorities to purchase compulsorily and clear unfit houses on a comprehensive scale, while part V allows them to acquire dwellings compulsorily in order to increase the quantity of housing. In both cases the compulsory purchase orders must be authorised by the Secretary of State.

The compensation payable on compulsory purchase in such cases has undergone various changes. In the case of unfit dwellings it was fixed at or near 'site value'; however, for certain cases it has been raised approximately to the level of the market price by the introduction of various supplements. No allowance is made for the fact that the purchase is compulsory, but there is a disturbance allowance. The market valuation also applies to non-residential property.

The legislation governing the powers and duties of new town corporations is the New Towns Acts 1946–65. The powers are available following designation by the minister of an area of land to be developed as a new town and the appointment of a corporation for the purpose. A corporation has 'power to acquire, hold, manage and dispose of land and other property'.[59] This empowers corporations to purchase the following categories of land for new town purposes:

1   any land within the designated new town area, irrespective of whether it is required for development;
2   any land adjacent to that area which is needed for purposes connected with the development of the new town;
3   any land, adjacent or not, required for the provision of services for the new town.

The acquisition of any land by the corporation within the designated area is thus settled in principle when that area is designated, even though the corporation intends it to remain in its existing state of development. For land outside the area needed for roads, sewerage, etc., the precise purpose has to be demonstrated. A corporation is free to buy by agreement but a compulsory purchase order requires the minister's express approval.

The procedure for a compulsory acquisition of land by development corporations is based on the procedure devised in 1944 primarily for the purchase of war-damaged land. This included 'expedited completion' – changed in 1967 to the 'vesting declaration' of the Land Commission Act – by which full ownership of land could be transferred to a development corporation without waiting for investigation of title, formal conveyance and settlement of compensation. This provision is useful if resale of the land or its leasing out to a developer is contemplated.

The minister may disregard objections to compulsory purchase orders which relate to land within the designated area if objection to that acquisition is merely that it is 'unnecessary' or 'inexpedient'. While this power has not been extensively used in practice, it echoes the underlying assumption of areas of comprehensive development under the Town and Country Planning Acts, i.e. the settling of the principle of acquisition once and for all at the outset.

Before 1953 the basis of compensation on compulsory purchase was existing use value, excluding development value brought about by the designation of the area as a new town area. All land for the mark-I new towns was acquired on this basis. This has not, however, been the case with mark-II new towns, where land has been acquired at open market values:

> Although new towns have been insulated up to a point from the more drastic effects, these changes in compensation law have nevertheless made a substantial difference to the finances of the new towns now starting. The high prices they are having to pay for land can easily add £100 million more to the capital costs of building even a small town, on which loan charges – some £9 million a year – have to be carried for 60 years. Higher rents are thus inevitable and a much longer period must elapse before the new towns become financially self-supporting.[60]

5.4.3 CONTROL OVER SPECIFIC DEVELOPMENT BY DIRECT PUBLIC AUTHORITY PARTICIPATION[61]

Whereas in the previous category the authority would intervene by making land available for use by any other development agency, on lease or sale, the emphasis here is direct participation in the development itself.

The clear use is the traditional provision of public-sector uses, such as roads or schools. But beyond this is the growing role of developing in fields which conventionally have fallen to the private sector – in industrial estates, commercial centres, middle-income housing, and so on.

The typical tenure is leasehold, whereby as landlord the authority will attempt to secure the development it seeks under leasehold as well as planning control. But as we have seen (section 4.2.5), this form has been extended into so-called 'partnerships' (whereby the authority takes a more active and involved role than the conventional landlord even to the point of participating in a joint company).

But more subtle and widespread than this is the participation with or without land ownership which has come through formal planning agreements and informal arrangements on 'planning gain'. Here the authorities have secured public facilities on the land in question without being a party in the development process.

In the new towns there is also a mix of public and private bodies participating in development. With respect to the development of its land, three courses are open to the corporation: (i) building for sale or let; (ii) renting the site on long leases to firms to build for their own use; (iii) renting the site to others to build for letting.

The decisions made vary from one town to another.[62] While to some extent corporations engage in commerce and industry development, they spend most on building houses (nearly two-thirds of their expenditure) and they provide about 85 per cent of all housing in new towns. However, they are not the only house-building agency, local authorities and private developers account for 9 and 6.2 per cent respectively of the housing built before 1962. Increasing emphasis is being placed on owner-occupation and private building for sale, while the proportion of local authority housing is decreasing.

The attitude towards the construction of industrial premises, offices and shops is more varied. In some instances corporations will lease the prepared land to developers, while in others they will develop themselves.

5.4.4   INFLUENCE OVER GENERAL DEVELOPMENT BY FISCAL MEASURES

In our review of taxes on land above (section 4.2) we introduced the site value tax and current use value tax. Despite decades of argument for the former in Britain,[63] it has not been introduced and thus does not come into this review.

In this category also come fiscal measures of central and local government which, while being designed for general purposes (e.g. price stabilisation or revenue collection), do influence the development process and thereby implementation. Examples are price controls (general rent control ceiling on rent increase following house improvement); taxes (local rates, capital transfer tax, estate and inheritance duty); discriminatory pricing (on cars in congested areas by high car-parking charges); and inducements (improvement grants, tax concessions and capital grants in development areas as part of regional policy).

Sometimes the effect on development is direct, such as price controls which discourage new investment, or local rates which discourage improvement. But, sometimes it is indirect, in having side-effects, as in encouraging a switch from one kind of development to another, e.g. shift of land uses through cost and difficulty of car parking.

5.4.5   INFLUENCE OVER SPECIFIC DEVELOPMENT BY FISCAL MEASURES

When we turn to fiscal means which influence specific development we come to a set of measures which are more directly related to the development process.

A clear example is the betterment levy which, prior to the Development Land Tax Act, existed in less familiar forms. The Development Gains Tax of 1974 taxed all development gains (including those recouped as rents) at a higher rate than all other capital gains. And although not part of the formal legal system, there are the contributions made on development permissions by formal or informal planning agreements.[64]

Of another kind are the payment of housing grants for improvements under the General Improvement Area and Housing Action Area schemes which are paid in respect of improvements to houses in selected areas (see section 5.4).

Under this heading can also be included the financial arrangements of the new towns since these have influenced their development (see section 4.4).[65]

5.5 SOME IMPEDIMENTS TO IMPLEMENTATION IN BRITISH LAND POLICY PRIOR TO THE COMMUNITY LAND SCHEME

The British land policies reviewed in this chapter are impressive and contribute greatly to the orderly implementation of urban and regional plans. But in the general debate on the issue in the early 1970s it was commonly recognised that they had serious weaknesses in effectiveness (see section 1.1): that is, what we have called *impediments to implementation*. It was this which led to the recognition by major political parties in Britain that some reform was needed, leading to the measures initiated by the Conservative administration in 1973 and the Labour administration in 1975–6.

We introduce these measures in Chapter 6, but before doing so, and in order to be able to assess the effectiveness of the new community land legislation, it is useful here to summarise the impediments to implementation as they have emerged from the previous sections. This review is necessarily personal[66] since, while there has been much debate, there is no authoritative description or analysis to which all would agree.

In presenting the impediments we could pursue the categorisation of land policy measures used in describing the current situation (section 5.4). But it would seem more helpful to do so by reference to inadequacies in the policies under the two major headings of (i) allocation of resources, i.e. the manner in which the planning and development process has worked, and (ii) distribution of resources, i.e. the manner in which the resulting land revenues have been distributed between individual landowners on the one hand and landowners as a whole and the community. In doing so we recognise that the two cannot be kept distinct but are intertwined; for example, if an authority needs to pay too high a price in buying land for schools, and thus distributes resources from the public to the private sector, this feeds back into the location of the school sites on the cheaper land, i.e. to allocation.

Development control as the cornerstone of 'negative planning' has come under considerable criticism from both the developers who find it time-consuming and frustrating (and so adding to the costs of development) and planners who find it ineffective for implementation.[67] Thus it is necessary to improve performance in this area. The Dobry Report[68] is only a preliminary one since it was concerned more with the machinery than the substance of control. Thus further inquiry is needed which would consider and make recommendations on development control in the context of positive planned development: to clarify the uncertainty of recent years which has grown up around such matters as the objectives of development control, the considerations which are and are not appropriate to planning in the Town and Country Planning Acts, the appropriateness and use of 'planning gain' and the appropriate reflection of public involvement in development issues.[69]

Coming back to the planners' criticism, development control has been inadequate to ensure the phasing and priorities of development according to the policies of the authorities. These have largely been dictated by the decisions of the landlords and developers, typically based on profitability in the private sector under the logic of development economics (section 3.5) and not by the planning authorities having regard to the interests of the community as a whole.

On another aspect, land assembly for suitable development units (in size, boundary, location, etc.) has been inefficient; it does not result in land being made available at the right time, in the right place and at the right price, when 'right' is considered from the community viewpoint and not just in terms of the working of the land market. There has been in consequence a waste of time, energy, money and other scarce resources by both planners and developers trying to steer the market. This situation has been overcome to a degree where the land has first passed into the ownership of the local authority, which is then able to use its powers of control upon sale, or lease or partnership. But even here there is no full solution, since it is the developer and financier who call the basic tune on the same criteria as those just mentioned. The results are seen in our town-centre redevelopment projects, with their emphasis on commercial development.

Accordingly, there have been gaps between views of the authorities as to orderly and controlled development in the town (and the schemes and budgets for infrastructure development in association) and the realities as seen by the landowners, developers and consumers in the town. Thus there has been pressure to release land for development which has not been allocated in the plans, in both quantity and location, out of accord with local planning policies. Such pressures have been accentuated in times of inflation of land prices, as part of the speculative fever of the market; the speculative dealing in land in effect withdrew some from supply, leading to the argument that there was a shortage of land which was inflating house prices, and therefore justifying allocation of more land.

The attempts by the planning authorities to bridge this gap in the interests of the orderly planning of their areas has not in general been backed by central government, despite formal approval of plans by the relevant ministers. This has flowed from the continued reluctance of government since development plans were introduced to form their own development strategies and programmes, and to underwrite the orderly phasing of local authority development programmes based on local plans, in terms of central government sanctions for borrowing, grants, approvals of programmes, and so on.

5.5.1   DISTRIBUTION

Planning concentrates development value into selected areas and selected projects. However, with the abandonment of the financial provisions of the 1947 Town and Country Planning Act in 1952, and the absence of any replacement beyond the short-lived Land Commission Act, 1967 (see section 5.3), rising development values flowed to the pockets of landowners and developers (both public and private) and not by way of betterment to the community as a whole, except through general taxation on both income and capital gains. Since such taxation has not absorbed the whole of the rise in land values, planning permissions have created windfalls for some and denied fortunes to others, in what to landowners as a whole is quite an arbitrary fashion. This has led to tension between the landowners and pressure on the planning system (section 4.5).

The denied landowner feels aggrieved not only in being denied the windfall but for other reasons as well. For one thing, he cannot get adequate compensation for the denial of the permission. For another, on compulsory purchase he is paid compensation which is less than the 'value to him', since market value and disturbance costs (the general rule) assume he is a willing seller and fail to recognise that he is not; he would often need to be paid more than the market value to induce him to go voluntarily. Furthermore, he suffers from delay in either fighting the refusal of permission or fighting the compulsory purchase order, all of which adds to his costs.

The authority which is denied betterment also feels aggrieved, for a variety of reasons. For one thing, while the rise in land values has gone to sectoral pockets, the financial burdens of providing the social overheads and infrastructure, without which the land value rise could not be reaped, have fallen on local and central government. Since these costs have been met through local and central taxation, they have been spread throughout the whole community to provide windfalls for the few.

For another, although the social overhead and infrastructure development has contributed towards the boosting of land values for those obtaining planning permission, the land costs to authorities for the provision of such facilities has been at market values. And since such market values have been increased by the very grants or expected grants of the planning permissions, and the provision or expected provision of the social overhead and infrastructure itself, the authorities are in a sense paying twice over. And given the limitations in public-sector budgets, it follows that in the attempt to economise on land costs authorities are forced to provide their facilities in poorer locations and on poorer land than would otherwise be desirable or not provide them at all. This again has contributed to the distortion of local authority planning and programming of land release.

All that has been said above about high prices being paid by public authorities is exacerbated by another consideration. Where an authority buys land for a public purpose (roads, schools, etc.), it normally, by definition, can expect a financial loss on the provision of public goods. But the compensation code fails to recognise this; on the whole it determines the compulsory purchase price on the basis of the use which would have been permitted had the local authority not wished to buy. Broadly speaking, this is the opportunity cost in the private sector. This is a practicable formula for valuation but hardly an equitable formula in terms of value in after use. Thus again there is price inflation for public purchases.

This necessity to buy land at market prices has a particular bite where the purchase is for the redevelopment of obsolete property. Here the market value of the land for the new use is the higher of two figures: the value of the property as it stands, or the value of the site if cleared of buildings. Although the latter could be higher for commercial uses, the former tends to be higher in the generality of obsolete property, including housing. Accordingly, the authorities are faced with a heavy land purchase price for clearing away property which is socially regarded as obsolete.[70] Such costs tend to be high even where there is no attraction in the market for the land in question, as in the inner urban areas, simply because there is a threshold related to historical cost below which prices tend not to go.[71]

5.6   THE COMPENSATION–BETTERMENT ISSUE

In our review above of British planned development and land policy (Chapters 4 and 5) we have touched many times on the financial implications and the related issues which have been discussed ever since planning was initiated at the beginning of this century: the degree of financial adjustment (if any) which should be made between government and landowners consequent upon the shift of development values resulting from planning (the compensation–betterment problem). So central is it that at this point we present an overall account.

Whereas compensation and betterment arose prior to statutory planning activities (for example, compensation in relation to the building of railways in the nineteenth century and betterment in relation to the provision of sea-defence works), they became of particular importance in relation to planning where the effects are more palpable and more easily observed and traced.[73]

We have seen (section 3.7) that without land-use planning land has certain potential uses dictated by market forces and that these uses lead to a certain structure of land values. When land-use planning is introduced, it operates by controlling or stimulating the potential use of land and will therefore influence the value of particular plots of land. Thus the introduction of planning measures will result in either a diminution or enhancement of current use and development value which may well, in the minds of the owners, seem completely arbitrary.

The central question is then posed: to whom should increases in land value accrue under each of these circumstances, and who should forfeit the losses? Such questions bring in others which, taken together, relate to the economic discussions above on the ethics of land rent, the concept of land ownership and the facilitating of plan implementation.

The issue has two dimensions which, though related, are separable. First, there are the actual effects on land value of implementation of projects or plans by authorities: how they are distributed in time, in geographical location and in amount. Second, there are the rights of the individual landowner as against the state, or other owners, and vice versa, in relation to compensation and betterment.

(It is useful at this point to compare our treatment, under the familiar British title of 'compensation–betterment', with another under the less staid name of 'windfalls for wipeouts'.[74] A 'windfall', broadly conceived, is an increase in property value caused by public action; a 'wipeout' is an analogous decrease. The windfall is equated with *betterment* and the wipeout with *worsenment*. As defined, these terms relate to the first of the two dimensions in compensation and betterment described above: the actual effects on land value of plan or project implementation by government, and also as between private landowners. But despite the definition the treatment (in great richness of detail) goes well beyond this into the second of our dimensions: the rights of the individual landowner as against the state or other owners (despite the reference to *public action* and *vice versa*) under various legal and institutional arrangements. Here the windfall relates to the possibilities of recapture of some of the increases in land value to those who cause them other than the owner; and the wipeout to measures for mitigation of the loss.)

Clearly the central question of the compensation–betterment issue had its roots in the first dimension, on the effects of planning on land value. But the heat and controversy come from the second, from the societal view of the rights of the various bodies involved. Whereas the former dimension is international in character, the latter is very national, since countries differ enormously in their attitudes in this respect, as also do the powers of the different classes in the country. Thus the diminution and enhancement of values resulting from planning has attracted rights to compensation and betterment which are circumscribed in individual countries according to codes relating to the rights of landowners as against the rights of the community. We now discuss these dimensions in turn.

Coming back to the first dimension, we have seen that the market value of land is the present value of the expected future stream of rents accruing to that land; and that the magnitude of this stream is a function of the actual and expected uses of the land, the demand function and the suitability of the land for these uses, i.e. the supply functions (section 3.5). It follows that a whole spectrum of causes may result in changes in the value of land. In the long run the overall economic, social and demographic evolution of a country or area will bring pressures to bear on land which will dictate the trend in land values. These will be subject to short-run cyclical fluctuations which may occur over a wide area or a small one. At the most local, the actions of one individual or firm may alter the value of surrounding, adjacent land. For example, the building of a factory may enhance values in the area because associated activities wish to congregate around the new works; or it may reduce values by creating pollution, cutting off light, and so on.

The influence of the community via the state through all these channels is fundamental. The existence of a state and the services it provides enables a people to multiply and prosper, so enhancing land value. For example, a government's fiscal policy (say, in relation to the balance of payments or inflation) could raise the overall demand function for land, and its regional policy could stimulate employment where it would not have occurred otherwise. The fact that a state can do the reverse only by disastrous policies emphasises the point.

More direct still, however, are those government actions related to land use. General legal restrictions may be imposed on the use of land: 'For the last hundred years owners of property have been compelled ... to comply with certain requirements regarding their property such, for example, as maintaining or improving its sanitary equipment, observing certain standards of construction, providing adequate air space around building.'[75] The British land-use planning system is an extension of these legal restrictions, a major extension certainly. Then the public sector may undertake development itself, for example the creation of infrastructure and the servicing of land, which will have a direct effect on the potential use of surrounding land, on the suitability of the land for these uses, and thus on its value.

This raises the second dimension: given these influences, what should be the financial adjustments between landowners and the state.

First, while a landowner would accept a fall in his expectations on land value were it to come from an economic slump (as an act of God), he will not do so from government and claims inequity among landowners. From the viewpoint of the individual landowner, it will seem completely arbitrary that his land is, say, not allocated for commercial uses while his neighbour's is, and that, as a result, he loses substantially while his neighbour is made rich. Again, it is completely arbitrary that a road will be built which will serve the land of others and not his.

But as against this, the same landowner, as taxpayer, would consider it inequitable that the community pay over the odds for land which is not his. This could arise when a local authority or public agency purchases land for public development, such as a new town. If this will have the effect of increasing the price of land in the vicinity, and this effect will operate as soon as the possibility becomes known, perhaps substantially before the land is bought, the public body, in paying the full market price for land, will in effect pay for values it will be creating, and which only it can create.[76]

Last, there is the matter of the general distribution of wealth. As a nation develops and its population, infrastructure and economy grow, the pressures on the national stock of land will increase. Since this stock cannot be increased, the price of land will tend to increase the real wealth of the landowning class, despite the fact that the costs of production of the 'raw land' are nil, the real costs being in infrastructure, mostly provided by the public purse. Is it right that a growing amount of a nation's wealth be channelled into the pockets of the landowners simply due to their ownership rights and despite the fact that strictly as landowners they have not contributed towards the stock of national wealth? As landowners they attract no economic rent because of their own productive efforts (except in so far as they act as land improvers or developers) but only as expropriators of profits made by others which their monopoly power (for that location) allows them to extract.[77]

The answer to the question 'Is it *right*?' has been answered trenchantly in the negative over the centuries. In this group was the young Winston Churchill in the early half of the century:

> Fancy comparing these healthy processes with the enrichment which comes to the landlord who happens to own a plot of land on the outskirts or at the centre of our great cities, who watches the busy population round him making the city larger, richer, more convenient, more famous every day and all the while sits still and does nothing. The roads are made, the streets are made, the railway services are improved, electric light turns night into day, electric trains glide to and fro, water is brought from reservoirs a hundred miles off in the mountains, and all the while the landlord sits still.

There has also been support for the view from certain economists, resulting in recommendations for the special taxation of land. In the eighteenth century Adam Smith proposed a tax on ground rents,[78] and a century later J. S. Mill advocated a system of taxing future rent increases 'to claim for the benefit of the State the interception of taxation for future increases in the value of land'.[79] Probably the most famous advocate of this school of thought is Henry George, who proposed a tax on rising land values, indeed a single tax since it would replace all others.[80] Arguments along these lines still continue today.

However, the introduction of such taxation raises related problems. First, there are the equity effects of moving into land taxation or increasing the rate drastically:

> Whatever the 'unearned component' of the present value of land, it is not necessarily in the hands of those who have received the 'unearned increments'; many present owners have paid full value for their investments. Thus, heavy taxation of site values, which appropriate a large part of the value of land, is, in

part at least, an unjustifiable discrimination against investors who happen to have put their funds in land rather than in other forms of wealth.[81]

One way to reduce this problem is to bring in (or increase) land taxation gradually, as was done in Pittsburgh, where twelve years was taken to introduce the full scheme.

Then there is the valuation problem whereby it

is difficult to distinguish in practice between the enhancement in value due to betterment proper and that due to more general causes; and between that part of the enhancement which is due to the manner in which a landowner or developer has used or created his opportunities, and that solely due to community influences and which he passively receives.[82]

This creates problems in maintaining the activity of the private sector in development. The very basis of the mixed economy is that it is accepted that both the public and the private sectors have a role to play. However, the private sector is essentially motivated by profit; thus to charge a rate of betterment which denies entrepreneurial reward is to reduce drastically the incentives to the private sector to take part in development. Thus, unless the public sector takes over a major role, the land and development market may be expected to dry up.

Thus land-use planning raises problems in respect of land values whether or not the state attempts to make appropriate financial adjustments. The resolution of the issue is of fundamental importance to the implementation of plans, and indeed holds a central place in any aspect of wider development policy which touches on land. Related to this is the fact that, since land and land ownership are such central features of daily life, there is wide public concern about the way in which the issue is resolved.

This is obviously important for plan implementation; unacceptable measures can kill planning stone dead. This can be seen as one of the frictional costs of implementation that will feed back, as we saw above (section 2.8), into the moulding of the plan proposals themselves.

5.7   TOWARDS CRITERIA FOR NEEDED CHANGES IN LAND POLICY

Having outlined the impediments to plan implementation existing in British land policy prior to the community land scheme, we now go on to generalise on some criteria for change in such land policy to make it more effective.

5.7.1   NEED FOR COLLABORATION BETWEEN PRIVATE AND PUBLIC ENTERPRISE

Local authorities plan for development but their ability to directly carry out all development is limited; in a mixed economy they must share this role with the private sector. Their behaviour is thus critical to the relationship between the aims of planning policy and development; authorities must therefore be involved in development in the workings of the process, in the private as well as in the public sector. We now present some relevant considerations which authorities need to bear in mind.

Private enterprise has much to offer in the way of skills, flexibility, finance, ability to take risks, etc., all of which are required if the development process is to function smoothly. But in offering this service it is essentially and necessarily motivated by the possibility of profits (section 3.5). Thus it does not, of its own free will, take account of the full range of the social costs of its actions which loom large in development. A failure to consider these externalities results in a misallocation of resources which is not in society's interest. It also exacerbates the financial situation of local authorities where it is they who have to take remedial action and so bear the social costs.

At present the public sector can only influence private development on a large scale through its powers of control. Despite its positive elements, development control being essentially negative, it can reduce the rate of a particular type of development when it is too high but it cannot increase it if it is too low. Indeed, it cannot secure any particular kind of development from the private sector, outside the limited sphere of 'planning-gain' agreements, and the like. It may have the effect of relocating development to socially more desirable places but this is largely a process of chance. It cannot actually initiate development but can only give developers an indication of where certain applications are likely to be accepted. In relation to a particular plan control alone cannot ensure that the development factors (land, finance, labour, expertise, etc.) are brought together at a time and in the quantities envisaged in the plan. This is especially serious at a time of economic depression and low development activity when encouragement is needed. Indeed, at such times not only does private development follow the cycles in the economy generally, but these cycles tend to be magnified in the development market. These fluctuations lead to cyclical unemployment, price variations and speculation in land.

Where there is the need for greater than negative control, one answer is in some form of alliance between the public and private sectors, which we have called 'partnerships' above (section 4.2.5). However, there are difficulties in such an alliance. The motivating forces of the two parties are fundamentally different – the social interest as against profit – and this often leads to an uneasy relationship. This is illustrated by the frequent claims of each party that it is not understood by the other. Thus the public sector is said not to understand the speed and swift decision-taking which is necessary if profits are to be realised, and to exhibit entrenched political views, often against the private sector. On the other side of the coin, the private sector is said not to understand the need for local authorities to remain accountable to the public, and professional officers to elected lay members, including inviting tenders from competing developers.

One reason for such partnerships is to allow the community a share in the profits from development, from which it follows that the developer's gain will be less than if he were to carry out the development completely alone. However, pressure for too great a share can dissuade the private sector from participating in development at all; some would argue that the profit is already taken up by the various capital gains taxes. If the private sector does have a role to play in development, the maintenance of an adequate role of profit is necessary. It is difficult to say whether the failure of some past land policies which restricted these profits was due to the restriction *per se* or to forecasts that the restrictions would be lifted. It is therefore difficult to say exactly what continuing profit rate is necessary to make the private sector participate. Another aspect of this is that long-term investment from the financial institutions has to be forthcoming for private development and this requires as much certainty as possible, both in terms of legislation and local and central government policies.

All these considerations enter into the debate as to whether the local authority system could provide all the necessary development ingredients if it were given the powers and the financial freedom; or whether the basic structure and *raison d'être* of local authorities, their committee structure and public accountability, militates against it. Where the authorities think they can displace the private sector, they must recognise the many problems associated with private-sector development.

5.7.2   INSTITUTIONAL CONSTRAINTS

We turn now to the constraints on land policy arising from such things as the availability of professional and political skills in administration and legal and institutional practicalities.

For land policy to be administratively efficient it must be within the capability of central and local government. Certain parts of the government machinery are overstretched, including those professionals who deal with valuation, compulsory purchase and the management of the public estate, precisely because our established land policies are over-complex in administration. A system which would conserve administrative resources should be simple, understandable and enforceable; it should certainly not require the impossible from any discipline, as currently demanded from valuers. There is thus strong reason for not burdening government with major new tasks connected with planning. There is a greater chance of success if existing institutions are used than if new bodies without managerial experience are especially created to handle the new system.

Additionally, such new institutions are particularly exposed to abandonment by a following government if they are *ad hoc* rather than all-purpose. This is in line with the short-sighted approach to the political implications of land policy. Investments in development and the development itself are, by their very nature, long-term operations and work within a long-term perspective.

Expectations of future land policy measures are just as important as current land policy in influencing the development process. For this reason a situation in which land policy swings, like a pendulum, between successive governments of different hue can create havoc in orderly development. A land policy must therefore command broad political support, and not only at the level of national government; since local authorities are the private agents in plan implementation, their support is fundamental.

This aspect is closely related to that of the difficulties created by a lack of co-operation between various public bodies. For plan implementation to function smoothly, it is essential that there be full co-operation within the public sector, both vertically between different levels of local and national government and horizontally at each level. All levels of government contribute towards implementation and the conflicts between these levels may seriously hamper implementation. Time and again this problem crops up. Two-tier planning authorities provide well-known examples, the relationships between the different parties being highly complex and often difficult, both politically and professionally. In many urban areas a great deal of land is owned by the public sector in one guise or another, yet the co-operation between many of them is often poor. Within local authorities the implementation process is under the jurisdiction of a variety of committees, and, even here, lack of co-ordination can severely impede implementation.

5.7.3 EQUITY

In concluding our discussion above on compensation–betterment we stressed the importance of resolving the issue (who gets what of the rise in land value) for land and development policy. The resolution must clearly be on some concept of social justice which is acceptable to the community.

Just what is acceptable in this context is the stuff of the ongoing debate, which we have briefly reviewed about (sections 5.2 and 5.3). There is as yet no agreement.

No suggestion is provided here, for it is only Parliament that can decide as between all the options, based on our long experience since the days of Uthwatt (see section 5.2.3). But to provide an acceptable answer there must be evolved in the first instance some criteria and objectives for land policy, rather than just solutions. This in turn requires consideration to such broadly ranging questions as the following:

1   Should all betterment go to the community, so leaving individuals and organisations in the private sector without the fruits of their enterprise, while reserving for the whole community all the benefits which flow from public authority decisions over land use? Or should this thesis, with its distinguished proponents of the past (see section 5.6), be set aside on the more recent argument that, since the community is not in fact a party to any transaction in the market (unless the government is actually buying interest in land), it cannot *claim* to create land value by, for example, the provision of public services and the control of land use? In other words, since it is the land market where the interplay of supply and demand around the proprietary land unit expresses the price of the land (and therefore its value), the whole of that value must flow to the participants in the market process.[83] Clearly these two statements are extreme, so should not a midway course be chosen, whereby the skill and enterprise of the landowner/developer is recognised for its contribution as is the input of the community (as well as its responsibility for paying compensation for those whose land values are 'worsened')?

2   Where gain stems from the action of the local community rather than central government, should not the betterment which is appropriated be directed to that community and not central government, and furthermore be distributed equitably as between local communities?

3   Since particular land is not necessarily in the hands of those who have in the past received the unearned increments (many present owners having paid full value for their investment), would not appropriation of a large proportion be an unjustifiable discrimination against investors who happen to have put their funds in land rather than in other forms of wealth?

4   Turning to equity between landowners, if betterment does not accrue to the

community at large, should there not be full compensation of a refusal of planning permission?

5   Again on equity as between landowners, should the landowner whose land be compulsorily acquired not be made worse off than one whose land is not? At present the rules require that the valuation assumes a willing buyer and a willing seller: 'This is blatantly not so and resentment which is very undesirable is generated. Studies have indicated an extra payment of thirty per cent is necessary in residential cases to reflect the unwillingness of the seller to sell.'[84]

6   Should not land policy be equitable as between generations? This does not occur, for example, in renewal of obsolete buildings since the present 'compensation for [the] public purchase [of buildings] is in effect paid by future generations from loan charges to be levied out of rates and taxes, and not by the past generations who have enjoyed the building and used them up'.[85]

7   Finally, there is the matter of equity between landlord and occupier. Should not land policy conform to the prevailing social view concerning the termination of tenure, eviction, rent levels and reviews, and so on?

5.7.4   SOME CRITERIA WHICH HAVE BEEN SUGGESTED

In discussing equity in the previous section we stressed the importance of having some criteria or objectives as a basis not so much for decision in the first instance but for ongoing debate. We close this chapter by recalling for this purpose some which have already been put forward by individuals or groups as a basis for their own views. The first was the basis for a review of compensation and betterment in the mid-1960s as a lead to what should happen next:[86]

Allocation
1   Since we live in a mixed economy which relies on the private and public investment in land, we must not stultify the forces which can be subsumed under the 'economics of development'.

2   But since land planning is vital, the rules must not make it impossible to carry out planning objectives.

3   Since resources should be conserved, any system should not waste time and skilled manpower. To this end the system needs to be administratively simple, understandable, enforceable and not require the impossible of valuers.

4   Any system should not result in a massive and rapid transfer of assets from the private to the public sector if this were to disturb the economy.

Distribution
5   Where a landowner is denied development, or his development is controlled, he clearly wants to know (i) that landowners are being treated uniformly, and (ii) the principles on which compensation is paid or denied.

6   Where land is bought for public purposes, i.e. for public use or for development initiated by a public authority, the price should be 'fair' to the community in that it should not pay one landowner for value which the public purchase will shift to another site.

7   Where land remains in private hands and its value is increased by public action, including a planning permission, there should be some means of collecting betterment.

8   Where the landowner enjoys 'unearned increment' even without specific public action, there should be some way of the community sharing the product.

The second group represents a more recent statement on what would comprise a satisfactory solution from alternatives:[87]

1   Permanent.
2   Acceptable.
3   A constant and continuing stimulus to investment and development in land. Not conducive to a stultification of the property market.
4   Administratively simple, understandable, enforceable, and not requiring the impossible of valuers.
5   Designed to avoid arbitrariness in accuracy or in equity.
6   Formulated so as to conform with the primary fiscal canons of feasibility, i.e. economic neutrality and distribution of equity.
7   Drawn up to facilitate planning machinery.
8   Intended to promote comprehensive development and redevelopment.
9   Conceived so as to enhance good public and private estate management.
10 Generally prepared to ensure more effective control of land.

Third, as a stimulus to what might be done for Britain, as a latter-day Uthwatt, comes the impressive statement of objectives of a National Land Policy for Australia which, as indicated above (section 1.3), grew out of an inquiry into land tenures:[88]

Efficiency
More specific criteria may be identified within these broad categories. In so far as efficiency is concerned, the following seem to be important:

1   Land policy must be geared to the requirements of community growth by helping to ensure that land is made available where and when it is wanted, for the purposes for which it is wanted, at a price which reflects its value in use and thereby excludes any speculative element.
2   Because unfettered development has proved so destructive of environmental and aesthetic qualities, development must be viewed not as an end in itself but as a means of achieving more fundamental goals of society, including improvements in the quality of urban living and in social relationships. Land development, use and redevelopment must therefore be controlled in the public interest.
3   Land policy must support and not conflict with other urban policies directed towards accommodating growth and improving living conditions in the cities.
4   Land policy must encourage and not stifle productive enterprise. But initiatives for development and redevelopment must depend on the prospect of gains from more efficient land use and not on gains which accrue to the private sector from permitted changes in land use.
5   Decisions on land use must be taken, in both the private and public sectors of the economy, with full regard to their social consequences, and not merely by

reference to their effects on the profitability of individual landholders or the budgets of public authorities.

6   Land policy must treat land as a scarce resource by ensuring that it is used effectively and not held idle for purposes of speculative gain. Society must insist that land is used as a productive asset and not as a store of value. Buying and selling land for purely speculative reasons does not serve any useful social purpose and is inimical to enterprise.

7   Land must be made available for any given purpose at a minimal cost in terms of labour and other resources. This means that costs of administering land policies must be kept as low as possible, consistent with the achievement of the aims of those policies, and more generally that policies must be administratively feasible.

8   The use of the market as a resource-allocating device must be reconciled with the application of social controls intended as far as possible to prevent the market from being exploited or manipulated by sectional interests.

9   Land policies cannot meet the efficiency criterion unless they are politically acceptable. Although the major political parties may have different philosophies and seek different goals, a particular policy must not evoke so much opposition as to lead to its eventual repeal. Nothing is so wasteful of resources as an attempt to impose a policy which, because it is directed towards sectional or short-term political goals, contains within itself the seeds of its own destruction.

Equity

1   A general objective must be to balance the rights and obligations of different individuals and groups in relation to land use. This involves recognition of the fact that private rights and obligations over land need to be set against those of neighbours and of the community generally.

2   Also of overriding importance is the need for land policy to contribute towards the task of providing all members of the community with acceptable standards of housing on terms which are both just and within their capacity to pay. Given the evident propensity for home ownership on the part of most Australians, this involves making land available for residential purposes at prices which on the one hand reflect the costs to society of providing the land for those purposes, and on the other hand have regard to levels of income and wealth and hence capacity to pay. By reason of social or economic disability, some members of the community will be unable to meet the full costs of land use and home ownership. Special provision must be made for these people, for example through subsidised government housing.

3   The equitable distribution of land requires appropriate provision of land for purposes of social housing, public services generally and the preservation and improvement of the public domain.

4   Equitable arrangements for the distribution of land must also extend to commercial, industrial and non-profit-making organisations. In each of these user categories the aim must be to make the price of land reflect its social cost in terms of the resources needed to justify its continuing use for the purpose in question. But the price must not reflect imperfections in the market arising from such factors as inadequate supplies relative to need, excessive demands generated by an over-abundant money supply, or speculative pressures arising from expectations about future price increases.

5   Inflationary increases in land prices must be minimised. Government policy must seek to stabilise land prices, because rising prices benefit some members of the community at the expense of others, for example existing landowners at the expense of potential landowners or tenants, and speculators at the expense of land users. There is a problem in equity even if the gains from rising prices are distributed by chance, but the problem is accentuated if speculators are able to manipulate the land market in their own interests, or if, because of widespread buying by persons seeking a hedge against inflation, a classical land boom develops which is followed by a collapse in prices.

6   Land policy must be directed towards ensuring that landholders are restricted to gains from the development or use of land and are excluded from gains associated merely with the passive holding of land. This involves action to leave individuals and organisations in the private sector with the fruits of their enterprise, while reserving for the whole community the benefits which flow from public authority decisions over land use.

5.7.5   CONCLUSIONS AND PRELIMINARY

From section 5.7 it has been seen how varied are the possible criteria for land policies and thus the consequential measures. These have been presented in exemplification of criteria that could be adopted in the political process, where the essential decisions are taken on land policy, with the aid of professional analysis.

From this point we go on to make our own suggestions for land policy reform in Britain. In so doing we will be adopting our own criteria. We will present their basis as explicitly as we can.

REFERENCES: CHAPTER 5

 1   McAuslan (1975, pp. 48–65).
 2   Ibid, pp. 34–9, and Scarman (1974, p. 53).
 3   Garner (1956).
 4   Scarman (1974, p. 53).
 5   Jowell (1977a), and Scarman (1974, pp. 59–60).
 6   Mishan (1967).
 7   Ministry of Works and Planning (1942b, p. 7).
 8   The Town and Country Planning Act, 1943.
 9   Royal Commission on the Distribution of the Industrial Population (1939).
10   Ibid, para. 248.
11   Coal Industry Nationalisation Act of 1946.
12   For a detailed account, see Cullingworth (1975, vol. I).
13   House of Lords, *Hansard*, vol. 118, 26 February 1941, cols. 507–8 'Post-war Planning'.
14   See Ministry of Works and Planning (1942b, pp. 10–16).
15   See ibid.
16   See ibid.
17   See ibid.
18   *France Fenwick & Co.* v. *The King (1927)*, IKB 458, quoted in Ministry of Works and Planning (1942b).
19   See Ministry of Works and Planning (1942b, p. 57).
20   Ibid, pp. 29, 135–54.
21   See ibid, ch. 10.
22   *The Times*, 1 October 1973.
23   Ministry of Works and Planning (1942b, ch. 10).
24   See Cullingworth (1975).

25 Ministry of Town and Country Planning Act, 1943; Town and Country Planning (Interim Development) (Scotland) Act, 1943; Town and Country Planning Act, 1944.
26 House of Lords, *Hansard*, vol. 118, 26 February 1941, cols. 507–8 'Post-war Planning'.
27 The final figure was £387 million. See *Report on Work of the Central Land Board 1958–59* (1959).
28 Ministry of Works and Planning (1942b).
29 Committee of Public Accounts (1951, Q. 6595 ff.), and House of Commons (1950, para. 32).
30 Sharp (1969, p. 143).
31 *Earl Fitzwilliam and Wentworth Estates* v. *Ministry of Housing and Local Government* (1952).
32 Ministry of Town and Country Planning (1951).
33 Cullingworth, vol. 4 (forthcoming).
34 See, for example, Chartered Auctioneers and Estate Agents Institute (1968).
35 For a general account, see Purdue (1977, ch. 4), and McAuslan (1975).
36 These adjectives refer to different kinds of brief with ascending order of selectivity of detail.
37 Town and Country Planning Act of 1971, section 29.
38 Ministry of Town and Country Planning (1949).
39 DoE (1973e).
40 Ministry of Housing and Local Government (1968).
41 McAuslan (1975, pp. 485 ff.)
42 DoE (1975g).
43 Royal Town Planning Institute (1978a).
44 Town and Country Planning Act of 1971, section 29.
45 Ministry of Housing and Local Government (1968).
46 Town and Country Planning Act of 1971.
47 Local Government Act of 1972.
48 Housing Act of 1974.
49 Jowell (1977a).
50 Ibid.
51 Scarman (1974).
52 For a general account, see McAuslan (1975).
53 Ibid, pp. 684 ff.
54 Craig (1964, p. 181).
55 Ibid, p. 181.
56 Ministry of Works and Planning (1942b).
57 Hagman (1971, pp. 323–8).
58 Garner (1956).
59 The following relies on Lichfield (1956, ch. 15).
60 Schaffer (1970).
61 Ibid, p. 80.
62 See DoE (1972b), DoE (1975a), and Lichfield (1976c).
63 Schaffer (1970).
64 Wilks (1974).
65 Jowell (1977a).
66 Lichfield and Wendt (1969).
67 Lichfield (1975a).
68 Royal Town Planning Institute (1978a).
69 DoE (1975a).
70 For an explanation of this reasoning, see Royal Town Planning Institute (1978a), and Lichfield (1979b).
71 Lichfield (1963).
72 Royal Town Planning Institute (1978b).
73 See Lichfield (1964a).
74 Parker (1965).
75 Hagman and Misczynski (1978, ch. 1).
76 Telling (1973).
77 Neutze (1973, p. 21).
78 Mill (1970).
79 Smith (1910).
80 Mill (1970).
81 George (1931).
82 Netzer (1966, p. 259).

83   Lichfield (1958a, p. 332).
84   Denman (1978, pp. 86–9).
85   Schaffer (1970).
86   Lichfield (1975a).
87   Lichfield (1964a).
88   Ratcliffe (1976, pp. 46–7).
89   Commission of Inquiry into Land Tenures (1976).

Chapter 6

The Community Land Scheme

6.1 THE POLITICAL-ECONOMIC CONTEXT

The objectives of the community land legislation (Community Land Act, 1975, and Development Land Tax Act, 1976) were given in the preceding White Paper:

(a) to enable the community to control the development of land in accordance with its needs and priorities; and
(b) to restore to the community the increase in value of land arising from its efforts.[1]

The first aim, which comes within the orbit of 'implementation of plans' (see Chapter 2), arose out of the difficulties in achieving 'positive planning' (see Chapter 5). The second aim was born of the need to do something in the face of mounting public pressure in relation to the rocketing land and property prices of the late 1960s and early 1970s, associated with the absence of any specific means of channelling some part of this increase into the public purse, other than through general taxation (see section 5.4.4).

The previous Conservative government had tackled the second aim in its own way: by strengthening capital gains tax to cover increases in land value during the 1960s; and by the stringent Development Gains Act foreshadowed in December 1973 (on all gains on sale or development of land with planning permission at the individual or corporate (not capital gains) tax rate) and introduced in the Finance Bill, 1974. But as we saw in Chapter 5, it was tackled somewhat differently by the Labour administration of 1974, which was the third attempt since 1947 to deal with these problems along its own ideological lines.[2]

But while the political programme on community land was predictable from Labour policy, what was not predictable was the complete change in the economy in general, and the land market in particular, in 1973–4, just about the time of the introduction of the legislation. During the early 1970s, when the scheme was maturing in Labour party circles, there was a phenomenal boom and inflation in land and property prices at a rate not known in this country since the 1890s.[3] In the two years between 1971 and 1973 owner-occupied dwelling prices increased by 80 per cent, house-building land prices by 160 per cent and commercial offices by 250 per cent. The only exception to this trend in the same period was the prices for industrial premises, which rose by only 30 per cent.[4] Concurrently there was a general growth in gains from development, improvement or changes in use.[5] Their size gave substantial impetus to any proposals for a new land policy, since it was generally accepted, including in Conservative party circles, that some at least of these development gains justly belonged to the community.

However, the downturn in the years 1973–4 saw a falling-off in real growth, and therefore in real incomes and demands; it saw rising unemployment, which again undercut demand; it saw inflation, which raised building costs to unmanageable levels; it saw rising interest rates, which made borrowing very expensive; and so on.[6] This undermined the economic basis of development, in particular that kind of development on which the development companies were concentrating, the commercial (mostly shops and offices).

An associated feature was the collapse of the property development companies and secondary banks. This occurred not simply because of the downturn in the economy (which could simply have led to a cessation of development pending better times) but because they had over-extended themselves when faced with mounting interest charges on the one hand and reduced revenues on the other, owing to the slackening of expected growth in revenues and the sudden introduction of the development gains tax.

All these factors had direct repercussions on financial institutions. On the one hand they found themselves, through foreclosures, with huge amounts of property from the companies which could not carry on; this was unprecedented for them not only in terms of the vast supply but in terms of the management role for which they were not equipped. On the other hand, despite the large supply of investment funds available, they lost enthusiasm for property development, both because of the lack of confidence in the former borrowers who had crumbled and because new developments were not attractive in terms of security and yield because of the economic downturn. Thus they were forced to look to other forms of investment.

But the supply of money for development was not to be made up from the public sector, for quite different reasons. Because of the economic difficulties there had to be a restriction on public spending, which cut deeply into the funds which could be borrowed and made available for development by local authorities and new town development corporations. This undermined the very launching of the community land scheme, which, as originally envisaged, involved heavy investment flows from central government to local authorities for land purchase for development. And it also undermined a possibility which had only just become available to local authorities in general legislation (as opposed to local Acts): to participate directly in developments as equity shareholders in companies.

These trends were associated with a situation in terms of land prices and development values which was quite different from that which had prevailed earlier in the 1970s. The price of housing land, which had risen by 1974 to nearly four times its 1968 level, fell drastically by over 50 per cent before the end of 1975.[7] In commercial property there was a fall of some 20 per cent in values in the first half of 1974.[8] Yet the costs of development continued to increase,[9] and these factors taken together caused a dramatic decrease in the scale of development and in development gains.[10] Land often assumed negative development value; if the local authority purchased land even at current use value for, say, housing development, it might have had to accept a loss for the development to proceed.

Within these general trends the depression of the market for new commercial properties was further exacerbated after 1973, by uncertainty owing to a period of modifications, actual and proposed, in the basis of taxing development. There were the 1973 Conservative proposals for a specific development gains tax; a tax on the capital value of first lettings – which was subsequently modified; the incorporation by Labour of the Conservative proposal into the Finance Bill, 1974; followed by the anticipation and fact of the development land tax. Thus on this account an investor considering commercial development was also deterred.

6.2   THE COMMUNITY LAND SCHEME IN ENGLAND[11]

The community land scheme, introduced by the Community Land Act (CLA), (1975), and Development Land Tax Act (DLTA), 1976, is novel and complex. We first give a simple account of its provisions for England before examining its implications as land policy for plan implementation (sections 6.3–6.5). We then consider Wales, where the powers are given to a new body, the Welsh Land Authority, rather than to local authorities as in England. This enables a revealing contrast to be made simply because of this institutional difference.

6.2.1   LAND ACQUISITION

Under the CLA a local authority can purchase land expressly for the purpose of *private-sector* development.[12] But whereas initially (after the 'first appointed day') the authority has a duty to *consider* the desirability of buying land which it thinks suitable for private 'relevant' development,[13] after the 'second appointed day' (and no one knows when this will be, although ten years was foreshadowed soon after the CLA became law) the authority has a duty to *purchase all* land for private, relevant development.[14] In the period between these two days the Secretary of State can impose a duty on authorities in *certain* areas to purchase land for *certain* kinds of development.[15] The land an authority purchases will have been identified in a 'programme for community land acquisition and disposal', or have been brought to its notice through a planning application; if the authority gives permission for relevant development, it has the option to acquire the land for subsequent disposal.[16]

The local authority may purchase land for private development either compulsorily or by agreement. If it is done compulsorily, the Secretary of State may disregard objections on the grounds that the acquisition is either 'unnecessary or expedient',[17] provided the proposed land use and/or development is included in a statutory plan.

The local authority will generally only be able to purchase land for private development compulsorily if this is 'relevant development'. This covers all development save 'exempt' development (which is outside the coverage of the community land scheme) and 'excepted' development (which may only be purchased in exceptional cases).

Very broadly *exempt* development comprises:

1   development for which permission is given by a General Development Order; and
2   development for purposes of agriculture and forestry.[18]

Excepted development includes:

1   that for which permission was granted before September 1974, or development on land owned by the developer or builder on that date;
2   industrial development up to 1,500 square metres or other building up to 1,000 square metres;
3   development of single dwellings and most recreational buildings;
4   extension of a building up to 10 per cent of its original size; and
5   all changes of use.[19]

Since the CLA system is effectively limited to land for private development, the new compulsory purchase order powers give no advantage in the case of land for other local authority statutory uses since here public powers of acquisition are obviously available. Should, however, land for local authority use be purchased under the CLA system and paid for out of the community land accounts either because

1   the local authority is uncertain of the final use of the land, or
2   the land for local authority use is part of a large parcel which the authority wished to purchase for disposal to the private sector,

then the relevant local authority account has to 'purchase' the land from the community land account as soon as possible.[20]

6.2.2   LAND-ACQUISITION AND MANAGEMENT SCHEMES

The local authorities should, by 1 January 1976, have drawn up land-acquisition and management schemes.[21] These are plans of the way in which the county and district authorities in an area will organise themselves in relation to their new powers and duties. Their actual acquisitions and disposals will be governed by 'programmes of community land acquisition and disposal' and by the possibilities of 'opportunity purchases' which arise from planning applications.

These programmes will include forecasts over a five-year period which considered the needs for a period of ten years. The programmes, together with full financial statements and projections, have to be submitted to the Secretary of State annually.[22] More specifically, authorities are required to prepare 'land policy statements' which will form the basis of the 'programmes of community land acquisition and disposal' and provide them with links to the planning objectives for the area.[23] This link with planning is emphasised by the obligation on authorities, in exercising their functions under the CLA, to consider the development needs of their areas,[24] and by the fact that the streamlined compulsory purchase order powers only apply to development included in a statutory plan.[25] In the early years the Secretary of State urged local authorities to concentrate on housing land, making sure there was sufficient land available for builders and on getting the community land accounts into surplus as soon as possible.[26]

6.2.3   LOCAL AUTHORITY DEVELOPMENT

The local authority has the power to undertake residential, industrial and commercial development itself on land bought under the community land scheme. For this it has to get separate loan sanctions from central government, but, to start with, such sanctions were not forthcoming.[27]

6.2.4 LOCAL AUTHORITY DISPOSALS

Disposals of land to the private sector for commercial or industrial development will be by lease, in general up to ninety-nine years.[28] But in the case of residential development, by freehold sale, to the occupiers of the housing, with the developer operating under a building agreement from the local authority, to the developer with the condition that the developer must convey the freehold on the purchase of the house.

The terms of the disposal must have regard to the need for:

1   a reasonable balance between planning considerations and freedom of scope for builders and developers to innovate and to apply their skills and knowledge of the market so that they might meet market requirements;
2   caution over untried methods of disposal and close consultation with relevant people as experience is developed; and
3   a policy to achieve a surplus in the land accounts as soon as was reasonably possible.[29]

The choice of developer to whom the local authority leases the land is affected by 'prior negotiating rights'. If there is a prior negotiating right claim from either

1   the previous owner of the land, or
2   the applicant for planning permission, acting with the consent of the previous owners (where a planning application initiated the public purchase

the local authority must first consider disposing the land to them.[30] However, if the local authority does not think that either of these is a suitable candidate, or that their offers are not reasonable, it may choose to dispose of the land to other developers on a competitive basis.

It is accepted in the advice to local authorities that the financial needs of the developer must be fully recognised. It must be made as easy as possible for him to obtain all the necessary finance – an important point if he is taking the land on building licence and wishes to own the land and so use it as collateral for the finance. Indeed, lending institutions may require the agreement to be assigned to them from the outset and authorities are urged to be ready to accommodate this.[31]

6.2.5 FINANCING

The financing of community land will, until it is fully profitable, be kept completely apart from other local authority endeavours.[32] Land acquisition will be financed by borrowing, and all the cost of this borrowing as well as the costs of management and of land improvements will be met from the proceeds of land disposal and further borrowing. Only when it is fully profitable will it be possible to transfer funds from the 'community land accounts' to other local authority sectors. However, this is the case with only 30 per cent of the surplus: 40 per cent has got to be paid to the central government (for general purposes) and the remaining 30 per cent will be paid into a fund from which allocations will be made to local authorities whose community land accounts are still in deficit;[33] the first call on any surplus will be to pay these allocations. The remaining 30 per cent which the local authority uses for its own purpose will correspond to a capital receipt, and its use will be subject to the normal central government approval for loans.[34] For instance, the government stated that in the economic circumstances of 1976 these capital receipts would not be allowed to swell local authority capital expenditure.[35] Accordingly, the main effect would therefore be a reduction in the rates and not an increase in public services.

6.2.6   DEVELOPMENT LAND TAX

Under the Development Land Tax Act development gains are, very roughly, the difference between the market value (the net proceeds of disposal) and either the current use value or the cost of acquisition plus special additions (whichever is the highest). The Act introduces a tax of 80 per cent on realised development gains (but, until 1980, at the lower rate of 66⅔ per cent in respect of the first £150,000 of development gain in any one year).[36] The rate of tax may increase over the years until, at the 'second appointed day', it will reach 100 per cent. There is a basic exemption on the first £10,000 realised in any one financial year. The tax will be levied when there is development on the land, or when the land is sold, or when it is leased.[37] It will apply to all sales of land and to all types of development, whether relevant development or not.

In the case of transactions between private parties the tax is simple and straightforward, with revenue being used for general central government purposes. However, when a purchase is made by a local authority, it will be credited with the amount of the tax, whether it is purchased for its own purposes or for disposal to the private sector under the Community Land Act. But as indicated above (section 6.2.5), the local authority will only gain 30 per cent of the development gains compared with 100 per cent on land outside the community land scheme.[38]

6.2.7   THE SCHEME'S PROGRESS

It is clear that in the early years the public expenditure axe has limited the scale of acquisition and disposal. However, the government proposed that the loan sanction should be some £75 million in 1977–8 and £100 million per annum for the two years after that.[39] The scheme is, in effect, a statement of intent that local authorities will be expected to be more active in this field than before.

6.3   THE COMMUNITY LAND SCHEME AND PLANNED DEVELOPMENT[40]

6.3.1   THE SCHEME AS A PLANNING MEASURE

The White Paper *Land*[41] clearly saw the new measures as a contribution to planning. Whether or not the fears which were expressed were justified, that the Act could be regarded as one relating to land purchase and development as opposed to one integrated into planning,[42] the concern has resulted in clarifying the issue. This is now specific: 'these functions are placed in the context of the authority's planning responsibilities, so that the planning framework will be a key element in the identification of development land'.[43]

The instruments for linking the land-acquisition and development proposals will be land-acquisition and management schemes (LAMS)[44] and the related rolling programmes of land acquisition and disposal for five years starting in 1977–8. More specifically, authorities will need to prepare 'land policy statements' (earlier called 'planning statements') to form the basis of their rolling programmes of operations under the land scheme which will provide policy links with the planning objectives of the area and orderly framework of operation, including the background for consideration by authorities of possible acquisition of land identified by the submission of planning applications.[45]

6.3.2 THE SCHEME AS A DEVELOPMENT MEASURE

Whether or not the planning framework for land acquisition and disposal was implicit or explicit in the earlier drafts of the Bill, there has been no doubt from the outset about the role visualised for authorities in respect of their land acquisitions. This is to make the land available for development, whether by themselves or others, to assist *positive planning* and the more orderly development of their areas: in brief, to assist plan implementation. This is emphasised in the obligation of authorities to exercise these functions in relation to the development needs of their areas and in relation to facilitating builders' programmes of development.[46]

The framework for using community land for the purpose of positive development, as provided in the Act, offers a significant potential for the purpose. For instance, there are the land policy statements which will give notice of the authority's intentions, looking ahead as far as ten years in identifying land needs. The specification of the five-year rolling programmes and the statement of intentions in relation to opportunity purchases under development control should, for the first time, give some indication to those concerned with the development of where they can expect to operate on their own and where there will be a presumption to purchase by the authority. Also, the identification of the ten-year land needs and the rolling programmes can only be worked out in relation to programmes of development (be it in the public or private sector) in the area, which will be the cutting-edge of the implementation proposals for the plans.

It will therefore be possible to see which land should be developed according to the priorities of the authority, which land can be developed without the use of the powers under the Act (where builders and developers are willing to implement the plan proposals on their own land), and which land will have to be acquired. Such programming will facilitate the provision of infrastructure in the areas in a more orderly sequence than in the past, and will make possible meaningful co-ordinated programmes with the various statutory undertakings responsible for infrastructure.

6.4   THE SCHEME AND THE PRIVATE-SECTOR DEVELOPMENT PROCESS

We now turn to examine in greater detal how the private-sector development process will be affected by the Act. We do this by considering in turn the roles of the various actors involved, bearing in mind that one actor may take on more than one role, and that roles may be subdivided:

1   landowner
2   developer
3   financial institution
4   occupier
5   local authority as planner

6.4.1   THE LANDOWNER

A landowner supplies land to the development process in the hope of receiving a profit in development value. Since under the land scheme these profits may to a greater or lesser extent be expropriated by the state, the private landowner's incentive to take part in development is less than with development gains tax. However, because of the nature of his role, the landowner can be displaced without the use of economic resources simply by transferring ownership, and under the community land scheme local authorities have the power to take over the landowner's role.[47]

Indeed, come the 'second appointed day', they will have no choice, since they will have a *duty* to acquire all land for relevant development. Until then, however, the change is not so much one of powers or duties as one of intent. Local authorities will have the duty to *consider* the *desirability* of bringing land into public ownership and there is a presumption that they will use powers of compulsory purchase for planning purposes on a much larger scale.[48] These changes clearly mean that, within the limits set by finance, the local authorities should become land dealers on a more extensive scale than before.

The approach which local authorities will take to the disposal of land to the private sector is still uncertain: for example, will they dispose by competitive tender, to one particular developer or financial institution subject to the prior negotiating rights of certain parties.[49] In residential development the local authority is generally advised to remain the landowner during development, giving the builder a development brief to build the houses under licence. The house purchaser then buys the dwelling from the builder and the land from the local authority. It is, however, accepted that in the first few years the local authority may wish to sell to the builder, and this is allowed for.[50] Another method of disposal, more applicable to commercial and industrial development, is that of lease up to ninety-nine years.

This local authority land supply role in the Community Land Act may be seen as an answer to the problems encountered under the 1947 Town and Country Planning Act. One of the reasons for the failure of the earlier Act was said to be that while the 100 per cent tax on the development gains from land kept the landowner from the market, nobody else was given the power to take over his role. It is difficult to assess the importance of this fact in the drying up of development after the 1947 Act, but it certainly was one influence,[51] and the new scheme should do better. This is recognised by the Department of the Environment.[52]

6.4.2 THE DEVELOPER

In contrast to the relatively passive role of the landowner, the developer is the active supplier of know-how, experience and entrepreneurial and project-management skills. There is no easy substitute for these skills and any alternative must clearly perform no less efficiently in this regard.[53]

The White Paper *Land* saw a continuing role for the private developer. 'The Government wish to see the skills and initiative of private developers contribute to the needs of the community in a positive way',[54] and the Act requires authorities to have regard to the needs of 'developers engaged in, or wishing to engage in, the carrying out of development in the area'.[55] Thus the local authority will not take over the development process completely. The developer will not become a mere building contractor. He will remain an interpreter of market indicators, on behalf of the local authority and the financial institutions.

Thus under the land scheme the developer will continue his classical role as the manager of the development process, ensuring that the various factors of production are brought together at the right time. His role has been:[56]

1 the perception and estimation of demand;
2 the identification and securing of sites;
3 the design of accommodation;
4 the arrangement of short- and long-term finance;
5 the management and design of construction; and
6 the management, letting or selling of the completed buildings.

In addition he will continue to accept risk, of two kinds. The first is that he may not obtain suitable planning permission, and the second is that he may have misinterpreted the market situation. The first type depends crucially on the relationships between the local authority and the developer, and the landowner and developer (in the sense that he could get an option to buy dependent on planning permission). With full co-operation between the local authority/landowner, this risk is greatly diminished. The second type of risk will always remain, though it can be very much reduced by, for example, greater certainty in intervention by the authority as planners (section 3.8).

The relative importance of these two types of risk is difficult to determine, but it is possible to say that with a buoyant economy the risk of planning refusal is likely to play a major part, while market uncertainty will increase with fluctuations in the economy.

Another distinction can be made as to whether the developer is looking for a land profit as well as a developer's profit. In the former he would gain by purchasing land at low value in areas where a substantial amount of negotiation has got to be done to obtain planning permission, with success leading to profit on the land. In the latter he would concentrate on areas where planning permission is more certain, but the initial land price is probably higher, and be content to take his return from the building.

The first type of developer is going to suffer under the land scheme; profits from land are going to be taxed progressively more heavily, and following the 'second appointed day', when the local authority purchases all land for relevant development, this role will have been superseded. The second type of developer should gain from the land scheme. One of the main problems he has faced is the securing of an appropriate supply of land from the landowner at the right time and in the right place without costly land banking. By active pursuit of its landowner function under the Act, even in the first stage, an authority has the potential of overcoming this problem, as long as there is co-operation between the public and private sectors. In this sense the scheme has been called a 'developer's charter'.[57]

In the period leading up to the 'second appointed day' the developer will still have a role to play in identifying sites. However, because of reluctance to sell on the part of landowners, he may find it more difficult to engage in site assembly than before. Even if this problem can be overcome, the prospective developer will remain concerned that attempts to initiate projects will not be worth the effort while there is uncertainty about whether the local authority will or will not purchase, and therefore permit him to undertake them if planning approval is received.

Thus developers will need to look to the authority to make land available for development. From the authority's need to look ahead for ten years, to specify five-year rolling programmes and the statement of intentions in relation to opportunity purchases and development controls, those concerned with the development should for the first time get some reliable indication as to which land could be developed according to the priorities of the authority, which land can be developed without the use of powers under the Act and which will be acquired by the authority and therefore can be developed only in partnership.

However, the initial identification of sites cannot be a purely local authority role. The private sector will have a part to play in this identification, not only in initiating a planning application as a preliminary to the local authority purchase, but also (though less directly) in the formulation of land policy statements. This will arise because the local authority has got to have regard to the needs of the private development sector in its land acquisition, and the private sector will be more willing to co-operate if it is consulted on land-acquisition policy. And since the possibility of easier compulsory purchase under the land scheme is tied to statutory plans, it is probable that interaction with the private sector will need to start with the process of plan-making.

Such programming should facilitate the provision of infrastructure in the areas in a more orderly sequence than has prevailed till now and make for meaningful co-ordinated programmes with the various statutory undertakings responsible for infrastructure.

But while developers can save time and money in avoiding land-banking operations, they will have another source of delay with the local authority as land supplier. There is little chance that the land scheme as such will speed up particular developments for which application has to be made to the local authority. On receipt of an application for relevant development the local authority is required to decide whether to acquire the land within the period it is allowed for judging application. Thus, if the local authority decides not to purchase, there will be no extra delay in the development. If the local authority decides to acquire, the planning permission will be suspended for up to a year while the local authority institute purchase proceedings. If it does not make a move within this period, the scheme goes ahead as before. If it does make a move and the purchase goes through, the local authority then holds the land until it has decided who is to develop it and what the terms of the lease are to be. This process could well take longer than straight private development.

6.4.3   THE FINANCIAL INSTITUTIONS[58]

Under the community land scheme the Treasury will supply the finance for land purchases. But institutional money will be needed for the actual development. The institutions have a tradition of, and necessity for, investing in firms and companies in whom they have confidence for identifying good schemes and making profits. The development collapse could only have reinforced their caution. Thus they will be willing to lend to local authorities, who without the collaboration of developers are relatively untried in this field and are not necessarily geared up (in terms of their committee structure, officers' capabilities, etc.) for the kind of commercial decision-making which is needed in many cases.

Moreover, institutions do not favour two features of the land scheme which are potentially in conflict with their investment requirements. These are:

1   that leasehold should gradually become the normal form of tenure for new commercial properties; and
2   that when redevelopment is proposed then existing freeholds will, as a result of acquisition by the community, at best be converted into leaseholds.

The resistance is not the principle of leasehold tenure (which has been accepted in partnership schemes) but the proportion of total investment in property that this form of tenure will represent in the medium and long term, in the light of its effect on the average value of property holdings in investment portfolios.

It could thus well be that the terms on which leases are offered by authorities assume a critical importance in the light of the institutions' freedom to adopt alternative avenues of investment which may seem more attractive. Such terms must be sufficiently attractive to persuade the institutions to hold a higher proportion of leaseholds than they have been willing to do so far and to compete with the large number of freehold property investments which will continue to be available.

The other problem affecting the roles of institutional investors under the scheme is that of short-term financing. As financier for the long term, they also increasingly supply short-term funds, the interest charges being allowed to accrue and added to the capital cost covered by the long-term finance. However, in many cases, to provide short-term funds the institutions require collateral. This has often been provided against the security of the freehold site, both undeveloped and partly developed, and against work in progress. Under leasehold development this collateral is clearly less valuable.

There is a need, therefore, to find a means of providing greater security for the short-term lender, particularly where the lease is preceded by an agreement for a lease. Alternatives are:

1   A local authority guarantee – but this presents the difficulty that in the event of default there would be an inescapable commitment to public expenditure requiring loan sanction.
2   The local authority could grant a lease earlier in the building operation rather than on completion of the development – but this would have the disadvantage then in the event of the developer's failure to fulfil the terms of the lease, it is more difficult and more costly in time and effort for the authority to exercise sanctions.
3   The agreement for the lease should be assignable, with covenants of good quality, to the institution providing the short-term funds.

6.4.4   THE OCCUPIER

There is nothing in the land scheme which will lead directly to a reduction in the price of final development, despite the suggestion in the White Paper that 'those buying their first houses should share in the benefits of the scheme'.[59] House prices will still be governed by the interaction of supply and demand in the market for finished development, and development land tax is being calculated on that proposition. Thus the only way in which the scheme could lead to a reduction in price is through an expansion of supply. The control of this supply will rest more and more with the local authorities until, at the 'second appointed day', it will rest completely with them for relevant development. This will perhaps not be significant in terms of slack demand. But in terms of high demand the release of sufficient land can stimulate the supply of housing by removing the scarcity element from land prices. However, price is not everything: 'Given good planning and development, the consumer should also benefit – not by lower land prices necessarily, but through the benefits of more positive planning and public estate management'.[60]

6.4.5   LOCAL AUTHORITY AS PLANNER

From the above it is seen that while the local authority will continue its planning function, it will also have a landowner/developer function. The combination will mean a mutation in the planning function, as follows.

The community will have greater ability to control the development of land more positively in three main ways. First, as well known from the experience of new towns and comprehensive development planning, the leasehold control can augment planning controls in a positive way. Second, it will allow the public sector to initiate private development in a way it was unable to do before, by identifying and preparing land and offering it on terms which will induce development. Third, even if the local authority does not purchase the land, it will none the less have the sanction of possible purchase, be this provided for in their general planning proposals or on the exercise of their prerogative following the grant of a planning permission. This possibility of purchase cannot fail to give the local authority a stronger position at the negotiating table.

However, there are problems, and these raise one of the most contentious issues in the new scheme. Prior to the community land scheme the application of controls did not hurt the local authority financially (except indirectly through the rate-assessment base). However, planning decisions on land which the local authority owns will affect their financial return.[61] Thus, for example, the more stringent the terms of the lease, the lower will be the disposal price to the private sector. Again, the only way in which the local authority can induce a developer to carry out a development which he would not otherwise do is to offer him the lease at a reduced rent. While the community land account may still gain because of the tax rebate, it will gain less than if the local authority disposed at full value.

The other side to this coin is that too great an emphasis on financial gain on the part of the local authority will undermine planning objectives, or equally well could so undermine the financial gain to the developers as to inhibit the carrying out of good development. Just as the resolute pursuit of planning gain has recently tended to somewhat distort the pursuit of undiluted planning objectives, so will any conflict which now arises between such objectives and the financial gain that might be obtained by authorities from planning decisions relating to land which they are likely to own.[62] Planning decisions may continue to be distorted, particularly because of the financial straits of authorities, despite the recognition that the Act is a planning, not a land measure.

For example, despite planning policy to the contrary (to minimise attraction of traffic), an authority could press for office buildings not only to add to rate income and have planning gain as before but also to create a surplus in the community land account.

There is therefore the possibility of conflict between financial and planning aims. This is reflected in DoE advice. This seems to stress profitability inasmuch as there is an emphasis on getting the best terms for disposal and on quick turnover.[63] But there is also stress that the new functions are to be placed 'in the context of the authority's planning responsibilities, so that the planning framework will be a key element in the identification of development land'.[64]

But if community land is seen in a planning framework, the reverse will also apply, and planning and the economics of resource use will come closer together. In this vein an important aspect of the scheme is in the fact that planning will not now tend to ignore the land value implications of plans, because in the new situation the financial outcomes of planning decisions will fall back into the planners' laps.[65] Ironically this could still lead local authorities to go for the easy sites – for the green-field sites instead of the areas of derelict or unused urban land – just as they did before when needing to buy at market value. In that case it was cost minimisation; in the new situation it is profit maximisation.

Coming to the 'negative' control, the successful operation of the scheme will require an integration of development control and other planning activities in the local authority. Development control should no longer be the Cinderella of planning.[66] It will have new critical duties in the negotiation of planning briefs and in the disposal of land in such a way as to conform to planning objectives.

6.4.6 GENERAL CONCLUSION

The general conclusion from the above is that roles in the development process will be changing. The critical changes will be (i) the reluctance of landowners to make their land available for development, both because of the possibility of the exercise of compulsory purchase powers and the liability for development land tax; (ii) the unwillingness and inability of the developers to undertake the obligations and risks of major schemes in the new climates; and (iii) the unwillingness of financial institutions to make funds available in the circumstances now prevailing following their experience with developers over recent years. Thus the development process itself will take on a new colouring and the key actors in the traditional process (landowners, developers and financiers) will no longer be so willing to play.

But new actors will emerge. Local authorities' growing duties and powers will compensate for the private landowners' reluctance. Alternative forms of development agencies and consortia, aiming to discharge the role of the developer, will compensate for the development companies' inability and unwillingness. Financial institutions will continue the development role that some have initiated of using their finance directly for developments undertaken by and managed by themselves. Groups of professionals will collaborate as project managers on behalf of landowner, financial institution or owner-occupier clients.

Whereas landowners and developers have combined to oppose the Act as a matter of principle, given the existence of the Act their distinctive functions and roles in development are emerging. The landowner is the supplier of the land which is already in existence, and his role can be displaced by mere transfer of ownership. By contrast, the developer is the supplier of knowledge, experience, entrepreneurial skill and project management. There is no easy substitute for these, and any alternative must clearly perform no less an efficient job than the development companies. But the downturn in financial viability of projects, and the difficulties of matching return and cost in current circumstances, have raised doubts about the size of the profit margin which development companies have conventionally commanded from development undertakings; and the financial institutions are reinforcing the doubts by pursuing the trends of recent years in demanding a greater return for their contribution.

So, the development process in contemporary conditions itself needs reconsideration, and it is in this general context that authorities will need to make arrangements with particular developers on particular parcels. In this they will need to digest the accumulated experience of 'partnership agreements' with private developers and to prepare policies on future arrangements.[68] For example, in what kinds of development agencies will they be intersted – conventional development companies, financial institutions, the various arrangements outlined in the 1972 Sheaf Report, joint companies of landowners, financial institutions, development teams? What will be their means for selection of development companies, including the planning and development briefs to be prepared, the kinds of competition envisaged between developers and the forms of disposal and, if by leasehold, the kinds of building leases? With this delicate matter of competition between developers, they will need to consider the implications of safeguards in the Act for prior negotiating rights attached to landowners and developers who have made planning applications. In all this there will be the need to resolve some contentious ethical problems in local government, such as open tendering as against the negotiated tender.

6.5   HELP OR HINDRANCE TO IMPLEMENTATION?

In all this the basic question with which we are here concerned is the extent to which, when fully operational after the 'second appointed day', the scheme will facilitate the implementation of plans, one of the two reasons for which it was introduced (section 6.1).

The first point to be made is that the land scheme will almost certainly alter the kinds of plans which are produced, since they will incorporate a greater recognition of the realities of the development process as the local authority plays a greater role in this process. Not only will the existence of a 'patchwork quilt of land ownerships'[69] be largely overcome, but the requirement to keep the private development sector buoyant, both because of DoE directives to do so and because of the effect on the community land accounts, will feed back into a greater co-ordination between the public and private sectors at the plan-making stage. By this token the plans will be more realistic and therefore more capable of implementation.

But there is a delicate balance to be struck between making plans realistic and compromising planning objectives to financial ends. This procedure may introduce market imperfections and inadequacies, vested financial interests, etc., or the sacrifice of planning objectives for financial gain, into an authority's plan preparation. The success in obtaining a proper balance will vary from authority to authority.

All other things being equal, the fact that a local authority can purchase land at a reduced rate, and at current use value after the 'second appointed day', will allow it to loosen its financial belt, and will thus lead to a reduction in the mismatch between local authority funds and the expenditure required for proper implementation. But there will still be large differences between current use values and therefore land prices, and the incentive or need will remain to steer local authority development to cheaper land. And removal of non-conforming uses will be no less expensive, as will be the compensation cost of 'zoning down' in built-up areas.

The answer to the question of how the private sector will react to the new scheme is complex. But some pointers can be given. The reduction in land profit through the development land tax will most seriously affect the landowner, who will therefore be less willing to play ball, and in that way will resist implementation of plans. And developers will be cautious on land assembly. This will matter little after the 'second appointed day', but until the local authorities are operating as suppliers of land in a large way it could have a serious effect in holding up land supply for implementation. This is especially so since the Conservatives may be expected to reduce the rate of tax even if only slightly, and there will thus be an incentive for the landowner to hold on to his land till there is a change of government. Accordingly, the local authority will need to be active in land supply. However, this decrease in the land profits to be made by the private sector, and the consequential holding back on land supply, means that there will be less development pressure on local authorities to allow developments which give high development gains.

At present, the emphasis in DoE advice is to collect development gains or betterment by the complicated means of public purchase and disposal so that a certain set of accounts, arbitrarily defined, may show a surplus. This gives rise to anomaly. If one of the parties to a transaction in land is a local authority, between 30 and 60 per cent of the development land tax remains (in the final analysis and before a change in the tax rate) with that tier of government. Yet, if the transaction does not include a local authority, all the tax accrues to the central government. This could influence an authority's judgement as to its approach. If, instead, a portion of the tax collected from private transactions were to accrue to the local authority, either directly or through the pool, it would have the general effect of allowing local authorities to slacken their financial belts, and furthermore concentrate on their purchases solely for implementation, and not as a roundabout way of collecting betterment.

Turning to other side-effects, the scheme is felt by many to be over-complex, involving local authority time and staff to a degree incommensurate with the benefit derived. How much of this is due to teething troubles is hard to judge – as is the position when the scheme has built up suitable staff and skills and the money allocated for purchase has grown.

As regards equity, while only time can tell whether the new distribution of development gains between the public and the private sectors is generally acceptable over a broad political spectrum, for the following reasons the greater equity in distribution should facilitate implementation: (i) the profits which the landowner makes while he sleeps are expropriated totally by the state; (ii) inequity within the private sector is reduced since large sums of money will not be arbitrarily given to certain landowners rather than others; (iii) it will not discriminate against those who have already purchased land, in that it will not reduce the value of these holdings since the base value of development land tax is at least as high as the cost of acquisition by the current holder; and (iv) while no final judgement can be made on the division of gains between the local and central government until it is known how the 'pool' is going to be finally distributed when all local authorities are in profit, the principle of sharing betterment is an improvement on the past – local government will get some of the betterment, and the poorer authority will share with the richer.

As for the effects on the rest of the economy, any decrease in the profits from investment in land, as there will be under the scheme, must reduce its attractiveness as a resting-place for investment at the expense of industry; the scheme will not fuel inflation by injection of funds into circulation, as would follow from compensation for the loss of development gains; and inflation of land prices will more and more come under the control of the public sector. All this will facilitate the work of the implementation authorities.

In summary, then, were the scheme fully operational it would be of great help for plan implementation. But unless it were backed up by large resources it will become a policy of marginal usefulness which local authorities may add to their existing battery of powers. And even if so backed, it will not be of help unless the powers are used wisely and with skill which fully comprehends the mixed nature of the British economy.

6.6   THE COMMUNITY LAND SCHEME IN WALES

As indicated above (section 6.2), when describing the community land scheme in the preceding sections we have confined ourselves to England where the powers and duties are placed on the local authorities, with division of responsibility resting with the counties and the districts. But an entirely different arrangement is provided for in Wales: in brief the aims, powers and duties of the Community Land Act are the same as for England, but instead of their being operated by the local authorities they are vested in the Welsh Land Authority, which covers the whole of Wales. This introduces significant differences in the community land scheme which are described in this section. However, development land tax is the same as for England.

The Land Authority for Wales is a body composed of a nominated Chairman, Deputy Chairman and seven members. They are served by a staff under a Chief Executive and Secretary.[70] Thus constitutionally the Land Authority is quite unlike a local authority in many respects: it can take a regional view of the whole of Wales, which (considering the trend towards devolution) is also in some respects a national view; since its members are nominated by the government, it can discharge its functions not as an elected body but in response to its own policies, under the control of the Welsh Office and the Secretary of State for the Environment; since it has been appointed to operate the community land scheme alone, it is not also concurrently operating, as do local authorities, a host of planning and other municipal functions.

Thus the objectives of the Land Authority are less complex than would be those of a planning authority. These have been listed as:[71]

1 To secure by intervention in the private development land market an adequate supply of land − serviced or capable of being serviced − to enable the construction industry to meet the needs of the community within the framework of adopted planning policies.
2 To contribute significantly to the implementation of redevelopment and rehabilitation policies in existing urban areas through site assembly, acquisition, servicing and disposal of land for private development.
3 To bring about the best use of land for private development, taking special care to avoid or minimise interference with agriculture and forestry.
4 To establish high standards of development through the preparation of development briefs based upon a balanced application of social, design and economic considerations.
5 To restore to the community in Wales a substantial part of the increase in value of land arising from its development potential.

In brief, the Land Authority has three main objectives: (i) to act as a broker between the private-sector developers in the development industry and the landowners, with the general aims implicit in the community land scheme; (ii) aid in the implementation of local authority policies; and (iii) securing betterment value to the community in Wales. But since it is doing this as an independent authority, it has certain advantages and disadvantages as compared with local authorities in England.

As to advantages, it is able to avoid the conventional local government political complexion of community land scheme decisions and concentrate on its single-purpose function; in particular it can avoid the complexities of the two-tier level of local government in England and the added complications that this brings to all local authority planning and development; and it is in receipt of all the money available for Wales under the community land scheme and can thus take a regional as opposed to a local authority view of the best ways of disposing of these funds. The Land Authority has freedom to negotiate both individual acquisitions and disposals within the overall approval of its budget, cash limits and land policy statement.

As to the disadvantages, there is a danger that the Land Authority might be tempted to apply its resources (particularly when these may be limited by the overall financial policies of the government) to those proposals which provide the most financially advantageous opportunities for development within the overall planning objectives, though the policies adopted by the Land Authority clearly indicate an intention to try to serve the best interests of the community – and these are not necessarily the most financially advantageous.

But in this situation it can be assumed that the planning authorities in Wales (the Welsh Office and the two-tier local authorities) will try to make sure that the Land Authority is 'planning led'. Indeed, it could be that the fact that the Land Authority itself does not have planning powers means that it would be more likely to operate within the planning structure than would a local authority in England which might temper its planning decisions by the financial considerations of land dealing. Because of the independent status of the Land Authority it can only influence planning matters by consultation with the local authorities, and this it clearly does in the preparation of its land policy statement and rolling programme. There are complexities in such consultations, but the system does ensure that in the end planning matters are decided by local planning authorities free of the influence of possible direct financial gain. The Land Authority is left to ensure that the land necessary for the implementation of the planning objectives is brought into development to the best financial effect within the planning constraints.

But generally the great advantage of the Land Authority is that it is able to take a regional as opposed to a local view of its land policy and dealings in a way which would not be practicable for local authorities. This includes the freedom to offset losses in one area against gains in another, and so directly redistribute land values as between the authorities in Wales, and not indirectly as in England in the redistribution of surpluses in the community land accounts.

6.7   MERIT OF A PARTIAL SCHEME[72]

6.7.1   WHY IS A PARTIAL SCHEME POSSIBLE?

So far we have considered the community land scheme in its entirety and have drawn conclusions as to its contribution towards implementation. But, as indicated above, the Community Land Act is to be introduced gradually over a period of about ten years and in three distinct stages; and the Development Land Tax Act also provides for a gradual increase in the percentage of the tax itself. Thus it is relevant to consider the basic question in this chapter, i.e. will the community land scheme help or hinder plan implementation, in terms of the three stages of the Community Land Act, which are:

1   the 'first appointed day (FAD)' covering all land and all authorities;
2   relevant and commencement dates (RCD) covering certain classes of development in certain areas, progressing to all areas; and
3   the 'second appointed day (SAD)' applied uniformly to all areas.

Since the three stages are to be introduced sequentially, in answering our basic question it is possible also to ask of the second and third stages: compared with the earlier situation, would the marginal benefits to the community of each extension be worth the marginal costs?

There are many possible approaches to answering the question. The simplest here is to return to the current land policy situation prior to the community land scheme in 1975 and frame our answer in relation to our summary of impediments to implementation which then existed, keeping the same subdivision of allocation and distribution (section 5.5). For each of the three stages we give our answer following a brief restatement of the conditions at each stage.

6.7.2   SYSTEM FOLLOWING 'FIRST APPOINTED DAY (FAD)'

In brief the system to be introduced will have the following salient features: preparation of land-acquisition and management schemes; duty to have regard to *desirability* of acquiring development land; acquisition will be much simpler and price will be at present compensation basis, net of development land tax; duty to develop acquired land, or make available for development; means of developing not made specific, and disposal will be at market value; land not to be bought will be developed subject to development control as at present, with rises in land value resulting from permissions to be subject to the development land tax.

On allocation, through development control the FAD system will assist in securing orderly development, for it offers the authority more scope for taking the initiative under conditions where owners are inclined to take less, and adds critically to the powers of 'persuasion'. Furthermore, the 'land policy statements' will, if used imaginatively, offer a basis for orderly development of the area. Taken together there should be better opportunity for securing the right land, at the right time, and so on.

On distribution, even at the initial rates the development land tax will go a great way to resolving the equity issue on land values as between authority and landowners as a class, but not as between landowners *per se*.

6.7.3   SYSTEM OF RELEVANT AND COMMENCEMENT DATES (RCD)

The significant difference from the preceding system is the gradual extension over the country, by type of development and area, of the *duty* (as opposed to the *desirability*) of acquiring all land for relevant development, whether the process be initiated in the private or public sector. And development land tax will rise to 100 per cent.

The fact that the authorities would be the owners of all the relevant development land would assist in the efficiency of land assembly and disposal and in the phasing and priorities of development. But where an authority is willing and anxious to carry out its positive planning functions under the first-stage system, the introduction of the *duty* will hardly add to its performance as a planning authority. What it will do is to force upon it the functions and costs of land ownership in a situation where, were it not under compulsion, it would by definition not have elected to adopt them. Such duty could impose costs by compelling them to take over land where economic prudence would dictate otherwise. A clear case here is the renewal site where redevelopment would lead to financial loss on the land value, which would need to be borne by the new landowner.

And where an authority, having considered the desirability under the first system, decides *not* to go ahead (for reasons of resources, ideology or politics), even if the desirability could be shown, then it will have to contend not simply with the minister's intervention in relation to its acquisition and management scheme but also with a duty enforced across the board. Will this make for harmonious and efficient planned development?

Thus this addition to the system will create difficulties for those authorities who are not willing and able to operate it effectively; and it cannot be seen to bring high marginal benefits for those who are so willing.

6.7.4   SYSTEM FOLLOWING 'SECOND APPOINTED DAY (SAD)'

The simple but significant change here is the introduction of current use value throughout the whole country for the purpose of acquisition and other compensation.

Given the claim that the 100 per cent development land tax should bring down the prices paid for development value to zero, (since acquisition costs will be net of the tax), it seems unlikely that there will be much difference between the price paid for acquisition before and after the 'second appointed day'. This, however, predicates that the development tax will act to remove development value from transactions; experience with the 1947 and 1967 Acts leads to questioning whether this will necessarily be so. Thus there could be an advantage in practice, if not in theory, in terms of prices paid on acquisition: current use value could be less than development value net of development land tax.

Thus the effect of the final step will be to remove all potential development value from acquisition prices for public purposes, and in so doing remove any need to buy development values created by the community on that land.

6.7.5   CONCLUSION

It is clearly too early to judge the workings of the community land scheme in practice. Not only is there the friction of the normal 'running-in' period, but as we have seen (section 6.1) the scheme has come into operation in a hostile environment, because of two factors which were completely unexpected by its authors: the slump in development and the heavy rationing of government loans on which the scheme depended. Furthermore, it is too early to see whether the Community Land Act will fulfil one of its main intentions (that authorities who have failed in the past to exercise the positive planning powers which have been available will be led to do so in the future) and thus dispose of the argument of the critics that the Act was not needed since all such powers were already available.

But in advance of our ability to review the working of the scheme from practice, our conclusion from the above analysis is that the introduction of the scheme following the 'first appointed day' could remove many impediments to planned development, though not all. But from the analysis it is not so apparent that the introduction of the next two stages would greatly add to the net benefits of planned development, and it could add to the net financial cost. Thus a case was made for not moving beyond the 'first appointed day' – certainly until the net benefits to be obtained from so doing were clearer – and for deferring indefinitely the 'second appointed day'.

Clearly such deferment would reduce the chances of the community land scheme being entirely scrapped by a Conservative administration. But whether or not the Conservatives do this, there would appear to be reasonable prospects that the collection of betterment would not be abandoned (as it was in the repeal of the financial provisions of the 1947 and 1967 Acts) even though the burden of the tax percentage of development gain could be reduced. Pointers in this direction are the changing mood in the country since the 1960s as to the rights of the community to some share in enhanced development value, which the Conservatives themselves appreciated when introducing the development gains tax of 1973.

Such betterment might not necessarily be in development land tax but in other forms, for example in normal capital gains tax, in development gains tax or, perhaps, in the betterment levy of the 1967 Act. As a guide to what might happen is the view of the British Property Federation, representing the property development industry.

The Federation accepts the principle that a fair proportion of the gain resulting from the granting of planning permission should accrue, through a suitable tax, to the community. But it is critical of the development land tax (DLT) and its predecessor, the development gains tax (DGT), and suggests instead a tax on betterment gains. They also present the following criteria which would, in their view, make it acceptable to the taxpayer:

1 It should not discourage landowners from making land available for development.
2 It should not be payable until the gain is realised.
3 It should be capable of quantification at the time that development commences.
4 It should be calculated by reference to the increase in value of the land only.
5 It should contain reasonably generous 'deminimus' provisions.
6 Where tax is payable as a result of the deemed realisation of a development gain on the completion of the development as envisaged in section 2 above, it should be possible to pay the tax out of the income stream.
7 There should be adequate relief for losses.

The Federation then recognises that there is another consideration concerning the position of local authorities as beneficiaries of the tax, and suggests that the tax should be accounted for separately into a betterment gain tax fund from which the authority should be entitled to receive (i) the whole of the tax in respect of land purchased by the authority for its own use; and (ii) a proportion, say 30 per cent, as at present on the tax of all other disposals of land in its area.

All this can be summarised as follows. Even if the community land scheme were to be *the total* answer to land policy in planning (something we are led to doubt below in Chapter 8), it has certain disadvantages in operation which suggest that it may not be fully implemented. Furthermore, it carries the unreality we saw above (section 6.1) of having been conceived at a time of economic boom and applied over a period of stagnation.

This suggests that the community land scheme cannot claim on this score to be the final word on British land policy, and that immediate consideration is needed to moving onwards from it. In Chapter 7 we turn to foreign experience to assess its contribution on this score.

REFERENCES: CHAPTER 6

1   DoE (1974, para. 16).
2   See, for example, Lipsey (1973), and Brocklebank *et al.* (1973).
3   DoE (1976f).
4   Ibid, p. 2.
5   See Marriott (1967).
6   The following relies on Lichfield (1976c), and DoE (1975a).
7   DoE (1975e).
8   Ibid.
9   Ibid.
10 DoE (1975a).
11 For a general account, see Royal Institution of Chartered Surveyors (1976), and Bristol University, School for Advanced Urban Studies (1976).
12 Community Land Act, 1975, sections 15(1) and 17(1).
13 Ibid, section 15(1).
14 Ibid, section 7(3); and DoE (1975c).
15 Community Land Act, 1975, section 18; and DoE (1975c, para. 5).
16 DoE (1975c), and DoE (1976b).
17 Community Land Act, 1975, schedule 4, para. 26(b); DoE (1975c, paras 34–5).
18 Community Land Act, 1975, section 3 and schedule 1.
19 DoE (1975c, annexe B).
20 DoE (1975d).
21 DoE (1975f, section 16).
22 Bristol Univeristy, School for Advanced Urban Studies (1976, paper 3).
23 DoE (1976c), and Bristol University, School for Advanced Urban Studies (1976, paper 3).
24 Community Land Act, 1975, section 17(1).
25 DoE (1976d, para. 29).
26 DoE (1975c, paras 53–8), and DoE (1976c, para. 52).
27 Community Land Act, 1975, section 17(1)(a).
28 DoE (1976c, annex E, para. 36).
29 Ibid, para. 52.
30 Community Land Act, 1975, schedule 6; DoE (1976c, paras 62–6 and annexe E).
31 DoE (1976c, annexe E, para. 15).
32 DoE (1975d), and DoE (1975b).
33 DoE (1976a, paras 28–33).
34 Ibid, paras 6–8.
35 Ibid, para. 29.
36 Board of Inland Revenue (1976, para. 3).
37 Ibid, para. 5.
38 DoE (1976a, paras 9–13).
39 The Treasury (1976).
40 This relies on Lichfield (1976c).
41 DoE (1974).
42 Ash (1975a), and Ash (1975b).
43 DoE (1975c).
44 Community Land Act, 1975, section 19 and schedule 5.
45 DoE (1976c, para. 69).
46 Ibid, para. 57.
47 Lichfield (1976c).
48 Bristol University, School for Advanced Urban Studies (1976, paper 2).
49 Bagnall (1976).
50 DoE (1976c, para. 50).

51 Bristol University, School for Advanced Urban Studies (1976, paper 2).
52 DoE (1976c, annexe E).
53 Lichfield (1975a).
54 DoE (1974).
55 Community Land Act, 1975, schedule 6.
56 DoE (1975a).
57 Lichfield (1975a).
58 This relies on DoE (1975a, ch. 5), and Lichfield (1976a).
59 DoE (1974).
60 Lichfield (1976c).
61 DoE (1976a), and DoE (1976c, para. 52).
62 Lichfield (1976c).
63 DoE (1976c, p. 3).
64 DoE (1975c, p. 12).
65 Eddison (1976).
66 Ibid.
67 Lichfield (1976a).
68 DoE (1972b).
69 DoE (1974, para. 18).
70 Community Land Act, 1975, part II and schedule 3.
71 Land Authority for Wales (1977, section 1.2.1).
72 This relies on Lichfield (1975a).

Chapter 7

The Foreign Experience

7.1 BASIS FOR COMPARISONS AMONG COUNTRIES

Conditions are alike in no two countries and comparisons between them are accordingly always difficult. However, we have attempted to reduce some of the difficulties of comparison by choosing for our investigation those countries with a similar level of socioeconomic development (advanced industrial countries) and a similar sociopolitical orientation (commitment to a welfare state in the framework of a mixed economy). Therefore, the main countries investigated are those of North-west Europe – and in particular Scandinavia (Sweden and Denmark), the Netherlands and (to a lesser extent) France and West Germany. Some more scattered examples, however, are drawn from other countries, particularly in other parts of Europe, but also from the industrialised countries of Northern America and Australia.

Land policy structure in the United Kingdom and in the other countries investigated is the result of differing patterns of historical experience, present socioeconomic structure, and planning orientation for the future. In analysing the difference and the factors specific to each country, we can, however, also emphasise some large areas of similarity in background and experience.

In spite of the predominantly private land-ownership patterns in the investigated countries, there is in all of them an historic legacy of a large amount of communal or state land ownership, resulting from the former feudal system and the traditional village rights of common lands. Both in the United Kingdom and Sweden large tracts of land were also owned by the Crown, but in Scandinavia, especially Sweden, the Crown transferred large sections of land to the municipalities.

Another similarity between all the countries investigated concerns trends of socioeconomic development. All show a high level of industrialisation and a dense population concentration – the Netherlands being the most overcrowded country in Europe, with Britain (England and Wales) the next. They also all have a high degree, not only of urban population, but of urban concentration (the percentage of urban population living in large cities). This concentration is most marked for Copenhagen and Paris, with England having slightly more secondary urban centres. In addition all show a high rate of development of the tertiary sector, which is concentrated in the big city regions; the pressure on space for growing commercial uses in the central business district is affecting all the major cities, Manchester, Amsterdam, Copenhagen, Stockholm, Rotterdam, but, most of all, Paris and London.

There is also in these countries unbalanced regional development with population concentrated in the advanced, urbanised regions roughly bordering on the North Sea – South-east England, West Holland, North Denmark, South

Sweden and North-west France. As a result of the faster development of these regions, there is a substantial socioeconomic gap between them and the rest of their respective countries.

But a significant difference between countries is *when* industrialisation occurred. In England, and to some degree France, this was much earlier than in Scandinavia. The implications are twofold: first, there was the need to pioneer in land-use regulations to deal with the problems of industrialisation and urbanisation; second, urban renewal becomes a more critical problem due to obsolescence of the housing stock. But this also means that the pioneers were unable to benefit from the experience of other countries in finding effective policy instruments.

Another difference is the importance of the Second World War. This had two contrary effects: increased state intervention, and also (through destruction) increased urgency of short-term as opposed to long-term development needs. On the first, the physical damage caused by the war pushed the state into a more active role in development policy, very strongly in Britain and, to a more modest degree, France and the Netherlands, but less in Scandinavia. On the second, the differing pressure of short-term needs hampered to various degrees in the post-war years the implementation of programmes for dealing with long-term needs (such as advance land acquisition).

Another effect of the war was to create pressures for a more egalitarian society, or at least one with more social justice and social services for the majority of the population. To pursue this the role of the state in the economy was greatly strengthened – both for welfare needs and for socioeconomic planning – continuing in some measure the unprecedented measures of the wartime state planning of manpower, production, and so on.

Following the war the United Kingdom was the first country to show the new post-war trends. Even during the war the various commissions and the creating of planning agencies anticipated the new role the state would assume in urban development, alongside the expanding role in health, housing and education which led to higher taxation. In France this trend emerged later, after the post-war political instability was resolved. In Sweden, which was neutral during the war, the establishment of a stable political order based on Social-Democratic party control in the 1930s encouraged the growth of economic planning and welfare measures.

Another important point of comparison is the structure of government administration in the different countries. England, the Netherlands and Scandinavia are similar in that the local authorities have traditionally played a prominent role as the essential unit for implementing social-welfare policies. In France there is an extremely centralised structure, with even provincial government being largely controlled from the centre through the prefectural system. The provincial or regional level is weakest in the United Kingdom.

The political system of the countries investigated also show differences. While in Sweden the same party held power until recently since the 1930s and France has had relatively stable governments in recent years, the United Kingdom, the Netherlands and Denmark have shown many fluctuations. The dominant political attitude has to some degree influenced the basic tenets of land policy in the various countries. In each there is the right of expropriation for public purpose. But the definition of *public purpose* varies. In the Netherlands and

Sweden it means all land needed for urban growth for all purposes. In the United Kingdom in theory the local authorities have the power to take land for any planning purpose, but in practice this has been circumscribed in that planning powers for purchase have tended to be seen as the residual for other purchase powers. The expropriation procedure shows similar differences. In the United Kingdom there are long delays for public inquiries and subsequent appeals, a reflection of a long democratic tradition. But in contrast, in other countries of the same tradition, there was greater political flexibility in speeding up the expropriation and compensation system in order to achieve planning aims.

In all countries there is a gap between the accepted principles of land policy (e.g. development value to be transferred to the community, the community to provide social housing) and the means of implementation of these principles: between the expressed principles of a programme and the actual programme. What should be in theory is amended or modified in practice to appease interests. Perhaps this gap is greatest in Britain because of Conservative reversals of Labour legislation. In France legislative amendments concerning implementation powers have changed the essential meaning of many proposals. In Sweden and the Netherlands this has happened to much less an extent. The political stability in Sweden has assured consistent implementation of land policy and made Sweden the outstanding example in the world. In the Netherlands, too, despite government changes, the basic approach to land policy is accepted by all political parties: land is a resource like water, to be controlled and owned by the community. It is likely that the peculiar topographical conditions of Holland, with most of the land below sea level, and the consequent need to defend and extend the land area, as a nation, have influenced Dutch attitudes.

For almost all countries there is, in public land acquisition, a lack of a comprehensive regional and national land-supply policy; exceptions are the Netherlands, Sweden and some socialist countries. Even in these countries there are unresolved conflicts between local, regional and national land needs on the basis of planned development schemes. But although in most countries public land-acquisition policies have been unsuccessful in affecting the growth patterns of the existing city regions, it should be emphasised that they have led to some substantial achievements in reaching limited objectives, such as new towns. But a comprehensive approach is needed to influence fundamentally the urban process.

Finally, we would emphasise that while the review is of interest in itself its purpose is to throw light on the situation in Britain. For example, an examination of the experience of public land ownership in other countries may give some valuable insight into the difficulties and advantages of such a policy in Britain. It may be useful to examine the experience of different countries in order to understand why one was successful and why in another place problems occurred.

This includes consideration of why the previous planning system has been found inadequate in most countries, what successful measures of public land supply have been implemented abroad, and what unsolved problems of land policy exist even in these countries.

One of the most important questions for Britain is the role of the private sector under the new conditions of municipal land ownership. In terms of acquisition, how effective is a mixed economy of both private and public land ownership for development? Is it possible to affect the private land market through municipal land supply? Relevant to disposal, the question is whether there will be a lack of private initiative under the new system, and whether new relationships can be forged between banks, developers, municipalities and others in the development process.

Another set of problems concerns financing. What are the effects of various methods of financing on the final goals of the municipal land-supply policy? Second, how is it possible to avoid paying exaggerated prices for land? What effect will the British system possibly have, and what other alternatives are there?

7.2 CONTROL WITHOUT TAKING LAND

7.2.1 THE LIMITATIONS OF NEGATIVE PLANNING CONTROL

Negative controls of land use were greatly strengthened in many West European countries following the Second World War. In particular Scandinavia and Holland followed the British example (section 4.3), whereas in Italy and Spain both plans and effective control were lacking for many years and development occurred on an *ad hoc* basis. But as we have seen (section 2.3), even where plans existed, implementation has been mostly on the initiative of the private market, which determines the actual course of development. And if the landowner/developer prefers a use not in accord with the plan, there is pressure on the public authorities to change it in order to release the land. Thus despite the legal authority of a plan authorities were not able to influence significantly the actual development. This was particularly true of the expansion of city regions where there was failure of the new planned development – in the context of predominant private land ownership – to attract a significant proportion of population growth.

In addition to the difficulty in controlling the actual development the common post-war experience of many countries has been the inability to ensure the supply of enough land to meet the needs of urban growth through the mechanism of the private land market even as regulated by public authority land-use controls, in the case of the decisions of private landowners to withhold land from the market in the expectation of future gains. Thus withholding of land as a long-term investment has been one of the main factors leading to the higher rate of land price increase in most countries than would be justified by the real determinants, among them the rapidity of urbanisation and the rate of economic growth. Particularly significant has been the increase in prices of agricultural land on the edges of city regions, as the largest proportionate capital gains are made from converting land from rural to urban uses.

The land price increase of recent years has in turn led to a number of countries introducing fiscal measures to reduce speculative pressure, and also to collect the unearned increment of land value for the community. These measures, too, have had limited success: as in Britain, both difficulties in collection and political opposition have made ineffective most land profits taxation and there has been even less success in overcoming market pressures which give rise to land price increases.

Our examination below of some of the more successful land and taxation policies in different countries may help to illuminate some of the common problems that even the best of these policies face. From a foreign perspective, what is noticeable in the British experience in planning is perhaps the ambitiousness of the post-war aims, and thus perhaps the size of the gap between plans and implementation. Such large-scale regional programmes only arose at a later stage in most continental countries – in the late 1950s – and then urban development policies were generally considered as a means implementing regional policy (for example, by creating growth poles in the regions).

7.2.2   EFFECTIVE NEGATIVE CONTROL : THE DANISH SYSTEM

The most successful example of negative planning control (without public land ownership) has been in Denmark. Through the use of macro-zoning, strict control on the provision of infrastructure, site taxation, and co-ordinated regional planning (including transportation), fragmented development of large towns in Denmark has largely been avoided. The system has been less successful in its social as opposed to its environmental objectives, i.e. in collecting the increased increment of land value from the community, in reducing land speculation, and in acquiring land for public purposes (social housing) in appropriate locations.

In brief, the Danish system is based on the preparation of sub-regional plans for urban growth for the next twelve years, within which detailed schemes are then drawn up for the provision of infrastructure works over a four-year period in areas designated for development. All development is forbidden in the rest of the zone of furture urban growth, and the local authorities are not allowed to provide infrastructure works for such areas. In addition the Danish authorities have introduced a series of tax measures in order to force the use of land according to their plans. These include a betterment levy that is collected at the time that the decision is made to designate an area as urban (and infrastructure works are begun). At this time the landowner must pay the increased value of his land as if it were urban. The authorities grant a mortgage if the owner is unable to raise the amount of the tax. But faced with such a high tax levy, the presumption is that many owners will have to sell for development in order to raise the taxes.

The urban zones designated by an urban development plan *shall be* of a size adequate to meet the estimated demand for land over a period of at least twelve years, to take account of the needs of the whole urban community (not necessarily of the individual municipality). Every four years the amount of land allocated for furture urban development over the following twelve years is re-estimated. The urban zones will consequently grow concurrently with the growth of the urban communities, so avoiding urban sprawl.

The Urban and Rural Zones Act also stipulates that it is the duty of municipalities within urban development zones to make land available for urban development for the coming five years, and to ensure that it is serviced with roads, sewerage, public amenities, etc., of a reasonable standard.

To complement the land designation, a betterment charge on the change of use from rural to urban has been introduced. This is charged on the difference between the (lower) valuation of a property in rural zone and its (higher) valuation after its transfer to an urban zone (the market value).

The basis for the betterment levy is a very efficient valuation system, first introduced in 1922, with a general valuation of all properties taking place every four years. There are a number of complicated rules about the assessment of these values. Farms and similar properties in rural zones are assessed with regard to the fact that such properties may only be used for agricultural and similar purposes and not for urban development. *When the properties are transferred to an urban zone*, they are reassessed at market value in view of the possibility of urban development.

The collection of tax at the time of a planning decision to change the land use, and not at the time of the sale of land, restrains the purchase of land for speculative reasons, and also encourages the supply of land to the market in line with planned development. Such methods for forcing development after a planning scheme has been prepared and infrastructure works begun are also found in Spain. Here relatively strong measures have been introduced to deal with this problem, involving both legal compulsion and tax mechanisms. If land is kept vacant in an urban area where a detailed land-use scheme has been prepared, it is subject to an increasing rate of tax over time. In addition the land can be expropriated by the public authorities after a certain time period and sold to some (public or private) body which is willing to use the land for construction purposes. However, the fact that the legal compulsion exists means that in practice it does not often have to be used and landowners do sell to construction firms – without sanctions.

7.2.3 REPARCELLATION: POOLING WITHOUT ACQUISITION

Where property boundaries would not facilitate orderly development, as when there are many small landowners with irregularly shaped parcels, one solution is comprehensive acquisition for development by either public or private agencies (see section 7.3 below). An alternative is by the mechanism of compulsory reparcellation, or the rearrangement of plots in built-up areas on which it is desired to build, in accordance with a town plan. In such a rearrangement each individual owner generally receives a plot smaller than his original one, not necessarily located in exactly the same place, as some land area is given over to an improved arrangement of streets, parks and other public facilities, with the remaining land divided equitably among all landowners on the former tenure. As the rearrangement generally leads to permission for development on an improved basis, the new smaller plots are generally more valuable than the old ones. If the owner actually suffers a loss, he is given cash compensation. But he remains a landowner.

This system of private landowner/public authority co-operation is widely used in West Germany under its Federal Building Law, dating back to the *Lex Adickes* of 1909, which established the legal right for the authorities to enforce a compulsory exchange of property.

The planning authority is responsible for the detailed site plan which contains the new street pattern, additional open spaces, and so on (the *Bebauugsplan*). Usually this lowers the total amount of land left in private ownership; for example, in Dortmund the redirection was of the order of 28 per cent. However, before this binding site plan is published, the authority attempts to reach agreement with the holders of proprietary interests voluntarily as the rearrangement of plots that is necessitated by the new plan and exemptions from rates and costs are made in the event of a voluntary agreement. The revised land-ownership plan (*Umlegungskarte*) thus fairly apportions the remaining plots among the landowners.

It should be noted that if the new plot is decreased in value, the owner receives compensation (either cash or other land); however, if there is a gain in value, betterment is charged, since this is the result purely of public activity with no action on the part of the landowners.

The German system has been copied in other countries, particularly in Japan. Since 1919 land-readjustment schemes have been widely used, particularly after natural disasters or war destruction. Approximately 27 per cent of the total urban land surface, or over 1,500 square kilometres, has been affected. Again, both public and private bodies are involved. In the latter case these are known as Land Readjustment Associations and they must hold a yearly public meeting (*sokai*) of all landowners to approve the scheme for rearrangement. The basic procedure is the same in the area as a whole; some land is designated for public uses (called *genbu*), while the remainder is pooled as the reserve to be apportioned between all the landowners (*horyuchi*). This procedure was used, for example, when the high-speed train line was built from Tokyo.

It should be noted, however, that reparcellation mainly applies either to non-built land lying in urban areas that is ripe for development, or to very major redevelopment. This gives it a relatively limited application for urban redevelopment, barring a major disaster which destroys the built structures on the land.

7.3   CONTROL BY TAKING LAND

7.3.1   THE GENERAL AIMS OF LAND ACQUISITION

The fact that negative land-use control measures alone have proved inadequate to ensure implementation of land-use planning schemes at the appropriate time has led to local authorities taking increasing responsibility for land supply following public acquisition. The general aim is to supply the land needed to implement urban development schemes in the right location and quantity at an appropriate time and price. The effectiveness of different strategies may be judged by the degree to which they meet these criteria. Different approaches have been adopted in different countries. And the extent of purchase by authorities also differs between countries.

In almost all countries the state has taken on the responsibility for supplying the land required for the development of infrastructure (roads, railways, water and sewage) as the essential precondition for urban development. For this purpose public authorities need to obtain land. Available methods include (i) forcing landowners of areas being developed to supply the required land for infrastructure as a condition of approval of a private development scheme; (ii) acquiring the land in the free market; or (iii) expropriating from the landowners.

Then in most countries authorities have sought to provide land for public buildings, services and facilities which arise from growth in urban development resulting from the general increase in the standard of living. Different requirements for land arise from the need to provide social housing for those with low income, and then in many countries for industrial development, commercial development, large parks, etc., and then whole new towns. Some countries pursue a more active acquisition policy, acquiring land which is then supplied to developers in accordance with a development scheme. In most countries public authorities have the power to acquire land, and in those cases where the land is needed for public purposes they have the power to expropriate the land. Since most countries are involved in at least some of these activities, it is possible to suggest that some kind of public land-acquisition policy exists almost everywhere.

Legislative power which limits public authorities to acquiring land for current needs has proved inadequate. The investment made by public authorities and urban growth itself brought an increase in land prices. Housing projects, public facilities and plans prepared for new urban settlements caused large increases in the land prices of land adjacent to the new developments. Thus the public authorities had to invest money to carry out development schemes and then pay higher land prices resulting from the influence of the previous development.

In addition land ordinarily available at a cheap price in the land market became difficult to purchase when development schemes were implemented, or even announced, because the landowners preferred to hold the land vacant rather than sell it for public development. In response some countries instituted a policy of advance acquisition by purchasing land in agricultural use which might be required for future urban development; this has happened in recent years in France, Spain and Sweden. Their experience shows that such policies economise on public spending and also provide an efficient tool for carrying out development schemes.

The land-acquisition policy of some countries (e.g. the Netherlands and Sweden, but not France, Israel and Spain) aims to encourage the creation of new planned neighbourhoods in the urban extension, combining housing with all needed services for a community and also some employment opportunities (i.e. to supplement those in the near-by big city which provides for the inhabitants of the planned communities the majority of employment and high-level services).

The effect of such new neighbourhoods on urban growth depends on the ability of such communities to absorb urban population growth, avoiding a fragmented development and ensuring a comprehensive city-region development. Such a policy in regard to the urban extension should be distinguished from the development of complete new towns through public land ownership; these may affect regional development without affecting urban-region growth.

7.3.2 PUBLIC LAND SUPPLY AND THE LAND MARKET

The planning aims of land-acquisition policy, which primarily relate to location, quantity, time and price, may be distinguished from the price effects on the land market, though of course the two are interrelated. In some countries land policy has been able to affect land prices and produce a lower rate of price increase than in other countries, and in some they have not succeeded. An analysis of the reasons is revealing.

Expectations about future use influence present land prices. Therefore, a degree of uncertainty as to political conditions, and the possibility of land policies being repealed, will inevitably mean that such a policy cannot hope to be effective on the land market. Where public land supply is long established and not politically contentious, the expectations of landowners are different. This limits the effectiveness of the municipalities' attempts to use their power to influence the land market.

The policy of public land acquisition is expected to lead to the municipality playing the dominant role in the execution of the development scheme, by acquiring land on a large-enough scale to serve as the basis for supplying the needs for the entire future expansion of the urban population. In cases where public land acquisition is restricted to some purposes and some locations only, it has no effect on the land market and on urban growth patterns. There is a danger that the public authorities (including the planning authority) may use their powers to adapt the planning scheme, not to the needs of the growing urban community, but to the needs of public vested interests (i.e. in order to promote specific schemes by functional authorities).

Another limitation of this kind, as in France, is restriction on only some areas of future development and renewal, leaving the majority of land for present and future urban development to the play of free-market forces. The same phenomenon may be observed in Israel and Spain, where land prices in the big cities show some of the highest rates of increase in the world. On the other hand, the land-acquisition policy of the Dutch and Swedish municipalities, which supply *all* the land needed for future development for *all* uses, has resulted in these countries having some of the lowest rates of land price increases in the world.

The experience of Israel, France, India and other countries has shown that a policy of public land acquisition or land ownership *on its own* does not necessarily affect the urban land market, and may not supply enough land for the growing areas of urban concentration. The most important part of a public land-acquisition policy is that it allows the public authorities to fix the timing of land-use development precisely, and thus they are able to implement effectively a long-term development scheme.

The extent, location and variety of land uses on publicly owned land is the decisive factor in the effectiveness of the public sector in influencing the private land market. Only if the public sector does not isolate itself from certain sectors of the land market will it have a significant economic impact. Obviously, the methods of administration and financing of publicly owned land has a considerable effect on the use of land according to the plan. And a decisive effect is produced by the allocation by the public authorities of sufficient funds to carry out comprehensive development of all land requirements and uses.

It has been argued by some that there is a risk for the public authority in committing itself to such a large-scale land acquisition over a long time period, as urban growth patterns and needs may be very uncertain over such a period. This may be correct for private land acquisition for long-term needs. There is uncertainty in forecasting the exact location of future growth. But it is possible to forecast the quantitative needs for different land uses over time in a large city region. It may be suggested that these developments would not be in opposition to a policy of large-scale land acquisition. On the contrary, the close co-ordination of the land-acquisition and planning authority in the same government agency could greatly diminish the risk, as the land acquired could be used either for urban or for recreational purposes.

In Holland the long experience of municipal land acquisition of the urban-extension type has so affected expectations that speculation in development land is considerably restricted. The Dutch land-acquisition procedure is based on the Expropriation Act which gives municipalities the power to expropriate land located in an area of an approved extension plan. While the purpose of the Expropriation Act is to ensure the availability of land needed for future development, it also defends the property rights of landowners. Compensation for expropriated land *must* be paid on the basis of existing market prices for current land use.

The basic difference between the Dutch experience and that of other countries lies in the area of land market price formation. Generally, transformation of agricultural land use to other uses near urbanised areas leads to high land prices, even for land remaining in agricultural use. Therefore, the public authorities in most countries have to pay relatively high compensation costs according to the principle of market prices. The Expropriation Act in the Netherlands, based on the original 1951 legislation, influenced agricultural land prices in a different way. The knowledge that future land planned as urban extension would be expropriated discouraged speculative investment in land. Rather, the planning procedure (i.e. the provincial government's right of approval of local development plans and its control of building permits) created continuous rural areas near the city frontiers, without urban extension into these areas.

Thus the planning procedure, by controlling the direction and location of growth, effectively kept some land in agricultural areas outside the building market. The net result was to create a situation where the municipalities themselves became the biggest land purchasers and developers. The municipality's monopolistic advantage in the suburban land market thus prevented payment of exaggerated prices.

A comparison of green-field site land prices for the Netherlands in 1969 with the development of land prices on the urban fringe in other European countries illustrates some of the economic advantages of a public land-acquisition policy (see Table 7.1).

The prices near the city may be only 100 per cent higher than the land in the purely rural areas. In comparison with other countries these differences are insignificant. For example, the prices of agricultural land near big cities within a distance of ten to twenty miles are about twenty times higher than rural prices in

Table 7.1 *Comparison of agricultural land prices near cities and in rural districts for selected countries, 1969*

Country	Land price near cities (US $ per m²)	Land price in rural Districts (US $ per m²)
Italy	1·5–5·0[1]	0·30
Switzerland	7·5–9·0[2]	0·20
Denmark	2·0[3]	0·20
West Germany	12·5	0·60
Spain	10·0–12·0[4]	0·05
The Netherlands	1·0	0·50

[1] Average near largest cities.
[2] Fifteen kilometres from Zurich.
[3] Average near largest cities.
[4] Near Madrid.

Source: United Nations (1973), *Urban Land Policies and Land Use Control Measures, Vol. III Western Europe.*

West Germany, ten times in Italy, fifteen times in Switzerland and thirty to forty times in Spain. Although the value of agricultural land away from urban areas is influenced only by the intensity of its use and the income derived from its use, for agricultural land near urban areas it is more common to find land price formation strongly affected by the prospects of future urbanised values.

The most important factor influencing the land development process and the price of building sites is the relatively small difference between the prices of raw land near the city and that in the rural areas.

7.3.3 METHODS OF ACQUISITION

The experiences of several countries have shown that it is possible to develop efficient new instruments of municipal land purchase which reduce public expenditure on land.

Basis of compensation and expropriation

The compensation system has an important influence on two aspects of public land-acquisition policy. First, it obviously influences the cost of such programmes and therefore is an important consideration in the allocation and distribution of resources. Second, it may also have significant planning effects. For example, an inefficient compensation system may involve long delays which impede implementation; and the level of compensation itself may influence decisions about where to acquire, particularly if the compensation is close to or related to market value. This brings in, as it were, the effect of the private market through the back door.

Sweden is an example of a country where the long procedure of expropriation and compensation was seriously delaying municipal land acquisition. For one thing the law provided that the government bear the cost of all private appeals; in addition it had to be proved that the landowners themselves were not ready to exploit the land themselves. This had an effect on the location of municipal land purchases.

Significant changes were introduced in 1972. It is no longer necessary to prove that the landowners themselves are unlikely to be capable of exploiting the land on reasonable conditions. It suffices now for the local government to show that the land may be required for planned community development. In principle, the municipalities have thus gained priority right to all land needed for this purpose, and also the legal means of acquiring it at an early stage.

More important was the creation of a fixed date as the basis of compensation. The law existing until recently did not fix exactly the date of land valuation for paying compensation. It was generally understood that the market value prevailing at the time of the Court decision was the basis of compensation. The expropriation procedure took place over a period of three to five years, and therefore the municipalities have had to pay an increased price for land. But following an amendment, compensation for the expropriation will be based on the market value ten years before the expropriation was decided by the municipalities, so that public authorities need not pay the additional value created during the ten years before the expropriation. But for a transitional period this regulation will only be realised gradually. Until 1981 the compensation will be based on the price prevailing on 1 July 1971, i.e. at a higher rate than if based on ten years previously. But for the future the expectation of compensation according to the land price prevailing ten years before the expropriation may influence the landowners to be ready for a voluntary agreement with the municipalities instead of starting a long expropriation procedure; and a landowner and the potential land investors might not be interested in keeping land unused or might invest in land purchases to gain the expected land price increases.

Priority purchase rights
The difficulties and delays of expropriation and compensation have made local authorities prefer to buy land by agreement rather than use compulsory purchase. One way to assist the local authorities is to give them priority rights – that is, the right of first purchase of any land that is offered on the market in (usually) designated urban development areas. If the local authority is not interested in buying, the owner is free to sell. The other side of priority purchasing is the obligation of the local authority to buy land designated for development when it refuses to give permission to the landowner to use the land.

Priority purchase rights are operative for different purposes in many continental countries, including Sweden, France, Switzerland, the Netherlands and West Germany.

Special zones of priority development
Another way to affect land prices that the public authorities must pay is to freeze private development for a designated area where the public authorities are interested in a future development project themselves, as in Sweden and West Germany, but most notably in France, where such zones (declared by the Prefect) are called ZADs. Development is frozen in such zones for sixteen years and both the compensation and priority purchase powers described above apply. Compensation in the case of expropriation is based on the prices one year before the zone is declared and the public authorities have priority rights to purchase any land offered for sale in the zone. These measures are important because they affect land prices without any widespread purchases. The knowledge that the public authorities have these powers gradually induce landowners to sell land at lower prices to the public authorities. Recently this method has been extended to all urban regions.

7.3.4 THE ADMINISTRATION OF PUBLICLY OWNED LAND

The public ownership of land created a problem for incentives of land development and land use. In the private sector the developer takes decisions on the basis of market forces, predicting future needs and land uses to satisfy these needs on the basis of achieving the highest profit from his activity. By contrast the incentive for land development for the public authority is based on achieving economic and social-welfare aims. These are two different approaches towards land development. But there are also common interests between these two approaches, based on the need of the developer to continue his economic activity on the basis of land ownership by the public authority, and it is in the interest of the public authority to use the experience of the developers in land development.

The Swedish experience in collaboration

Experience in Sweden shows that it is possible to introduce co-ordinated action between the public authority and the developers.

Different municipalities have introduced the participation of the developers in land-use planning and in the planning of building schemes. At the same time the municipalities encouraged the establishment of municipal building societies and co-operative housing societies in order to create a basis for a strong public building sector. The municipality is therefore able to act as a co-ordinating agent between the private co-operative and municipal building sectors. The policy of the municipality is to co-ordinate the land purchase and the long-term land-use planning with the developers in order to allow the developer to prepare his long-term activity schemes based on the municipality ensuring that the needed land for three to five years' activity is available. Such a policy of co-ordination also makes the land-acquisition policy of the municipality more efficient by eliminating the competitition of the private developer, who is not interested in bidding for the land since he is able to get the needed land from the municipality.

Obviously, the level of co-ordination and participation of the developer as well as the citizens in the development is not similar in all the municipalities. An interesting example is that of Marsta in the Stockholm region. The Stockholm municipality built in Marsta a complex of high-rise buildings. The developers provided few amenities and the municipality few community facilities to the residents. There was growing opposition among the residents against the high-rise buildings. The municipality therefore decided to initiate a participation exercise between the residents and five planning firms with a view to developing an alternative plan. A group of families worked together with each of the five planning firms. As a result of co-ordination between the planning firms and the citizens, it was decided to plan mixed housing types, to introduce more family housing and to ensure the needed community services.

The example of Marsta is not unique: there is a readiness on the part of the community to execute its powers on the basis of co-ordination with the residents and developers, a policy which makes planning closer to the needs of the population.

The French experience of mixed companies

French policy has created a range of institutions specifically concerned with different urban policy goals. In this the most interesting aspect is that these institutions have generally been in the form of public land development companies, which are mixed companies in which local authorities are represented together with private interests, generally limited to 50 per cent of total capital. These companies were created in order to secure greater flexibility and greater financial resources than development through the conventional government agencies, and to cut through administrative delay and mobilise resources for specific development projects, including the securing of more favourable financial terms for loans for development work. To this end the companies are given powers for the acquisition of land through negotiation or expropriation, the clearing of the area, allocation of different land uses, and the siting of industrial buildings. Every stage of the company's activities comes under close public inspection, and must be co-ordinated with the regional development plan.

Mixed-economy companies for urban activities also exist for construction purposes (particularly of social housing), where public participation is usually more limited. Such companies are limited in the amount of profit they can make; in return, they are granted especially favourable terms of credit. Finally, urban-renewal activities can also be undertaken within the framework of a mixed company, whereby the owners of slum areas contribute their land to the company and the municipality undertakes the rehabilitation of the area.

One instrument through which the French attempted to increase the useful participation of private interests in urban development schemes was the plan for the leasing of land *from* private owners. Under a law enacted in 1964, and in view of the delays inherent in expropriation procedures, the public authorities have the right to conclude a leasing agreement with a private landowner for a limited number of years (eighteen to seventy) for building rights on his land, for housing or for infrastructure works. The public authority may pay the lessee either through rent (linked to the building cost index) or securities; or they may place part of their construction project at his disposal. The lessee undertakes to maintain the buildings for the period of the lease and restore full ownership rights to the land after its expiration.

Another part of this law provides for the joint participation of landowners in urban-renewal schemes in the framework of the mixed companies for urban renewal described above. The law provides for notification and publication of the detailed scheme for the redevelopment of an area. A choice is then presented to all affected landowners between expropriation or participation in the urban development project through a mixed company.

The Dutch experience in local consolidation
The problem of an appropriate structure of a land authority is connected with the general problems of public administrative structure. One of the problems of co-ordination is the link between the planning, financing and landowning authorities, including that between the agencies representing different public functions. Differences between them result from the conflict between short-term and long-term needs as well as between local, regional and national requirements. For example, while the local planning authorities are the main factor in establishing the location of different land uses according to the general plan, there is often a conflict of interest between their requirements and those of national planning.

One way through this conflict can be seen from the experience of Holland. The Amsterdam municipality (as well as Stockholm) show that positive urban growth is possible when the land authority is a part of the same municipality, acting in co-ordination with the planning department, the financial department and the public-works department. Obviously, co-ordination does not mean no conflict, as there might always be different approaches by different agencies dealing with specific fields of action. But the deciding factor influencing the implementation of the planning process is the ability to narrow the differences in the conflicting short-term interests of the different agencies by a dominant public authority, which should draw the lines of compromise between the long-term plans and short-term needs.

A feature of the administrative structure associated with Amsterdam's land-acquisition policy is its ability to shorten the time periods of both land acquisition and construction, so reducing time and money costs. No more than six to eight years passed from initial land acquisition to completion of housing construction. Certainly, the combined authority of the municipality's planning division, land-acquisition department, and so on within the same organisational framework has been a positive factor in shortening the time needed for total execution of development plans.

The French experience in regional land purchase

The Real Estate and Technical Agency of the Paris Region was founded in accordance with the Decree of 14 April 1962. Its purpose is to proceed within the Paris region with the purchase (if need be through expropriation, or through the legal right of pre-emption) of the land necessary for the various urbanisation operations, and to carry out these operations itself.

Thus the mission of the Agency is twofold. As a real-estate agency, it purchases land on behalf of itself (only in the areas appointed by the Administrative Head of the Paris Region), or on behlf of the state or of other public bodies. As a technical agency, it is empowered to proceed on the improvement, equipment or renovation of buildings required for the carrying out of urbanisation of any kind, or that necessary for the installation of public services or facilities.

In addition to the juridicial means at the Agency's disposal, such as sales by private contracts, through expropriation for public purposes, or through the right of pre-emtion, the Agency possesses financial means based on the loans granted by the National Fund for Real Estate Improvement and Urbanisation – and to this must be added the district loans, and the loans and financing operations on the part of future occupiers. The Board of Directors consists of twenty-two members, eleven of whom represent the state (senior officials of the Ministries of Economy and Finances, of Equipment and Housing, of National Education, of the Interior, of Welfare, and of Transportation) and eleven represent the local public bodies: two for the city of Paris, two for the district of the Paris Region, and seven for the administrative subdivisions of the Paris Region.

Hence the Real Estate Agency is a service that can be used by the state, by the local public bodies and by the district. However, it is with the district that the Agency entertains closer relationships, since it can operate only in the sectors assigned, or agreed, by the Administrative Head of the Paris Region, the Administrative Head assuming also the function of General Delegate to the district by the Decree of 10 August 1966.

A regional land authority may overcome the shortage of knowledgeable experts in land acquisition and land valuation. It is difficult for small municipalities to take responsibility for land acquisition themselves; besides the lack of qualified staff, they lack bargaining power with landowners if they are too small. Land acquisition by many independent authorities may also lead to increased administrative costs through duplication, and also leads to difficulties in creating a comprehensive regional land-use policy. On the other hand, land acquisition without the active participation of the local authorities may lead to an administrative allocation of land which ignores local interests. Therefore, a regional authority, with the participation of local authorities in its management, may be an appropriate framework for efficient land-use policy. Obviously, the financing of such a regional agency is an important question. It may be suggested that this might be done on the basis of co-ordination with a national land agency. The creation of such an agency may be a precondition for the widespread success of regional and local land authorities, as a high percentage of land is used for national needs (agriculture, transport, some recreation). The national authority would be able to reconcile conflicting interests of different regional authorities for certain areas which it might not be in the national interest to develop in the way the regional authority wanted.

7.3.5   DISPOSALS: TO SELL OR TO LEASE ?

One of the most discussed problems of public land administration in market-economy countries is the question of leasing or selling the land to users. In the Netherlands and Sweden some municipalities use the system of leasing and others use selling. In Sweden the government gives preference to leasing by fixing better terms for their loans for land acquisition when land is leased. In France, generally, the land acquired by the public land-acquisition agencies is sold to the developers. Israel has a long tradition of leasing land, but in some cases Parliament has allowed land to be sold. The capital city of Australia (Canberra) has been using the leasehold system since its founding in 1924.

More favourable conditions of leasing public land for development by the authorities, and frequent revaluation of land (to collect part of the incremental increase as tax) may strengthen the financial structures of public land-acquisition agencies, enabling them to finance future land purchases from income from publicly leased land, and collecting for the community the additional value created by the urban growth process.

It should be emphasised that the leasehold system is used in some countries with long experience of such a system even in private land market transactions. This is the case in Norway as well as in some other countries. Private landowners sometimes are interested in holding the ownership rights to land rather than selling it in order to gain the increase in land value which can be realised at the expiration of the lease term. Sometimes, especially in the case of commercial enterprises, they are interested in insuring the real value of their rent through receiving some percentage of the profit or the turnover of the lessee as part of the lease payment.

There are obviously pros and cons in each of these systems. The leasehold system allows the public authority to keep for the community the permanently increasing urban land values. But this system requires more investment of public capital than when land is sold. The leasehold system should allow the public authority to obtain land more easily for changing needs and consequent land-use changes. On the other hand, it is suggested that efficient land-use legislation and taxation methods that control development may serve as a partial substitute for public leaseholding of land.

The system of selling land acquired by the public agencies may provide more money for additional land acquisition, and at the same time may still allow the assembling of large land parcels for carrying out future development schemes. In France financial groups, together with the public authorities, participate in large-scale land acquisition. This is done in the framework of public mixed societies with at least 50 per cent public capital. The system of selling publicly owned land has the disadvantage, not only of losing for the community the prospective additional land value, but also losing flexibility in the case of changing future land-use needs. It is desirable, even when land is sold by the municipality, not to transfer rights to the land until the land is used for building purposes (in order to prevent the holding of vacant land). One of the advantages of public ownership is the ability to fix the timing of land use according to development schemes. Public land ownership is needed, not only to ensure the immediate needs of human settlements, but also to create the needed land reserve for furture development, including such a vital need as recreation (e.g. national parks) which have no commercial importance. Therefore, the system of selling public land may only influence short-term needs and is less in keeping with long-term development.

It may be suggested that the essential factor in the choice of system is the method of financing land acquisition, and especially the appreciation by the public authorities and by public opinion in general of the role of land as an essential factor in establishing the patterns of urban growth and the quality of urban life.

One of the means of financing land acquisition is the system of capital payment in advance, rather than entirely by annual rent. Such a system requires the future leaseholder to pay off part of the rent in cash in advance in addition to yearly payments. This system allows the public authorities to keep land in their possession, but to get part of the land value immediately in order to have resources available for early further acquisition — but losing some of the ability to change the financial terms of the lease. This system is used in Amsterdam and Israel, and has been proposed as a solution to the financial difficulties of most of the Swedish municipalities.

In the discussion about the advantages and disadvantages of the leasehold system conducted in many countries the essential problem is seen as how to encourage a large-scale public advance land-acquisition programme in order to create a land reserve for future urban development. Obviously, it is advisable to lease the land in such a way that the public authorities will obtain the additional value of the land resulting from general urban growth, and so that they will also have the ability to change the land use if needed or take it for public purposes. Without effective lease conditions the public authorities have lost the main advantage of the leasehold system, for which they have forgone the immediate financial advantage of selling the land.

Recently, different countries using the leasehold system (Sweden, the Netherlands, Australia, Israel) have introduced amendments to leasehold legislation in order to ensure that the rents from leases are adjusted for inflation, and to ensure that rents are adjusted if use changes.

7.3.6   THE SWEDISH EXPERIENCE

One of the most successful public land-acquisition policies has been carried out for over fifty years in Sweden. This is based on a combination of policy instruments, the most important being advance municipal land acquisition in order to supply the needed land for urban growth. The operation of large land reserves has ensured the integrated development of the large municipalities in co-ordination with planned neighbourhoods linked by public transportation. The success of the Swedish policy depends on efficient administrative and financial instruments. Land purchase is carried out by the experienced land agency for each municipality, acting (like large private buyers) swiftly and often secretly. The central government has tried to encourage advance land acquisition through its loan system: positively, loans are given for acquisition of land; and negatively, as a condition of loans for public housing, the condition is that a reserve of land be prepared for the next five years and that reasonable prices be paid for land. These measures, strengthening the Swedish system, were added recently after historical experience showed that the speed of urban development was increasingly straining the capacity and desire of municipalities, particularly smaller ones, to control positively urban growth through planned land ownership.

The Swedish land policy has succeeded in generally ensuring the supply of land necessary to fulfil the needs of urban growth. It has also been successful in allocating the land at the right locations for the needs of the permanently growing urban population. One of its main achievements might be seen as the attempt not only to ensure the appropriate housing conditions but also to combine the appropriate environmental conditions and services within the residential location.

One of the main achievements of the land policy has been the advance land acquisition of large quantities of land combined with legislation making land acquisition the basis for the implementation of urban development programmes. The expropriation legislation and the priority rights purchase allow the municipalities to acquire the land at prices which do not include speculative price increases; they also shorten the delay in acquiring land in cases of expropriation and encourage voluntary agreements thanks to the efficient expropriation legislation.

The Swedish experience has shown that policy must go through an historical evolution and show flexibility to be successful.

7.3.7 THE FINANCIAL BASE FOR ADVANCED LAND ACQUISITION

Financial difficulties are often seen as the main obstacle to the implementation of a public advance land-acquisition policy. Those countries with a long experience of public land acquisition have financed their programmes through normal municipal budget sources, with the assistance of long- and medium-term loans from the central government (Sweden, the Netherlands). France and Spain have financed land acquisition directly from national government revenues allocated to the national land-acquisition agencies, with additional funds from private financial groups interested in participating jointly in development schemes. In the Netherlands and Sweden it is sometimes the case that private builders will transfer land to the public development agencies in order to participate in development schemes.

Experience in the Netherlands and Sweden shows that an advance land-acquisition policy economises on public money, by supplying land for building when needed on the basis of prices paid many years earlier. But in order to test the general applicability of the practice it is necessary to know more about the relationship of certain variables which have been discussed in the economics of development (section 3.5): the rate of increase in the real and monetary price of land in a growing urban region; the interest rate on loans to finance the advance land acquisition; and the rise in cost of infrastructure works needed for development.

But this apart, a detailed study may suggest that some of the difficulty in financing advance land acquisition is a result of a lack of understanding of the importance of such a policy for urban growth patterns, and not purely a result of financial difficulties. It may also suggest that the interests of developers and landowners – interested in continuing to get high profits from the permanent rise in land prices resulting from reliance on the private market to supply land – should not be neglected as a factor creating an unfavourable climate of opinion for advance land acquisition.

A cost–benefit analysis may show that the part of GNP needed for advance land acquisition is not substantial and has little to do with the real financial difficulties. The Netherlands and Sweden started advance land acquisition before the First World War when their GNPs were considerably lower than that of the then most industrialised countries and even of some of the developing countries today. The financial difficulties in advance land acquisition stem mostly from the power of the land-ownership concept, and the underestimating of the deciding role of private land ownership in determining urban growth patterns, where only some uses are profitable (e.g. commercial as opposed to recreational, cultural and other public land uses).

The understanding of the importance of the role of advance land acquisition in assuring more desirable urban growth patterns may lead to the mobilisation of greater financial resources to carry out such a policy, not only from general revenues, but also by collecting a proportion of the increase in land prices throughout the city as a result of the development of new areas (through an appropriate property tax on the additional value). In addition it might be possible to institute a greater degree of partnership between landowners and the development agency – whereby landowners put their land at the disposal of the public development agency, either by granting a lease or simply construction rights, with financial provisions to reflect the nature of the agreement.

Another suggested approach for financing a land-acquisition programme is the encouragement of the investment of private savings in the public land-acquisition and development agencies. The bonds so issued could be indexed to the land prices or rents in the areas of public land administration. Such a method of financing may ensure that the real purchasing power of invested money is maintained, as the leasehold conditions of rent are also adjusted for the consumer price index (or sometimes the GNP level), and also that the increase in value resulting from the general process of urban growth is realised.

The experience of other countries has shown that an important element in the success of land policy carried out by the municipalities is that they have a strong financial basis of revenue. In Holland and Sweden the local authorities receive some fixed percentage of the national revenues from income tax. This amounts to a very substantial sum – in Sweden the local authorities control some 20 per cent of GNP and their revenue exceeds that of the central government. This has made their decisions about land acquisition less dependent on central government financial attitudes. Furthermore, the tax base is also related to land policy, in the sense that it is hoped that a suitable land policy will itself strengthen the financial base of the local authorities. This leads us into taxation.

7.4   TAXATION AND LAND POLICY

The efficiency of taxation methods might be measured by their effects on the financing and planning of urban growth. Taxation on land, like other types of taxation, has a fiscal purpose to assure income for the public authorities; at the same time in some countries the additional aim of taxation is to redistribute income and wealth in order to reduce inequality. Taxation of land has two additional aims: to give to the community the additional value created through public authority planning decisions and investment, and to increase the supply of land needed for urban development.

The effectiveness of all land taxation is ultimately dependent on the valuation system. For example, the rate of betterment tax may be very high, but if the valuation system does not function appropriately the actual tax rate (based on the difference between the original purchase price and the selling price) may be far lower.

An ineffective valuation system is also likely to be an unfair one. Where there does not exist a system which limits the freedom of a valuer to rate property as he sees fit, and also allows public comparison of the valuations of different properties, there is no guarantee that every citizen will be paying the tax equally. This problem of equity in turn creates resistance to payment.

In order for tax methods to be efficient a periodic valuation carried out by the same system for the whole country would be appropriate. This would ensure that there was a check on the estimates of individual valuers and would also show all citizens that they have the same rights and the same obligations. It would also be useful for determining compensation in the case of public appropriation procedures.

Betterment taxes include taxation of the additional value created through 'normal' urban growth and general price increases as well as the profits resulting from specific public authority development works and planning decisions. Legislation in some countries distinguishes between these two categories, and there is a special tax on increases in value connected directly with the carrying out of development work. In some cases this is called a *betterment tax*, and is based on the collection by the public authorities of a part of any additional value resulting from planning decisions but not necessarily as a direct result of infrastructure works. There are special categories of taxes on the profits resulting from public decisions to change land use from agricultural to urban, or to allow more intensive use of land than accepted in the planning schemes.

Other countries use the term *land increment* or *land profit* tax, which is based on collecting a part of land profits without defining the cause of increased land value. Such a tax includes the collecting of a tax on land profits resulting from the impact of 'normal' urban growth as well as those due to the public authorities' planning decisions. It is based on the general concept of capital gains taxation. However, in general it is difficult to separate the additional land value resulting from public authorities' investment and planning decisions and that increase caused by general inflation and urban growth processes.

Special taxation of the additional value created through land-use changes, depending on the methods of valuation and collection of such taxes, may be of major importance in ensuring a supply of land to the market. The taxation of 100 per cent of the additional value created through higher densities (as in France) should restrict the granting of exaggerated densities in urban areas. But there is a danger in such a tax of a contradiction between the financial and planning aims: that is, the local authority may actually be encouraged to allow greater densities and overcrowding in the city in order to gain the additional tax revenue. The calculation of the additional value in such cases may also be arbitrarily adjusted to fix a lower rate of tax than expected so as to benefit developers.

There are some public authority decisions whose effect on price land increases might be measured easily. The planning decision to change land use from agricultural to urban, or from residential to commercial, or increase the building densities, leads to such a high rate of price increase that is quite comparable with creating a new land value.

The calculation of land profit is usually based on the difference between the sale and the purchase price of the land. The maintenance expense of holding the land (taxes, improvements) are added to the purchase price. Recently some countries decided to link the purchase price and other expenses to the cost of living index in order to eliminate the effect of inflation on the sale price.

Land profit taxation based on the distinction between 'normal' capital gains and those stemming from planning decisions is limited in most countries to planning decisions changing use or increasing densities; in some countries, however, the costs of additional infrastructure works (roads, etc.) are included, making the calculation of the impact of betterment on land prices rather complicated.

Some countries fix a lower rate of land profit taxation if the owner has been in continuous possession for a long time. Such an approach is based on the assumption that land transactions after a short holding period are basically commercial transactions to be taxed as other profits, while land sales after a long ownership period are a kind of savings which should be taxed at a lower rate. For example, in some cantons in Switzerland land profit taxation does not apply after fifteen to twenty years of ownership. This generally increases withholding of land, as owners wait for the specified period before selling.

Taxes which are not intended to have planning effects may nevertheless have unintended consequences. A property tax based on the concept of the current rental value is only paid when real property produces income. This offers no incentive for occupation or development. Such a system also means that a small house with a large garden that is centrally located is not heavily taxed. The capital value of a vacant or built site is based on the expected income from construction on the site, while taxation on rental value only taxes the *present* use value of a site. Rental value taxation can lead to such inequities as low-value suburban property rented out to low-income, overcrowded residents having a higher tax burden than central-city vacant sites.

Some countries which use rent as the basis of property tax do not use the real income from property but, rather, an estimate of the potential rental value in the prevailing market conditions. In this case empty buildings are taxed, but the level is determined by the estimate of the potential rent of the space in its current use, which may be less than the current market value, which takes into account the potential rent from prospective changes in use or density.

In order to encourage the use of land for construction and to reduce the amount of vacant land in urban areas some countries (e.g. the USA, Australia and Denmark) have introduced a different rate of tax for land and buildings, sometimes even taxing the value of land separately (site value taxation).

Other countries have, with the same objective, introduced a high rate of taxation on vacant land in urban areas. Syria has introduced a progressive rate of taxation of vacant land which depends on the value of the site. Spain has an increasing rate of tax for each year the vacant land is not used for construction.

The reason for taking account of the amount of time the land is held vacant or the value of the site is to avoid the taxation of individuals holding land for themselves and their children rather than for speculative reasons. An increasing rate with time is intended to force development. The effectiveness of such measures, however, also depends on the nature of the valuation of the property and the efficiency of collection of taxes. In some countries where there are many long-standing taxation debts and a high rate of inflation, tax debts are index-linked to inflation, and there may also be additional time-linked penalites for non-payment.

The impact of vacant site taxation on land prices and the supply of land to the market depends on the rate of tax in comparison with the rate of increase of land prices. Where land prices are increasing quickly, a low rate of vacant site taxation will not encourage owners to sell when they can gain much larger profits if they can afford to wait a few years. Thus sometimes such taxation only forces small owners to sell and leads to the concentration of vacant land in the hands of large financial groups who can afford to pay the tax and hold the land until the public authorities authorise a more profitable land use on the site, thus realising large profits. But in general a land property tax on built sites which is based on the land value only, or land which is more heavily taxed if it is not used according to approved planning schemes, may lead to the use of land nearer to its full capacity.

It may also be suggested that it might be appropriate to tax commercial land at higher rates than residential land; the reason is that commercial land prices lead to higher land prices in adjacent residential areas through an expectation of change of use, which in turn tends to increase other urban land prices. A high rate of tax on centrally located commercial sites, combined with a tax on the turnover of business enterprises, may (if high enough) make land expensive enough in the central business district to reduce demand for land there and effect a redistribution to other areas.

This review of taxation methods adopted in different countries shows that there are various attempts to adjust the taxation system to the growing needs of public expenditure on urban services which are permanently increasing in cost. But it may be suggested that in no country has the taxation system succeeded in collecting the major part of the additional value created through the urbanisation process.

It is suggested by some that the land price increase may be slowed through the introduction of some taxation methods which reduce the possibility of gaining high profits from land. One of the reasons for the high rate of land price increases is the restricted supply of land in areas where there is a high demand. Therefore, it is suggested that a taxation system which makes it expensive to hold land vacant will increase the supply of land to the market and hence reduce land prices. The introduction of a high rate of tax on vacant land, with an increasing rate for each year the land remains unbuilt, may lead to an increase in supply of land to the market. Obviously, it is necessary to collect this tax regularly and to expropriate the land of those owners who avoid the tax.

Another useful device is the differential assessment of land and buildings in order to encourage the use of land to the fullest extent possible according to planning regulations. For example, buildings may be taxed at half the rate of land.

An additional factor influencing the efficiency of tax collection, discouraging excessive land price increases and stimulating development is the timing of the payment of a tax on the additional value created through planning decisions. If this is not at the time of transfer of land ownership but at the time the public authority decision to change land use was made, it will secure earlier income for the public authority and at the same time diminish the attractiveness of capital investment in land.

The method of taxation in the city and city region is related to the general structure of a city/regional government. There are few city regions with strong metropolitan regional authorities. The lack of such an authority with overall responsibility for urban growth expenditures leads to planning decisions being taken by some local authorities based on short-term fiscal necessities which are in conflict with long-term planning goals.

The basis of successful implementation of taxation policy is the existence of an efficient valuation system. The experience of different countries using particular valuation systems is that a system of periodic and public valuation is relatively inexpensive in relation to the advantages that such a system has. When landowners perceive that the system of valuation is fair and based on common criteria, there is less evasion of taxes and less scope for corruption than when decisions about valuation are made relatively arbitrarily. Therefore, the establishment of a land register and a systematic and periodic tax-assessment system are the most important measures which must be introduced for a successful taxation system.

7.5 THE COMMUNITY LAND SCHEME FROM THE FOREIGN PERSPECTIVE

This broad review of foreign experience has had one main aim: to show what foreign experiments could be helpful in new British land policy. Since so much in this regard is now based on the community land scheme (see Chapter 6), it is thought helpful here to make some pertinent comments on the scheme based on the foreign review.

One of the most important questions concerning the community land scheme is its effect on the land market. The Community Land Act makes it the specific duty of the local authority to enter the land market. But the financial structure puts pressure on keeping prices high. As it is intended that all acquisition of land be financed from the proceeds of disposal, the local authority has an interest in high land prices in order to make a large profit from betterment gains.

It is impossible to tell at this stage exactly what effect it will have on land prices but it is possible to make some suggestions based on the foreign experience.

In so far as there is the expectation that the Act will be repealed, it may have a limited impact on the existing land market, as it is expectations about the ability to use land in the future that have a large impact on present prices. The other factor which may limit the effect of the scheme on land prices prior to the 'second appointed day' system (when land must pass through local authority hands) is that the most profitable land, presumably, and especially commercial land, will still be bought and sold through private transactions. Here it is the rate of the new development land tax that is the relevant factor; but as we have seen above, the tax system alone is unlikely (in this form) to influence market patterns. The local authorities do have an incentive to take more land through their own hands, as they get a lower price than before (i.e. gain the equivalent of development land tax), while they get nothing if private transactions occur (the revenue goes to the central government). But they are limited in the amount they can spend.

There is no doubt that the Community Land Act will make land that the local authority acquires itself cheaper (especially green-field sites). But the price effects on the private land market, as the local authority is selling or leasing at market prices to private owners, are difficult to predict – it depends whether they adopt an essentially 'sectoral' approach concerned primarily with their own acquisition, thus possibly acting as speculators, or whether they move quickly to supply all land for all private needs as required.

One of the most important aspects of the Community Land Act is the degree to which it will encourage land banking, i.e. advance acquisition of land for future urban development. While in theory the Act provides an instrument for public authority land banking, in practice it discourages it. As the Act is intended to be financed from receipts on disposal, there is every incentive to the local authority to release land as quickly as possible. As the pressure of the private sector is likely to be for this as well, it is likely that most land will be released to meet short-term needs. Thus there is a danger that such a policy will ignore long-term development strategies in favour of such immediate and tactical considerations. There is an inevitable conflict between short-term and long-term needs, but the financing of the Act increases this and shifts the balance to short-term needs. This has serious implications for the land-use planning aims of the Act.

The experience of other countries has shown that when the public authorities only acquire land for present needs, the selection of sites is heavily influenced by private developers. The CLA specifically encourages this. But the needs of private, immediate development may not be consistent with a long-term development plan. And as local authorities have often not worked out their long-term comprehensive development plan in Britain, there is the possiblity that the Act will lead to the consideration of land administration and price influencing the plan (in a way similar to that described as happening before the Act).

One of the potential problems in the current Community Land Act is the problem of local–regional co-ordination. Whereas in Wales there is a regional authority which can avoid the issue, in England all power for executing the Act is given to the local authorities. This raises two problems: first, the experience of many countries carrying out public land acquisition has shown that the smaller municipalities do not have the expertise or interest to carry out such programmes, and must get outside assistance in some form; second, there are often conflicts between different authorities in a metropolitan region over the priorities of development – small communities sometimes do not like to develop. The Community Land Act has no mechanism for resolving such conflicts; in theory there could be joint land-management schemes between authorities, but in practice it is precisely those urban authorities where conflict is likely which have shied away from such schemes.

7.6 SOME UNRESOLVED PROBLEMS IN LAND POLICY

Even the most advanced countries have still not fully resolved all the problems of land policy.

7.6.1　CO-ORDINATION IN A CITY-REGION FRAMEWORK

The purpose of land acquisition and the role of the central and local public authority in the government structure affects the character of the land-acquisition agencies. In a country with a strong central government or no strong local authority tradition there were established national land-acquisition and land-development agencies, as in France, Spain, Israel, Singapore and Hong Kong. The countries with a long tradition of local government autonomy have developed municipal land-acquisition agencies, as in the Netherlands, Sweden and Britain. Here, the experience shows that the lack of regional land-acquisition and land-development agencies is a serious obstacle for carrying out not only national and regional development schemes but even an efficient land development policy of a city with a long tradition of land acquisition (as in the case of Dutch cities). The lack of regional land-acquisition and land-development agencies may be seen as one of the obstacles for the further development of human settlements in countries with long public land-acquisition experience (the Netherlands, Sweden, Denmark).

It is by the transformation of the city function from the city to the city region which makes a separate city land-acquisition and development policy impossible, since urban growth occurs mostly in the city region.

The UK experience also shows that the lack of co-ordination between the former (national) Land Commission and the municipal authorities, and the lack of regional land-acquisition agencies (with participation by the municipalities), is one of the major weaknesses in effective land policy; and this is being perpetuated in the community land scheme for England. But the experience of Israel shows that the operation of a national land authority administering public land, without co-ordination with municipal authorities and without establishing regional land authorities, may involve a contradiction between the needs of the urban growth and the fiscal vested interests of the land authority. The regional land-acquisition and land-development agencies in France, which have the participation of the municipal authorities in the region, as well as that of the representatives of some private economic institutions, may serve as an example of such a regional executive.

In countries where the land authority is autonomous and even independent financially it may attempt to demonstrate its efficiency by showing large financial surpluses. It can happen then that the public land agency is acting as a small vested interest in contradiction to the planning requirements of other public institutions. The examples of the land authority in Israel (the New Delhi Land Development Agency) and the French implementation agencies of ZACs (zones of concentrated action) show what might be the dangers of a public agency activity if its policy is not part of a comprehensive development process closely co-ordinated with other public authorities.

There are several well-known examples which received much public criticism, such as the changing of the face of Paris by allowing extraordinary high-rise building along the *Seine*, and the high-rise building erected on the hills of Jerusalem. One of the deciding factors in these public decisions was the higher immediate income for the public land authority from a decision allowing higher densities than fixed by the planning authorities. In such a way these public agencies are carrying out a policy based on short-term profit, which is the basis of the private economy, and neglecting the destructive effect on urban growth patterns of such policies. Some in France and Israel suggest that this short-sighted financial policy by the land authorities does not increase (even in the short term) government revenues but only increases the revenues of private financial interests by giving them conditions more favourable than those formerly possible on the basis of free competition.

There are of course difficulties in deciding how to take into account conflicting views between local and city-region needs and also between different strata of the population. One such conflict is between the short-term needs of housing stock and the long-term development scheme for a planned city region. Large-scale land acquisition could reduce this conflict by making available land for housing purposes in the context of an overall planning scheme with properly developed infrastructure and public services at the same time.

The situation in the Stockholm region illustrates some of the problems of regional co-ordination. The close relationship between Stockholm and the localities in the region created a need for regional co-operation and the establishment of institutions capable of co-ordinating the activity of Stockholm and the municipality in the region. The reality of people living in the region and working in Stockholm created a need for the establishment of a regional authority to plan the region's activities and to execute the plans. The Stockholm region succeeded in creating a regional planning association. Although a voluntary authority, it has a strong influence in planning the housing activities and negotiating with the National Housing Board to get the needed government loans to subsidise the housing and the distribution of housing among the municipalities of the region. This planning association acts on the basis of co-ordination with Stockholm and the municipalities of the region. Obviously, there are some conflicting interests between different municipalities in connection with the allocation of housing needs. But those different interests are generally solved in the framework of the co-ordinated activity of the regional planning association.

A more difficult situation has been created regarding land supply and land use. There exist differences between the financial possibilities of Stockholm in comparison with the small municipalities. The Stockholm municipality succeeded in purchasing large quantities of land located outside Stockholm and within the administrative framework of the small municipality in the region. The land use for satisfying the needs of the Stockholm citizens depends, therefore, not on the available land purchased by Stockholm but on the readiness of the other municipality to use the land on the basis of agreement with the Stockholm municipality.

Obviously, there exist some conflicting interests between Stockholm and the other municipalities interested primarily in satisfying the needs of their citizens. These conflicting interests might be expressed either in the wish of the municipality to use more land for satisfying the needs of their citizens rather than Stockholm's residents. Sometimes the municipalities are not interested in growth and are refusing to develop land located in their administrative area. Such conflicting interests between the separate municipalities are an expression of the existing conflict between a group of citizens and a large strata of citizens, and also a result of conflicting interests between the present generation and the needs of the future generation. The institutional aspect of this conflicting interest may receive a solution through the establishment of regional institutions with executive power, but also on the basis of participation of the different municipalities in the regional institutions' decision-making and on the basis of an active participation of citizens of the region in the planning process on the basis of co-ordinated activity between planners and citizens.

As another example, the favourable experience of the last twenty-five years of Amsterdam municipality's acquisition policy is primarily based on the planned development *within* its municipal jurisdiction. There may be difficulty in planning future extension because much of the land needed for new development schemes is located in the broader city region, and includes land within other autonomous municipalities. Therefore, new development plans will require close co-ordination with those of other municipalities.

Such regional co-ordination may not come easy, however. The basic problem centres on the need to take a regional development approach without the regional institutions with the authority to do so. Close co-ordination does take place at the provincial level, where each of the seventeen provincial governments co-ordinates the activities of the municipalities in their respective provinces. The provincial governments cannot, however, initiate and direct the municipalities to execute provincial development plans. As the provinces have no agencies for land acquisition or implementation, all plans must be executed by the separate municipalities. The propensity for contradictions between local and regional interests is also quite high. For example, some of the smaller municipalities may be more concerned with maintaining existing 'town character' rather than allocating land to build roads for increasing access between other towns. Similarly, some municipalities may be opposed to some forms of industrial development because of the wish to retain the residential features of their towns. In like manner, there is a potential contradiction between local and national interests in that national planning to promote balanced development of different parts of the Netherlands may result in some decisions which are completely distasteful to certain municipalities (e.g. a decision to locate a 'needed' industry somewhere on the basis of minimising environmental impact).

In summary, while the achievements of the Amsterdam municipality's land-acquisition policy has met with remarkable success to date, it is now having difficulties in acquiring additional land outside its own administrative frontiers. This problem, in particular, points out the structural and administrative difficulties involved in formulating efficient, long-range, land-use policy in the Netherlands. As a result, the need for a regional land-acquisition and land-use authority is becoming an urgent problem, a problem which will require further adaptation of the existing administrative structure so as to better respond to the new needs resulting from the extension of the city's functions into a broader city region.

7.6.2   URBAN RENEWAL

The greatest problems in urban land policy relates to urban renewal. In no mixed-economy country has the problem of the high probity costs been solved; and in no country has the problem of allocation of central-city land use according to proper social criteria been completely resolved successfully. This may be a contributory factor to the shift in emphasis in many countries in recent years from redevelopment to rehabilitation.

Britain has been in many respects a pioneer in the field of urban land policy for redevelopment. However, the same difficulties of cost have reappeared again and again in the history of British urban land policy. In this respect the Community Land Act is not likely to change the position very much. Although it applies the compensation criteria of current use value (rather than speculative value), it is not likely in general to result in reduced prices for central-city land. A look at the experience of other countries in the field of urban renewal shows that they have encountered similar difficulties.

In Holland, for example, it was originally planned to carry out a comprehensive redevelopment of the inner-city core (other than the old historic quarter). In 1969 a plan for comprehensive demolition and reconstruction was drawn up (*First Memorandum on Urban Renewal*). This was envisaged as a forty- to fifty-year project, similar in scope to Amsterdam's urban-extension programme, which would systematically reconstruct the old districts of the city one by one, starting with the very worst ones. In 1971 the specific districts that it was proposed to reconstruct were outlined. Approximately 18,000 dwellings were scheduled for destruction in the first stage of the plan. As part of the plan would involve the lowering of densities within the inner city, it was understood that the plan would have to be co-ordinated with the urban-extension programmes already undertaken in the city.

But the main difficulty with urban renewal is the high cost of the land to be acquired in the city centre. Amsterdam's preliminary estimates for the urban-renewal programme showed that the rebuilding of an area only one-quarter of the size of their newest urban extension (500 hectares as opposed to 2,000 hectares in the south-east extension) would cost two and a half times as much. The unit land costs were 600 to 1,350 guilders per square metre as opposed to 37·5 guilders for the municipal extension. This is because for already urbanised land, as opposed to newly developed green-field sites, it was not possible to control the price of land through municipal acquisition policies.

In the light of these considerations, and also in order to gain a more participatory approach which took into account the views of the residents of these areas, Amsterdam now has a project approach to renewal as opposed to comprehensive redevelopment and rebuilding. Project groups, consisting of representatives of the different city departments, as well as citizen involvement, have been set up in a number of selected inner-city areas marked for renewal. The project group itself decides what mixture of renewal, rehabilitation or new building will take place and includes considerations of social as well as physical reconstruction. For example, in one area it was decided to demolish approximately eleven blocks (some 1,200 dwellings in four premises) and rehouse the families, constructing a park and various youth and community centres in a part of this reconstructed area. But the major emphasis has now been placed on rehabilitation, as when a series of back-yards for tower blocks were reconstructed to allow for a communal play space.

We now turn to the USA, which has some very interesting institutional arrangements for urban renewal. The Federal urban-renewal legislation, which began in 1949, has provided for a federal subsidy for the municipal acquisition, assembly and disposal of land for private redevelopment in dilapidated areas of the inner city. Although the cost-sharing formula has proved effective, the programme has run into a good deal of political criticism and is now greatly curtailed in scope.

The basic system in the USA is that the Federal government will underwrite two-thirds of the 'net project costs' of the local urban-renewal authority. The net costs are basically the losses made by the agency in the disposal of land at its fair market value; thus the government is subsidising most of the land-acquisition costs. The government also makes loans available, both short-term (for providing the capital to begin the project, which is then paid back out of proceeds from sale, and federal and local revenues), and long term in the case of leasing. However, loans are often obtained from private sources for the redevelopment. This does not affect the federal capital grant subsidy.

This urban-renewal legislation was intended to improve the quality of residential housing available in cities, and it was specifically written into it that an urban-renewal project must involve a 'predominantly residential' character. This was originally opposed by those advocates of urban planning who argued that there should be a possibility of preparing a more comprehensive shceme. In practice, however, the requirement has been whittled down so that about 20 per cent of redevelopment takes place on industrial or railroad land, and certain specific exemptions have been given. But this requirement has legally been interpreted to apply to areas before redevelopment; and thus in some cases it is possible to reconstruct the area in a more commercially orientated manner.

One of the most important provisions is that its purpose is to encourage private-enterprise redevelopment. This meant that the renewal agency, having acquired a large parcel of land, had to dispose of it to a private developer who was willing to bid for it. This has created several problems. While there is a legal requirement that the redevelopment be carried out according to an approved plan by the municipality, there is also the possiblity that if the city goes ahead by its own it will not be able to dispose of the parcel by itself. It will also lose out financially if it designates too much of the parcel for public land, because it will have less to sell. For these reasons there has generally been close co-ordination between private developers and public agencies in planning such projects. Cities have often been forced to give tax relief and other incentives to developers in order to attract them to their area.

Another important effect is that, generally, it is not commercially possible to build much low-income housing in the redeveloped blighted area. This has led to the greatest political controversy, with charges that urban renewal has been 'negro removal', or just the replacement of the poor by richer residents in certain choice areas of the city. Others have also argued that the working-class communities displaced have not been relocated elsewhere, and that the rehousing provisions have been totally inadequate. Although there are legal provisions requiring provision being made for rehousing, uptake has been low. This is partly because of bad communication and the fact that many have left the area before the actual renewal, but also because there is little public housing available for use as rehousing, and therefore rehousing at equivalent rents cannot be guaranteed.

7.6.3   ALLOCATION OF LAND WITHOUT THE MARKET MECHANISM

While public land supply may assure enough land, there is still the question of what uses are appropriate for what locations. Whereas the market has its own mechanism for this task, the relationship between the public land authority and the other government agencies, especially the planning authority and the financial departments, are of the highest importance in the administration of the publicly owned land. The criteria for answering this question may be seen as relating to the unsolved problem of public land administration. An examination of the practical problems, including those in the socialist countries who have reached the point at which this problem is acute, may be illustrative.

The basis for estimating land prices in the area of land acquired by the public authority varies from one country to another. Generally, it is admitted that the calculation of price should be based on the costs of land acquisition plus the investment in the infrastructure costs. In some cases the investment in the social overhead (public facilities) is also included in the costs, as well as the interest on loans for land acquisition and the infrastructure investment. But the problem arises in the distribution of these costs according to the different land uses and land users.

Generally, in most countries the price of land for low-cost housing is based on the costs of the public authority, and in some cases the price is estimated lower than actual cost, on the basis of a special subsidy from the central government for low-income housing.

In a case where the land authority is supplying land for middle-income groups and for commercial enterprises there are different approaches in different countries. The Netherlands and Sweden put the land cost as the same for residential purposes, without distinction between levels of housing standard, with the price differences based on location and density of use. Australia (Canberra) fixes a low price for social housing and leaves to competition among builders the price for high-level residential use.

The same approach is established in the New Delhi Land Development Corporation in Israel. The land for residential purposes is fixed administratively by the land authorities, establishing lower prices in new towns and less-developed regions and higher prices for residential use in the big cities and in already developed urban areas.

Commercial land prices are established in most countries by competition, but some countries fix them administratively lower than the market price in order to attract commercial services in new areas. While such a system may achieve this objective, it may also result in discrimination in favour of some commercial enterprises which succeed in locating in an attractive area. On the other hand, if there is no prospect of a sufficient turnover in new areas, even low (administratively set) prices will not be attractive enough. Some cities have solved this problem adequately by erecting needed commercial services in new areas directly, by public or co-operative institutions, subsidising prices at first and establishing higher land prices and rentals after some time.

An interesting example of fixing criteria for commercial land prices in new towns is the French legislation for new town centres. It is suggested that the commercial enterprise should pay land rental not on the basis of land value but as a part of the turnover. This system is based on an assumption that commercial land prices are influenced by the location and size of the human settlement (which influences the turnover). Therefore, the commercial services would pay a lower rent than actual land cost in the first period of new town development, and a higher rate in further stages of development.

There are differences in the approach to the evaluation of land for urban uses in the socialist countries, especially that used by public institutions and economic enterprises. In the USSR, where all land is nationalised, those enterprises financed directly from the central government budget use land without payment. Private persons and companies pay rent for the use of agricultural land, and individual and co-operative owners of housing pay rent based on the agricultural rent plus the estimated additional urban value (depending on location). The part of the rent due to location is collected by the local authorities.

The approach of the USSR was influenced not only by theoretical considerations but also by the generous availability of unused agricultural land and potential urban land. Recently the high rate of urbanisation and industrialisation in the USSR has also increased the pressure to fix criteria for rents based on an economic calculation of costs. This is based on the theoretical approach that urban land is not only a natural resource but is also an economic good whose value is fixed by the amount of investment in a particular area creating a physical and social infrastructure which makes a location valuable.

A different approach has been adopted by Poland, Czechoslovakia and East Germany, no doubt influenced by the smaller amount of potential agricultural land available in these countries than in the USSR (from 0·5 to 0·63 hectares per inhabitant as compared with 2·33 hectares in the USSR). The reasoning on land valuation in a socialist economy (as it is seen in Poland) has been presented as follows:

> No more doubts are still caused by the consideration that land as a means of production or of services should be introduced in the economic account and that the price paid for land used for production or services should be an economic regulator and stimulate rational investments. On the other hand opinions on the principles of pricing and its functions are highly controversial (e.g. whether the price should perform its allocative and distributive role or ought to be restricted to inventory and informative functions only). Some countries are also doubtful if the price for land use should be paid by everybody including public land users or whether this duty should be – as in the Soviet Union – limited to private and co-operative users. Finally there exist different solutions as to the way of collecting payments for the benefit of national or local self-government.

In Poland there was introduced in several cities a system of payment of rent on the basis of location value but not agricultural use value. Although the rate is low, the importance lies in the acceptance of the principle of charging land rent according to location, and using the rent for the execution of infrastructure works for urban growth. From the institutional aspect, what is important is that the rent is collected by the local authorities which are responsible for providing the infrastructure works. On the other hand, as the rate is low because well-defined criteria do not exist, such rent does not play an important role in the economic calculations of cost for housing construction or industrial enterprises.

Probably a more comprehensive approach should take into account a more differentiated set of criteria for the evaluation of land values without the market mechanism. Some parameters may be introduced to evaluate the economic impact of location (as expressed in distance from the city centre), the turnover of commercial firms, and the relation between land value and construction and infrastructure costs.

The distance may be measured by the time and discomfort of travelling (i.e. the cost of time to people commuting to the city centre), as well as by the ratio of land to total housing costs, which may be of value in fixing land values according to different locations in the city region.

A coefficient of city size may also be introduced as an additional factor in estimating land value (i.e. land in a big city is more valuable than in a small or medium-size town). Such a coefficient may be seen as part of a policy of balanced growth, making land more expensive in large human settlements than in rural areas and in new towns planned for future growth (where the coefficient could reach zero).

The value of land for services may also be based on some coefficient, raising its value in comparison with residential values. Obviously, such a system will make land in the central-city area more expensive; this may be useful for enforcing lower norms of land allocation in the central city than at some distance from it.

Generalising from this for a non-market economy, the calculation of the total costs invested in infrastructure (physical and social) as well as of the structures erected above the land may serve as the basis for the estimation of the total production cost of a human settlement in new towns and new neighbourhoods. This aggregate would then be distributed, according to different social criteria, to the various users of the space of the human settlements. There would need to be taken into account the amortisation of the costs – whether it should be over one generation or over the entire estimated life of the settlement, i.e. over many generations. Thus the establishment of appropriate land values based on costs also depends on the general approach to natural resource conservation in an overall socioeconomic framework.

7.7 SOME CONCLUSIONS ON PLANNING AND THE MARKET

Our initial question was whether it is possible to leave the initiative for the development of land in private hands and still avoid undesirable side-effects. Do local authorities need the instrument (land) in their hands in order to implement their planning schemes effectively?

If left to private initiative, development tends to be implemented in bits and pieces, and the overall development strategy gets lost. This leads to side-effects due to the interrelationship of land uses. For example, if, due to commercial pressures and the lack of any other policy of office development, planning permission is given to high-rise buildings in the central business district, this leads to excessive traffic congestion and noise in the central area and the deterioration of near-by residential communities. Shopping centres in residential areas have a similar effect. Even more significant is the side-effect on social housing – public authorities are forced to obtain land where they can, and as cheaply as they can, and this leads them to build housing without services located far from the city centre, with increased travel time, with its direct and indirect costs. Such are the effects on the development of the city region if a planning system exists but is not able to impose land use according to plan.

Another side-effect concerns national land-use planning. There have often been excellent sectoral land-use programmes, such as for the creation of national parks, forest preservation, and so on. But too often these efforts have not been properly co-ordinated with city and regional planning. The result is that national parks and recreational areas are located too far from large population concentrations and recreation land near metropolitan areas is not preserved.

In general the planning system makes decisions about the acquisition of land a function of the land market, rather than releasing land according to the stages of plan implementation.

Theoretically it may be possible to influence the land market without public ownership, through those comprehensive measures which absolutely forbid any building in rural areas but designate enough for urban uses, coupled with a high-enough rate of property tax or other measures to force the use of vacant land in the areas designated for development. The example that approaches this most closely is that of Denmark. It should be noted that effective legal controls often do not have to be applied to be effective – it is the *belief* that they will be applied that is crucial.

But in practice most tax measures have been ineffective. This has been partly due to weaknesses in administration, such as the lack of a good valuation system. But it is also due to the lack of a comprehensive approach, in understanding the side-effects of measures and combining different types of measures to gain the desired outcome.

The classic example is the high rate of land profits tax in Britain which has increased prices through the withholding of land in order not to pay the tax. The ineffectiveness of such measures has led the public authorities to consider public land acquisition as a way of meeting their objectives of land policy. It is to this that we now turn.

The goals served by urban land policies may be achieved in different ways, and the machinery of planning may serve as an efficient means of fixing the kind, location and use of land. The land-acquisition policy conducted in different countries to a large extent allows for creating a basis for realising the urban land planning aims.

Detailed land-use planning, i.e. fixing the different land categories of the country according to the actual and future needs, is a basis for land policies mostly in countries using planning machinery as a framework and a basis for general economic and social development. One of the difficulties in using planning as a tool for urban land policies is the changing character of the needs. The land-use schemes prepared for actual needs may be useless and even an obstacle to development if they are not continually adapted to the current and the forecasted needs. Therefore, the use of planning machinery may be of highest importance, but at the same time it may be a burden if the adequate conditions for using planning in an efficient way are non-existent. One of the crucial problems of using the planning machinery involves adapting planning methods and purposes to the peculiar conditions of a country.

The planning machinery demonstrates its role in land-use policies particularly in densely populated or small-sized countries, as in the Netherlands, Hong Kong, Singapore, Taiwan and Israel. In larger countries efficiency is often a result of it being a part of comprehensive planning, as in England, France and the USSR.

The land-acquisition policies employed by central governments and local authorities are essential to an efficient land policy, because they can permit the acquisition of land reserves for future urban development of city regions and new towns.

An active land-acquisition policy permits land to be transferred from private to public ownership without using political power to overcome the opposition of landowners who may try to hold on to the rights of private land ownership. Furthermore, a land-acquisition policy allows public authorities to become a regulating force in the land market by supplying needed land to the market at appropriate times and restraining land speculation. A land-acquisition policy will show positive results when it is closely co-ordinated with the implementation of the work programmes of public authorities. The efficiency of a land-acquisition policy depends on the extent of the land purchases by public authorities, and the supplying of needed land to the market at the right time and at the appropriate location.

The extent of land acquisition is one of the deciding factors influencing urban development and also justifying the economic calculation. In the conditions of a free market and the free movement of the population and with limited comprehensive economic, social and physical planning, there exists a danger that the public funds invested in land acquisition may be partially unjustified economically, when taking into account the permanently changing needs of the society. In these circumstances it may be difficult to anticipate which locations the public will value most at some time in the future. Rapid technological changes influencing economic and transportation developments may make some regions more desireable in the future than they are today. Thus the creation of land reserves by private interests may involve taking a considerable economic risk. On the other hand, public acquisition of land, co-ordinated with overall development schemes, may ensure the efficient use of created land reserves for the future.

Planning authorities, by fixing open space as well as residential, commercial and industrial land uses, may avoid the economic risks when creating land reserves since these land-use prescriptions will be based on the changing needs of the society.

The planning measures fixing detailed land uses and policies, and developing the necessary land for implementing the planned land-use schemes, are able to achieve positive results when combined in a framework of land-use development policies.

The effectiveness of policy measures depends to a great extent on the co-ordination of policy measures in order to minimise the side-effects due to the interrelationships between different policy measures. The results achieved by a particular policy measure are a function not only of its efficient implementation but also a result of the effects provided by other different measures.

The role of the institutional structure as a framework for implementing policies is one of the factors influencing policy results.

The policy programme is implemented on national, regional and local levels; therefore, conflicts between national, regional and local authorities may hamper implementation. The effective participation of the local level in establishing the regional plan, and the efficient control by the national and regional level of implementation at the local level are important factors leading to policy efficiency. Local authorities must have restricted competence to change land use, yet the ability to influence the release of land needed for urban extension and renewal. The allocation of adequate financial resources for the implementation of local and regional plans by the national or regional authority is important for the implementation of policy plans according to the policy programme.

Based on past experience, the establishment of public agencies responsible for carrying out different land-development schemes might be seen as one of the factors leading to efficient policy implementation.

Chapter 8

Some New Land Policies for Britain

8.1 SOURCE OF NEW LAND POLICIES

We saw above (section 4.5) that there were certain general impediments to the implementation of development plans and programmes in Britain, and then, more specifically, that there were such impediments in land policy measures in the country prior to the community land legislation (section 5.5). We then showed how the new community land scheme went a long way to meet these impediments in land policy (section 6.5), particularly when the 'second appointed day' stage of the Community Land Act would be reached, and to a considerable degree before then (section 6.7).

From this review it was concluded that were the scheme fully operational it would be of great help for plan implementation (section 6.5). Thus, given the appropriate political atmosphere and adequate funds, the coming to fruition of the scheme after the 'second appointed day' would set us on a new course as regards land policies needed for land-use planning and implementation.

But we noted doubts about whether the scheme *would* be implemented were the Conservatives in power; and, even if Labour is in power, whether it *should* be fully implemented beyond the 'first appointed day' stage (section 6.7.5). Furthermore, any view that with the full scheme we had reached the end of the road in land policy measures in Britain was undermined when, following our review of land policies around the world in Chapter 7, it emerged that there were many measures in existence in various countries of a kind not practised in Britain, and which on *prima facie* evidence would be valuable in terms of implementing land-use plans in Britain.

To summarise briefly, our analysis suggests that the pre-community land scheme measures did not go far enough for effective plan implementation (Chapters 4 and 5); the scheme itself goes too far (Chapter 6); and yet, with an eye to foreign experience, not far enough in other directions (Chapter 7). Against this background this chapter makes proposals for additions to our land policy measures, taking as a starting-point the current (1978) situation on the Community Land and Development Land Tax Acts (see section 8.3). But such policies are only measures for the achievement of objectives. Thus before summarising what might be introduced, it is necessary first to restate the aims of such land policies. This is attempted in the next section.

8.2 THE OBJECTIVES OF BRITISH LAND POLICY: FROM 'NEGATIVE' TO 'POSITIVE' PLANNING

If the essential differences between the systems of urban and regional planning as practised in Britain before and after the Second World War were to be described briefly, it would be that there had been a move from 'negative' to 'positive' planning: that is, from the attempt to build towns mainly by negative control over the activities of others to a system in which local and central government could take a more positive and active role. This was recognised as long ago as 1943, when the newly formed Ministry of Town and Country Planning was finding its way, as the following shows:

> whereas, in the past, planning schemes settled the pattern which development should take if it was carried out at all, in future they will map out the programme of development which planning authorities should promote or themselves undertake. The whole basis of planning legislation will need review in order to give statutory expression to this new conception of the objects of planning.[1]

This important change of emphasis was seen in the great array of statutes in town and country planning in the post-war Labour administration (section 5.2). But despite the powers for the purpose provided in the 1947 Act, somehow the positive aspects of this post-war planning became eroded. Perhaps it was inadequate for the purpose; perhaps it was the emasculation of the financial provisions of the 1947 Act in 1952 by the Conservative administration; perhaps it was the change in philosophy and ideology in the country as a whole, as a reaction against positive planning, associated with the all-to-recent war, which brought the Conservatives to power in 1951 and gave blessing to the erosion of positive planning.

Whatever the reasons, this positive aspect of planning was inadequately emphasised or encouraged after the Act came into force and local planning authorities organised their planning departments accordingly. Planning activities were centred on preparing development plans, giving day-to-day decisions on planning applications and fighting the thousands of appeals to the minister against refusal. In short, the interim development control of the 1932 Act became the development control of the 1947 Act. And it became consolidated as the changing economy put more and more development activity into the private sector, while the repeal of the financial provisions of the 1947 Act took the steam out of positive action by the authorities (see section 5.3).

This situation can be given emphasis by contrasting the objectives of John Silkin, when introducing Labour's new land policy in 1974, with statements of Lewis Silkin, when introducing the comparable policy of the 1945 Labour administration. Whereas the father spoke about the need to introduce positive planning,[2] the son spoke also of the same need without dwelling on the differences;[3] in other words, some twenty-five years later it was necessary to try and put the planning machine back on the road where it had started in 1947.

But while it has been useful so far to pose the continuing search in planning for something more 'positive', this very word is of itself not very constructive for what is needed to make plan implementation more effective. For one thing, even negative planning has its positive side, for example in using the power of refusal to steer the developer towards better development; and when this is accompanied by the publication of standards, design briefs, creative discussions, etc., the results have been quite positive (see section 5.4.1). For another, even the most positive of planning has its limitations in implementation, having regard to the essential fact that we are a mixed economy, where much of the drive for development comes from the calculus of the private sector as regards profitability and of the public sector as regards cost minimisation. And indeed, even if we were not in a mixed economy, but there were collective ownership of all the resources, our experience of public-sector development agencies does not suggest that they would automatically collaborate to implement a centrally conceived plan.

Given this mixed economy, if positive planning means anything, it means the ability of the implementation authorities to secure the orderly implementation by development and operating agencies of such plan for its area as has emerged from the planning process, which has regard *inter alia* to the evaluation of feasible alternatives taking into account the community interests and the views and wishes of the people. And given, as described above (section 2.3), that in urban and regional planning it is *development* which is the instrument by which change, economic progress, social well-being and environmental satisfaction are all made possible or denied, it is the appropriate 'programmes of development' which are at the core of what the authorities are trying to achieve.

Thus it is of significance that this move away from the concept of positive planning to the negative has been mirrored, in the evolution of post-1945 planning, in the relaxation and virtual abandonment of the *programme* provided for in the development plans initiated in the 1947 Act. By contrast to the original concept, a plan for development, whereby the development programme *was* the plan,[4] we still use the term 'development plan' but it is in practice used interchangeably with the term 'structure plan', and the framework for development outside the local plans is so much the weaker.[5]

The purpose of such a development programme is to provide a focus for implementation of plans; and within such implementation that land policy has a critical role. Accordingly, if we are to draw conclusions on the objectives needed for changes in the land policy beyond the situation described above (Chapters 5 and 6), then we must devise them within the framework of the implementation of development programmes.

But any such development programme prepared by local government is heavily dependent in its realisation on the backing of the central government, whose specific authority is needed for so much local government activity (authorisation of land purchase, specific grants, sanctions for borrowing money, and so on). However, it has been the practice that central government is not prepared to commit itself to back any local authority programmes included in their development plans, even if it had been approved by the relevant ministry responsible for that sector (now the Department of the Environment). Accordingly, for development programmes to be meaningful central government must find some way for underwriting, backing and finding funds for the basis of the local development programmes, i.e. infrastructure, social overhead and housing. While recognising the difficulties of such commitment and the reasons for central government reluctance, it must go as far as possible along these lines if orderly local development is to be pursued.

In addition to its other centrally formulated policies central government could take on the new implementation influence which has been advocated, controlling the investment policies of the institutional funds.[6] Public ownership of such funds is not contemplated here but rather the imposition of controls over them in the same spirit as the imposition of controls over private use of the land. The reasons are that following prudent investment policy for their beneficiaries, this critical resource is currently being syphoned into development primarily on the criteria of long-term profitability. As a result, vast resources have been given to financially profitable schemes to the neglect of less profitable or unprofitable schemes, not only in the public sector but in the private (e.g. industrial development and rehabilitation), with the result that development priorities throughout the country have been distorted in the light of social objectives.

8.3   STARTING-POINT FOR SPECIFIC PROPOSALS FOR NEW LAND POLICIES

In putting forward specific land policy proposals within the objectives mentioned above (section 8.2) we do so in the same broad categories followed in describing the weaknesses of British land policy prior to the community land scheme: policies which will improve the allocation of resources for the implementation of plans, and those which will change the distribution of the output of the allocation. As mentioned, this categorisation is not particularly watertight (allocation measures result in a certain redistribution, and redistributive measures feed back into allocation) but it does provide a useful framework for our purposes.

In putting forward the proposed reforms in legislation and practice there clearly needs to be some point of departure. The natural point would normally be the established legislation of the country, but in this case the Community Land Act and Development Land Tax Act are not fully in operation. And in the light of the discussion above (section 6.7) there is clearly the possibility that these Acts will not mature in the form intended by the government at the time: for one thing they could well be repealed by a Conservative administration; and for another there is doubt whether even under Labour the Community Land Act would proceed precisely as visualised to the 'second appointed day', and whether the development land tax would reach the 100 per cent of development value. Just where the ball will settle under these influences is impossible to predict. Accordingly, for the purpose of exposition of our proposals we take the current position, i.e.

1   the Community Land Act is in its initial phase after the 'first appointed day'; and
2   the Development Land Tax Act is in its initial phase, with the tax itself being 60 per cent.

In considering the new measures we are again faced with the need for categorisation. Since this varies in each of the sources of our new land policies, it is necessary to be selective. It seems most helpful to divide between allocation and distribution.

8.4   PROPOSALS RELATING TO ALLOCATION

Under this head it is clearer to deal first with the most comprehensive and positive, then to move to the more specific, and conclude with the most negative, development control.

8.4.1. DEVELOPMENT PREVENTED IN NON-PRIORITY DEVELOPMENT ZONES

Whereas in our land allocations in development plans there is some attempt to restrict the supply according to estimated needs and demands over a foreseeable period (say, ten to twenty years), and whereas there is shown some order of priority in the use of such land, in practice authorities find it difficult to ensure the release of the land in some sequence in accordance with the priorities. In a typical case they could refuse permission on grounds of prematurity, in the light of infrastructure developments, but in practice they may not always succeed on appeal, and would then need to put in the infrastructure out of phase.

On the proposition that priorities in development locations and types, and the ability to control the sequencing, are desirable objectives in a development plan, one measure which would assist is to enable the authority to prevent development in areas allocated but where it is not 'needed', in the interests of the town, for another, say, five to eight years. This would concentrate the development on the early phases; the resultant increase in development value which would result on that land could be siphoned off through the development land tax.

But for such measures to be acceptable it would be necessary for the authorities to work out a programme of sequencing which is credible in practice, i.e. that it takes account of land ownership, infrastructure supply, thresholds, programmes, and so on. This kind of advance programming has not been strong in development plans so far; for one thing the support of central government and associated utility undertakings has not always been available (often a result of failure in consultation), and for another the authorities have often not shown a full understanding of the developers' criteria in site selection. But the possibilities have certainly advanced with the introduction of the 'land policy statements' of the Community Land Act which in themselves, to carry credibility, require this kind of programming approach.

Once such a programme has been prepared, it will be necessary for the associated infrastructure and social-overhead programme to be geared with it accordingly. This in turn requires a corporate approach to its services by the local authority in question, a joint corporate approach by the county and district authorities, and collaboration with central government departments and its arms who are together responsible for infrastructure and social overhead (such as the water authorities, the Ministry of Transport, the Ministry of Education, and so on).

Also associated with these moves would be acceptance of the authority's right to be able to prevent development in areas where it or other public agencies had proposals for development but where they had not themselves so far obtained ownership of the land in question. Such rights are currently within the purview of development control, authorities being able to refuse development of land reserved for public purposes, though the intention is often undermined in practice.

In brief, the price of the freedom to manage the orderly development of a town is the ability and willingness of authorities to understand better the land and development market in a mixed economy, and the collaboration in executing programmes by all those agencies which have responsibility for infrastructure and social overhead.

8.4.2   ALL-PURPOSE PURCHASE AUTHORITY OR AGENCY

In Britain the puchase of land for a public purpose is typically undertaken by the agency which requires it for that purpose (e.g. housing, education). While this is clearly sensible, since it is for the authority which will use the land to make up its mind on areas, purchase price, etc., the logic becomes eroded where the various purchases are needed to complement each other within a planned framework, as, for example, in the building of a residential neighbourhood. Here the overriding purpose is the whole neighbourhood. Therefore, should individual authorities pursue their own purposes, they may come into conflict as regards the land they wish to buy, boundaries, etc., and may be bidding up the price against one another by their competition.

In this connection the advantages of the purchase being pursued by a single authority has been seen in Britain in the case of new towns or comprehensive redevelopment areas (although even in new towns there are also purchases by local authorities). But such advantages could also be gained in land purchase for the orderly development and expansion of a town, be it on open land or for renewal. Judged merely from its title, this could be the approach in the community land scheme. But there the potential advantage is constrained by the authority being able to include only land meant for private development and then to select which of its purchases goes into the community land account and which does not. Since this division is primarily a financial one (related to the distribution of community land profits), it clearly could be prejudicial to the concept of the all-purpose purchasing authority.

Thus the concept in the community land scheme needs to be changed to attain the principle of one purchasing authority for all purposes, for local and central government, whatever the financial outcome. All purchases would then go into one account for disposal to the relevant functional committees or private agencies with the advantages of efficiency in, for example, being able to have a specialist department with trained manpower.

Given this approach, individual decisions could still rest with the functional agencies as to the purchases to be pursued (specification of land required, locations, areas of search, price levels, etc.), with the actual purchase being undertaken by the all-purpose purchasing agency. But clearly, in order to achieve the benefits of rationalisation, the latter would need to have some powers of review over the requirements of the former rather than simply act as their executive arm in land purchase.

8.4.3   REGIONAL OR NATIONAL LAND PURCHASE AUTHORITY OR AGENCY

But even where a local authority consolidates its land purchase activities, its functions in this respect could still be undermined. By confining its administration to particular authority areas, and by definition having another authority exercising the same function in competition, it may not be able to take a sufficiently wide view in relation to its acquisition policy. Thus there would appear to be an advantage in having all the purchasing functions centralised in a regional agency as opposed to a local authority; an analogy here is the setting up of the Welsh Land Authority to take on the functions under the Community Land Act which are exercised by local authorities in England.

The relations between the individual agencies seeking land and the regional agency would be similar to that described in relation to an all-purpose purchasing agency. Thus the regional authority would have some review powers over local authorities. This certainly raises complications of its own, as was seen above in the short-lived experience of the Land Commission set up by the Labour administrations for central purchasing (see section 5.3.3).

8.4.4   REGIONAL OR NATIONAL LAND ACCOUNTS

The centralisation of land purchase and disposal on the lines just indicated would bring with it the possibility of cross-subsidisation from high development to low development land values. This could facilitate development in areas of slack demand where there is difficulty in securing development at all, simply because land could have negative development value. Thus there is need for subsidy if adequate development or renewal is to take place here.

Subsidisation from local authorities in such areas is difficult, for by definition they are low in local taxation assessment and financial resources. This leads in practice to the subsidy coming from central government in the form of equalisation grants or regional policy subventions. But a parallel measure would be in the redistribution of the development values themselves. This principle is enshrined in the Community Land Act, whereby profits in the community land account are subject to distribution throughout the country (section 6.2.5). But, for the reasons just mentioned (section 8.4.2), while this is a welcome principle, the execution has limitations, partly because the community land account reflects only part of the development values which have been created and also because not all purchases go through the account. Thus a regional or national land account geared to the principles of an all-purpose purchasing authority could make a significant contribution to the redistribution of development values.

This process could have a particular significance for urban renewal. In parallel with the problems of authorities having more or less growth, and therefore more or less development value, there is the historical co-relation that it is slow-growth authorities which have the oldest towns and also the biggest backlog in terms of urban obsolescence (section 4.1). Thus their needs in terms of renewal are greater as a proportion of development activity in the area. Accordingly, if development values were chanelled to them through the workings of the regional or national land account, they would, by definition, have subsidies towards the backlog of urban renewal.

8.4.5   CO-ORDINATED LAND PURCHASE AND DEVELOPMENT

As mentioned above (section 6.3), under the Community Land Act authorities will need to prepare 'land policy statements' to form the basis of their rolling programmes of land acquisition and disposal, and the instruments for linking the land-acquisition and development proposals will be land-acquisition and management schemes (LAMS).

In order to prepare such land policy statements and rolling programmes it is apparent that the authorities would need to consider the likely and desired development programme of their areas, for it is this which will give the clue to the land assembly, the priorities and the sequence needed. In this it is clearly not only the local authorities' own development which is at issue but that of all agencies, including the private sector. For this purpose the authority will need to work closely with the agencies in this sector to discuss their intentions, needs and requirements.

This particular principle is clearly most important in preparing and carrying out a programme of development for an area, which is the expression of positive planning (section 8.2). But to fulfil its purpose more effectively, the land policy statements and rolling programmes should not be expressed only in land-acquisition and disposal terms, for this is only one factor in comprehensive development, but also as a basis for more integration of all the factors of production in the area. In this connection could be visualised some ongoing discussions with the development industry as a whole, to ensure that it has some measure of the total calls on its capacity which will be made over the ensuing years.

Thus taken to its full, what is here envisaged is more like 'development policy' than 'land policy'; the 'land policy' in the community land scheme can offer only part of the total picture.

8.4.6 IMPROVED PARTNERSHIPS

The arrangements just described indicate the possibilities of closer collaboration between the authority and the development industry. Such collaboration is of a kind which has been called 'partnership' over recent years. While the term has been somewhat loose, it is none the less clear in its intention: that the different factors of the development process see advantage in working together (section 4.2.5). They do so because, while each retains its own objectives, they are voluntarily collaborating with others to undertake a common enterprise to achieve common objectives, with agreement as to respective inputs, liabilities, responsibilities and share of the output.

Given the extended public land ownership of the community land scheme, and the decline in conventional development company activity, there needs to be introduced the new forms of partnership which have been described above (section 4.2.5). Within this, appropriate land policies are and can be devised.

8.4.7 DIFFERENTIAL LOCAL TAXATION

Having prepared our development programme with priorities, how can taxation help? Here we consider three current features of local property taxation in Britain which make it neutral as regards the carrying out of development, and therefore offer no specific stimulus or restriction in that regard. These are (i) the absence of local rates on agricultural land; (ii) the absence of local rates on undeveloped land which is vacant and available for development; and (iii) the pressure for uniformity in rating assessments throughout the country.

On the first, while agricultural land is derated, there is not the pressure which exists in other countries for farmers to sell for development simply to avoid the burden of land taxes. As we have seen, such pressure can be counterproductive in terms of planning where the tax relates to potential and not current use, and where the assessment has regard to the 'market' but not to the future development of the land as visualised in some plan which allocates land realistically in relation to the expected demand. But where, as in Britain, there is such tight land allocation (and indeed some would say under-allocation) of land for development, then there is planning advantage in being able to stimulate the transfer of land from agriculture to development, to stimulate its use in accordance with the plan, at least for the areas of early priority.

This same argument applies even more to land which has already passed out of beneficial use (such as agriculture, sports fields, etc.) and is ready for development but is kept vacant and unused for one reason or another, as in (ii). This situation is encouraged by the absence of land taxes, whereas an appropriate tax on the potential value of the land would stimulate development. Clearly in such cases there would need to be some appeal on the grounds of prematurity or the like, since there could well be reasons whereby the landowner would wish to proceed with the development but is held up by reasons outside his control.

In the third case, if the principle of uniformity in rating assessment could be relaxed, then it would be practicable to introduce differential local rates which could stimulate development where needed in certain areas and of certain kinds and be restrictive in others. This would mean departing from the principle of equity between owners in favour of reallocation; but this is a principle already recognised in regional policy. And clearly such discrimination would need to be geared to planning objectives which had been approved in government regional policies, for otherwise a means would be offered of following local planning policies which would be in conflict with them.

8.4.8 TAKING OF LAND FOR INFRASTRUCTURE AND SOCIAL OVERHEAD ON GRANT OF PERMISSION

It is axiomatic that in any urban area there is a need for both infrastructure (e.g. utilities) and social overhead (e.g. open spaces) alongside the places for living and working. And in a mixed economy there is a general tendency for the former to be provided out of the public purse and the latter out of the private, though there are significant overlaps (notably in Royal Parks or public-sector housing). Furthermore, it is axiomatic that the value of the land used for these private-sector purposes must be enhanced by the provision of the appropriate infrastructure and social overhead; residential areas with no access to schools could not be as highly valued as those (other things being equal) where schools are available.

Therefore, what would appear to be anomalous is that in Britain the land needed for infrastructure and social overhead by public agencies needs to be paid for as though it were to be used for revenue-earning purposes,[7] and not simply as service land to the residential, industrial and commercial uses.

Given the anomaly, what would be needed is that any land developed for revenue-earning purposes (including those in the public sector) yields up on the grant of planning permission its proportion for public use of the kinds described. This would be a general rule which would override the present somewhat arbitrary rules, whereby, for example, the private developer yields up land for local streets to the authorities (having made up the streets) but not for major roads, or small open spaces and not major ones, following negotiations on particular applications in terms of 'planning gain'. Such general rules, judging from other countries (see the appendix), would demand a generous yield from the landowner of around 40 per cent in typical cases. But clearly the percentage take would need to vary with the density of development to be permitted; and there would need to be a form of financial levy on owners of, say, small sites where a percentage take would not be sensible, or of sites which are so located that the land is not needed within it for schools, open spaces, and so on.

8.4.9   COMPULSORY PURCHASE ON BEHALF OF PRIVATE OWNERS

It is generally assumed that compulsory purchase by a public body is for public purposes and in the public interest, and equally that this could not apply to compulsory purchase on behalf of the private sector, since it would (by definition) make financial profit.

But the securing of such profit might none the less go with public gain — as where a private developer wishes to redevelop for housing on a pooled land ownership which he has acquired by negotiation, but on which one recalcitrant owner obstructs. The exercise of public purchase in such cases has been occasionally entertained in Britain. But it could be more widely used — where clear net public advantage is to be seen.

8.4.10   COMPULSORY REPARCELLATION OF PRIVATE LAND

Under the planning system in Britain, where land remains in private ownership, the landowner has the development rights but can only exercise them within the constraints of specific planning permission. This situation is unlike that prevailing prior to the Second World War[8] (and still prevailing in other countries such as the USA),[9] whereby a 'statutory scheme' or 'zoning ordnance' stipulates the constraints on the development which the landowner is legally entitled to follow, and can be denied only on payment of compensation. Accordingly, in Britain the landowners' rights as to form and type of development comes into existence on the grant of a specific planning permission, be it outline or detailed, outside his established development rights for reinstatement of current use (see section 4.3.2). Here in general any wish by the authority to diminish these rights brings with it liability for compensation. So severe can this be in financial terms that authorities rarely incur it.

This situation results in the detailed planning of land being fixed by planning permission, even to some extent on outline permission through the conditions imposed, leaving little room for authorities to change their attitude subsequent to the granting of the permission without liability for compensation. It therefore reduces flexibility. The situation was relieved to a major extent in the Town and Country Planning Act, 1968, when all permissions were given a life of four years, following which there needed to be a further application and consent to restore the owners' position. Even so inflexibility still exists, both during the period of the life and to some degree thereafter; there is a presumption against change in the original terms of consent.

This situation can be met by the introduction of the land policy measure familiar in certain countries around the world, and of considerable antecedents in West Germany, described above (section 7.2.3). Here the rights of the landowners to develop in a certain layout, roads, parcellation, densities, etc. can be rearranged compulsorily according to contemporary ideas, even to the degree of rearranging land ownership and transferring to public ownership certain land needed for social overhead or infrastructure. With such rearrangement there goes the need to keep the owners in a similar financial position compared with previously, either on an absolute or relative basis; in principle the intention is that no one loses and all would gain. Such a measure clearly has application in undeveloped areas. But it perhaps has greater application within built-up areas, where there is greater difficulty in securing departures from the established past in accordance with comtemporary ideas.

Such a measure would be of help where it was intended to permit development. But where it were not, or it was intended to remove current rights, a measure which has attracted popularity in the USA, the transfer of development rights,[10] could be of help. The owner is not denied development to the point of compensation. Rather he is allowed to transfer such rights as he has to other property under his control – where it would accord with the plan. In passing it should be noted why the scheme has less potential in Britain than the USA. As pointed out above (section 8.4.10) landowners here do not have rights relating to potential development and value which need to be bargained above, on pain of compensation, if no satisfactory conclusion is reached.

8.4.11   WIDER POWERS OF PLANNING CONTROL

Under the Community Land Act, after the 'second appointed day' all development land will pass into municipal ownership so that the local authority can give consent as landowner, having regard to planning considerations. But until then, whereas such control will apply in certain instances, mostly there will be the normal planning control on development. This could be strengthened in three ways.

First, it is the criticism against the ineffectiveness of this 'negative' form of planned development which is one of the main pressure points for the community land scheme. Thus all the while it remains it will still be necessary to improve performance in this area, as discussed above (section 5.5.1).

Second, should the Community Land Act ever reach the 'second appointed day', then the situation of the local authority will become reasonably clear; it will have all the powers and rights it needs to control development, for example, in the new towns or in comprehensive redevelopment areas. But until then there is likely to be even more uncertainty than at present (see section 5.5.1) in the minds of the authorities and development applicants as to what control is appropriate for planning (bearing in mind the reserve powers under the Community Land Act to buy should the authorities so wish and the murky area of 'planning gain' (section 5.4.1).[11] There would also be anomaly as between applicants whose land is bought and those whose land is not (both in terms of the authorities' powers and the extent to which the betterment levy is collected). And indeed there could be pressures by an authority to purchase compulsorily or threaten to do so simply in order to exercise the ultimate control.

Third, it was argued above (section 8.4.3) that one objection to the partial municipalisation of land which would be inherent in the 'first appointed day' system of the community land scheme is the mixture of land tenures which could result without apparent rhyme or reason. Where the authority chooses not to exercise its option to purchase, the owners would be freeholders, whereas the exercise of the option would create leaseholders. Since the criteria of desirability could vary from area to area, even though the basic considerations would be common, there would be 'untidiness'. This has its drawbacks, not simply in geographical patterns (which could have estate-management implications), but also as towards equity between individuals in the 'two tenures'.

In order to strengthen planning control to meet all these three weaknesses the following ambitious measure might be adopted.

In respect of planning permission the initiative would still be with the landowner/developer. But where he wishes to obtain development permission, and public purchase is not to be exercised, he can do so only by offering to the authority his freehold subject to the granting of an immediate lease of an interest appropriate for this development (on which there could be arguments for any period of between 80 and 150 years). Both planning permission and the grant of a building lease would be given concurrently on the conclusion of negotiations. The lease would contain provision for ground-rents rising beyond an initial peppercorn. There would be no compensation for the acquisition of the freehold, on the valuation proposition that the long deferment of possession would result in zero value. There would be relevant 'lease-renewal' provisions.

The adoption of this system would have several features. Comprehensive community land scheme purchases would be avoided. Estate management as well as planning conditions could be applied to the development of the land. The landowner could proceed as before, surrendering his interest at the close of lease, subject to the renewal conditions.

Given this authority/landlord combination of powers, the new 'development control' would not be simply the traditional practice but would have added other dimensions to make up a package as follows, subdivided between allocation and distribution (measures 1–7 exist and 8–9 are proposed here).

Allocation
1   Traditional development control.
2   Planning by agreement.
3   Priorities and programmes under land policy statements and LAMS.
4   Landlord control on acquisitions outside the community land scheme.
5   Landlord control on acquisitions within the community land scheme.

Distribution
6   Financial contributions to infrastructure and dedication of streets.
7   Development land tax under the community land scheme.
8   Land take by the authority for infrastructure on zero payment (section 8.4.8).
9   Rental payment under the 'compulsory lease' in respect of some proportion of the rise in land value.

The complexity of this package derives from various sources. First, it would no longer be simply based upon the Town and Country Planning Acts but would involve other departments of the municipalities, thus increasing the co-ordination requirements. Second, since many of the provisions themselves are overlapping in intent and effect, there is room for confusion. Third, certain important elements of the package are in process of evolution so that the learning process must proceed concurrently in respect of them and their relationship with other elements (for example, the new community land scheme). Fourth, the package contains the dilemma as to whether it should be 'planning-led' or 'finance-led', the issue which has arisen under the community land scheme (section 6.3). Fifth, there is the growing political involvement with control decisions of this kind, with the 'black box' of politics needing to be clarified and understood (section 2.9). Finally, there is the growing involvement and interest of the public in these measures, within the mainstream trend of opinion which wishes to see less and less control over the individual and his rights.

As a simple instance of the uncertainty, there is the question of whether the development land tax might or might not undermine the practice of the authorities levying 'specific' betterment as 'planning gain' in the grant of planning permissions. The possibility that these might disappear arises from the fact that some applications have doubtful basis in law; that they grew up in the absence of some overall betterment provisions in the statutes and were condoned as the authorities bid for some betterment from development specific to each situation; and the certainty that the levy of betterment would leave less margin for contribution of planning gain, particularly when development values are slack. Thus in logic a 100 per cent betterment tax would avoid the need for planning gain. But if the betterment tax is to be less than this, it could be that planning gain would still be negotiable in circumstances where it would produce fruitful results for both authority and developer.

All this requires that there be clarity on the purpose and substance of the development control measures and the objectives towards which the development control decisions are being exercised. This is necessary not simply because of the new untried package of controls which is emerging but also because, as pointed out above (section 5.4.1), there is still a lack of clarity on this point in development control. Perhaps the reason lies in the fact that the development control provisions in legislation are much the same today as they were when initiated in the 1947 Act, by contrast with the changing procedures in plan-making. Although a very early attempt revealed the lack of consistency and purpose,[12] there is still obscurity.

Perhaps the way forward is to return to the simplest of concepts in this regard, as follows. In planning we have a mixed economy in at least two senses: the contributions to development of the private and public sectors (accepting that these terms are themselves quite obscure in reality and cover a broad spectrum),[13] and the role of town and country planning in initiating, stimulating, regulating, controlling, etc., both private and public development as an intervening force, as described above (section 3.7). Thus there should be a presumption that the development agencies in their proposals have the benefit of the doubt, since they are pursuing their own functions and objectives with their own resources, and will be taking the responsibilities for their actions and investments, something which no planning authority can hope to supersede with any prudence. Given this, the implementing authority thus has certain simple questions when faced with the proposals, such as:

1   Considering the proposal 'internally', is it to be carried out in accordance with the standards which should be observed in such a development, for example the car-parking provision for a shopping centre, or the provision of amenities for a housing layout?
2   Considering the proposal on a spatial and time scale, will it fit into other projects and programmes?

3   What are the 'external' effects on both neighbours and the community at
large, on the impacts which the development will have, be it environmental,
social, aesthetic, economic, and so on?

Given these questions, criteria need to be formulated for the answers to be
provided on them. As regards the first, there is the battery of 'standards' with
which public authorities are armed. On the second, what costs arise from untidy
sequence of operations? On the last, there are sub-questions of the following
kind: Are the social costs and benefits which will be generated by the impacts
acceptable or should they be reduced? How can the divergence be narrowed
between private and social benefit? How can the total of private and social costs
and benefits be minimised? To what degree should the social costs be internalised
on the development and operating agencies who would implement the permitted
development?
    For the purpose of development and land policy controls these questions are
simple, but they require methods and techniques which are not. They are at the
complex root of how we manage our mixed economy. However, if the questions
are correct, the methodology can be found; if the questions are not correct, there
can only continue endless confusion.

8.5   PROPOSALS RELATING TO DISTRIBUTION

Specific betterment at a reasonable percentage, with or without planning gain,
will go a long way to getting round the distributive or equity aspects of
development value, as between the landowners and the community on the one
hand, and as between individual landowners on the other (section 5.6). But it by
no means goes the whole way. Following are some suggestions for going further.

8.5.1   ADVANCE PURCHASE AT LOWER PRICES

Given that authorities will have all the powers they need for purchase at any time,
for whatever purpose, there is no need for them to buy in advance simply in order
to secure the land (subject to the exigencies of administrative procedures). But in a
developing town there is clearly some point in thinking about advance purchase
for another reason: where the price which would be paid at that moment in time
would be economical in terms of the likely price at the time the land is needed for
development, bearing in mind interest rates and inflation in the meantime.
    This practice has come to be known as *land banking*. In the private sector it is
the prudent reserve for operations by, say, a house builder needing to buy against
competition in the market. In the public sector it is 'a public programme for the
acquisition of a land reserve for future use'.[14] But in addition to providing the
opportunity for purchase at favourable terms, it generally has two other
objectives: providing a mechanism by which public agencies can direct where
development can take place and the nature of that development; and exerting an
influence on land prices in order to keep them at a reasonable level.
    There has been considerable experience of such land banking,[15] and all that
needs be added here is the emphasis to one point made above. In certain
circumstances, in the growth of a town during which land prices rise as maturity

dates advance and with some degree of inflation, it is normally good sense to buy in advance. But the case is not always self-evident. Accordingly, some calculation is needed as to the comparative costs and benefits of advance purchase as opposed to biding time, as a guide to whether or not to add to the land bank, for example when a particular estate comes on to the market.

8.5.2 FREEZING LAND PRICE ON PURCHASE

Whether or not land banking is pursued, the price which is paid by the authority in Britain is that prevailing at the time of the decision to buy, normally at the date of agreement to buy or on the making of the compulsory purchase order. But without specific control over purchase price levels this could work to the disadvantage of an authority. The classic example is in new towns, or in comprehensive redevelopment or town development, where it is the authorities' announced intention to carry out large-scale investment of a kind which would not otherwise be undertaken in the area and which clearly would increase land values and expectations. To overcome this the law provides in Britain for the land prices for acquisition to be pegged to the development potential which exists (and not those which are prospective) at the time of the designation of the new town, comprehensive development area or town development agreement.

This, however, does not 'freeze' the purchase price since this could later increase, owing to inflation, heightened economic activity in established uses, and so on. As a means of getting round this in favour of the authority there has crept in the notion of *actually freezing* the prices to the level prevailing at the time of the decision to designate or expropriate, as the case might be.

But in certain countries, for example Sweden, the measure is even more severe: the price which is actually paid would be that prevailing ten years before the expropriation takes place (see section 7.3.3). This seems to be too stringent for British practice, but it does emphasise the point: there must be some cut-off between what the authorities are expected to pay and what the landowners are entitled to receive.

The current formula in Britain would appear reasonable but could be extended in practice in two respects. First, it could apply beyond the limited cases mentioned to a wider range of cases, for example to any major project for development, redevelopment or rehabilitation initiated by an authority. Second, it could be extended in time to take account of unforeseen events, like the additions to designation in a new town beyond the initial area which in practice have failed to attract the controlled price on purchase.[16] Such extension would still be well behind the concept of the Town and Country Planning Act, 1947, whereby it was *all* development rights in existence on 1 April 1948 which, as it were, became vested in the authorites, so that there could be no question of obtaining compensation for such development rights beyond the levels of value prevailing at that date.

8.5.3 AVOID COMPENSATION FOR OBSOLESCENCE

The preceding discussion relates to development values, those related to potential for future growth. But other considerations arise in respect of the acquisition price to be paid for current as opposed to development values. On these it is the practice in Britain, and one that is rarely departed from, that acquisition price should be no less than the values of current use of the property in question. It is this which the owner has in his pocket, as it were, and for which he should be compensated. This is in contrast to the development value, which, Uthwatt argued (see section 5.2), he does not own and to which there is some doubt as to whether he is entitled, until such time as the value is in his pocket.

But the anomaly of paying 'current use value' in *all* circumstances was grasped a long time ago in Britain in relation to residential properties designated as 'slums'. Here the principle was as follows: if society condemned such properties as slums (i.e. as socially disgraceful), then it would be illogical for society to pay the owner for the bricks and mortar as opposed to the value of the land on which the dwellings stood.[17] However, this principle has wavered in its application to slum property in recent years. And furthermore, the principle has not been applied to property which is not a residential slum in the growing practice since then of the purchase for redevelopment for renewal of obsolete property of all kinds (section 4.5).

It is this principle which needs reaffirmation. There is clearly some anomaly in having a social concept of obsolescence which demands that conditions be swept away at the same time as paying the established landowners at a market value which does not reflect the social valuation. This is particularly so since in certain conditions the properties which are socially obsolete may none the less have high values on the market, such as the slum or near-slum property which can have high occupancy rates in the premises, even though the payment per unit of occupancy is low. There is clearly some divergence here between private and social costs and benefits. The principle of 'social discounting' for obsolescence needs to be pursued.[18]

8.5.4   AMORTISATION FOR SOCIAL OBSOLESCENCE

A cogent argument against the preceding would be by emphasising inequity against the owner; he could have bought without knowledge of any impending acquisition which would take into account the 'social-obsolescence criterion' in the purchase price. Whereas his claims could be and are dismissed in the case of properties which are obviously slums, this might be more difficult with respect to properties which are simply considered 'obsolete', particularly if non-residential, since the rules for defining this are notoriously imprecise.[19] One way round this objection, which would protect the established owner as well as society, is for owners of property to recognise from the outset that it will inevitably become obsolete, and for them to make provision for amortisation against this eventuality.

This is something often done by an individual owner for the purpose of ensuring that he can accumulate the funds for renewal when the conditions are ripe. In so doing he reduces net income; but if not, he consumes capital during the life of the property. It is up to each owner to decide. But even if he does, the benefits of such funds do not accrue to society. Accordingly, the proposal is for a compulsory amortisation fund for all property into which owners would pay, with the fund being at the command of the relevant authority, as a basis for liquidating obsolescence in financial terms as the occasion arises.[20] In any particular year the amortisation for all property would be available for renewal of selected obsolete areas. This would offer some kind of justice as between generations: those that live in and so consume property would be contributing out of their incomes towards its replacement, as opposed to leaving the burden to the future. Furthermore, on actuarial calculations over the typical life of property, sixty to one hundred years, the annual burden on occupiers would not be great (even on current as opposed to historical cost), whereas the burden on the current generation of liquidating obsolescence is certainly heavy.

8.5.5 REGULATING THE MARKET THROUGH PUBLIC LAND SUPPLY

So far we have been concerned with minimising the land-acquisition costs to authorities. We here move to a new aspect: the possibilities open to authorities of keeping down land price to the public as a whole, and not simply the acquiring authorities, through its role as a landowner or land purchaser.

Given that the land market is made up of the supply and demand elements discussed above (Chapter 3), and given that on occasions land prices rise to levels which impose burdens on both the acquisition authority (and thereby the ratepayers and taxpayers) and the individual consumers (e.g. house buyers or tenants), it follows that any action that can be taken by an authority to minimise the injurious effects would be welcome. It is here that the authorities can play a role as interveners in the land market.

One possibility lies on the demand side: the central purchasing agency (section 8.4.2), not only for all public needs but for those of the private sector, could exert influence as a monopolist. To some extent this is done in the new town by the development corporation. But this is a special case. On the supply side, if such an authority had a 'land bank' of sufficient size (section 8.5.1), it could offer funds at competitive levels so as to keep down prices. Intervention in the broader scene on these lines is attempted by the Land Commission in Australia.[21] It is also pursued in a different form in Holland, where the certainty of acquisition on the urban fringe by the authority has been notably successful in keeping down the prices of land (section 7.3.2).

Thus the positive role in this connection is the ability of the public landowner to 'manipulate the market' by judicious intervention, with a view to both keeping down land prices and making land available at the right time, at the right price, in the right locations and on the right tenure. This clearly needs both considerable land ownership, actual or potential, and considerable estate-management skill.

8.5.6 NATIONALISATION OF THE REVERSION

From the vesting of the freehold on grant of planning permission (section 8.4.10 above), it is a short step to return full circle to the suggestion made by Uthwatt of the desirability for a simple Act of Parliament turning all land into long-term leases from the state (section 5.2). Compared with the previous suggestion, the event would not be partial and dependent on the landowner/developer initiative for development but be concurrent for all property. More particularly established buildings would still remain in private ownership; the leases could be bought and sold; and where the condition of a building justifies it, leases could be extended.

It is a highly controversial proposal, there being many arguments for and against. It is probable that no government would take such a step that would not yield immediate benefit, political or otherwise. But if and when total public ownership of land becomes accepted policy, it is the most painless way of achieving it.[22]

8.6   THE APPROPRIATE MANPOWER FOR THE JOB

Land policies on the lines suggested will need an enhancement of current expertise and teamwork, and this for the following reasons.

We have argued at the outset of this chapter (section 8.2) that positive planning means bringing into plan preparation a firmer grasp of plan-implementation measures, and that the plan is seen as a programme for implementation. Planning for implementation thus means that those concerned with planning must work intimately with those concerned with implementation; and implementation itself must be seen not simply as a series of measures aimed at carrying out the plan but also as a series of tests and considerations introduced during the preparation of plans to ensure that they are capable of implementation (section 2.8). In particular, programmes will have to be based much more firmly than hitherto on an accurate estimate of economic demand, and on the supply side will have to be scrutinised on the grounds of viability, if only to establish that the private-sector development industry will co-operate in the programme. This can produce quite a different plan from the formulation of generalised objectives with only general ideas as to how the objectives will, in fact, be translated into practice (section 2.8).

To achieve this, it has been argued, there is a lot to be said for making the body responsible for preparing the plan also responsible for implementing it; experience shows that to ask a body to implement a plan it has not itself prepared usually causes difficulty. But this is hardly the way forward, for an extension of its logic would be that planning authorities and departments take over not simply key development but all development — an untenable hypothesis.

But given the separation of plan-making and plan implementation, we need skills appropriate to their collaboration, particularly if the community land scheme stays and there are extensions of land policy in the directions suggested here.

This means, within the framework of local authority planning, closer working between what have conventionally come to be regarded as the planning and estate-management skills. Not only must each have regard to the responsibilities and interests of the others (and not consider themselves in watertight compartments) but each must effectively collaborate in practice. From this follows the need to strengthen the economics and implementation aspects of planning in the planning offices as a means of communication with the implementation agencies; and also the need for surveyors and valuers concerned with estates advice to broaden their skills to operate within the orbit of planned development for the public sector and to seek the collaboration of the urban economists and financial analysts. Such skills must figure not only in the plan preparation and implementation work of the authorities, but also in the dialogue that will need to take place between the public- and private-sector interests in development partnerships on land to be owned by the authority.

Put another way, the greater opportunity for ownership, management and disposal of land which the Community Land Act offers to planning authorities can solve many of the problems of planning which have been ventilated in recent years.[23] But as in all social reform, the solution of certain problems creates new problems in the application of the measures which have been introduced. Where land in a town is in multi-ownership, then land-pooling is needed for effective plan implementation. But where all the land is in public (or private) ownership, then new issues arise.[24]

This applies to the introduction of the Community Land Act. It solves certain problems. We must now get on with solving the problems that it creates, and grasping the opportunities it offers.

REFERENCES: CHAPTER 8

1 Cullingworth (1975).
2 House of Commons, *Hansard*, vol. 432, 1946–7, cols 947–1975 'Second Reading of Town and Country Planning Bill, 1947'.
3 House of Commons, *Hansard*, vol. 891, 29 April 1975, cols 236–382 'Land Bill'.
4 For a contemporary view see Lichfield (1956, chs 20, 21).
5 DoE (1979).
6 This policy is already practised in such unlikely countries as Nigeria and Brazil.
7 Under a Certificate of Alternative Use (Town and Country Planning Act, 1971).
8 Town and Country Planning Bill, 1932.
9 Delafons (1962).
10 Rose (1975).
11 Jowell (1977a).
12 Telling (1973).
13 Dahl and Lindblom (1953).
14 Kam (1970).
15 Strong (1971).
16 Schaffer (1970).
17 Housing Act, 1930.
18 Lichfield (1963).
19 Cowan (1967).
20 Lichfield (1958b).
21 Troy (1978).
22 Lichfield (1965).
23 Lichfield (1976c).
24 See, for example, Lichfield (1975b).

Part Three

Which Land Policy?

Chapter 9

Selection of Land Policies

9.1 NEED FOR IMPROVED SELECTION IN LAND POLICY

Chapter 8 has summarised our conclusions from Part Two as to the additions of
land policies which are appropriate for introduction in Britain as an aid to the
better implementation of urban and regional plans.

For these additional measures to become available they would need to be
incorporated into current practice. The nature of the incorporation would vary
with the particular measure in mind: some could require the repeal or
amendment of current legislation or the introduction of new legislation; some
could be effected by changes in administrative law; some simply by variations in
practice. If the changes were introduced, they would be added to the vast array of
measures which already exist. From this array the plan-implementation authority
would select those measures suitable for its purpose.

In this sense the addition of the new powers would make no difference to the
situation of authorities, for they have always been faced with such problems of
selection: for example, when to attempt to implement renewal by control or by
land assembly. From our critique of implementation through land policy which
has been running throughout this book, it has been apparent that the selection
process has not been particularly rigorous in terms of the effectiveness of the
measures chosen. In some instances the measure has hardly been appropriate to
the purpose; in some it has been a sledgehammer to crack a nut; in some the costs
of introducing the measure (in the broadest sense) has not been matched by
benefit from the planning proposals which have been implemented; and some
have even been counterproductive in undermining and frustrating the proposals
intended for implementation.

If this be so, then some guidelines are needed as to the mode of selection of land
policies for the purpose in mind, in a manner which will aid and not impede the
implementation of plans. The purpose of this chapter is to contribute to such
guidelines. We start by reviewing some possible approaches to selection.

9.2 POSSIBLE APPROACHES TO SELECTION OF LAND
POLICIES

9.2.1 CURRENT PRACTICE

There seem to be few studies which show how land policies are selected in Britain
for use in plan implementation. In their absence we present the following
impressions (from general observation and experience) as to how the selection
takes place in practice.

The modes, procedures and practices of urban and regional planning are heavily directed in Britain by central government. Accordingly, the initiative for the introduction of new measures, (by statute or administrative law) has come from the relevant ministry, though often in response to pressures from localities for their introduction, and often in general legislation following pioneer experiments in local Acts. For example, the introduction of comprehensive redevelopment through large-scale acquisition in the inner areas of Birmingham under a private Act was a laboratory for the formulation of general legislation in the Town and Country Planning Act, 1944.

Most of these additions to legislation are permissive rather than mandatory, so that the selection to adopt each addition rests with the authority in question. In such selection they are influenced by their political or ideological approach to plan implementation. If this were very interventionist, then any new power might be seized upon as a means for better and stronger implementation of plans – the more power the better. If, on the other hand, the authority were more inclined to leave development decisions to the market, and were light-handed on intervention, then they might prefer not to use the powers. They would prefer, for example, to achieve urban redevelopment by a plan which acted as a guideline for those wishing to develop on its particular land rather than by comprehensive acquisition for land-pooling.

Coming to the array of implementation measures which rely more on voluntary initiative than statutory power (for example, dissemination of information, consultation and co-ordination (see section 2.6), then again the authority's approach would be critical: there could be greater activity amongst those authorities more anxious to influence the future and less with those who were not; and a non-interventionist authority wishing to influence the future might push such measures in preference to the more direct ones.

Without empirical study it is not possible to say how effective this process of selection has been, in the sense of introducing implementation measures which achieve their intent. But, again, general observation and experience lead to the impression that they have been only partially effective; indeed, this is the widely supported view which led to the emphasis above on the general failures of plan implementation in practice (see section 2.7).

9.2.2   LIMITATIONS ON TRANSFERABILITY

As just indicated in relation to permissive powers, a considerable element in selection in current practice must be the consideration of land policies which have been tried in other parts of the country or abroad, currently or previously, in order to consider their appropriateness to the locality in question. This in essence is one of the methods of selection used in this book, in respect of the array of planning powers available around the world (see Chapter 7).

This question of transferability in planning applies not only to land policy measures but also to a whole array of other aspects, for example the kinds of studies which are carried out in plan-making (e.g. transportation/land use); the normative goals which should be reflected in the plan-making (e.g. standards for housing, open space, road intersections, etc.); and the kinds of design which are adopted (linear and concentric urban forms, neighbourhood layouts, mixture or non-mixture of competing uses). On this there is the widespread view that there has been a tendency to import and export such planning ideas around the world; the transfers are sometimes extreme (from developed to developing countries, or temperate and rainy climates to dry and arid), which only serves to emphasise the limitations of transference and the caution that needs to be employed in it.

And this is even more so in relation to land policy. Whereas it could be argued that in many of the matters just mentioned the common denominator is the human being, his tastes and needs and aspirations, there can be no doubt that international transfer in land policy must be amongst the most difficult. Enough has been said in Chapters 5 to 7 to show that such policies are rooted in the situation prevailing in each country in relation to concepts about land – its ownership, tenure, rights of individuals versus the state, absolute scarcity in relation to the development needs of the country, and so on. And this has been reflected in our suggestions for adoption of land policies in this country from the foreign experience (section 7.1).

9.2.3   BASED ON THEORY AND REVIEW

Given any problem of selection, a theory could be evolved, then be applied in practice, and the results then used as a basis for refinement of the theory and continued use in selection. In developing such theory there could be two possible approaches. The first is to work intensively in its formulation before putting it into practice; the second is to devise a concept which would appear to be operational, and then apply it with a view to testing and learning.

The first approach is clearly necessary as a preliminary to large-scale and expensive production where performance depends upon the soundness of the theory, as in the building of a bridge, aeroplane or motor-car. But even here this pure approach is diluted: the testing of theory in bridge construction will have been carried out on bridges built previously, or indeed in other kinds of structures; and for aeroplanes and motor-cars there is the testing of prototype models prior to large-scale investment in production. Thus even here there is some leaning towards the second approach. And this would appear to be the only one that can be adopted in those areas where a firm theory is most difficult to achieve and test. This applies in the social sciences, and in urban and regional planning. The difficulties come from the very complexities of the human being, particularly in the mass as in towns and regions, and the absence of the laboratory conditions which are available for the natural sciences. Thus the aim is served by some conceptual model which can then be tried out, under as rigorous conditions as social science experiments can offer.

This has been the approach in this book in discussing the implementation of plans and policies. There is no robust theory; there is by common consent land policy selection of a somewhat hit-and-miss character; and there is disappointment in performance. This led to the evolution of a conceptual model (section 2.3) and the demonstration of how it could be applied in practice to improve plan implementation (sections 2.6–2.9). In the process there would arise a conscious and controlled selection of land and development policies.

A natural extension of this method is the testing of the concept through case studies of actual planning processes, both plan-making and plan implementation, the empirical studies referred to above (section 9.2.1). This has been tried in other contexts in planning, for example the case studies of decision-making which have then been fed back to improve concepts of the plan-making process, some on the basis of a conceptual model and some less so.[1] There are attempts also in relation to implementation, again with greater or less reliance on a conceptual model.[2]

Whatever the variations in these approaches, they all benefit from an actual review of practice. This can be *ad hoc*, as in the examples just noted; but it could also be more systematic, in the monitoring and review process typically carried out in planning, as indicated above (section 2.9). As pointed out there, the essential purpose is to explore any gap which may have arisen between what the plans visualised and what, in fact, has been taking place as a preliminary to describing the remedial action needed. In planning practice the action relates to plan review; within our context it is the improvement of the theory for the selection of land policy.

9.3   A MODEL FOR THE SELECTION OF LAND POLICY

But whatever the approach to the selection of land policy, amongst those indicated or others, there is needed a formal process for land policy selection which can be tried out, in detail or in principle, in particular instances and tested on review. Such a model is described in this section, which aims at closing the planning–implementation gap. But for simplicity in exposition the closing of the gap has only one of the variables in mind: the land policy itself aimed at implementation of a plan as opposed to modification in the plan because of the limitations to implementation, but it could be adapted for the two variables; and also for monitoring and review as well as plan-making.

The model presented here consists of five steps. They are described in this section in general terms, as they might be applied in the selection of a land policy at any particular stage in the planning process.

9.3.1   DEFINE THE IMPEDIMENTS TO IMPLEMENTATION WHICH MAKE UP THE PLANNING–IMPLEMENTATION GAP

The nature of the impediment to plan implementation was described above as the 'planning–implementation gap': that 'gap' which exists between what the planning authorities would wish to see implemented and what they could, in fact, achieve under the current implementation measures which are available (section 2.8). It was also stated that the definition and measurement of the gap is not easy. We now proceed to show more precisely how these could be defined.

Initially limits must be set. At the one extreme is what would result from the implementation of planning proposals if any of the current implementation measures were used; and at the other extreme is what proposals the decision-makers would like to see achieved if they had the freedom to select measures which were not currently available. In setting these, limited use could be made of the model of the plan-implementation process described above (section 2.3). From this it is apparent that the gap could arise from impediments to implementation, which derive from either:

1   In carrying out the physical development itself via the development process, or in operating the finished development as carried out (implementation agencies).

2   In the plan-implementation measures which are available and used by the plan-implementation authorities (implementation authorities).

Examples of the first impediment relating to physical development could be in external constraints on the development process (a ban on investment in buildings of certain kinds during a financial crisis, leading to a refusal to issue a building licence, which would stop an office development which would otherwise go ahead); or in some impediment within the development process (the absence of an essential supply factor, such as the site or finance). Examples relating to operating the finished development could come from the absence of an institution which would be capable of operating, say, schools, such as an educational authority, or of the resources needed by that authority (such as teachers, income for the necessary equipment, etc.).

On the second impediment, the inadequacy of plan-implementation measures, again there could be different kinds. The measure may not be available; the measure could in fact be available but its sanction might not be forthcoming from a higher-level authority (for example, the unwillingness of a ministry to approve a compulsory purchase order made by a local authority); the ministry might be willing to sanction such an order, but there may be difficulties in the way of the local authority taking advantage of the order (for example, when they would not have the necessary finance or the technical manpower necessary for carrying out the complex processes of land transfer); or the authority could have all these resources but not the necessary political knowledge or will to carry through the compulsory purchase against the interests and expressed opposition of the population which is to be displaced.

9.3.2   PREPARE CRITERIA (DESIGN SPECIFICATIONS) FOR THE LAND POLICY MEASURE

Thus in order to define the nature of the impediment it is necessary to have full regard to the actual cause of the impediment, whether *ex ante*, i.e. when preparing the plan, or *ex post*, i.e. from experience of the actual workings of the implementation process (section 2.6). And defining the cause leads to defining criteria for formulating the appropriate land policy measure for overcoming the impediments. This we call here the 'policy design specification'. For this purpose we need to distinguish between the constraints on implementation which come from outside the plan-implementation process itself (i.e. by the implementation agencies or implementation authorities), and those that come from within it. As to the latter, we are looking for a land policy implementation measure *per se*; for the former we are seeking ways of breaking the constraints.

Coming to the criteria themselves, some examples will illustrate. If, for example, the impediment is the absence of legal processes to facilitate compulsory purchase of land within a reasonable time, then an alteration to statute is needed. If the gap relates to, for example, the inability to secure the orderly development of a town around the programme of infrastructure expansion (as opposed to a common situation of the infrastructure needing to be provided by the authorities to follow planning permissions), then clearly no alteration of statute is required, but rather a firming up of the possibilities of using refusals of planning permission, or conditions of planning permission, to secure the orderly development of the town. But if this measure were inadequate (for example, from failure to secure support of the minister on appeals against planning decisions) and the orderly development were thought desirable, then the only course might be the 'land banking' by the authorities of the available land for the town, well in advance of needs, so that the selection of priorities in development could be based here. Thus from this process 'design specifications' of the missing and desired land policy measures can be evolved.

9.3.3   SELECTING THE LAND POLICY

From the design specifications it is now possible to proceed to identify the appropriate land policy measures. This could be done either for a specific proposal in which the impediment arises or it could be applied to a plan as a whole, or for a particular project or programme of projects. Clearly there will be variations in the scale of the analysis from the particular to the whole, but the same process could apply.

In identifying the land policy measure it would be important not only to isolate the points of friction in implementation which the measure is designed to overcome (visualising the development/operation and plan-implementation processes described above) but also the possible side-effects which could occur from the removal of the impediment to implementation. To trace this through, regard would be had to the discussion above on direct and indirect (side) impacts from implementation measures (section 2.5). From this it can be seen that the side-effects might be beneficial or adverse. For example, land banking to secure the orderly development of a town would be beneficial in economising on infrastructure expenditures and in improving accessibility to urban facilities from the pockets of development which take place over the years; but it could clearly have adverse financial effects on the land-holding sector of the community who would feel that they were being deprived of the enhancement in land values which comes about through land ownership.

9.3.4   TESTING THE LAND POLICY

The above process would result in the specification of land policy measures designed to remove impediments. But for the same reasons given above in relation to testing plans (section 2.8), it will also be necessary to check that the land policy measures so evolved would, in fact, meet the requirements. This is done in answer to the following:

1   *Effectiveness in conformity with the design specification*
Having evolved the land policy measure from a design specification it is necessary to ensure that the measure is likely to meet the specification, i.e. be effective in terms of its objectives. For example, given the wish to secure the orderly development of a town through land banking, will the operation of the measure itself achieve this, or will there be frictions in the process (for example, through the side-effects) which will in practice frustrate the process. If so, then modifications of the measure would be required, bringing with it modifications of the proposed plan, that is, provision for less orderly development.

2   *Enhances welfare*
Even if the land policy measure would appear to conform to design specification,

it still might not be desirable in terms of the impact on the welfare of the community. To test in this respect, it is necessary to follow the approach in evaluation of public acceptability which was described above (section 2.8). Here the question is raised: would or would not the benefits to the community exceed the costs of implementing the plan in accordance with the land policy measures chosen? Again, in the example of the land banking proposal compared with the proposal without land banking, there could be different locations for private housing development. The question arises: would the advantages to the community as a whole outweigh the disadvantages, bearing in mind that the costs and benefits would not be evenly distributed over all sectors. To do this, it is necessary for the alternatives to be put within a benefit–cost evaluation framework, to which we return below (sections 9.4 and 9.5).

9.3.5   DRAW CONCLUSIONS FROM TESTS

Having answered both these questions, a conclusion can be drawn. This could be that neither of the alternatives are sufficiently attractive to be adopted and that a further option or options should be devised. For this purpose the findings from the actual tests would be used for the 'redesign' of the land policy and the plan, in their mutual interaction, and the result would then be tested along the same lines until there is satisfaction.

9.3.6   CONFIRMATION OF LAND POLICY

Given the above tests, and the adaptation of the land policy measure as appropriate from it, the way is now clear for the confirmation and adoption of the land policy in question.

Thus the impediment to plan implementation will have been reduced, the 'gap' closed, and the way forward to smoother plan implementation would have been advanced.

9.4   CASE STUDY IN LAND POLICY SELECTION: REDEVELOPMENT OR REHABILITATION IN CITY-CENTRE RENEWAL

In the previous section we outlined a model for design and selection of land policy aimed at overcoming a defined impediment to the implementation process. We now conclude with a case study. Within the general approach of the model, this study enters the planning process at a different point. We have a plan within which associated implementation measures are considered to have undesirable side-effects. The problem is to reduce the side-effects through altering the implementation measures which, while necessarily resulting in a different plan, would none the less produce acceptable conditions in the area. The study thus considers both variables (the plan and the implementation measures) and not simply the latter, as in the example studied in section 9.3.

Since the study has been published, we present here only the highlights.[3] It starts with the proposal by a consortium of the Greater London Council, City of

Westminster and Borough of Camden to remove to a new location the fifteen acres of the historic produce market of Covent Garden.[4] Because of this removal the Greater London Council anticipated considerable pressures for redevelopment of the surrounding areas, since the location was in the heart of London and the surrounding development could be considered as 'obsolete'. To meet this situation they prepared a comprehensive redevelopment plan for the 100 acres surrounding, involving wholesale clearance and replacement, both as a means of controlling the pressures in the public interest (as landowners as well as planners) and also to provide for a much-needed restructuring of the area which could not be carried out otherwise.

But, as mentioned above (section 4.5), around this time there was in Britain a move against such comprehensive redevelopment in favour of a more conservative approach. The study reflects this contemporary controversy; more particularly it expressed the concern that the comprehensive redevelopment measures which were proposed would be exploited for their own ends by the private property development companies which would be undertaking the scheme as ground lessees of the authorities and result in heavy displacement and relocation of current occupiers.

Following this different emphasis of the public interest, the study therefore proposed an alternative form of renewal which would overcome these and other objections, i.e. by 'the gradual piecemeal renewal of the area and conversion of existing structures within the existing framework of roads and services'. There would thus be minimum acquisition with implementation through planning controls. This would clearly result in a quite different plan for the area from that proposed under comprehensive development. The plan devised in the study, through simulation of the private development market, led to differences in total floor space and an entirely different layout.

The question then arose: which of the two alternative plans would produce greater net advantage to the community as a whole? Put another way, would the net advantages to the community of the comprehensive redevelopment solution compared with that of piecemeal redevelopment outweigh the additional frictional costs of implementing through the comprehensive development process?

The study then went on to consider the relevance of three alternative evaluation methods for the purpose, namely conventional cost–benefit analysis,[5] the goal-achievement matrix,[6] and the planning balance-sheet.[7] It concluded against the first (as producing only a partial result) and against the second (as leading only to conclusions on pre-weighted and pre-set goals), and came out in favour of the third (as overcoming the major disadvantages of cost–benefit analysis while retaining its favourable features).

It then proceeds to use this method of analysis for the evaluation of the alternatives. The components of the two alternatives and the planning balance-sheet analysis are fully presented, but only the conclusions are given here:[8]

In general terms therefore, the analysis undertaken indicates that in the case under examination the alternative of comprehensive redevelopment is inferior in comparison to the situation produced by controlled gradual piecemeal redevelopment, in terms of its effects on the welfare of the community. Whilst the comprehensive scheme does offer the community greater benefits, these are outweighed by far greater costs (social and financial) that it involves. Furthermore these costs fall on the less well off members of the community'.

But a further conclusion is drawn, that:

there are grounds for concluding that neither scheme is particularly satisfactory from this point of view of promoting the welfare of the community, since the piecemeal scheme also bears heavily on the lower income groups of the community and tends to produce an area that is dominated by activities of an intensive and profit-oriented nature at the expense of uses such as housing and public facilities.

Accordingly, the scene is set for the evolution of a third alternative which would overcome these disadvantages to the best possible extent. This is an example of the reference in our model to the use of the land policy tests as design tools to improve upon the alternatives which have been under consideration (section 9.3.5).

The study then goes on to consider the implications of the analysis, both in terms of evaluation methodology and approach to city-centre redevelopment.[9] On the former, it concludes that 'the analysis does give an indication of the most appropriate method of implementing redevelopment plans in the best interests of all those involved'. On the latter it makes recommendations for changes in the form and content of redevelopment schemes.

The study ends with a postscript which refers to the Secretary of State's decision on the public inquiry into the plan for the comprehensive redevelopment of Covent Garden[10] which was subsequent to the case study. While approving the general objectives of the plan and the declaration of the comprehensive development area, the decision letter requested the Greater London Council to make substantial modifications to both the scale and volume of the redevelopment originally contemplated. In effect this would have lessened the comprehensive nature of the redevelopment proposal and would have tended to overcome many of the objections to this process which had been investigated in the case study.

All that needs to be added is that since then the renewal of the Covent Garden area has proceeded on lines which are nearer to the spirit of the piecemeal as opposed to the comprehensive redevelopment approach.[11] And 'Covent Garden' has since then symbolised not simply the famous produce market but also the great change in the 1970s in the style and approach to city-centre redevelopment in Britain.

REFERENCES: CHAPTER 9

1 Meyerson and Banfield (1955), and Altschuler (1956).
2 Pressman and Wildavsky (1973), and Alexander (1979).
3 For details see Alexander (1974).
4 Consortium (1968).
5 Prest and Turvey (1965).
6 Hill (1968).
7 Lichfield (1962).
8 Alexander (1974, p. 28).
9 Alexander (1974, ch. 4).
10 DoE (1973a).
11 Covent Garden Development Team (1974).

Appendix

An International Survey of Land Policy Measures

A.1   INTRODUCTION

This appendix comprises a listing and brief description of all the land policy measures which have been drawn on in Chapter 7, with an eye to their relevance for Britain.

The survey itself is given in section A.5 below, covering twenty-eight countries from all continents (see section A.4 for list). Since it covers such a wide geographical range and a great variety of measures, it was necessary to categorise. The scheme is presented in sections A.2 and A.3. It helps to bring out and compare the different characteristics of the measures, but clearly it cannot be completely watertight.

A.2   CLASSIFICATION SCHEME FOR LAND POLICY MEASURES

The policies are given a three-tiered hierarchical classification.

The first tier is the six types of land policy measure introduced in sections 1.6 and 3.10 as follows:

1   Control over specific development without taking land.
2   Control over specific development by taking land.
3   Control over specific development by direct public authority participation.
4   Influence over general development by fiscal means.
5   Influence over specific development by fiscal means.
6   General influence on the land market.

The second tier gives seven specific characteristics of each of the six types, i.e. within each of the types there are listed seven specific characteristics of each type of policy. The first number (e.g. 1.1, 2.1, etc.) is the specific power or detailed specification of a particular policy. The next six numbers (e.g. 1.2–1.7) are the modifiers and conditions attached to each type of specific measure. In most cases, therefore, the actual policy measure will be described under *powers*, while in the other categories the main concern will be with problems or varieties of implementation. However, in some cases where another characteristic seems to be crucial to a policy measure, it is described in that section (for example, environmental zoning is described in section 1.2 under 'scope' and also cross-referenced in 1.3 under 'agency', as often special agencies – like river-basin authorities – were set up to carry out this type of policy measure).

The six modifying characteristics are uniform in all sections:

   .2 refers to the *scope*, i.e. where the measure is applied.
   .3 to the *agency*, i.e. the administering body of a particular policy.
   .4 refers to the *timing* of the application of a particular policy measure.

.5 to the *basis of the land value* relevant to each general category – thus it is compensation in the case of land-use controls and land acquisition, valuation in the case of taxation and disposal terms in the case of public land supply.
.6 concerns the *methods of financing*, and applies only to land acquisition and disposal.
.7 relates to *enforcement* of the particular policy measures; again this is applicable only to some types of policy.

The third tier is a subdivision which is particular to the policy under discussion. It can refer to types (e.g. of powers), actors, specific factors or issues (e.g. local versus regional, separate land authority versus integration with planning department).
Even with such a comprehensive classification, there will clearly be gaps under particular heads.

A.3   LIST OF CLASSIFICATIONS

From this classification scheme we can now enumerate a comprehensive list of classifications for each of the six types of land policy measure:

1.0   CONTROL OVER SPECIFIC DEVELOPMENT WITHOUT TAKING LAND

1.1   *Powers*
    1.1.1   Standards and norms
    1.1.2   Permits
    1.1.3   Zoning
    1.1.4   Compulsory reparcellation
1.2   *Scope*
    1.2.1   National
    1.2.2   Selective
    1.2.3   Discretionary
1.3   *Agency*
    1.3.1   National
    1.3.2   Regional
    1.3.3   Local
1.4   *Timing*
    1.4.1   In relation to private application
    1.4.2   In relation to public authority decision and revision
1.5   *Compensation/betterment*
1.6   No
1.7   *Enforcement*
    1.7.1   Conditions on control
    1.7.2   Penalties on defiance of control

2.0   CONTROL OVER SPECIFIC DEVELOPMENT BY TAKING LAND

2.1   *Powers*
    2.1.1   By agreement or exchange
    2.1.2   By compulsory purchase
    2.1.3   Pre-emption on sale
    2.1.4   Forced dedication

2.1.5   Compulsory pooling
2.1.6   Default on non-development

2.2   *Scope*
2.2.1   Stimulate private development
2.2.2   Secure better private development
2.2.3   Public development
2.2.4   Reserve for future development

2.3   *Agency*
2.3.1   Local
2.3.2   Regional
2.3.3   National
2.3.4   Functional

2.4   *Timing*
2.4.1   Before expropriation (establishing legal right)
2.4.2   After expropriation procedure (possession before compensation)

2.5   *Compensation basis*
2.5.1   At market value
2.5.2   At current use value
2.5.3   At frozen value

2.6   *Financing*
2.6.1   Loans
2.6.2   Profits from disposal
2.6.3   Participation of private capital
2.6.4   General revenues

2.7   No

3.0   CONTROL OVER SPECIFIC DEVELOPMENT BY DIRECT PARTICIPATION

3.1   *Powers*
3.1.1   Infrastructure
3.1.2   Statutory functions
3.1.3   General development

3.2   *Scope*
3.2.1   New towns
3.2.2   Urban extension
3.2.3   Existing city

3.3   *Agency*
3.3.1   Public authority
3.3.2   Public corporation
3.3.3   Mixed public–private corporation
3.3.4   Co-operative associations

3.4   *Timing*
3.4.1   Of release of land
3.4.2   Of construction

3.5   *Valuation basis*
3.5.1   Freehold disposal: economic cost or market value
3.5.2   Leasehold system

3.6   *Financing*
3.6.1   From rent revenues
3.6.2   From general revenues
3.6.3   Participation of private capital

3.7   *Enforcement*
3.7.1   Conditions and terms on development
3.7.2   Right of retrieval

4.0   CONTROL OVER GENERAL DEVELOPMENT BY FISCAL MEANS

4.1   *Powers*
    4.1.1   Land profit taxes
    4.1.2   Property taxes
    4.1.3   Transfer taxes
    4.1.4   Municipal income tax
    4.1.5   Municipal sales tax
    4.1.6   Death/inheritance tax
    4.1.7   Wealth tax
    4.1.8   Subsidies (locational or functional, e.g. housing)
    4.1.9   Price and sales controls
4.2   *Scope*
    4.2.1   Location differentiation (e.g. USA, not allowed in Britain)
    4.2.2   Revenue-sharing
4.3   *Agency*
    4.3.1   Local or regional
    4.3.2   National
    4.3.3   Functional (e.g. water board)
4.4   *Timing*
    4.4.1   During transactions
    4.4.2   Periodically
    4.4.3   As a one-time levy
4.5   *Valuation*
    4.5.1   Basis of valuation (annual, capital, site, gradated)
    4.5.2   Procedure of valuation (periodic, uniform, public, published)
4.6   No
4.7   *Enforcement*
    4.7.1   Availability of information and use of self-reporting

5.0   CONTROL OVER SPECIFIC DEVELOPMENT BY FISCAL MEANS

5.1   *Powers*
    5.1.1   Infrastructure charges
    5.1.2   Taxation of vacant land
    5.1.3   Taxation based on development scheme
    5.1.4   Conditional loans and subsidies
    5.1.5   Transport pricing policy

6.0   CONTROL OVER GENERAL DEVELOPMENT BY GENERAL MEANS

6.1   *Powers*
    6.1.1   Indicative planning
    6.1.2   Co-ordination of development
    6.1.3   Information on land holdings (land registry)
    6.1.4   Information on land transactions

A.4   COUNTRY INDEX

For each of the countries surveyed below (section A.5) we now present an index showing its land policy measures in the survey, cross-referenced to the categorisation scheme of section A.3.

A.5   AN INTERNATIONAL SURVEY OF LAND POLICY MEASURES

We now present the comprehensive survey of measures, using the schema of section A.3. For each there is a general statement on the measure and then a brief description of the measure in particular countries, with a bibliographical source (see the Bibliography for full details).

1.0   CONTROL OVER SPECIFIC DEVELOPMENT WITHOUT TAKING LAND

1.1   *Powers*

1.1.1   *Standards and norms*
The simplest form of control over development are specific regulations on, for example, the height, plot ratio, etc., of buildings. This type of regulation applies a fixed standard to new development. In some cases it may also apply to the general layout (subdivision) of the land, specifying a percentage of green space, and so on. Recently flexibility has been introduced, in order to avoid monotonous subdivision of standard plots, by allowing the developer to meet certain requirements evaluated by the planning department. Norms are also an important tool in some countries for the central government to regulate the actions of the local planning authorities and reduce their freedom of action when it has been considered that they are too vulnerable to local political and landowner pressure.

France   Fixed building coefficients
In 1975 the Giscard d'Estaing administration sponsored legislation which fixed a building coefficient maximum of 1.0 for all of France except Paris, where it is to be 1.5. This law was influenced by the Gilli's concept that some property rights belong to the community. 100 per cent of the additional value created if development exceeds these norms is to go to the local authorities.
Source: Gilli (1976).

Italy   Fixed norms
The provisional Act of 1967 fixed standards on building density, height, the ratio between industrial and residential quarters and the provision of areas for public services for all urban plans. A building licence is necessary throughout the whole area controlled by the local council, and can be granted only if primary infrastructure works exist or the developer promises to create it. All private plans

must have the approval of central, regional and local authorities, and the private builder must contribute to the cost of infrastructure in new urban areas. These provisions were in response to the situation in Italy of rapid unplanned growth on the outskirts of cities in response to industrialisation, where most local authorities had no detailed 'executive plan' and accepted that of the private builder even when there were no infrastructure works on the new estates.
Source: Bastianini and Urbani (1975).

USA   Planned unit development
One measure which is increasingly popular in the USA is the specifying of planning norms in areas about to be subdivided, leaving the developer the freedom to divide his land as he wants as long as he satisfies the specified norms (e.g. a certain percentage of green space). This avoids standard plot size subdivisions; it is only really practical, however, on large-scale developments.
Source: Reilly (1973).

1.1.2   *Permits*
Permits or licenses are a system of control in which each case of development must be examined separately and given legal approval. Such approval may be on the basis of conformity with development schemes, or may relate to other matters (such as building licences to control materials' shortages, or location permits to regulate agriculture in flood-prone areas). In theory permits are the strictest system of control, as the landowner has no automatic legal right to develop. On the other hand, in practice they may be applied in an arbitrary or delayed fashion which holds up development, and through *ad hoc* adjustment result in major unplanned changes in the development scheme.

1.1.3   *Zoning*
Zoning is the most common form of legal land-use control measure in the world. It implies the designation of certain areas for certain types of development. Within these areas (and within specified norms) automatic legal authority is given for the proper type of development. The most common categories are commercial, residential and industrial. Zoning has been generally given legal authority as an extension of police power. Its purpose has sometimes been seen as social as well as environmental segregation.

1.1.4   *Compulsory reparcellation*
In some cases it may be possible to rearrange land uses without going through the mechanism of actual acquisition by one central body (public or private). If landowners (or a majority of them) can agree on a scheme, this would involve the rearrangement of plots in the context of large-scale redevelopment which would, for example, increase road access and green space. If this makes the area more attractive, it may actually increase land values, despite the fact that redistributed plots would be smaller. Such schemes are mostly used on vacant land or in areas where great destruction has already occurred or where very derelict structures exist. This may be a highly flexible planning tool, but it depends to a degree on the active initiative of landowners. It often involves compulsory dedication of land for public uses (see 2.1.5).

France   'Lotissement'
Private mixed companies for urban renewal have the right of expropriation of land. In addition landowners may enter into voluntary agreement to rearrange plots, but this must be authorised by the local authorities. Since 1967, if two-

thirds of the owners by number and three-quarters by area approved a reparcellation, it could be carried out (formerly unanimous consent had to be obtained). The local authorities may attach conditions of provision of public services (roads, etc.) to the lotissement scheme.
Source: Lemasurier (1975, p. 138).

Japan   Compulsory reparcellation
Land-readjustment schemes have been used with considerable success since 1919, based on the German *Lex Adickes* (1909). Approximately 27 per cent of the total urban land surface has been affected, or over 1,500 square kilometres. Readjustment has been used to rebuild after the great earthquake disaster of 1923 in Tokyo, along the new rail line, and following war destruction. The schemes are carried out within a city planning area to provide adequate public facilities and to rearrange uses. Land is acquired for public uses (e.g. roads) (*genbu*) and also as a reserve (*horyuchi*) to redistribute to landowners who have lost land through the scheme. Both public bodies and private land readjustment associations can carry out such schemes; in the latter case, a yearly public meeting (*sokai*) of all owners must approve the scheme.
Source: United Nations (1973, vol. II, p. 45).

West Germany   Reparcellation
The municipalities have the right to allow land parcelling by private landowners, on the condition that they execute infrastructure works at their own cost and dedicate open space for green space, public buildings and public services. This has been widely used for co-operative planning of comprehensive redevelopment between public and private authorities, for example in Dortmund. Usually the area reallocated is reduced (e.g. in Dortmund 28 per cent less land due to street-widening and car-parking), but compensation is provided either in cash or in rights to land, and increased land values usually result (and betterment is charged). While the planning authority is responsible for the detailed site plans (*Bebauungsplan*), the map of revised land ownership patterns (*Umlegungskarte*) is negotiated with holders of proprietary interests before the legally binding site plan is published.
Source: Denman (1974).

1.2   *Scope*

1.2.1   *Comprehensive*
Planning schemes for the entire country are often in the form of macro-zoning legislation. The intent is to prevent fragmented development of residential areas by fixing some areas as designated for urban use and future urban growth, and leaving the rest fixed in agricultural use. Of course, such schemes must be revised frequently to account for changes in forecasted growth. National planning has also been introduced in order to deal with the problem of recreational use and second-home development.

Denmark   Macro-zoning
Denmark has formulated the most advanced national planning legislation, in which the country is divided into zones of urban, rural and recreational use. The release of land for urban development is forbidden in a rural zone, while urban zones contain areas for future expansion. All plans are binding on the municipalities, but must be revised every four years.
Source: Tolstrup (1975).

USA   Hawaii: land-use law of 1961
The American island state of Hawaii has instituted a state-wide system of macro-zoning, dividing up the entire state into four districts: conservation, rural, agricultural and urban. Land use in the non-urban zones is regulated by special commissions. The purpose of the law is to preserve agricultural land and tourist-attracting sites of natural beauty while ensuring compact and efficient urban development. The latter goal has been threatened by the fact that due to speculation on the restricted amount of land left for urban development, land and housing prices have risen dramatically. Another issue has been the degree to which *ad hoc* decisions are made by the Land Use Commission without any established criteria.
Sources: Bosselman and Callies (1971, p. 256); Freund (1965).

1.2.2   *Selective*
In some cases control measures on land use may be applied not throughout the whole country or in municipalities but in selected areas, particularly those of natural beauty or of ecological significance. Such 'environmental' zoning has been applied, for example to bay-shore areas and coastal areas, as well as mountains and areas of natural beauty. Where national macro-zoning has not been introduced, this limited type of measure may be of use in preventing undesirable development, particularly in non-urban areas.

Switzerland   Environmental protection
In 1972 the Federal Assembly created provisionally protected zones in which urgent restrictions on land use were necessary; these included the shores of rivers and lakes, picturesque sites, historical places and recreation areas near urban areas. The law requires the cantons to create recreation zones. In addition another law forbids construction in any area which does not have an authorised sewage-project plan. Such plans are further restricted to take into account no more than fifteen years' future growth. Some cantons have energetically applied their powers: Geneva, for example, has forbidden the construction of villas on rural property even exceeding 40,000 square metres in order to prevent elevations detrimental to the harmony of the environment.
Source: Lendi (1975).

USA   Environmental land-use regulation
Recently several areas of the USA adopted regulations protecting vulnerable areas from over-development. The best example is the San Francisco Bay Conservation and Development Commission, which has prevented the filling-in of threatened wetlands on the shore which threaten the ecological balance of the bay, and has preserved the bay for water-orientated uses. The Vermont Environmental Control Law of 1970 requires a permit for all development in certain areas of natural beauty and of all development above a certain size, in order to control second-home buying from the nearby Atlantic Urban Region. Maine, Massachusetts and Wisconsin have similar statutes.
Source: Bosselman and Callies (1971).

1.2.3   *Discretionary*
In some cases special legal land-use controls may be applied on a rolling basis (i.e. for a limited time) by designation of some official in co-ordination with the planning department. Typically this may be for a future development project where it is desired to prevent development until such time as the whole scheme is ready for execution. It is particularly appropriate to development on the urban

fringe, and in a sense represents the other half of a macro-zoning scheme (if selective zoning is generally used to preserve environmentally needed rural areas, it regulates areas of future urban or recreational growth). The discretionary power of an official is the converse of the constant revision of plans and may be appropriate where plans are non-existent or not updated for an area.

France Special designated zones
In France the prefect of a district can declare a certain area a 'zone of deferred development' (ZAD) where a future development (e.g. a new town) is planned. In such a zone no new development is allowed and public authorities have pre-emption rights. This devise has reduced land prices without widespread public purchase. Within urban areas, ZAD areas can now be created, involving the suspension of the normal plan, where (mainly private) developers have more freedom in return for carrying out certain housing and road rights for the public authorities. This has led to large-scale commercial development in cities (e.g. Maine Montparnesse and La Defense in Paris).
Sources: Lemasurier (1975, pp. 140–1); D'Arcy and Jobert (1975); Pottier (1975).

USA Florida Environmental Management Act
In 1972 Florida established an environmental commission with the powers to designate (subject to confirmation by the Governor) certain areas of 'critical concern' – i.e. environmentally important areas threatened by development – in which the state requires the implementation of detailed land-use controls. Such areas are limited to 5 per cent of total state area. Additionally any land development impacting on more than one county must have a regional impact study and a development permit.
Sources: Bosselman and Callies (1971); Freund (1966).

1.3 Agency

1.3.1 Local
Normally land-use planning is carried out by local authority units. In particular actual detailed site plans, or building plans, or layout (subdivision) plans, are the responsibility of local authorities. The fragmentation of land-use control among many small units in most large city regions has led to conflict between differing goals and difficulties in effective control.

USA Fragmentation of local planning authorities
Lack of co-ordination among different local authorities hampers effective planning in the USA. In the first place, planning authorities (i.e. master plans) are often not the responsibility of those in charge of zoning (zoning commissions), the actual legal authority. Thus even detailed plans are merely indicative. Second, main city functions are often in the hands of semi-autonomous agencies (e.g. highway commission, sewer commission) which do not co-ordinate their policies.
Source: Hall (1975, pp. 262–3).

1.3.2 Regional
Regional planning authorities exist in many areas: however, those with effective power are fewer. Often regional-level planning is carried out on an *ad hoc* basis by planning teams from central government (which may be in conflict with the actual site planning of local authorities). Regional planning is usually far more indicative, and carries little legal authority. However, in some countries the provincial level is strong enough to exercise effective control over planning.

Regional land-use planning is often quite closely tied administratively and in objectives to other types of regional planning, with economic development of less advanced regions the principal aim. Regional planning authorities may also be based on natural boundaries rather than on administrative boundaries. In this sense they are closely related to the 'environmental' selective land-use controls discussed in 1.2.2.

France   Regional planning (DATAR)
Regional planning in France has been highly developed through the Regional Planning Board, which prepares indicative plans and public expenditure allocations for the regions. In terms of urban policy, DATAR has encouraged the creation of 'equilibrium cities' whose development is to be stimulated in order to reduce the attraction of Paris and central France.
Source: Gremion and Worms (1975).

The Netherlands   Provincial planning
In the Netherlands provincial planning authorities must approve local plans, and therefore have the opportunity of co-ordinating city-regional development.
Source: The Netherlands – Ministry of Housing and Physical Planning (1976).

USA   River-basin and bay-shore regional authorities
Most regional land-use planning in the USA has been carried out in the context of environmental concern. One example is the San Francisco Bay Commission (see 1.2.2). Another is the New England River Basins Authority, which has the task of developing a comprehensive land-use planning scheme for the major river basins in order to co-ordinate pollution control and amenity preservation among many local and state authorities.
Source: Bosselman and Callies (1971).

1.3.3   *National*
Control at the national level may be twofold: first, the power to oversee and approve local plans (which varies in different countries, particularly if they have a Federal structure), which included the power to force planning; and second, the actual carrying out of legal land-use controls by such means as macro-zoning or norms.

1.4   *Timing*

1.4.1   *In relation to private application*
The time that it takes to reach an administrative decision concerning land use, including the time taken in appeals, can be a significant impediment to plan implementation. Characteristically, long delays are related to greater control powers by the local planning authorities, particularly through the permit system of scrutinising individually in detail each application for planning permission.

1.4.2   *In relation to public authority decision and revision*
Often plans are dead letters, because by the time it takes to make them they are obsolete. Many countries did not have developed or frequently revised plans, and thus had to depend on *ad hoc* systems in their absence. France, Spain and Italy all suspended or ignored legally established planning controls in their rapid urban development. The frequent revision of plans is important if planning is to be able to supply enough land to the market, as in Denmark where four-year revisions are required.

1.5   *Compensation*

1.5.1   *Private ownership of development rights*

Traditionally, if legal restrictions on private development of land were promulgated, the owner was entitled to compensation for his loss. In Britain this was ended in 1947 by the nationalisation of development rights and the payment of a global sum in compensation; the Uthwatt Committee had argued that normal compensation involves over-payment because not everyone could actually realise the 'hope value' that each property has (floating values). In the USA freedom of land use has been eroded by a wider interpretation of the police power, but this has limited in turn the scope of land use to, in the main, zoning.

1.5.2   *Public ownership of development rights*

Public ownership of development rights may lead to more efficient procedures for appeal in the case of expropriation as well as a justification for wide-ranging development controls. The Swedish experience has been that the recent reform (not requiring that the public authority prove that private owners cannot develop) has been an important part of their total land policy.

1.7   *Enforcement*

1.7.1   *Conditions on control*

In some cases legal controls on the use of land, particularly permits, can be accompanied by specific conditions that the owner must meet in order to be allowed to develop and gain the approval of the authorities. These may be specified building and road arrangements in urban areas, or types of agricultural practice in rural areas.

1.7.2   *Penalties on defiance of control*

Generally stiff legal penalties exist for the defiance of control in most countries, including the demolition of buildings. Enforcement has been notably lax, however, partly because local authorities do not always have their own plans ready in time, and partly because there are often complicated administrative procedures before proof of non-compliance can be gained. The possibility of corruption and the malleability of planning authorities before business and political pressure has also led to lax enforcement or changes in the planning scheme retroactively.

Italy   Enforcement of planning
Up until the Bridge Law of 1967, the maximum penalty for illegal subdivisions was only $640, far less than the possible profit.
Source: Fried (1973).

2.0   CONTROL OVER SPECIFIC DEVELOPMENT BY TAKING LAND

2.1   *Powers*

2.1.1   *By agreement or exchange*

It is usually quickest for a public authority to acquire land directly through a sale purchase than to go through the various legal expropriation procedures with the lengthy delays. It is the purpose of public policy to encourage private owners to sell, rather than to actually have to use the expropriation procedure. It is sometimes possible to encourage owners to sell by giving them land-use rights in another site rather than cash compensation. If such agreement is voluntary, it may be called an *exchange* or *treaty*.

2.1.2   *Compulsory purchase*

Expropriation or compulsory purchase is the most important legal power of the public authorities for taking land. The legal authority for expropriation rests on the definition of public purpose, which may vary between countries. In some countries it is based on the 'police power' of the public authorities of eminent domain. Definitions of public purpose have expanded in recent years but still vary among countries: in most countries it now includes housing as well as infrastructure (France since 1958, Spain since 1962, but this was rejected in Denmark). In some cases it is permitted only if private interests cannot carry out the purpose for which expropriation is used (West Germany). Increasingly the needs of urban development are seen as a legitimate reason for expropriation. (See section 2.4 on the timing of expropriation).

2.1.3   *Pre-emption of sale*

Pre-emption rights give the public authorities the right of first purchase of land that is offered for sale. The landowner must offer his land to the public authorities, who then may or may not declare their interest in buying. If mutual negotiations fail to produce an acceptable price, normal compensation procedures may be invoked. Pre-emption rights may be also a useful device in monitoring the land market (by what prices land is offered to the public authorities, since all land subject to this provision must be so offered).

Denmark   Compulsory Offer Bill
Denmark has recently introduced a Bill to allow the municipalities the right to purchase first any land above 6,000 square metres. There are generally weak powers of compulsory purchase in Denmark, but a referendum had rejected an earlier and more comprehensive proposal.
Source: United Nations (1973, vol. III, p. 47).

France   ZAD pre-emption
In the French ZAD zones pre-emption rights of the public authorities apply and have helped to lower land prices. Even though these are areas of future government development, less than half the land offered is generally acquired. Recently the pre-emption rights were introduced in all urban areas in France.
Source: Darin-Drabkin (1977).

Sweden   Pre-emption rights
In Sweden since 1968 the public authorities have had the right of first purchase of any land coming on the market in parcels larger than 3,000 square metres or with a rentable value of less than 200,000 kroner. The municipality is able to monitor land transactions through this method. There is a set period during which the municipality must declare its interest in buying, or else the owner is free to sell elsewhere.
Source: United Nations (1973, vol. III, p. 46).

Switzerland   Rural pre-emption rights
In rural villages in some cantons farmers from that village have the first right to

purchase any land being sold in their village in order to preserve village ownership.
Source: Darin-Drabkin – information supplied.

2.1.4 *Forced dedication*
Sometimes the public authorities require that a developer gives, without cost, some portion of his land on which to construct infrastructure works. This may be just primary works (sewers, streets, etc.) or may include secondary infrastructure as well (schools, health centres, etc.). This, in a sense, is an infrastructure charge taken in kind, as the presumption is that the developer is benefiting from public provision of services, and that his land values will increase as a result of this.

Israel　Forced dedication
In Israel the public authorities require a developer to give 40 per cent of his newly subdivided land for public purposes. This is for both primary and secondary infrastructure.
Source: Darin-Drabkin *et al.* (1972).

Poland　Compulsory dedication
In Poland one-third of land being developed must be given to the authorities for infrastructure works.
Source: Darin-Drabkin, information supplied.

2.1.5 *Compulsory pooling*
In some cases landowners are forced to form one company for the large-scale development or redevelopment of an area. Other factors may also participate in such a development company. This generally applies to large-scale urban redevelopment, in contrast to forced readjustment (1.1.4), which is the rearrangement of plots without forming one unified landowner in the area.

2.1.6 *Default on non-development*
In a few countries the public authorities have the right to take land which has not been developed in areas designated as for development (urban zones) after some years. Usually the threat of such positive planning measures is enough to force development according to plan.

Spain　Positive land-use controls
In Spain the public authorities have the right to expropriate any landowner who does not use his land for construction within two years from the publication of a planning permit for his site or within three years of the commencement of urban infrastructure works. If the municipality does not expropriate, the central government has the power to do this.
Source: United Nations (1973, vol. III, pp. 132–3).

2.2 *Scope*

2.2.1 *Stimulate private development*
One purpose of public authorities taking land may be to stimulate private development by rapidly supplying the land to private builders or developers. Where high land prices and problems of land assembly are inhibiting private development, such public policy may aid private development.

2.2.2 *Secure better private development*
In some cases, particularly for urban renewal, it is only through public powers of

land assembly that a comprehensive plot for private redevelopment can be assembled.

USA   Urban renewal
Federal funds are provided on a matching basis (75 per cent to 25 per cent state funds) for large-scale central-city comprehensive redevelopment for land acquisition and assembly. The land is then disposed of to private developers at generally write-off prices, in order to stimulate development, on a comprehensive scale that would not otherwise be possible.
Source: United Nations (1973, vol. VI, pp. 63–6).

2.2.3   *Public development*
One of the main reasons for acquiring land is to build various statutory public functions, particularly housing, but ranging all the way to complete new towns.

Australia   South Australia Housing Trust
The South Australia Housing Trust was set up in the 1930s in order to promote economic development through the provision of public housing and infrastructure services. The Trust is a semi-autonomous public corporation and has acted as a major developer of both rented accommodation and lots for owner-occupiers, building about one-third of all housing in the Adelaide region in the post-war years, including a complete new town of 60,000 people. Land price inflation has been reduced in the city region.
Source: Harrison (1971, pp. 244–5).

Canada   Federal–provincial land assembly for housing
The 1954 Housing Act authorised the Federal government to provide 75 per cent of the cost of land for residential public housing projects. Over 23,000 acres have been acquired with Federal help.
Source: United Nations (1973, vol. VI, pp. 69–79).

USA   Land acquisition for green space
Federal and state funds are available for the purchase of recreation areas, particularly near metropolitan regions, and this has been increasing rapidly in recent years, as existing facilities are clearly becoming overcrowded.
Source: Reilly (1973).

2.2.4   *Reserve for future development*
The Netherlands   Amsterdam advance acquisition
The city has acquired nearly all the land needed for various projects of urban extension since before the Second World War, and has built a series of continuous extensions – the south, south-east and north extensions on municipally owned land.
Source: Amsterdam Public Works Department (1973).

USA   Puerto Rico: Advance land acquisition
The Puerto Rico land administration has in the last few years acquired substantial areas of land for eventual planned development in eleven urban areas. The legality of such advance acquisition for general development needs was upheld by the US Supreme Court in 1968.
Sources: Puerto Rico Planning Board (1968); Puerto Rico Act no. 13 (1962).

Sweden Advance acquisition
In Sweden government policy encourages the creation of large land banks in the city region in order that future growth is planned on the basis of public land ownership in planned new communities with integrated transport connections and adequate services. This policy has led to widespread land banking and an expenditure of about $100 million a year for peripheral land purchase.
Source: Doebele (1974, p. 38).

USA Advance acquisition of highway rights of way
Advance acquisition of land needed for large motorways is specifically authorised by the Federal Interstate Highway Programme (which is 90 per cent funded by the Federal government). The advantages include the saving of money, but no special funds have been set up for advance acquisition. Of the twelve states practising such programmes, only California has acquired in advance on a large scale (some $30 million a year) to produce significant savings.
Source: United Nations (1973, vol. VI, pp. 67–8).

2.3 Agency

2.3.1 Local
Canada City of Red Deer, Saskatchewan and Edmonton, Alberta
The rapidly growing city of Red Deer (20,000 people) has practised advance acquisition of land needed for urban development since 1953, and has found that the subdivision and selling of serviced lots has been a viable means of financing needed infrastructure works in a period of rapid growth. Some other western Canadian cities (Edmonton, Alberta and Saskatchewan) also practise advance land acquisition, originally based on land acquired by the city through tax default. They have been able to have a more compact development pattern, which, for instance, improved the efficiency of their public transport.
Sources: Cole (1963); United Nations (1973, vol. VI, pp. 147–55).

The Netherlands Amsterdam Planning Department
In the City of Amsterdam responsibility for the acquisition and development of land and the preparation of the plan (which serves as a legal document of expropriation) are all in the same Department of Planning and Public Works. This department sometimes has the task of helping the smaller municipalities.
Source: Amsterdam Public Works Department (1973).

2.3.2 Regional
Australia Metropolitan Perth Regional Planning Authority
Since 1965 the Perth (Western Australia) Metropolitan Regional Planning Authority has had the power to acquire compulsorily and develop land on a wide scale. This was in response to a situation of widespread land speculation due to the rapid development and strict subdivision control which pinpointed the direction of future growth. The land was to be purchased by the public authorities at rural value only.
Sources: Harrison (1971, pp. 244–8); Western Australia (1968).

2.3.3 National
Israel National Land Administration
In 1960 all state-owned land in Israel was consolidated into one national agency, chaired by the representative of the Ministry of Agriculture. Some conflicts have

arisen, however, between this agency and the Housing Ministry.
Source: Darin-Drabkin *et al.* (1972).

Spain   Central Land Authority

In 1958 the Real Estate Development Management Office (*Gerencia de Urbanizacion*) was established as an autonomous body within the Ministry of Housing. This agency was responsible for supplying land for the fifteen-year National Housing Programme (1961–76) which involved the creation of polygones, centres of industry and residence in the urban region. The agency has acquired about 25,000 hectares and spent some $50 million.
Sources: Spain – Ministeria de la Vivienda (1975); United Nations (1973, vol. III, pp. 145–6).

2.3.4   *Functional*

The question of whether a public land agency should be autonomous or part of the planning machinery is an important one for the effectiveness of implementation. A semi-autonomus agency has the advantages of (usually) efficient and swift action unhampered by bureaucratic delay. On the other hand, it may lead to conflicts between different authorities, as the land agency attempts to be self-financing and therefore is not interested in releasing land for public housing (Israel), or pays exaggerated prices in order to get efficiency (France). The co-ordination of land administration and planning in one department leads to planning aims controlling acquisition, rather than the other way around. The difficulty is that such arrangements may only be feasible at the municipal level (with the lack of a city-region authority).

France   Paris Region Land Acquisition Agency

L'Agence Foncière et Technique de la Region Parisienne was established in 1962 to purchase land required by public bodies for urban development projects (including new towns). The agency has powers of expropriation and is jointly managed by representatives of central government ministries and local government districts. By 1973 the Agency had acquired some 20,000 hectares, including 8,600 for new towns. Financing is by a special loan fund (FNAFU – National Fund for Real Estate Development).
Sources: Pottier (1975); United Nations (1973, vol. III, pp. 144–5).

Sweden   STRADA (municipal land-buying agency of Stockholm)

A special autonomous public company was created by the city of Stockholm in 1954 for the specific purpose of cutting red tape and ensuring confidentiality in city real-estate transactions. In order to assemble large land reserves cheaply, the company operates secretly, not even informing officials of the towns it is buying land in. It is even forbidden by the Official Secrets Act to publish information which might lead to land price speculation (town plans). STRADA and other public companies accounted for 30 per cent of all municipal land purchases in Sweden in 1971.
Source: Doebele (1974).

2.4   *Timing of expropriation*

2.4.1   *Before taking land*

The establishment of legal grounds for the right of the public authorities to take land may take a good deal of time, and thus be an impediment to implementation. Therefore efficient expropriation procedures are essential for plan implementation, especially as delays often run to years.

The Netherlands   Expropriation
In the Netherlands the structure plan of the municipality, approved at the provincial level, is a legal document giving the right to expropriate land for urban development.
Source: Darin-Drabkin (1977).

2.4.2   *During the taking of land*
The ability of the public authorities to take possession of land while compensation proceedings are taking place, (which are often even more subject to appeals than expropriation) is important for speeding up the execution of development.

Sweden   Changes in expropriation procedure
Recently Swedish expropriation procedure has been streamlined in order to avoid situations such as the Stockholm expropriation that took six years to gain possession. The 1972 reforms are: first, the local authorities do not now have to prove that the private owner was not capable of creating reasonable development himself; second, the payment of court costs of the private party, even if he lost, was eliminated; and third, the legislation now permits quick taking of possession of land before exact compensation payment is settled.
Source: Doebele (1974, p. 17).

2.5   *Compensation*

2.5.1   *At market value*
In most countries compensation is at the basis of the prevailing market value − based primarily on comparing transaction prices in recent years. The market value may of course contain an element of hope value for future new development, and not just reflect the replacement costs of the capitalised value of the rental income from a particular activity on a particular site. In a few countries strict planning control has eliminated this development value from the market price of certain types of land.

The Netherlands   Compensation
Compensation for land expropriated by the authorities is on the basis of market value. In addition, for agricultural land (e.g. taken for conversion to urban use) there is provided ten years' income from farming. But the market price of agricultural land near the large cities in Holland is little different from its value in other areas: a situation which contrasts to nearly every other country. The public land supply and automatic expropriation procedure for urban extension land has so influenced the market as to eliminate development value of agricultural land.
Source: Darin-Drabkin (1977, pp. 349 ff).

2.5.2   *Current use value*
Some countries are attempting to exclude the hope value of future development from the calculation of compensation, paying only the current use value, which may be expressed as the capitalised value of the expected stream of benefits from the current use. This is relatively easy to calculate in the case of agricultural land on the basis of fixed criteria, though it may be more contentious in theory for land in urban uses.

2.5.3   *Frozen value*
A few countries are attempting to solve the difficulty of a lack of financial means of public authorities to carry out widespread land acquisition, due in recent years

to the great increase in all land prices, by paying compensation on the basis of the land prices prevailing at a fixed date (with an adjustment for inflation and sometimes a reasonable degree of profit). This is an attempt to exclude the speculative increase in prices from compensation, something that current use value still takes into account (the general rise in land prices).

France   Compensation in ZAD
Within the French zones of future urban development (where no current development is allowed) compensation for land acquired by the public authorities is payable on the basis of prices prevailing one year before the declaration of the ZAD.
Source: Lemasurier (1975, pp. 147–9).

Sweden   Compensation
In 1972 compensation for expropriated land was set at the prices prevailing on 1 January 1971. This will be in effect until 1981, at which time the prices prevailing ten years earlier will be the basis of compensation.
Source: Doebele (1974).

2.6   *Financing*

2.6.1   *Loans*
Land acquisition, as part of the capital budget, is usually financed, at least in its initial stages, by some type of loan. The type and conditions of loan are very important for their consequences on the land-acquisition programme: whether the authorities have to go to the regular capital markets or whether some special arrangements for long-term, low-interest loans can be made (amortising the costs of urban development over all the generations that will use it). The role of the central authorities in relation to local bodies when they are actually acquiring land is central to the use of loans – they are a means of regulating local authority activity. In some cases loans are used as an indirect means of controlling land prices, through review of purchase prices paid by higher authorities.

Sweden   Loans for land acquisition
The government started to grant special loans in 1968 to assist municipalities with land acquisition on the basis of acquiring a reserve ten years in advance. There is an additional low-interest loan fund for municipal investment in land disposed of with leasehold rights and developed with the assistance of government housing loans. Finally, some check on the reasonableness of land prices is made as a condition of receiving a government housing loan (which loans account for 90 per cent of housing production).
Source: Odmann and Dahlberg (1970, pp. 148–9).

2.6.2   *Profits from disposal*
The money from the sale or lease of public land can be used to finance the purchase of more land. In some cases land schemes attempt to be self-financing in this way, even keeping separate accounts. The conditions of loans have an influence on the extent to which the local authorities feel obligated to make a quick profit from proceeds of disposal, rather than keep capital tied up in land.

Italy   Bridge Law, 1967
There was an attempt in Italy to create a self-financing programme of municipal land acquisition for low-cost housing. The land was to be acquired at fixed prices

and resold at market prices, with the proceeds of sale of land going to private residential and commercial builders to finance the condemnation of more land. However, the key compensation provision was declared unconstitutional, and little acquisition was actually made.
Source: Fried (1973, p. 131).

2.6.3 *Participation of private capital*
One way for the public authorities to raise the capital needed for land purchase is to involve private capital through the creation of some form of mixed company which allows for profitable investment in development projects. Another type of participation is the issuing of shares for such companies for landowners in compensation for taking their land.

France   Mixed companies for urban development
In France mixed public–private companies are widely used as a means of financing urban development. Urban-renewal companies include landowners, and issue shares, while in the new ZAD zones private mixed companies carry out the actual development and have authorities to expropriate land.
Source: Lemasurier (1975, pp. 139–40).

2.6.4 *General revenues*
Large authorities, and some regional and local authorities with a secure financial base, may be able to finance land acquisition at least partly out of their normal revenues. It should be noted that revenue from income is generally a more secure base than revenue from property, attempting to directly link betterment and land purchasing.

3.0 CONTROL OVER SPECIFIC DEVELOPMENT BY DIRECT PARTICIPATION

3.1 *Powers*

3.1.1 *Infrastructure*
In nearly all countries the public authorities have the primary responsibility for providing infrastructure, both primary (roads, sewers) and secondary (schools, health centres), and acquiring land for these purposes.

3.1.2 *Statutory functions*
In most countries the public authorities carry out a number of different public functions, besides the provision of infrastructure, for which they need land. The chief of these is housing.

Australia   South Australia Housing Trust
The South Australia Housing Trust has acquired land for housing which it has sold for single-family housing plots as well as developing itself. About one-third of all housing, mainly at the lower end of the market, is in the Adelaide city region.
Source: Harrison (1971).

Canada   Ontario Housing Corporation
The Ontario Housing Corporation has been most active in acquiring land for statutory functions, on the basis of Federal/provincial/municipal agreements. The Federal government provides 75 per cent matching funds, and also authorises loans.
Source: Amato (1973).

3.1.3   *General development*
In some cases the public authorities may directly carry out urban development themselves. This may be in the case of a new town, in the creation of new neighbourhoods in the urban extension, or in comprehensive redevelopment of existing urban areas (less frequent).

Chile   CORMU
In Chile an autonomous corporation was set up to acquire land for urban development, issuing bonds and getting general government revenue.
Source: United Nations (1973, vol. IV).

India   Delhi Development Corporation
This was created in the 1960s with the power to buy up all the land needed for future development in the New Delhi region in order to stop land speculation. Unfortunately, as it was not co-ordinated with housing policy, the disposals tended to favour more expensive housing uses (through auction of leases).
Source: Bose (1975).

The Netherlands   Land policy
In the Netherlands the public authorities acquire all the land needed for urban extension through expropriation, with the structure plan for urban expansion being the legal authority for public ownership.
Source: Darin-Drabkin (1977, pp. 349–51).

Sweden   Municipal land policy
The declared government policy in Sweden is for the local authorities to acquire all the land needed for urban growth and lease it out themselves. This policy was first introduced in Stockholm in 1907.
Source: Darin-Drabkin (1977, pp. 310–14).

3.2   *Scope*

3.2.1   *New towns*
In recent years the creation of new towns on green-field sites or from small villages has been one of the most important types of public development. New towns may be situated in areas of growth in order to decant population from existing centres, or they may be located in depressed regions in order to stimulate development. Recently the size of a new town defined as a self-sustaining economic unit has been increasing, from around 50,000 (1940s) to 200,000–500,000 (1970s).

Australia   New towns
The South Australia Housing Trust constructed a complete new town at Elizabeth, fifteen miles from Adelaide, to take overspill from the existing city and to provide housing in the context of complete community services for industrial workers (see 2.3.2).
Source: Harrison (1971).

Brazil   Brasilia
The capital of Brazil was moved to a complete new town of Brasilia in the interior in order to encourage development away from the coastal areas. The town was to be completely planned and constructed, but rapid influx of migrants still created

adjoining shanty towns. None the less it has stimulated development of the interior, without, however, reaching the scale to reduce concentration in the south-east Metropolitan areas (Rio and Sao Paulo).
Source: United Nations (1973, Vol. IV).

France New towns in the Paris region
The regional plan for Paris envisages the creation of five new towns on two axes north and south of the existing metropolitan area to absorb virtually all the forecasted population growth of the region until the year 2000 (some several millions). The towns are to be linked to the centre by new high-speed metro lines, and each town will have a large self-sustaining commercial centre and services as well as housing. The first new town, Cerg-Pointoise, planned to reach 500,000 eventually, has begun to be settled.
Source: Merlin (1971).

India Bombay
A complete new centre for Bombay is being constructed by the Metropolitan Bombay Planning Authority, in order to decentralise overcrowded industrial and commercial development.
Source: Correa *et al.* (1965).

Israel New towns
A number of new towns have been constructed in Israel since 1949 as regional growth poles, integrated into a pattern of small rural settlements and middle-sized rural agro-industrial centres. The most impressive achievement is Beersheba, which has grown to over 100,000 and greatly stimulated the development of the Negev desert. The location of high-level educational services as well as employment has been an important ingredient in success.
Source: Lichfield (1978a).

USSR New towns
In order to encourage the development of Siberia, the Soviets have constructed a number of new settlements which are major educational and industrial centres. One of the most important incentives which encouraged their successful development was the existence of wage differentials (higher in the less desirable regions).
Source: Underhill (1978).

USA New towns
New towns were supposed to be encouraged by the 1968 Urban Development Act, but few have been built. Two new towns in the Washington–Baltimore area have been constructed by private interests (Columbia, Maryland, and Reston, Virginia). A few new towns were established with the help of government agencies during the 1930s Depression as green-belt towns, and another small group were constructed during the Second World War as housing for special projects, like atomic-energy installations.
Source: McLaughlin (1978).

3.2.2 *Urban extension*
In some countries the area of urban extension from the large city is developed by the public authorities in order to ensure non-fragmented development and an appropriate housing and services mix. The creation of planned new neighbourhoods in the city region, with adequate services, on the basis of public land ownership allows co-ordinated transportation planning and general

infrastructure development. The new neighbourhoods are an integral part of the economy of the big city, and are planned as sub-units.

The Netherlands   Amsterdam extension
The whole of Amsterdam's growth since the First World War has been planned and laid out by the city's planning department on the basis of public land ownership. The South Amsterdam extension was completed between the wars, while the general extension plan of 1935 approved the layout for the west Amsterdam extension (completed 1947–59), the south-west extension, and the north extension (both still under completion). The general pattern is for a mixture of flats and low-rise houses with much green space and good transport connections. There is no urban sprawl, but an abrupt break between city and country.
Source: Amsterdam – Public Works Department (1962).

Sweden   Stockholm's new neighbourhoods
In the post-war years Stockholm has constructed a number of new neighbourhoods in a planned pattern on the basis of public land ownership. Such new neighbourhoods are planned along the new public transportation lines. Within the neighbourhoods it is arranged that everyone is within walking distance, with a hierarchical planning system of commercial services and public services around the transport point, with high-rise buildings adjacent, and low-rise housing laid out so that road-traffic disturbance is minimal. The central commercial centres are sometimes developed by the public authorities, and sometimes done privately.
Source: Odmann and Dahlberg (1970).
See also **Chile,** CORMU, and **India,** Delhi Development Corporation in 3.1.3.

3.2.3   *Existing city*
In some cases the public authorities are able to carry out public development within the existing city, most frequently for statutory functions, such as housing, but also for comprehensive development.

France   ZAC
The French Zones of Concentrated Development are an administrative device used to suspend building regulations in a city region in order to carry out comprehensive redevelopment, usually by a public–private mixed company. Such schemes have been both for commercial centres and public housing (in the latter case, usually by a public agency alone). The land is leased and acquired by the public authorities, which must also approve the scheme and in theory take into account the social consequences. In practice this has resulted in the efficient construction of large-scale and profitable office blocks (e.g. Maine-Montparnesse and La Defense in Paris) with few social goals being realised.
Source: Pottier (1975).

Spain   Polygones
In Spain the main government policy has been to create polygones, urban industrial centres around which housing is constructed. In addition government has constructed special 'decongestion centres' for commercial development in the urban extension in Madrid and Barcelona.
Source: United Nations (1973 vol. III).

USA   New York State Urban Development Corporation
This public corporation, established in 1969, carries out land-acquisition and

assembly operations for comprehensive new town and new neighbourhood development in new areas and within existing cities. It has the power to override existing city ordnances to carry out redevelopment, but these powers are not usually invoked. Among the projects constructed have been two new towns and a new neighbourhood on formerly derelict land in New York City (on Welfare Island).
Source: Reilly (1973, pp. 251 ff).

USA Urban renewal
The 1949 Housing Act established comprehensive redevelopment of city centres on the basis of local acquisition of land and resale to developers on the basis of approved schemes for all purposes, including industrial and commercial development as well as public housing (first authorised in 1937). The programmes have been widely criticised for displacing poor people in favour of commercial development without adequate provision of public housing for them.
Source: Wilson (1967).

3.3 *Agency*

3.3.1 *Public authority*
The most common source of public development is the public authorities themselves, either at the local level (Netherlands, Britain) or through central government (Spain, France).

France Administrative direction of new public development
In France most public development projects (e.g. the new towns in the Paris region) have been carried out by the Ministry of Equipment of the central government, and have been specifically planned and administered by the Prefect (representative of the central government at the provincial level). A special institution of the Prefecture of the Paris Region was created partly for this purpose.
Source: Darin-Drabkin (1977, pp. 389–92).

Spain Gerencia da Urbaninacion
In Spain the agency which carries out polygones is an autonomous part of the Ministry of Housing of the central government.
Source: United Nations (1973, vol. III).

3.3.2 *Public corporations*
Autonomous public corporations are often used as land-acquisition and development agencies. One advantage is that they can raise money themselves on the market, and it is also thought that they can keep separate accounts and perhaps operate more efficiently and with less bureaucracy.

Australia South Australia Housing Trust (see 3.1.2)

Chile CORMU (see 3.1.3)

India Delhi Development Corporation
The Delhi Development Corporation is an autonomous public company charged with providing land for all future development in New Delhi. It may lease or sell, and ultimately (though it may borrow loans) should be self-financing.
Source: Bose (1975).

USA   New York State Urban Development Corporation (see 3.2.3)

3.3.3   *Mixed public–private corporations*
France   Mixed private–public companies
Since the 1950s mixed companies have been an important way of carrying out development in France, via mobilising capital for public purposes. Such companies include housing companies which construct social housing, and urban-renewal companies which include landowners in their development schemes. Recently these have been made easier by the provision that only a majority and not all landowners have to agree to form such a company.
Source: United Nations (1973, vol. III, p. 161).

Spain   AZCA
An interesting example of the participation of landowners in development schemes is the Association de la Zone Commercial de Avenida del Generalissimo Franco. This is a mixed private–public company (made up of landowners and government representatives) to develop a commercial centre on a fifty-acre site two miles from the centre of Madrid. All land ownership in the area is pooled into this company, which then participates with state powers of expropriation to develop the site.
Source: United Nations (1973, vol. III, pp. 162–4).

3.3.4   *Co-operative associations*
In some countries the role of co-operative associations for construction and development is important, and they may be given semi-official standing and subsidies.

Sweden   Co-operative housing associations
In Sweden a significant part of new development has been carried out in recent years by co-operative organisations of tenants of trade unions, authorised in policy statements made in 1945. Public housing corporations number 300 in different municipalities; in addition there is the nation-wide National Association of Tenants Saving and Building Societies (HSB) and the co-operative organ of the trade unions (*Svenska Riksbygogen*). The co-operative sector owns 24 per cent of the housing stock of flats and accounted for 17 per cent of new construction in 1969.
Source: Odmann and Dahlberg (1970, pp. 185–6).

3.4   Timing

3.4.1   *Timing of release of land*
The timing of release of land is important for the effect that public land ownership actually has on urban land prices and urban development. Public ownership without release in the right quantity and time does not alone solve the problems of urban life. The local authority may be tempted to act as a speculator itself, gaining higher prices through withholding land, if financial and administrative arrangements encourage this.

France   Timing of release of land
The need for quick return on short-term financing has led to widespread quick disposal for sale (see 3.2.3).

Israel   Conflicts among authorities
In Israel there exists a conflict between the land Authority, which was interested in selling its land at market prices, and the housing ministry, which wanted to create public development in certain areas immediately. As a result, public land ownership in Israel, not being able to supply land in the urban areas or urban extension in sufficient amount or time, has not affected urban land prices.
Source: Darin-Drabkin *et al.* (1972).

3.4.2   *Timing of construction*
The question of whether public land ownership speeds up the building process or not is important in deciding what the final results of public development will be. The speed of use of land depends on (i) the size of land reserves (if large, a smaller amount of land can be released, and some land can be held longer, in advance); (ii) the financing arrangements which favour a quick return; and (iii) the costs of infrastructure and the difficulties of construction.

Sweden   Use of land for building
In Sweden, despite advance land acquisition, publicly used land was used for more housing than planned, reaching 76 per cent of all housing built on publicly owned land by 1970, as opposed to a planned 54 per cent. Thus land reserved had to be used more quickly than originally planned, with 25 per cent of housing built on public land acquired in the last four years and 53 per cent on land held for less than ten years.
Source: Doebele (1974, pp. 51–2).

3.5   *Valuation of disposed land*

3.5.1   *Freehold disposal*
In many cases the public authorities sell the land that they have developed to private owners, especially home-owners who either get freeholds or perpetual leaseholds. This method produces a smaller capital debt for the public authorities, but denies them the flexibility of either taking back land for changed purposes or collecting betterment through the leasehold terms.

Australia   Land tenure
The Commission of Inquiry into Land Tenures recently suggested that private residential households should be treated as freeholds at peppercorn rent, a suggestion accepted by the Conservative national government.
Source: Commission of Inquiry into Land Tenures (1973).

France   Freehold disposal
In France land which is acquired by the public authorities and developed is usually sold, or the total amount of a lease collected, at once. This has been done because most projects must be self-financing. It has led to large profits for developers (see 3.2.3).
Source: Pottier (1975).

3.5.2   *Leasehold system*
The leasehold system may be an efficient tool of planning (by fixing conditions on the lease) and collection of betterment (by readjustment of the terms). However, the actual type of the lease, first the length of time of the lease, and second the terms and conditions, are important as to whether this aim is in fact realised. There are usually distinctions made in this regard between residential and other

property. The use of leasehold often depends on the financial strength of the public authority concerned to raise the necessary capital. One method is, formally, to have a lease but ask for the total amount or some proportion of it in advance. This, however, means that the possibility of benefiting from increases in value is gone. Another issue is whether leasehold terms should be calculated on the economic cost to the local authority – raw land plus infrastructure – whether they should be subsidised even more and for what uses, or whether they should be based on market rents.

Australia   Leasehold system in Canberra
The capital city of Australia was planned from its beginning in 1924 on the basis of public land ownership leased to private developers. Leases are offered at public auctions for residential, commercial and profit-making activities; land for public purposes, however, is allocated without auction (including that for voluntary bodies such as churches). Some land auctions are reserved specifically for owner-occupier buyers. The system has led to very strict control and planning of development and return to the community of land value increments. But some problems have arisen over the speed of release of land, as land reserves left open tend to be used as parks, and residents are opposed to developing them.
Sources: Harrison (1971, pp. 241–4); Archer (1972).

Hong Kong   Leasehold system
All land in Hong Kong is Crown land, and it is generally administered on ninety-nine-year leases, which are auctioned off regularly and generate some part of the government revenues.
Source: United Nations (1973, vol. II).

The Netherlands   Leasehold
Amsterdam generally leases all its publicly owned land, while Rotterdam has sold some land in the city centre after its comprehensive redevelopment. One of the most discussed questions is the calculation of costs, as infrastructure costs are very high due to the need to fill the weak sub-soil with sand. Currently, economic costs fully include these infrastructure costs, as well as the costs of interest on the capital tied up in land purchase before construction is finished. This has tended to make social housing expensive in the urban extensions.
Source: United Nations (1973, vol. III).

Sweden   Leasehold system
In Sweden the government policy is to encourage leaseholds. The larger municipalities, such as Stockholm, now primarily use this, as they have large land reserves to draw revenue from, while the smaller ones do not. In Stockholm originally leases were made for up to sixty years and commercial land in the city centre was sold. Now, however, the tendency is to give leases for commercial purposes for only seven to ten years, with frequent revisions to take into account the cost of living, land prices, and so on. However, leases are still generally quite undervalued, particularly for residential uses. Municipalities based leases on the economic cost of their land acquired plus infrastructure, not on the market value of land.
Sources: Doebele (1974, pp. 54 ff); Carlegrim (1966).

3.6   Financing

3.6.1   From rent revenues

The most common source of financing is from the proceeds of development. This requirement for self-financing sometimes has a significant effect on the pattern of development, either in location or social effects, and often in the long run is not economical, either because long-term betterment collection is forgone or because high prices are paid for initial land assembly. This is related to whether or not leasehold is used (3.5.2) and the general release policy (see 3.4.1) and is often the case with public comparison (3.3.2).

3.6.2 *From general revenues*
An important source of financing is the base of the public authority itself. If it has large-enough funds, either through its own loans or government revenues (its own or free from the appropriate government body), its scope is much increased. The degree of government involvement in final development is important in affecting and regulating land assembly and release policies.

Sweden Financing of development
In Sweden the government finances over 90 per cent of development through housing loans which give a various proportion of the total mortgage on new housing (more for social housing and co-operatives in comparison with private single-family homes). In addition the municipalities themselves have a secure financial base due to the municipal income-tax system.
Source: Doebele (1974, annexe A–I).

3.6.3 *Participation of private capital*
One important way that the public authorities can ensure that development occurs when they lack resources is to involve private capital and landowners in development schemes through public mixed companies (see 3.3.3) and sometimes through land pooling or readjustment schemes (see 2.1.5). The use of shares instead of monetary compensation is one possibility.

France Participation of private capital
A major means of finance due to weakness of urban financing by the state (see 3.3.3).

Spain See 3.3.3

3.7 *Enforcement*

3.7.1 *Conditions and terms of development*
One of the most effective ways to enforce planning codes in a detailed way is to require and approve planning briefs as a means of leasing publicly owned land. This is more positive than just forbidding certain types of development, or having to justify a reason for rejecting a planning application that does not meet minimum standards.

Australia See 3.5.2 for leasehold system in Canberra

3.7.2 *Right of retrieval*
In theory one of the advantages of the leasehold system is that it gives the right of retrieval to the public authorities for a new development or use of land due to changing needs. In practice, however, political opposition has meant that this has not been widely used.

Australia   See 3.5.2 again

Sweden   Condemnation of leases
In practice, if a municipality wants to expropriate a leaseholder, the compensation determination and procedure is much more complex than in the case of owned land, as the fee for the unexpired term is of variable value, and with different forms of subsidies to complicate matters disputes are very complex.
Source: Doebele (1974, pp. 63–4).

4.0   CONTROL OF GENERAL DEVELOPMENT BY FISCAL MEANS

4.1.1   *Land profit taxes*
Land profit taxes are designed to tax the *increase* in land values over time. When this increase is generally attributed to the actions or investments of public authorities, this increase is generally known as *betterment*. A direct charge for a specific public authority investment is considered in section 5.1.1 as an infrastructure charge; this section includes those measures which attempt to collect general betterment due to public authority decisions (i.e. allowing urban use) and those measures which do not distinguish the cause of the rise in land values. Such measures also have as their purpose a desire to reduce speculation in the land market. Land profit taxes may be collected at the time of land sale (in which case they could be either capital gains or income taxes), or they may be levied periodically (after revaluations), in which case they are commonly called *land value increment taxes*. Finally, they may be collected as a one-time charge at the time of a public authority decision, in which case they may be called a *betterment levy*. When land transactions are taxed, adjustments to the original purchase price are usually made to adjust for inflation and other factors. Sometimes it is considered that land held a long time is not 'speculative', and a different rate or type of tax applies.

Australia   Betterment levy
A tax on the land value increase resulting from a public authority decision to allow a change of use is assessed at the time of the decision in New South Wales at the rate of 30 per cent. The first A$15,000 of property sold is exempted in order to protect the small landowner. However, the tax was not actually collected until development was begun; therefore, it was widely evaded as landowners refused to develop even when planning permission had been granted. The tax was repealed in 1973.
Source: Neutze (1973, p. 233).

Denmark   Land value increment tax
A tax on the increase in value due to a public authority decision to allow a change of use (from agricultural into urban) has been introduced in Denmark. The tax rate ranges from 40 to 60 per cent, and it is collected at the time the public authority decision is made rather than at the time of transfer (i.e. realised capital gain). A mortgage for twelve years is available if the owner cannot pay cash for the tax.
Source: Denmark Taxation Office (1962, p. 14).

Finland   Land profit tax
Land owned for less than ten years is subject to profits taxation on the basis of income-tax rates. 'Professional' selling of building lots is also taxed as income;

however, in some cases if the buyer is a public body, this tax is forgone.
Source: United Nations (1973, vol. III, p. 109).

France   Land profit tax
Land profits are taxed as income if the sale is made within five years of ownership of any buildable land. After five years, land sales are treated as capital gains and taxed at a rate of 60 per cent. The purchase price, in calculating the profit, is increased by 25 per cent plus cost of living escalator plus 3 per cent per year (for land maintenance).
Source: United Nations (1973, vol. III, p. 108).

Israel   Land profit tax
In Israel land transactions carried out within two years of purchase are taxed as normal commercial transactions on the basis of income-tax rates reaching 80 per cent maximum. Land transactions on land owned for more than two years are taxed as capital gains at special rates of between 20–40 per cent of profit. The land profit is calculated by adjusting the original purchasing price by the cost of improvements, the amount of taxes paid, and 3 per cent per year land maintenance costs. The rate varies according to the length of time of ownership.
Source: Darin-Drabkin *et al.* (1972).

Norway   Land profit tax
Land profits are taxed as income in Norway. It has been stated that this has led to some withholding of land from the market, as the property tax is low in comparison with progressive income-tax rates.
Source: United Nations (1973, vol. III, p. 109).

South Korea   Real property speculation check tax
This tax was instituted in 1967 to apply to 'marginal profits from land transfers'. It was intended originally to apply to vacant land (or underbuilt land, defined as that on which building space was less than 10 per cent of land-surface area), but this was exempted in 1968 due to political pressure. Owner-occupied homes were also exempted, and thus the tax only applies to sales of, for example, offices and factories. The tax rate is 50 per cent of the 'net assessable marginal profit', which is the difference between the sale price and the purchase price adjusted for 10 per cent return on capital invested, the value of capital improvements, and any brokers' fees. There are very minor penalties (5 per cent) for late payment or underpayment, and the self-declaration of taxpayers is the general basis for collection. Thus revenues from this tax have been small, amounting to less than 0·5 per cent of government tax revenue (about $7 million) in 1971.
Source: Grimes (1974).

Spain   Land profit tax
In Spain 25 per cent of the profit from land sales is taxed on the basis of the periodic reassessment of land values by municipal index zones (every three years).
Source: United Nations (1973, vol. III, p. 109).

Sweden   Land profit tax
Land profits in Sweden are treated as income and taxed on the basis of (progressive) income-tax rates. Adjustments are made as follows:

1   after two years, only 75 per cent of the profit is taxable (before 1968, after ten years no land profit tax was payable);

2   the original purchase price is adjusted for inflation in calculating the amount of profit, and any improvements are also deducted;
3   a further deduction of $600 per year is made for owner-occupied residential property.

For property that has been in ownership a long time, the purchasing price can be arbitrarily assessed as 150 per cent of the 1940 assessment, or the owner can choose to use the estimated value twenty years before the sale.
Source: United Nations (1973, vol. III, p. 110).

Switzerland   Land profit taxes
Each canton is autonomous in setting the rate of tax on land profits. The highest is in Zurich, at 40 per cent of profit on sale, and 60 per cent if the sale was within two years of purchase; however, the rate is reduced to 12 per cent if ownership was for over twenty-five years. In some cantons there is no capital gains tax if the land is owned for longer than ten years (Geneva) or fifteen years (Valais).
Source: United Nations (1973, vol. III, p. 108).

Taiwan   Land value increment tax
This tax is designed to capture the unearned increases in land value for the public authorities. It is payable either at the time of transfer of land or ten years after the date of the previous assessment. The tax is a gradated one, ranging from a 20 per cent rate if the increase in land value is less than 100 per cent of the previous land value, 40 per cent on the increment from 100 to 200 per cent, 60 per cent on the increment from 200 to 300 per cent, and 80 per cent on any increment of over 300 per cent. A special rate of 10 per cent applies to owner-occupied sites, and the rates are halved for factories. The calculation of the increment is made by adjusting the purchase price of the land for inflation and improvements. Publicly owned land, land acquired through compulsory purchase and some inheritance of land is exempt from taxation. This tax has become an important source of municipal finance, averaging some 13 per cent of provincial tax receipts with a total revenue of T$977 million in 1972.
Source: Grimes (1974).

USA   Land profit taxes
Land profits are considered as normal capital gains, which are taxed at half the income-tax rate to a maximum of 25 per cent. The real level of real-estate profit taxation is much lower, however, because of the favourable provisions for depreciation deductions at an accelerated rate on buildings. Land, however, is not depreciable for tax purposes.
Source: United Nations (1973, vol. VI, pp. 108–9).

4.1.2   *Property taxes*
Property taxes generally have a fiscal aim: to provide revenue for local government. For other bases of municipal finance, see sections 4.1.4, 4.1.5 and 4.2.2 (municipal income and sales taxes, and revenue-sharing from the central government). But they often have side-effects on the land market, sometimes intended. Property taxes may be based on the capital value or the rental value of property; in the latter case unused land is not taxed and the maintenance costs of holding land as a long-term investment are reduced. Property taxation may also differentiate between land and buildings; this generally has the effect of forcing development of valuable sites by taxing their most profitable use rather than current use. The differences in tax rates between different local authorities may also have an effect on the location of human activity; therefore, the size of the

taxing authority is significant. Finally, varying treatment of property taxes on agricultural land in urban areas may affect speculation and urban development patterns.

Australia   Site value taxation
In Sydney there is both a progressive tax on land values levied by New South Wales and a flat-rate city tax. The combined rate ranges from 2·5 per cent on a site value of less than A$17,250 to 5·66 per cent of site value of more than A$147,250. Numerous exemptions are given to certain classes of landowners, and no tax is payable below the minimum amount (A$17,250). All land taxes are deductible for income-tax purposes. In the opinion of Archer this tax has had a significant effect in forcing large-scale redevelopment in Sydney's central business district.
Source: Archer (1972).

Denmark   Property taxes
The land value tax is 2 per cent of assessed periodic valuation, with an additional rate set by the country at between 0·5 and 8·5 per cent, so that the average landowner pays 4 per cent of assessed value. This is deductible for income-tax purposes, however, and this has encouraged the holding of property for tax-deduction purposes. From 1926 to 1956 a separate rate was levied on improvements and land; now improvements are only taxed for non-residential uses.
Source: Denmark Taxation Office (1962).

France   Property taxes
Land taxes are the basis of local government finance. They are collected from both built and unbuilt land on the basis of rental value. The rates vary from between 0·3 and 0·7 per cent of assessed value. Recent legislation has been introduced which would force the municipalities to enforce a higher rate of tax (1–3 per cent of capital value). These taxes yielded about 15 per cent of local government revenues in the 1960s.
Sources: United Nations (1973, vol. III, p. 107); Grimes (1974, pp. 25–8).

Israel   Property tax
The property tax is collected both for the central government and for local authorities (combined since 1968). The rate is 1·5 per cent of the market value of buildings and land, except for vacant land, which is taxed at 2·5 per cent, and buildings which are rent-controlled (most multi-family rented accommodation), which are taxed at 0·7 per cent of market value per year. Up to 1972 built land was taxed on the basis of annual expected income (i.e. rental income) rather than market (i.e. capital) value. The property tax accounted for only 3·8 per cent of total government revenues in 1970–1.
Source: Darin-Drabkin *et al.* (1972, pp. 33–4).

Norway   Property taxes
In Norway there is a very low rate of property tax, varying in 1960 from 0·4 to 0·7 per cent of assessed valuation.
Source: United Nations (1973, vol. III, p. 109).

Sweden   Property tax
The property tax is based on the annual income from rental; however, if this is less than 2 per cent of assessed real-estate value, the tax is based on that amount. Sweden is relatively unique in attempting to tax the imputed rental value of

owner-occupied housing, calculated as from 2–8 per cent of the value of the house (the lowest rate applies to up to a £15,000-value house). The calculation of rental value is an underestimate that results in an estimated tax loss of about £100–200 million annually. No depreciation, however, is allowable for tax purposes in the case of the owner-occupied property tax. Gross yield for tax purposes from co-operative housing is set at 3 per cent of assessed value. All this income from property is taxable as part of normal income-tax rates.
Source: Neutze (1975, pp. 66–7).

Switzerland   Property tax
The property tax is variable in different cantons, ranging from 0·5 to 2 per cent of taxable value, which is only a small part of real market value.
Source: United Nations (1973, vol. III, p. 106).

USA   Differential assessment of agricultural land
In some states of the USA land in agricultural use in urban areas is assessed not on the basis of current market value (which would include hoped-for urban development) but only on the basis of current use value as agricultural land. In other states the taxes due if the land were used for urban uses are deferred until change of use actually occurs, at which time back payments for three to five years become due. In a few states the authorities have the discretion of approving the use of land as agricultural, in which case taxes are reduced. But the land must be used as specified, or all back taxes are immediately due, and five years' notice of cancellation must be given. These provisions, especially simple preferential assessment, have increased speculation by reducing the costs of not developing land.
Sources: United Nations (1973, vol. VI); Hady (1970, pp. 25–32).

USA   Graded tax
In Pittsburgh, Pennsylvania, a graded tax law has applied since 1913 where buildings are taxed at half the rate of land. This has encouraged recent central business district redevelopment and reduced average tax bills. In 1963 Hawaii introduced a graded property tax which aimed to reduce tax on improvements to 40 per cent of tax on site values by staged reductions every two years of 10 per cent. The rate of tax of improvements is presently 80 per cent, as the Governor has exercised his discretion in delaying the further reduction in the rate.
Source: United Nations (1973, vol. VI).

USA   Property taxes
Property taxes are a major source of local revenue, accounting for 88 per cent of local tax revenue and 47 per cent of all revenue for local authorities. State governments in some cases also rely heavily on property taxes. Property taxes are based on assessed value of property, land plus improvements, and the rate (set locally) varies from roughly 0·5 to 2 per cent.
Sources: Netzer (1966); United Nations (1973, vol. VI, pp. 108–9).

4.1.3   *Transfer taxes*
In many countries there is a flat-rate tax on the transfer of land. This generally has a fiscal purpose. The rate varies from 7 per cent of every land transaction (whether built land or not) in West Germany, and 7·4 per cent of the real value of real estate in Spain, to 1·25 per cent of real-estate valuation in France.
Source: United Nations (1973, vol. III, p. 110).

4.1.4   *Municipal income taxes*
Municipal income taxes have a fiscal purpose, and generally they provide the most secure financial basis for urban finance. This enables cities to carry out development programmes, including land purchase, on their own initiative without relying so much on outside government assistance. Income taxes can even be collected by the national government revenue service and returned to the municipalities.

Denmark   Municipal income tax
The local authorities receive their main revenue as a flat-rate income tax of 15 per cent, which is collected by the central government and redistributed. Some problems have occurred because the basis of collection is the taxpayer's residence rather than place of employment; thus city centres receive a low proportion of tax.
Source: Denmark Taxation Office (1962).

Sweden   Municipal income tax
In Sweden the municipalities have an exceptionally strong tax base due to the fact that they receive a flat-rate income tax as well as a property tax. The municipal income-tax rate varies from 10 to 16 per cent, with Stockholm at 17·5 per cent. The regional county councils also levy a flat rate, which raises the total non-national income-tax rate to an average of 24 per cent. This makes local income taxes higher for most individuals than the highly progressive national income tax, and their yield exceeds that of the national income tax. Local government received 46 per cent of all public receipts in 1972, and the percentage has been rising. This represents 20 per cent of total Swedish GNP as local government income.
Source: Doebele (1974, annexe A–1).

4.1.5   *Municipal sales taxes*
These generally have a fiscal purpose, to increase the tax base of the community. However, they may have locational effects if they are different in one community from another. In addition sales taxes or taxes on the turnover of commercial firms could also be used specifically for planning goals, by reducing rates in new towns or new commercial centres and raising rates to discourage commercial concentration in the central business district. Sales taxes also have the advantage of taking into account locational effects, in the sense that the turnover (and the basis for a high land value) is at least partially dependent on location.

France   Taxes on the turnover of commercial firms
In the new towns around Paris commercial firms are taxed in the new centres on the basis of turnover. The rate is differentiated by time, however, and is low (or non-existent) at the beginning of the new town, when there is a small catchment area, in order to encourage firms to locate there.
Source: Darin-Drabkin (1977, ch. 15).

USA   Municipal sales taxes
Sales taxes have long existed in many states and cities in the USA as a means of finance. However, where metropolitan areas cross state lines, or where the central city boundaries include only a small portion of the city region, sales taxes in the inner city have encouraged relocation of retail trade to suburban areas and raised the cost of living in inner-city areas. For example, New York City has a combined state–municipal sales tax of 8 per cent, while adjoining Connecticut suburbs have

a rate of 3 per cent. Sales taxes provide 7 per cent of city tax revenue (general sales taxes).
Source: Siegan (1972).

4.1.6   *Death/inheritance taxes*
The ability to accumulate large holdings of property over a long time period to some extent depends on the nature of inheritance taxation in a country, which might make it difficult or easy for families to hold large tracts of land. The effectiveness of such taxation is often dependent on its timing; if it is collected only at the time of death, it may be possible to evade its provisions through complex trust or other arrangements.

4.1.7   *Wealth taxes*
The periodic taxation of wealth is generally aimed at redistribution. However, it may affect the ability of the wealthy to hold land over a long time period if this asset is included in the calculation of wealth. Sometimes owner-occupiers are exempted from this tax.

Sweden   Wealth tax
In Sweden land is included in the annual taxation of wealth at the rate of 0·2 per cent annually and is gradated. The first £15,000 of wealth is exempt.
Source: Neutze (1975, p. 66).

4.1.9   *Price and sales controls*
Governments have sometimes attempted to control the price of land directly through price freezes. This has more often been applied to the components of the demand for land, e.g. rent control or control of the price of building materials. Generally this has been accompanied by some method of rationing and has been in conditions of scarcity (i.e. rent control during both world wars). For the accompanying controls on building, see section 1.1.2 on building licenses. Governments have also attempted to regulate the demand for land by controlling the demand through restriction on sale, for example in many developing (and other) countries not allowing sales of land and property to foreigners, who often have greater resources and are able to bid up prices.

Sweden   Rent control
Sweden has had rent control since 1942. It is now being gradually lifted in those areas which no longer have a shortage of housing. Rents may be raised if improvements are made and if rent tribunals exist. Housing built with subsidised loans had a different form of rent control between 1946 and 1969.
Sources: Odmann and Dahlberg (1970, p. 181); Neutze (1975, pp. 64–5).

Switzerland   Restriction on sales of land to foreigners
In recent years Switzerland has not allowed the registration of titles to land or buildings to non-Swiss citizens, in order to reduce the demand for land. While this has not stopped purchases (which can still be registered in the name of a lawyer) entirely it *has* reduced them.
Source: Darin-Drabkin (from the Swiss daily press).

4.2   Scope

4.2.1   *Location differentiation*
In some countries and some areas local taxes are reduced in certain locations as an incentive for investment, particularly industrial investment.

4.2.2 *Revenue-sharing*
Revenue-sharing is the redistribution of funds from the central government to local or provincial units. It has recently been given consideration in a number of countries in order to strengthen the financial base of the local authorities, as central government revenues are usually on a more secure basis.

Netherlands Revenue-sharing
Municipal authorities in the Netherlands, have since 1960, received a percentage of funds from the central authority as their main source of revenue. The central government also collects and redistributes some local taxes. Income from taxes directly collected by the municipalities comes to less than 10 per cent of their budgets. The municipal fund is a fixed percentage of the central government's revenue. In 1968 it was about 13 per cent of total revenues. It is distributed to the municipalities on the basis of population, area, built-up area and costs of social services. In addition municipalities with extra burdens can receive 'subjective', i.e. discretionary, extra amounts. Amsterdam, The Hague and Rotterdam have received such increases.
Source: United Nations (1973, vol. III).

USA Revenue-sharing
A number of proposals have been made to redistribute Federal government revenues to the cities and states. At present, a relatively small amount is returned to the states on the basis of population.
Source: Reilly (1973, p. 117).

4.3 *Agency*

4.3.1 *Local and provincial taxation*
Generally the tax base and sources of the local and national governments vary considerably, with more emphasis at the local level on property as opposed to income taxation. However, the tax base of the local authorities may in exceptional cases be just as strong as that of the national authority, if local income tax is collected. However, it is interesting to note that redistributive goals are mainly carried out at the national level, so that local taxation assumes primarily a revenue-raising function for local government services. The degree of authority assumed at the local or state level, as opposed to the national level, has some effect on the division of taxation, but perhaps less than might be assumed (e.g. US weak tax base of state units compared with Federal authority).

4.3.2 *National taxation*
Generally land taxation which has a non-revenue purpose is primarily carried out at the national level. Thus land profit taxes are the same throughout each country; otherwise, the effect on a national land market would be negligible. Occasionally the central authority collects property taxes, often as part of wealth taxation. Most regional and other types of development projects are applied fiscally by national controls as well.

4.3.3 *Functional tax authorities*
Often there are different authorities which each collect a tax rate for the specific service they provide, such as education, water, sewage, and so on. Such overlapping jurisdictions often do not have the same boundaries as the municipal boundaries; while this may be a substitute for regional municipal authorities, it may also lead to conflict between different functional taxing authorities, whose

concerns may be solely on their revenue base and may not be subject to very much public control.

Colombia   Overlapping jurisdictions
In administering special assessments, one problem in Colombia (5.1.1) has been that each different agency which is carrying out a major development project (which may be the city, or may also be a Federal agency, e.g. for highways or airport) assesses its own charge. Thus a number of overlapping charges may occur which are not co-ordinated.
Source: Doebele (1977).

4.4   Timing

The timing of taxation may have a significant effect on its results, particularly in the case of land profit taxation. Such taxes are usually collected at the time of transactions; this, however, may act as a disincentive to supply land to the market. Therefore, periodic levies (analogous to the way that property taxes are collected) may be more appropriate in collecting the unearned increment and forcing development. Most effective in theory, however, would be a one-time charge at the time of development permission. This is analogous to the frequent revaluation of property taxes on the basis of site values, which also attempts to increase the maintenance costs of holding land vacant when the authority wants it developed.

4.4.1   During transactions
Examples: land profit taxes (see 4.1.1) in Finland, France, Israel, Norway and Sweden.

4.4.2   Periodic
Examples: all property taxes (see 4.1.2), and land value increment taxes (4.1.1) in Taiwan.

4.4.3   One-time levy
Examples: betterment levy (see 4.1.1) in Australia and Denmark, and infrastructure charges (5.1.1).

4.5   Valuation

4.5.1   Basis of valuation
The basis of the valuation of real property and land has a significant effect on the actual role of the taxation instrument as a measure in urban land policy. One of the most important is assessment on the basis of estimated annual rental value versus valuation on the basis of the capital value (i.e. the income that would be raised from the sale of the property). The basis of rental value does not take into account expected future gains from changes in use, and thus tends to increase speculative holding. For example, vacant land would have no value for tax purposes under that system. Another important issue is the separate rating of property and land, with sometimes separate tax rates applying to each (graded tax, site value taxation, single tax). Again, the separate rating of land value tends to take into account the expected future value of the land with a change in use, where the actual buildings on a site may not be an asset for that purpose.

Australia   Rating system
In Australia three different valuations of property are made every six years: the

unimproved capital value (which serves as a basis for site value taxation); the improved capital value; and the assessed annual value (which serves as the basis for property taxes). Every class of land is valued including strata and air rights and mineral-bearing land. The assessed annual value must be at least 5 per cent of the improved capital value, and corresponds to the annual rental value. In cities it is difficult to assess the unimproved capital value due to lack of sales data, but both the Bridge Report of 1960 on the Valuation of Land Act and the Royal Commission of Inquiry into Rating, Valuation and Local Government confirmed that the unimproved capital value seemed the fairest basis of taxation.
Source: Commission of Enquiry into Land Tenures, final report (1976).

4.5.2 *Procedure of valuation authority*
The procedure of valuation has an important influence on the effectiveness of taxation. Without accurate assessments, any tax of land will be ineffective. Yet assessments are often infrequently revised, and even worse are often arbitrary or only a percentage of actual market value. In addition different authorities sometimes assess the same property differently. Yet fairness in standards is important in gaining compliance with land taxation, which is so often not enforced in many countries. Finally, self-assessments are a useful basis for beginning valuations, particularly if they are published so that no one believes his neighbour has lied.

Canada   Valuation procedure
The Smith Committee and the Select Committee of the Ontario Legislature both recommended that all property should be reassessed at current market value, and that residential and business property should not be assessed differently. It was suggested, however, that residential property should be taxed at 60 per cent of assessed value, and working farms at 40 per cent.
Sources: United Nations (1973, vol. VI, pp. 111–12); Adler (1971).

Denmark   System of valuation
Denmark has perhaps the most sophisticated valuation system. Every four years every site in the entire country is evaluated, and the results are published as land value maps. The same criteria are used everywhere and assessors are elected by the municipalities and supervised by the Ministry of Finance. Transaction prices and planning and development works charges constitute the main criteria for assessment, and such information is required from each landowner (every real-estate sale must be recorded). In addition to the four-year valuation, there is a special valuation of property that has undergone major changes in status. Land value maps are open to inspection and objection by landowners, who must appeal within four weeks.
Source: Denmark Taxation Office (1962).

USA   Valuation authorities
Serious problems have arisen in the administration of the property tax in the USA because of the 'extreme geographic fragmentation of this function' into some 15,000 local tax units. Often a full-time qualified assessor cannot be afforded for such small units, or else is a political appointee. In addition political pressures have led to lower assessments of single-family houses than other types of property. Some experiments in consolidating assessments have begun to take place in Nashville, Tennessee, in Maryland and in Hawaii.
Source: Netzer (1966, pp. 48–9).

4.7 *Enforcement*
Difficulties of actually collecting land taxes, particularly land profit taxes, hamper

policy in many countries, particularly in the less-developed world. Valuation is only an element, albeit an important one, in such difficulties. Problems of reporting of sales, reporting of sales prices, registration of ownership and delays in collection are also important. Added to this is the fact that inefficiency in collection and inadequacy of assessment leads to cynicism among landowners and corruption among officials. Much of the problem is due to the lack of a strong administrative structure capable of enforcing legal decisions, i.e. by penalising delay in payment of taxes or by forcing the reporting of all land transactions.

Colombia   Difficulties in collection
The major difficulty in administering the special assessment tax system in Colombia is the problem of overdue taxes. Arrears range up to 30–40 per cent unpaid after five years. There are generally low penalties for non-payment and it is difficult to collect from public bodies.
Source: Doebele (1977).

Mexico   Self-assessment procedure
Mexico has attempted to overcome some of the difficulties connected with lack of adequate administrative structure for the collection of land taxation by using a system of self-reporting of land and property prices. However, the self-assessment is used both for tax purposes (where presumably there is a tendency to under-report) and for the price of compulsory purchase in the case of expropriation (where the bias is towards higher prices).
Source: Darin-Drabkin (information from interviews).

South Korea   Enforcement of taxation
Land tax administration and collection procedures, even after the 1967 reforms, are reported to be seriously inadequate. Because cadastral maps are incomplete, accuracy of self-assessment cannot in many cases be checked. Even those properties which are checked are not done by professionals, and unsystematic techniques have stiffened public resistance. Local officials are reluctant to revalue one property when they know that all others in one area also need revaluing. There is also evidence that taxes are being evaded through under-reporting of sales prices.
Source: Grimes (1974, p. 59).

5.0   CONTROL OF SPECIFIC DEVELOPMENT BY FISCAL MEANS

5.1.1   *Infrastructure charges*
Infrastructure charges are attempts by the public authorities to charge the cost of infrastructure works directly to the users; they are called 'special assessments' in the USA. In theory they have a betterment component, the attempt to recover the increase in land values due to a very specific public investment, as well as being a means of financing the development. In practice, however, they have tended to concentrate on recovering the costs of development works; even where, as in Colombia, the apportionment of charges is proportionate to estimated gains in land value, the actual amount collected is less than the estimated increase in value due to the development.

Colombia   Infrastructure charges
A major method of financing infrastructure works in Bogota, Colombia, is through the use of valorisation charges collected by the municipality through a

special agency. These charges are based on the cost of the project and apply to all those within the 'zone of influence' of the scheme (usually a road and associated sewer and other works). This zone generally extends some 500 metres on either side of the scheme; however, within the zone, charges are distributed according to a complex calculation of the betterment value that each site received from the scheme, and this in a highly flexible fashion. The valorisation tax has been responsible for financing nearly all of Bogota's major sewer and highway projects and has allowed for a much greater expansion than would have otherwise occurred. It was estimated that property taxes would have had to have been 50 per cent greater to pay for such programmes. On the other hand, it is found that nearly all landowners gain a greater increase in their land value than the amount of the tax. Administrative problems have centred around difficulties in collecting the tax, rather than the expected problems of calculation.
Source: Doebele (1977).

France   Infrastructure charges
In France, the development works tax, called the 'equipment tax', was introduced in 1961 and its rate was determined proportionally to the volume of building that can be erected on any given land (according to a 1964 amendment). The tax is set at 10 francs per cubic metre of building that can be erected, and it is collected when the landowner applies for a building permit or when he sells the property. The Land Orientation Law introduced a new system of taxation, with the aim of ensuring that the municipalities obtain the necessary financial means to meet urbanisation costs. An article of the Land Orientation Law, issued on 1 October 1968, normalised the taxing procedure and fixed the rate of tax. This law is in effect in all municipalities possessing any legal physical plan. In other localities the tax may be adopted by a vote of the local council. The basic tax rate is, as a rule, 1 per cent of the value. Local authorities are authorised to raise it to the maximum rate of 3 per cent; but for further augmentation, there must be government approval. The local authority can fix different rates of tax for various categories of construction; but they have to be equal for each category throughout the authority's area. The law forbids any other form of constructor's participation in financing public accommodations. However, there exist three exceptions: delivery of part of the construction land for public road development; an extra payment for exceeding density; and a special payment for sewerage connection.
Source: United Nations (1973, vol. III, p. 111).

West Germany   Tax for development works
In 1961–2 West Germany introduced a special tax for development works under which owners of land not yet in areas that had been urbanised had to remit the tax when the municipality decided to carry out a development scheme. This tax has been seen as efficient in preventing land speculation and in influencing the landowner either to build or to sell to someone interested in using the land for construction. However, the tax was abolished in 1964 because of public opposition.
Source: United Nations (1973, vol. III, p. 111).

Italy   Infrastructure charges
In Italy, until the enactment of the *Lege Pente* in 1967, municipalities had the right to fix the rate of participation of landowners in development works. In practice, the political structure of the municipalities affected the rate of this tax. Since 1967 the landowner must pay the municipality all the primary development costs. The landowner must also concede a gratuity to the municipality for

primary development works. For secondary development works, the municipality has the right to decide the rate of landowner participation.
Source: United Nations (1973, vol. III, p. 111).

5.1.2   *Taxation of vacant land*
This generally is a penal tax, designed to force the use of vacant land in urban areas and therefore deter speculative withholding of land from the market.

Belgium   Taxation of vacant land
Property which has been parcelled out or provided with infrastructure works but is still vacant may be taxed on a yearly basis.
Source: Suetens (1975, p. 64).

Chile   Taxation of vacant land
A tax on vacant land was introduced in Chile of 3 per cent of assessed value of vacant or unproductive land in urban areas. This rate is increased by 1 per cent annually until a maximum of 6 per cent is reached. Once the rate is reached it is maintained until the site is built upon. Newly subdivided land is tax-exempt for five years. When building starts, no taxes have to be paid, but if building is stopped for more than six months the tax applies again.
Source: United Nations (1973, vol. IV, p. 53).

Spain   Taxation of vacant land
The urbanisation ordnance in Spain introduced a tax on empty sites which is applied according to the state of the development scheme. The landowner must pay 0·5 per cent of the land value from approval of the scheme until the urban works are completed. The basis of evaluation is the expected value of land which was transferred from agriculture to urbanised land. After completing the urbanisation works, he must pay 2 per cent of the land value on the basis of the value of urban land. After some time, in built-up areas, the rate for plots used as private parks and gardens may be up to 5 per cent per annum.
Source: United Nations (1973, vol. III, p. 112).

Syria   Taxation of vacant land
There is a tax on unbuilt sites that is progressive, ranging from 1 to 5 per cent depending on the value of the site. Such property on which taxes have not been paid for three years can be auctioned by the municipality; if a building permit has been obtained, construction cannot be delayed for more than two years.
Source: United Nations (1973, vol. V, p. 35).

5.1.3   *Taxation based on development scheme*
Like taxation of vacant land, this type of taxation is intended to force development according to a planning scheme or to penalise non-conformity with one (e.g. in regard to densities).

West Germany   Taxation based on development scheme
The new law of the Federal Republic of Germany, in recognition of the growing building needs, allows for a more intensive land use of 20 per cent in the centre of the town, but introduces no special tax for the increased intensiveness of land use; therefore, the landowners receive an extra profit resulting from the rapid development.
Source: United Nations (1973, vol. III, pp. 111–12).

France   Taxation based on development scheme
In 1967 a French law introduced a tax of 90 per cent to be paid if land were used more intensively than accorded by the land occupation coefficient. For example, if because of pressing needs, a municipality permits a ten-storey building where only nine storeys are allowed, the landowner pays a tax of 90 per cent of the value of that land used more intensively. Recently this tax was raised to 100 per cent and made mandatory. This kind of tax was also introduced in Spain, though the tax rate for land more intensively used is not more than 8 per cent in urban areas and 2 per cent in rural areas.
Source: Gilli (1976).

Spain   Spanish land law
The Spanish Land Law of 1956 allowed municipalities to apply a tax for planning purposes on empty plots in the centre of the city, on plots under compulsory sale and on buildings of insufficient height (below permitted storey level according to the planning scheme). The law is very important because most taxes and land-use regulations tax only the use of the land, whereas this law imposes use of land according to the development scheme. The landowner, however, is free not to use the land. In addition this law introduces a measure permitting the public authority to expropriate land in new urbanised areas when it is not used according to the development scheme.
Source: United Nations (1973, vol. III, p. 112).

5.1.4   *Conditional loans and subsidies*
Central government supervision of the land acquisitions through loan sanction of local authorities can be a tool to enforce land policy goals.

Norway   Conditional loans and subsidies
Loans from the central government for land acquisition contain the provision that land must be bought at a non-speculative price (as judged by the central authority). This has led, however, to the purchase of outlying areas by the local authorities without regard to planning considerations, as this is where the cheapest land is to be found.
Source: United Nations (1973, vol. III).

Sweden   Government loan fund
There is a special government loan fund available to those municipalities which purchase land with the intention of leasing rather than selling it. In addition some check on the reasonableness of land prices is made by the government in connection with housing loans. Finally, special low-interest loans are available for land acquisition only if the municipality has prepared an advance acquisition scheme at least five years in advance.
Source: Odmann and Dahlberg (1970, pp. 148–9).

5.1.5   *Transport pricing*
The price of transport, if differentiated or subsidised regionally, can be a tool of regional development policy and will affect land in those areas. Also, within cities, road transport pricing could be used to control the development of certain areas, for example encouraging decentralisation from the central business district through road charges for travel into the central area.

6.0   CONTROL OVER GENERAL DEVELOPMENT BY GENERAL MEANS

6.1   *Powers*

6.1.1   *Indicative planning*

In some mixed-economy countries the public authorities set planning targets which are not primarily to be met by the public sector but rather by the private sector. Such planning may be sectoral (i.e. by sectors of the economy) or may focus on regional development. The targets, though mainly to be met through private forces, are also affected by the allocation of public resources on a priority basis. In terms of urban development, indicative planning (which is largely economic rather than physical) may set economic targets to be reached, and may also lead to specific urban redevelopment projects as a result. In some sense urban structure plans which do not have legal force, i.e. projections of general development trends, may be considered indicative plans for private-sector production of housing, and so on.

France   Indicative planning
An elaborate system of indicative planning exists in France, starting with the Planning Commission, which prepares four-year plan targets for various sectors of the French economy. There is a sub-section of this group which is the Commission on Urbanism, whose task it is to co-ordinate various public and private efforts in urban development. Finally, regional growth (including the creation of attractive metropolitan areas) is the responsibility of DATAR, the regional planning authority, which has representative advisory committees (CODERs). At the local level Programmes of Modernisation and Investment (PMEs) are drawn up for each city. The entire structure is highly centralised.
Source: Gremion and Worms (1975).

6.1.2   *Co-ordination of development*

Consultation and exchange of information between public- and private-sector planning and development actors may be an important general means of improving the efficiency of implementation of both, regardless of special arrangements (such as partnerships) made, as described in sections 2.6.3 and 3.3.3. Formal and informal contacts generally flow from the builders to the local authorities in most planning systems, but better channels (and possibly publication of plans) may be important improvements. Another issue is the co-ordination of development in a wider sense than just the intermeshing of investments, i.e. co-ordination with the goals and needs of the wider community. The procedures of public hearings vary widely among countries, but generally are too complex to be properly evaluated.

The Netherlands   Publicising plans
In the Netherlands plans for a new development are made into a model, which is displayed in public shopping places, in order to give people a chance to respond with criticisms of the design.
Source: Darin-Drabkin (personal information).

6.1.3   *Land registry*

Information on land holdings is an important precondition for an effective public land policy. Cadastral maps, showing division of plots and ownership, are vital for efficient expropriation procedures. Land value maps are essential for establishing compensation, especially in the case of fixed-date compensation (see

2.5.3). They are also crucial for an efficient taxation system as well, and particularly for the periodic collection of betterment (see 4.4.1). A periodic, published, uniform valuation may, as being seen to be fair, improve collection procedures. Compare Denmark in section 4.5.2.

6.1.4   *Information on land transactions*

Information on prices in the land market may be an aid to both public and private actors in the development process. Accurate information may improve the efficiency of the land market, and may allow the public authorities to monitor trends and also improve the efficiency of their own operations on the land market. Finally, accurate information about transactions is closely related to the problem of valuation; there is generally a time lag when valuers' assessments are not reflecting sharp changes (particularly downwards) in the land market.

Sweden   Information on land transactions

In Sweden there is the requirement that every seller of land first offers his land to the public authorities at a specific price. This allows them to monitor the land market and operate effectively as municipal purchasers.

Source: Doebele (1974).

Bibliography

ABERCROMBIE, E., *Greater London Plan 1944* (London: HMSO, 1945).

ADLER, G., *Land Planning by Administrative Regulation: the Policies of the Ontario Municipal Board* (Toronto: University of Toronto Press, 1971).

ALEXANDER, F., 'Policy planning and implementation: the missing link', in Soen, B. (ed.) *New Trends in Urban Planning* (Oxford: Pergamon Press, 1979).

ALEXANDER, I., *City Centre Redevelopment: an Evaluation of Alternative Approaches*, Progress in Planning Series, vol. 3, pt 1, (Oxford: Pergamon Press, 1974).

ALLISON, L., *Environmental Planning: a Political and Philosophical Analysis* (London: Allen & Unwin, 1975).

ALONSO, W., *Location and Land Use* (Cambridge, Mass.: Harvard University Press, 1964).

ALTERMAN, R., 'Selected aspects in the implementation of urban plans: measurement and identification of influencing factors', B.Sc. Dissertation in the Technion (Haifa: Israel Institute of Technology, 1974).

ALTSCHULER, A., *The City Planning Process: a Political Analysis* (New York: Cornell University Press, 1956).

AMATO, P., *Urban Land Policies and Land Use Control Measures: Vol. VI, Northern America* (New York: United Nations, 1973).

AMBROSE, P. and COLENUT, B., *The Property Machine* (Harmondsworth: Penguin, 1975).

AMSTERDAM PUBLIC WORKS DEPARTMENT, *Town Planning and Ground Exploitation in Amsterdam* (Amsterdam: Public Works Department, 1962).

AMSTERDAM PUBLIC WORKS DEPARTMENT, *Planning and Development in Amsterdam* (Amsterdam: Public Works Department, 1973).

APGAR, M. (ed.), *New Perspectives on Community Development* (New York: McGraw-Hill, 1976).

ARCHER, R. W., 'Urban planning and the property market: notes for a course of lectures' (unpublished, 1971).

ARCHER, R., *Site Value Taxation in Central Business District Redevelopment in Sydney, Australia* (Washington, D. C.: Urban Land Institute, 1972).

ARROW, K., *Social Choice and Individual Values* (New York: Wiley, 1951).

ASH, M., 'Viewpoint: the end of the affair', *Town and Country Planning Journal*, vol. 43, no. 5 (May 1975a).

ASH, M., 'Viewpoint: Planning Reprieved', *Town and Country Planning Journal*, vol. 43, no. 10 (October 1975b).

ASHTON, M., 'Highest-best use', *Journal of the American Institute of Real Estate Appraisal* (January 1939).

BAGNALL, K., 'Are partnerships between local authorities and developers feasible under the Community Land Act?', Blundell Memorial Lecture organised by the Senate of the Inns of Court and the Bar and the Royal Institute of Chartered Surveyors (May 1976).

BARLOWE, R., *Land Resource Economics: the Political Economy of Rural and Urban Land Resource Use* (Englewood Cliffs, NJ: Prentice-Hall, 1958).

BASTIANINI, A. and URBANI, G., 'Land-use planning in Italy', in Watson, M. and Haywood, J. (eds), *Planning Politics and the Public Interest: the French, British and Italian Experience* (Cambridge: Cambridge University Press, 1975).

BATOR, F., 'Capital, growth and Welfare: essays in the theory of allocation', Ph.D. thesis (Cambridge, Mass.: MIT, 1956).

BAUER, R. and GERGEN, K., *The Study of Policy Formation* (New York: The Free Press, 1968).

BAUMOL, W. S., *Welfare Economics and the Theory of the State*, 2nd edn (London: G. Bell, 1965).

BECKMAN, N., 'The planner as bureaucrat', *Journal of the American Institute of Planners*, vol. 30 (November 1964).

BOARD OF INLAND REVENUE, *Development Land Tax Bill* (London: Inland Revenue, 1976).

BOSE, A., 'Some aspects of rising land prices and land speculation in urban Delhi', in United Nations Regional Preparatory Conferences for the Habitat Conference on Human Settlements (Vancouver, Canada, 1975).

BOSSELMAN, F. and CALLIES, D., *The Quiet Revolution in Land Use Controls* (Washington, DC: Council of Environmental Quality, 1971).

BOWLEY, M., *The British Building Industry: Four Studies in Response and Resistance to Change* (Cambridge: Cambridge University Press, 1966).

BRISTOL UNIVERSITY, SCHOOL FOR ADVANCED URBAN STUDIES, *Community Land Training Programme: Background Papers nos 1–11* (Bristol University, 1976).

BROCKLEBANK, J. et al., *The Case for Nationalising Land* (London: Campaign for Nationalising Land, 1973).

CARLEGRIM E., *Survey of Land Policies of Municipalities* (Stockholm: Ministry of Housing, 1966).

CATANESE, A., *Impossible Dreams: Planners and Local Politics* (London: Sage Publications, 1974).

CENTRAL OFFICE OF INFORMATION, *Britain: an Official Handbook* (London: HMSO, 1978).

CHADWICK, G., *A Systems View of Planning: Towards a Theory of Urban and Regional Planning* (Oxford: Pergamon Press, 1971).

CHARTERED AUCTIONEERS and ESTATE AGENTS INSTITUTE, *Compensation for Compulsory Acquisition and Planning Restrictions* (London: Estate Agents Institute, 1968).

CHESTER, D., *Central and Local Government: Financial and Administrative Relations* (London: Macmillan, 1951).

CHEUNG, S. N. S., *The Myth of Social Cost* (London: Institute of Economic Affairs, 1978).

CLAWSON, M. (ed.), *Modernizing Urban Land Policy*, Paper Presented at an RFF Forum held in Washington, DC, (13–14 April 1972) (Baltimore: Johns Hopkins Press for Resources for the Future, 1973).

COMMISSION OF INQUIRY INTO LAND TENURES, *Final Report* (Canberra: Australian Government Publishing House, 1976).

COMMISSION ON INTERNATIONAL DEVELOPMENT, *Partners in Development: Report of the Commission on International Development*, Chairman: Lester B. Pearson (New York: Praeger, 1969).

COMMISSION ON THE THIRD LONDON AIRPORT, *Report*, Chairman: Mr Justice Roskill (London: HMSO, 1971).

COMMITTEE OF PUBLIC ACCOUNTS, *First Report: Treasury Minutes* (London: HMSO, 1951).

Community Land Act 1975 (London: HMSO, 1975).

CONSORTIUM OF THE GREATER LONDON COUNCIL, CITY OF WESTMINSTER, BOROUGH OF CAMDEN, *Covent Garden's Moving: Covent Garden Area Draft Plan* (London: The Consortium, 1968).

COVENT GARDEN DEVELOPMENT TEAM, *Covent Garden Local Plan: Report of Survey – Discussion Papers 1–6* (London: Greater London Council, 1974).

COWAN, P., *The Office – A Facet of Urban Growth* (London: University College Joint Unit for Planning Research, 1967).

CRAIG, D., 'Regulation and taxing: two governmental ways to obtain planned land use', in Haar, C. (ed.), *Law and Land: Anglo-American Planning Practice* (Cambridge, Mass.: Harvard University Press and MIT Press, 1964).

CROSSMAN, R., *Diaries of a Cabinet Minister* (London: Hamish Hamilton, 1975–7).

CULLINGWORTH, J., *Problems of an Urban Society. Vol. II: The Social Content of Planning* (London: Allen & Unwin, 1972).

CULLINGWORTH, J., *Town and Country Planning in Britain*, 5th edn (London: Allen & Unwin, 1974).

CULLINGWORTH, J., *Environmental Planning. Vol. 1: Reconstruction and Land Use Planning 1939–1947* (London: HMSO, 1975).

DAHL, R. and LINDBLOM, C., *Politics, Economics and Welfare: Planning and Politico-Economic Systems Resolved into Basic Social Processes* (New York: Harper, 1953).

D'ARCY, F. and JOPERT, B., 'Urban planning in France', in Hayward, J. and Watson, M., *Planning, Politics and the Public Interest: the French, British and Italian Experience* (Cambridge: Cambridge University Press, 1975).

DARIN-DRABKIN, H., *Land Policy and Urban Growth* (Oxford: Pergamon Press, 1977).

DARIN-DRABKIN, H. and LICHFIELD, N., 'Land utilisation', in Goldsmith, M. *et al.* (eds), *A Strategy for Resources: a Science Policy Foundation Symposium, Eindhoven, September 1975* (Amsterdam: North-Holland, 1977), pp. 20–40.

DARIN-DRABKIN, H. *et al.*, *Patterns of Land Use and Land Tenure in Israel* (Tel Aviv: Ministry of Housing and Land Use Research Institute, 1972).

DAVIDOFF, P., 'Advocacy and pluralism in planning', *Journal of the American Institute of Planners*, vol. 31 (November 1965).

DAVIDSON, A. and LEONARD, J., *The Property Development Process* (Reading: Centre for Advanced Land Use Studies, 1976).

DELAFONS, J., *Land Use Control in the United States* (Cambridge, Mass.: Joint Center for Urban Studies, 1962).

DENMAN, D., *Land Use and the Constitution of Property* (Cambridge: Cambridge University Press, 1969).

DENMAN, D. and PRODANO, S., *Land Use: an Introduction to Proprietary Land Use Analysis* (London: Allen & Unwin, 1972).

DENMAN, D., *Prospects of Cooperative Planning: The Warburton Lecture Delivered at the University of Manchester November 1973* (Berkhamsted: Geographical Publications, 1974).

DENMAN, D., *The Place of Property* (Berkhamsted: Geographical Publications, 1978).

DENMARK TAXATION OFFICE, *Report of the Director* (Copenhagen: Taxation Office, 1962).

DEPARTMENT OF ECONOMIC AFFAIRS, *The National Plan* (London: HMSO, 1965).

DOE/SOUTH EAST JOINT PLANNING TEAM, *Strategic Plan for the South East. Studies Vols 1–5* (London: HMSO, 1971).

DOE, *Local Government Act 1972*, (Circular 121/72 (London: HMSO, 1972a).

DOE. WORKING PARTY ON LOCAL AUTHORITY/PRIVATE ENTERPRISE PARTNERSHIP SCHEMES, *Report*, Chairman: P. R. Sheaf (London: HMSO, 1972b).

DOE, *Covent Garden: Geoffrey Rippon Proposes Changes to GLC Plan*, Press Notice, 15 January 1973 (London: HMSO, 1973a).

DOE, *Greater London Development Plan: Report of the Panel of Inquiry*, Chairman: F. H. B. Layfield (London: HMSO, 1973c).

DOE, *Local Government Act 1972. Town and Country Planning: Cooperation between Authorities*, Circular 74/73 (London: HMSO, 1973d).

DOE, *Streamlining the Planning Machine*, Circular 142/73 (London: HMSO, 1973e).

DOE, *Land* (Command 5730) (London: HMSO, 1974).

DOE, ADVISORY GROUP ON COMMERCIAL PROPERTY DEVELOPMENT, *First Report*, Chairman: Sir Dennis Pilcher (London: HMSO, 1975a).

DOE, *Community Land Accounts*, GNLA/3 (London: HMSO, 1975b).

DOE, *Community Land Circular 1 – General Introduction and Priorities*, DoE Circular 121/75 (London: HSMO, 1975c).

DOE, *Community Land Circular 2 – Community Land Accounts 1975–76*, DoE Circular 128/75 (London: HMSO, 1975d).

DOE, *Housing and Construction Statistics*, no. 13 (London: HMSO, 1975e).

DOE, *Land Acquisition and Management Schemes*, GNLA/1 (London: HMSO, 1975f).

DOE, *Review of the Development Control System: Final Report*, Chairman: George Dobry (London: HMSO, 1975g).

DOE, *Community Land Circular 3 – Scheme of Accounts for Land Bought for Private Development*, DoE Circular 5/76 (London: HMSO, 1976a).

DOE, *Community Land Circular 5 – Planning Applications and Permissions for Relevant Development*, DoE Circular 23/76 (London: HMSO, 1976b).

DOE, *Community Land Circular 6 – Land for Private Development: Acquisition, Management and Disposal*, DoE Circular 26/76 (London: HMSO, 1976c).

DOE, *Community Land Circular 7 – Compulsory Purchase Procedures*, DoE Circular 30/76 (London: HMSO, 1976d).

DOE, *Planning in the United Kingdom: National Report Prepared for Habitat, United Nations Conference on Human Settlements, Vancouver 1976* (London: HMSO, 1976e).

DOE, *The Recent Course of Land and Property Prices and the Factors underlying it*, DoE Research Report 4 (London: HMSO, 1976f).

DOE, *Memorandum on Structure and Local Plans*, Circular 55/77 (London: HMSO, 1977a).

DOE, *Monitoring for Development Planning*, DoE Research Report 23 (London: Tavistock Institute of Human Relations, 1977b).

DOE, *Local Government Moves Swift*, Press Notice no. 483 (3 August 1978a).

DOE, *Windscale Inquiry: Report by the Hon. Mr Justice Parker* (London: HMSO, 1978b).

DOE, *Transport Policies and Programme Submissions for the 1980/81 TSG Settlement*, Circular 4/79 (London: HMSO, 1979).

DOEBELE, W., *A Commentary on Urban Land Policy in Sweden: Preliminary Draft Report for the World Bank.* (Cambridge, Mass.: Harvard University Press, 1974).

DOEBELE, W., *Valorization Charges as a Method For Financing Urban Public Works: the Example of Bogota, Colombia*, World Bank Staff Working Paper no. 254 (Washington, DC: World Bank, 1977).

DUNKERLEY, H. *et al.*, *Urban Land Policy: Issues and Opportunities* (Washington, DC: World Bank, 1977).

'Earl Fitzwilliam's Wentworth Estates Co. Ltd v. Ministry of Housing and Local Government', *Planning and Compensation Reports*, vol. 2 pt 6 (April–June 1952), pp. 385–99.

EDDISON, R., 'The challenge of community land 2: exploring the ground', *Municipal Journal*, vol. 84, no. 5 (30 January 1976).

ELY, R. and WEHRWEIN, G., *Land Economics* (New York: Macmillan, 1940).

ENGELS, F., *Condition of the Working Class in England* (London: Blackwell, 1971).

FOSTER, C., 'Planning and the market', in Cowan, P. (ed.), *The Future of Planning* (London: Heinemann, 1973).

FOSTER, C. and GLAISTER, S., 'The anatomy of the development land tax', *Urban Studies*, vol. 12, no. 2 (1975), pp. 213–19.

FREUND, E., *Past, Present and Emergent Problems and Practices in Land Use Control* (Chicago: University of Illinois, Bureau of Urban Planning, 1965).

FRIED, R., *Planning the Eternal City: Roman Politics and Planning since World War II* (New Haven, Conn.: Yale University Press, 1973).

FRIEDMANN, J., *Retracking America: a Theory of Transactive Planning* (New York: Anchor, 1973).

GALBRAITH, K., *The Affluent Society* (Harmondsworth: Penguin, 1958).

GARNER, J., *The Public Control of Land* (London: Sweet & Maxwell, 1956).

GEIGER, R. L., *The Theory of the Land Question* (London: Macmillan, 1936).

GEORGE, H., *Progress and Poverty.* 52nd edn (London: Henry George Foundation of Great Britain, 1931).

GILLI, J., *Towards a New Definition of Property Rights* (Paris: International Federation for Housing and Planning/Centre de Recherche d'Urbanisme, 1976).

GOLANY, G., *New-town Planning: Principles and Practice* (New York: Wiley, 1976).

GREATER LONDON REGIONAL PLANNING COMMITTEE, *Second Report* (London: Knapp, Drewett, March 1933).

GREGORY, R., *The Price of Amenity* (London: Macmillan, 1971).

GREMION, P. and WORMS, J., 'The French regional planning experiments', in Haywood, J. and Watson, M., *Planning, Politics and the Public Interest: The French, British and Italian Experience* (Cambridge: Cambridge University Press, 1975).

GRIMES, O., *Urban Land and Public Policy: Social Appropriation of Betterment*, World Bank Staff Working Paper no. 179 (Washington, DC: World Bank, 1974).

GUTTENBERG, A., 'A multiple land use classification system', *Journal of the American Institute of Planners*, vol. 25, no. 3 (August 1959), pp. 143–50.

HAAR, C., *Land Use Planning: a Casebook on the Use, Misuse and Reuse of Urban Land* (Boston: Little, Brown, 1959).

HABITAT: United Nations Conference on Human Settlements, Vancouver 1976: Report (New York: United Nations, 1976).

HADY, T., 'Differential assessment of farmland on the urban–rural fringe', *American Journal of Agricultural Economics*, vol. 52 (February 1970).

HAGMAN, D., *Urban Planning and Land Development Control Law* (St Paul, Minn.: West Publishing, 1971).

HAGMAN, D. and MISCZYNSKI, D., *Windfalls for Wipeouts: Land Value Capture and Compensations* (Chicago: American Society of Planning Officials, 1978).

HALL, P., *Urban and Regional Planning* (Harmondsworth: Penguin, 1975).

HALL, P. et al., *The Containment of Urban England* (London: Allen & Unwin, 1973).

HARRISON, A., *Economics and Land Use Planning* (London: Croom-Helm, 1977).

HARRISON, P., 'Urban land policy: some Australian experiments', in Woodruff, A. and Brown, J. (eds), *Land for the Cities of Asia* (Hartford, Conn.: John C. Lincoln Institute, 1971).

HAUSER, P. and SCHNORE, L., *The Study of Urbanization* (New York: Wiley, 1965).

HAYEK, F. (ed.), *Collectivist Economic Planning* (London: Routledge & Kegan Paul, 1979).

HAYHOW, H., 'Financial administration in American cities', *Public Finance and Accountancy*, vol. 67, no. 2 (February 1963).

HEAP, D., *Introducing the Land Commission Act, 1967* (London: Sweet & Maxwell, 1967).

HILL, M., 'A goals achievement matrix for evaluating alternative plans', *Journal of the American Institute of Planners*, vol. 34 (1968), pp. 19–29.

HILLEBRANDT, P., *Economic Theory and the Construction Industry* (London: Macmillan, 1974).

HOLLIDAY, J. (ed.), *City Centre Redevelopment: a Study of British City Centre Planning and Case Studies of Five English City Centres* (London: Charles Knight, 1973).

HOUSE OF COMMONS, *Report of the Central Land Board for the Financial Year 1949–1950*, HC 148 (London: HMSO, 1950).

JOHNSON, S., *The Politics of Environment* (London: Stacey, 1973).

JOHNSON, V. and BARLOWE, R., *Land Problems and Policies* (New York: McGraw-Hill, 1954).

JOWELL, J., 'Bargaining in development control', *Journal of Planning and Environmental Law* (July 1977a).

JOWELL, J., 'The limits of law in urban planning', *Current Legal Problems*, vol. 30 (1977b).

KAM, S., *Land Banking: Public Policy Alternatives and Dilemmas* (Washington, DC: Urban Institute, 1970).

KAPP, K. W., *The Social Costs of Private Enterprise* (Cambridge, Mass.: Harvard University Press, 1950).

LABOUR PARTY, *Labour's Programme for Britain: Annual Conference 1973* (London: Labour Party, 1973).

LAND AUTHORITY FOR WALES, *Land Policy Statement and Rolling Programme 1977* (Cardiff: Land Authority, 1977).

Land Commission Act 1967 (London HMSO, 1967).

LAND ECONOMICS INSTITUTE, *Modern Land Policy* (Illinois: University of Illinois Press, 1960).

LEMASURIER, J., 'Town and country planning in France,' in Garner, J. (ed.), *Planning Law in Western Europe* (Amsterdam: North-Holland, 1975).

LENDI, M., 'Swiss planning law', in Garner, J. (ed.), *Planning Law in Western Europe* (Amsterdam: North-Holland, 1975).

LEVIN, P., *Government and the Planning Process: an Analysis and Appraisal of Government Decision-making Processes with Special Reference to the Launching of New Towns and Town Development Schemes* (London: Allen & Unwin, 1976).

LICHFIELD, N., *Economics of Planned Development* (London: Estates Gazette, 1956).

LICHFIELD, N., 'Capital formation and land value', *Estates Gazette* (February 1958a).

LICHFIELD, N., 'Economic problems of central redevelopment', *Housing Review* (September–October 1958b), pp. 133–41.

LICHFIELD, N., 'Resources for renewal', *Planning Outlook*, vol. 5, no. 4 (1962), pp. 22–34.

LICHFIELD, N., 'A pure theory of urban renewal: a further comment', *Land Economics* (February 1963), pp. 100–3.

LICHFIELD, N., *Compensation and Betterment – What Next?* (London: Town Planning Institute, 1964a).

LICHFIELD, N., 'Planning and the land market', in Denman, D. (ed.), *Contemporary Problems of Land Ownership* (Cambridge: University of Cambridge, Department of Land Economy, 1964b).

LICHFIELD, N., 'Land nationalization', in Hall, P. (ed.), *Land Values* (London: Acton Society Trust, 1965).

LICHFIELD, N., 'Economics of conservation', in Esher (ed.), *York: a Study of Conservation* (London: HMSO, 1968).

LICHFIELD, N., 'Evaluation and methodology of urban and regional plans: a review', *Regional Studies*, vol. 4, no. 2 (April 1970), pp. 151–65.

LICHFIELD, N., 'Cost benefit analysis in planning: a critique of the Roskill Commission', *Regional Studies*, vol. V (1971), pp. 157–83.

LICHFIELD, N., 'The Community Land Bill: some alternatives', *Estates Gazette*, vol. 235, no. 5736 (5 July 1975a), pp. 29–35.

LICHFIELD, N., 'Some economic aspects of the planning and development of Canberra 1974: National Capital Development Advisory Commission' (1975b, unpublished).

LICHFIELD, N., *Are Partnerships between Local Authorities and Developers Feasible under the Community Land Act?*, Blundell Memorial Lecture Organised by the Senate of the Inns of Court and the Bar and the Royal Institute of Chartered Surveyors (May 1976a).

LICHFIELD, N., 'The Israeli physical planning system: some needed changes, part 1', *Israeli Annual of Public Administration and Public Policy*, (1976b).

LICHFIELD, N., 'A positive approach to land development', *The Planner*, (April 1976c).

LICHFIELD, N., 'National strategy for the new-town program in Israel', in Golany, G. (ed.), *International Urban Growth Policies; New-town Contributions* (New York: Wiley, 1978a).

LICHFIELD, N., 'Role of land use planning in development', *International Technical Co-operation Review*, vol. 7, no. 1 (January 1978b).

LICHFIELD, N., 'From urban planning to settlement planning', in Soen, B. (ed.) *New Trends in Urban Planning* (Oxford: Pergamon Press, 1979a).

LICHFIELD, N., 'Towards an acceptable planning system: the Warburton Lecture, University of Manchester, March 1978', *Town Planning Review*, vol. 50 (January 1979b).

LICHFIELD, N., KETTLE, P. and WHITBREAD, M., *Evaluation in the Planning Process* (Oxford: Pergamon Press, 1975).

LICHFIELD, N. and MARINOV, U., 'Land-use planning and environmental protection: convergence or divergence?', *Environment and Planning*, vol. 9, no. 9 (September 1977), pp. 985–1002.

LICHFIELD, N. and WENDT, P., 'Six English new towns: a financial analysis', *Town Planning Review*, vol. 40 (October 1969).

NATHANIEL LICHFIELD & PARTNERS, *Bath Minimum Physical Change Study* (Bath: County of Avon, 1977).

NATHANIEL LICHFIELD & PARTNERS, *The Effect of Increased Tertiarisation of Central Urban Areas and Policies to Control it*, European Regional Planning Study no. 10 (Strasbourg: Council of Europe, 1978).

LIPSEY, D., *Labour and Land*, Fabian Tract no. 422 (London: Fabian Society, 1973).

LIPSEY, R., *An Introduction to Positive Economics* (London: Weidenfeld & Nicolson, 1966).

LITTLECHILD, S. C., *The Fallacy of the Mixed Economy* (London: Institute of Economic Affairs, 1978).

Local Government Act 1972 (London: HMSO, 1972).

MCAUSLAN, P., *Land, Law and Planning: Cases, Materials and Text* (London: Weidenfeld & Nicolson, 1975).

MCCRONE, G., *Regional Policy in Britain* (Glasgow: Glasgow University Press, 1969).

MCEVOY, J. and DIETZ, T. (eds), *Handbook for Environmental Planning: the Social Consequences of Environmental Change* (New York: Wiley, 1977).

MCLAUGHLIN, F., 'National growth policy and new communities in the United States: an overview', in Golany, G. (ed.), *International Urban Growth Policies: New-town Contributions* (New York: Wiley, 1978).

MCLOUGHLIN, J., *Urban and Regional Planning: a Systems Approach* (London: Faber, 1969).

MCLOUGHLIN, J., *Control and Urban Planning* (London: Faber, 1973).

MARGOLIS, J., *The Public Investment Model and the Public Choice Process: Proceedings of the Conference of the International Institute of Public Finance*, Hamburg, 1978 (to be published).

MARRIOTT, O., *The Property Boom* (London: Hamish Hamilton, 1967).

MARSHALL, A., *Principles of Economics: an Introductory Volume*, 8th edn (London: Macmillan, 1927).

MASSEY, D. and CATALANI, A., *Capital and Land: Landownership and Capital in Great Britain* (London: Edward Arnold, 1978).

MEADE, J., *The Intelligent Radical's Guide to Economics Policy: The Mixed Economy* (London: Allen & Unwin, 1975).

MERLIN, P., *New Towns: Regional Planning and Development* (London: Methuen, 1971).

MEYERSON, M. and BANFIELD, E., *Politics, Planning and the Public Interest* (New York: Columbia University Press, 1955).

MILL, J., *Principles of Political Economy* (Harmondsworth: Penguin, 1970).

Minister of Town and Country Planning Act 1943 (London: HMSO, 1943).

MINISTRY OF HEALTH, DEPARTMENTAL COMMITTEE ON GARDEN CITIES AND SATELLITE TOWNS, *Report*, Marley Report (London: HMSO, 1935).

MINISTRY OF HOUSING AND LOCAL GOVERNMENT, *Green Belts*, Circular 42/55 (London: HMSO, 1955).

MINISTRY OF HOUSING AND LOCAL GOVERNMENT, *South East Study 1961–1981* (London: HMSO, 1964).

MINISTRY OF HOUSING AND LOCAL GOVERNMENT, *The Use of Conditions in Planning Permissions*, Circular 5/68 (London: HMSO, 1968).

MINISTRY OF HOUSING AND LOCAL GOVERNMENT, COMMITTEE ON PUBLIC PARTICIPATION IN PLANNING, *People and Planning: Report of the Committee*, Chairman: A. M. Skeffington (London: HMSO, 1969).

MINISTRY OF TOWN AND COUNTRY PLANNING, NEW TOWNS COMMITTEE, *Final Report*, Command 6876, Chairman: Lord Reith (London: HMSO, 1946).

MINISTRY OF TOWN AND COUNTRY PLANNING, *Town and Country Planning (General Development) Amendment Order, 1949*, Circular 67 (London: HMSO, 1949).

MINISTRY OF TOWN AND COUNTRY PLANNING, *Town and Country Planning 1943–51: Progress Reports*, Command 8204 (London: HMSO, 1951).

MINISTRY OF WORKS AND PLANNING, COMMITTEE ON LAND UTILISATION IN RURAL AREAS, *Report*, Command 6378, Scott Report (London: HMSO, 1942a).

MINISTRY OF WORKS AND PLANNING, EXPERT COMMITTEE ON COMPENSATION AND BETTERMENT, *Final Report*, Command 6386, Uthwatt Report (London: HMSO, 1942b).

MINNS, R. and THORNLEY, J., *Local Government Economic Planning and the Provision of Risk Capital for Small Firms*, Policy Series no. 6 (London: Centre for Environmental Studies, 1978).

MISHAN, E., *The Costs of Economic Growth* (London: Staples Press, 1967).

MUSGRAVE, R., *The Theory of Public Finance* (New York: McGraw-Hill, 1959).

MYRDAL, G., *Beyond the Welfare State* (London: Duckworth, 1960).

NATIONAL ECONOMIC DEVELOPMENT OFFICE, *New Homes in the City: the Role of the Private Developer in Urban Renewal in England and Wales* (London: HMSO, 1971).

NEEDLEMAN, L., 'Comparative economics of improvement and new buildings', in Ministry of Housing and Local Government, *Improvement of Old Houses and their Environment: Two-day Conference held in Cambridge, 27th and 28th June 1967*, Chairman: Lord Kennet.

NETHERLANDS – MINISTRY OF HOUSING AND PHYSICAL PLANNING, *Third Report on Physical Planning. Part II: Urbanization Report* (The Hague: Government Printing Office, 1976).

NETZER, R., *Economics of the Property Tax* (Washington, DC: Brookings Institution, 1966).

NEUTZE, M., *The Price of Land and Land Use Planning: Policy Instruments in the Urban Land Market* (Paris: OECD, 1973).

NEUTZE, M., 'Urban land policy in five Western countries', *Journal of Social Policy*, vol. 4, no. 3 (July 1975).

NEWELL, M., *An Introduction to the Economics of Urban Land Use* (London: Estates Gazette, 1977).

ODMANN, E. and DAHLBERG, G–B., *Urbanization in Sweden: Means and Methods for Planning* (Stockholm: National Institute of Building and Urban Planning Research, 1970).

OFFICE OF POPULATION CENSUSES AND SURVEYS, *Census 1971: Great Britain Summary Tables* (London: HMSO, 1973).

OLSON, M. and LANDSBERG, H. (eds), *The No Growth Society* (London: Woburn Press, 1975).

PARKER, H., 'The history of compensation and betterment since 1900', in Acton Society Trust, *Land Values* (ed. Hall, P.) (London: Sweet & Maxwell, 1965).

PIGOU, A., *The Economics of Welfare*, 4th edn (London: Macmillan, 1948).

PLANNING ADVISORY GROUP, *The Future of Development Plans* (London: HMSO, 1965).

POTTIER, C., *La Logique du Financement Public d'Urbanization*, La Recherche Urbaine, 8 (Paris: Mouton, 1975).

PRESSMAN, J. and WILDAVSKY, A., *Implementation* (Berkeley: University of California Press, 1973).

PREST, A. and TURVEY, R., 'Cost benefit analysis: a survey', *Economic Journal* (December 1965).

Puerto Rico Act no. 13 (1962), quoted in Reps, J., 'Public land, urban development policy and the American planning tradition', in Clawson, M. (ed.), *Modernizing Urban Land Policy* (Baltimore: Johns Hopkins University Press, 1973).

PUERTO RICO PLANNING BOARD, *Urban Land Policy in the Commonwealth of Puerto Rico* (Santurce: Planning Board, 1968).

PURDUE, M., *Cases and Materials on Planning Law* (London: Sweet & Maxwell, 1977).

RABINOWITZ, F., *City Politics and Planning* (New York: Atherton Press, 1969).

RATCLIFFE, J., *Land Policy: an Exploration of the Nature of Land in Society* (London: Hutchinson, 1976).

RATCLIFF, R., *Urban Land Economics* (New York: McGraw-Hill, 1949).

RATCLIFF, R., *Real Estate Analysis* (New York: McGraw-Hill, 1961).

REILLY, W. (ed.), *The Use of Land: a Citizen's Policy Guide to Urban Growth*, a Task Force Report sponsored by the Rockefeller Brothers Fund (New York: Thomas Y. Crowell, 1973).

RENNE, R., *Land Economics*, 3rd edn (New York: Harper, 1958).

RICARDO, D., *The Principles of Political Economy and Taxation* (London: Dent, 1911).

ROSE, J., *The Transfer of Development Rights: a New Technique of Land Use Regulation* (New Jersey: Rutgers University Centre for Urban Policy Research, 1975).

ROYAL COMMISSION ON THE DISTRIBUTION OF THE INDUSTRIAL POPULATION, *Report*, Command 6153, Chairman: Montague Barlow (London: HMSO, 1939).

ROYAL INSTITUTION OF CHARTERED SURVEYORS, *The RICS Handbook of Community Land and Development Taxation* (Brentford: Kluwen-Harrap, 1976).

ROYAL TOWN PLANNING INSTITUTE, *The Land Question* (London: RTP Institute, 1975).

ROYAL TOWN PLANNING INSTITUTE, *Development Control: the Present System and some Proposals for the Future. Report of the Working Party* (London: RTP Institute, 1978a).

ROYAL TOWN PLANNING INSTITUTE, *Land Values and Planning in the Inner Areas: Report of the Working Party* (London: RTP Institute, 1978b).

SAMUELSON, P., *Economics: an Introductory Analysis*, 4th edn (New York: McGraw-Hill, 1958).

SCARMAN, SIR L., *English Law – the New Dimension*, Hamlyn Lectures, 26th series (London: Stevens, 1974).

SCHAFFER, F., *The New Town Story* (London: MacGibbon & Kee, 1970).

SCHIAVO-COMPO, S. and SINGER, H., *Perspective of Economic Development* (Boston: Houghton-Mifflin, 1970).

SCHUBERT, G., *The Public Interest: A Critique of the Theory of a Political Concept* (New York: The Free Press, 1960).

SCHUMACHER, E., *Small is Beautiful: a Study of Economics as if People Mattered* (London: Blond & Briggs, 1973).

SEERS, D. and JOY, S., *Development in a Divided World* (Harmondsworth: Penguin, 1968).

SELF, P., *Econocrats and the Policy Process: the Politics and Philosophy of Cost–Benefit Analysis* (London: Macmillan, 1975).

SHARP, E., *Ministry of Housing and Local Government* (London: Allen & Unwin, 1969).

SHONFIELD, A., *Modern Capitalism: the Changing Balance of Public and Private Power* (Oxford: Oxford University Press, 1965).

SIEGAN, B., *Land Use without Zoning* (Lexington, Mass.: D. C. Heath, 1972).

SIMMIE, J., *Citizens in Conflict: the Sociology of Town Planning* (London: Hutchinson, 1974).

SIMON, H., *Administrative Behavior* (New York: Macmillan, 1947).

SMITH, A., *The Wealth of Nations* (London: Dent, 1910).

SOLESBURY, W., *Policy in Urban Planning: Structure Plans, Programmes and Local Plans*, Urban and Regional Planning Series, vol. 8 (Oxford: Pergamon Press, 1974).

SOUTH EAST JOINT PLANNING TEAM, *Strategic Plan for the South East Studies Vol. II: Social and Environmental Aspects* (London: HMSO, 1971).

SPAIN – MINISTERIA DE LA VIVIENDA, *Gerencia de Urbanizacion* (Madrid: The Ministry, 1965).

STRONG, A., *Planned Urban Environments: Sweden, Finland, Israel, the Netherlands, France* (Baltimore: Johns Hopkins University Press, 1971).

SUETENS, L., 'Town and country planning in Belgium', in Garner, J. (ed.), *Planning Law in Western Europe* (Amsterdam: North-Holland, 1975).

TELLING, A., *Planning Law and Procedure*, 4th edn (London: Butterworths, 1973).

THOMAS, D., *London's Green Belt* (London: Faber, 1970).

THORNCROFT, M., *Principles of Estate Management* (London: Estates Gazette, 1965).

TOLSTRUP, F., 'Town and country planning law in Denmark', in Garner, J. (ed.), *Planning Law in Western Europe* (Amsterdam: North-Holland, 1975).

TOWN AND COUNTRY PLANNING, Command 3333 (London: HMSO, 1967).

Town and Country Planning Act 1971 (London: HMSO, 1971).

TRANTER, N., *Population since the Industrial Revolution: the English Experience* (London: Croom-Helm, 1973).

TREASURY, *Public Expenditure 1979–80*, Command 6393 (London: HMSO, 1976).

TROY, P., *A Fair Price* (Sydney: Hale & Iremonger, 1978).

TURIN, D., *Aspects of the Economics of Construction* (London: Godwin, 1975).

TURNER, D., *An Approach to Land Values* (Berkhamsted: Geographical Publications, 1977).

TURVEY, R., *The Economics of Real Property: an Analysis of Property Values and Patterns of Use* (London: Allen & Unwin, 1957).

UNDERHILL, J., 'Soviet policy for new towns and its implementation, achievements and problems', in Golany, G. (ed.), *International Urban Growth Policies: New-town Contributions* (New York: Wiley, 1978).

UNHEALTHY AREAS COMMITTEE, *Second and Final Report of the Committee Appointed to Consider and Advise on the Principles to be Followed in Dealing with Unhealthy Areas* (London: HMSO, 1921).

UNITED NATIONS, DEPARTMENT OF ECONOMIC AND SOCIAL AFFAIRS, *Urban Land Policies and Land-use Control Measures: Vol. I Africa; Vol. II Asia and the Far East; Vol. III Western Europe; Vol.IV Latin America; Vol. V Middle East; Vol. VI Northern America* (New York: United Nations, 1973); *Vol. VII Global Review* (New York: United Nations, 1975).

VAIZEY, J., *Revolutions in our Time: Social Democracy* (London: Weidenfeld & Nicholson, 1971).

VICKERS, G., *The Art of Judgment: a Study of Policy Making* (London: Methuen, 1965).

WALKER, R., *The Planning Tradition in Urban Government* (Chicago: University of Chicago Press, 1941).

WALTERS, A., 'Land speculator – creator or creature of inflation', in Walters, A. *et al.* (eds), *Government and the Land*, IEA Reading 13 (London: Institute of Economic Affairs, 1974).

WELLS, H., *Planning by Lease Control: Report of the Town and Country Planning Summer School at St Andrews* (London: Town Planning Institute, 1944).

WESTERN AUSTRALIA, *Land Taxation and Land Prices in Western Australia: Report* (Perth: Government Printer, 1968).

WHITEHOUSE, B., *Partners in Prosperity* (London: Pion/Shaw, 1964).

WILKS, H., *Some Reflections on the Second Valuation of Whitstable* (London: Land and Liberty Press, 1974).

WILSON, J. (ed.), *Urban Renewal: the Record and Controversy* (Cambridge, Mass.: MIT Press, 1967).

YONE, H., 'Planning as Control' Ph.D. dissertation in the Technion (Haifa: Israel Institute of Technology, 1974).

Index